The Songs of Elizabeth Cronin, Irish Traditional Singer

Bess singing at the fireside in Lios Buí, 1952
(Photo: George Pickow)

The Songs of Elizabeth Cronin, Irish Traditional Singer

The Complete Song Collection

COMPILED AND EDITED BY

Dáibhí Ó Cróinín

FOUR COURTS PRESS

Typeset in 12 pt on 15 pt Bembo by
Carrigboy Typesetting Services, County Cork for
FOUR COURTS PRESS LTD
Fumbally Court, Fumbally Lane, Dublin 8, Ireland
e-mail: info@four-courts-press.ie
and in North America for
FOUR COURTS PRESS
c/o ISBS, 5804 N.E. Hassalo Street, Portland, OR 97213.

© Dáibhí Ó Cróinín 2000

A catalogue record for this title is available
from the British Library.

ISBN 1–85182–259–3

SPECIAL ACKNOWLEDGMENT

This publication was grant-aided by The Arts Council/An Chomhairle Ealaíon,
the Publications Fund of the National University of Ireland, Galway and also by the
Heritage Council of Ireland under the 1999 Publications Grant Scheme

Printed in Ireland
Betaprint, Dublin

CONTENTS

LIST OF ABBREVIATIONS

The following abbreviations have been used in the notes to the songs:

BBC	British Broadcasting Corporation	*JIFSS*	*Journal of the Irish Folk Song Society*
BC	Bess Cronin	JR–GP	Jean Ritchie & George Pickow
CBÉ	Cnósach Bhéaloideas Éireann	MÓB	Mícheál Ó Briain
CUL	Cambridge University Library	SE	Seamus Ennis
DH	Diane Hamilton	SÓC	Seán Ó Cróinín
DÓC	Donncha Ó Cróinín	RTÉ	Radio Teilifís Éireann
IFC	Irish Folklore Commission	RIA	Royal Irish Academy
JFSS	*Journal of the Folk Song Society*	UCD	University College Dublin

Note: all CBÉ references are formally IFC materials.

LIST OF ILLUSTRATIONS

CREDITS

Editor's collection: 1, 2, 3, 4, 5, 6, 10, 11; George Pickow: frontispiece, 7, 8, 9, 12

PREFACE

The purpose of this publication is to make available, for the first time, the complete collection of songs noted down or recorded from the singing of my grandmother, Elizabeth (Bess) Cronin. The book contains everything that I have been able to recover of Bess Cronin's repertoire, and it is hoped that, by making this material accessible once again, the unique voice and style that were the hallmarks of her singing will inspire present-day singers and lovers of Irish songs and ballads to learn (or relearn) the different songs, in Irish and English, published here.[1]

Some of the songs in this collection, such as *Siúil, a rúin*, or *Lord Gregory*, will be familiar already to many people. Others in the collection are appearing here for the first time in the public domain. Each of them bears the distinctive stamp of Bess Cronin's style, of which one authority on the subject, Bill Meek, has said: 'The voice of Mrs Cronin of Macroom could only be described in terms of tranquil power. A most unique singer... a voice which somehow embodies a whole culture'.[2] More recently, Dr Angela Bourke, an eminent writer and Irish scholar, has remarked that 'there could be a [summer] school for Bess Cronin, covering singing and storytelling, because she did both'.[3] It is my intention to publish a separate volume containing Bess Cronin's storytelling and *seanchas*, which will give a further insight into the wealth of local lore and knowledge that she had, and the wonderfully rich and idiomatic Irish in which she recorded it.[4]

This volume, therefore, is the first instalment in a projected two-part study of one of the most remarkable figures in modern Irish folklore and traditional music.

The following individuals and organisations have assisted or encouraged me in this project: *Aer Lingus* (Artflight); *Prof. Bo Almqvist*, formerly Head of the Department of Irish Folklore, University College Dublin; *The Arts Council*, Dublin; *Anna Bale*, Department of Irish Folklore, University College Dublin; *David Bland*, Halifax; *Harry Bradshaw*, RTÉ, Dublin; *Peter Browne*, RTÉ, Dublin; *Marie Boran*, Special Acquisitions, James Hardiman Library, NUI, Galway; *Dr Philip Butterss*, Department of English, University of Adelaide; *Fionnuala Byrne*, formerly Special Acquisitions, Hardiman Library, NUI, Galway; *Nicholas Carolan*, Director, Irish Traditional Music Archive, Dublin and the staff of the Archive; *Anna Chairetakis (Lomax)*, New York; *Glenn Cumiskey*, Irish Traditional Music Archive, Dublin; *Maura Eaton*, The Arts Council of Ireland, Dublin; *D. Ellis-King*, City & County Librarian, Dublin Public Libraries; *Sarah Faulkner*, BBC Enterprises, London; *The Fulbright Foundation*, Dublin; *Eilís Gallagher (Cronin)*, Mallow, Co. Cork; *Clare Gilliam*, English Folk Dance & Song Society, London; *Cathal Goan*, ceannasaí, Teilifís na Gaeilge; *Diane Hamilton* (†) & *John Hamilton-Darby*, Dublin; *Dr Joseph Hickerson*, Archive of Folklife, Library of Congress, Washington, D.C.; *Sally K. Hine* (†), BBC Sound Archives, London;

---

1   In a letter sent to Bess Cronin in 1951, following the recording trip to Ireland by Alan Lomax and Robin Roberts, the latter remarked: 'I'm just writing a little note to tell you ... how lovely the songs turned out. They're really beautiful. It must take a long while to learn how to sing so well ...'

2   'Heartland singer', *Irish Times*, 23 April 1990.

3   'Not for want of women', *Irish Times*, 5 July 1995, 13.

4   Bess Cronin was one of the native speakers consulted by Prof. Brian Ó Cuív when he was editing the collection of rare and unusual Irish words entitled *Cnósach focal ó Bhaile Bhúirne* (Dublin 1947).

Prof. James Houghton, Department of Microbiology, NUI, Galway; *The Houghton Library*, Harvard University; *Sandra Joyce*, Irish World Music Centre, University of Limerick; *Tommy Keane*, Maree, Oranmore, Co. Galway; *Niall Keegan*, Irish World Music Centre, University of Limerick; *Peter Kennedy*, Gloucester; *Seán Mac Íomhair*, Audio-Visual Services, NUI, Galway; *Máire Kennedy*, Librarian, The Gilbert Library, Dublin; *Donal Lunny*, Dublin; *Pat Mackenzie & Jim Carroll*, London; *Bríd-Rose Lynch*, Cork; *Mamie and Dinny Lynch*, Renamaree, Co. Cork, *Liam McNulty*, Na Píobairí Uilleann, Dublin; *Sarah McQuaid*, Dublin; *John Moulden,* Portrush, Co. Antrim; *Mairéad Mulligan*, Letterkenny, Co. Donegal; *Tom Munnelly,* Department of Irish Folklore, UCD; *The National Library of Australia*, Canberra; *The National Library of Ireland*, Dublin; *The National University of Ireland; Seosaimhín Ní Bheaglaoich*, Dún Chaoin, Co. Kerry; *Pauline Nic Chonaonaigh*, James Hardiman Library, NUI, Galway; *Patsy Nic Fhlannchadha*, Audio-Visual Services, NUI, Galway; *Eilís Ní Shúilleabheáin*, Limerick; *Íde Ní Thuama*, Royal Irish Academy, Dublin; *Dr John Nolan*, National University of Ireland, Dublin; *Mícheál Ó Catháin*, An Spidéal, Co. Galway; *Prof. Séamus Ó Catháin*, Head of Department, Department of Irish Folklore, UCD; *Dr Seán Ó Cillín*, Department of Geography, NUI, Galway; *Seán & Nora Ó Cróinín*, Baile Mhic Íre, Co. Cork; *Ian Ó Laoi*, RTÉ, Dublin; *Maighréad & Mícheál Ó Lionaird*, Gort na Scairte, Co. Cork; *Dr Tim O'Neill*, Department of History, UCD; *Muiris Ó Rócháin*, Milltown Malbay, Co. Clare; *Brian O'Rourke*, Galway; *Prof. Mícheál Ó Súilleabháin*, Irish World Music Centre, University of Limerick; *Eilís Bean Uí Thuama (Ní Chróinín)*, Béal Átha an Ghaorthaidh, Co. Cork; *Prof. Gearóid Ó Tuathaigh*, Department of History, NUI, Galway; *Jeff Place*, Archivist, Smithsonian Institution, Washington, D.C.; *Marie Reddan*, Librarian, James Hardiman Library, NUI, Galway; *Jean Ritchie, George Pickow, & Jon Pickow*, Port Washington, New York; *The School of Irish Studies*; Dublin; *Dr Alan Seeger*, Curator, Folkways Collection, Smithsonian Institution, Washington, D.C.; *Dr Hugh Shields*, Department of French, Trinity College Dublin; *Jackie Small*, Galway; *Dr Seán J. White* (†); *Dr Ríonach uí Ógáin*, Department of Irish Folklore, UCD.

The Arts Council of Ireland, the National University of Ireland, Dublin, the National University of Ireland, Galway, the Heritage Council, Údarás na Gaeltachta and The School of Irish Studies are gratefully thanked for generous financial assistance towards publication.

Although their names are mentioned in the acknowledgements, the efforts of several people in particular made this collection possible: Harry Bradshaw, RTÉ, who expertly transferred the original recordings for the CDs which accompany the book; Glenn Cumiskey, Irish Traditional Music Archive, who compiled the CDs; Nicholas Carolan, who edited and produced the CDs, who made available the superb bibliographical resources of the Irish Traditional Music Archive, and who provided much-needed encouragement when the project appeared to be in difficulty; Sandra Joyce and Niall Keegan, who provided the computer-arrangement of the music; John Moulden, who was generous with his great store of knowledge about broadside ballads; and Tom Munnelly, who also went through my text and added many helpful comments and improvements.

I wish also to record my particular thanks to Sarah Faulkner, BBC Enterprises, London, and Michael Adams, Four Courts Press, for their patience.

BESS CRONIN
1879–1956

THE EARLY YEARS

Bess Cronin was born on 30 May 1879, the eldest of five children of Seán 'Máistir' Ó hIarlaithe and Maighréad Ní Thuama. Her father was headmaster in the school of Barr d'Ínse (hence the epithet 'Máistir', schoolmaster), in the Fuithirí (Fuhirees) area of West Cork, near the Cork-Kerry border.[1] Bess had four sisters, Mary Anne (b.1882), Johanna (b.1885), Nora (b.1890), and Ellie (b.1891), and one brother, Tom (b.1888), as well as two half-brothers, Dan and Tim, by the Master's first marriage. In her mid-teens, however, Bess was sent to help out on the farm of her uncle, Tomás Ó hIarfhlaithe (Tomás Bheity), and his wife, who were childless.[2] It was during those formative years, first with her parents, then with her uncle and aunt, that she acquired most of her songs.

BAILE MHÚIRNE AT THE TURN OF THE CENTURY

My father has described elsewhere[3] how the activities of the Irish language movement at the turn of the century galvanised the community of Irish-speakers in Baile Mhúirne and in neighbouring Cúil Aodha. With the foundation of the *Oireachtas* (the all-Ireland gathering of Irish speakers) in 1897, its annual competitions attracted the finest singers and storytellers from all the different Irish-speaking regions in the country. So successful were the Baile Mhúirne contestants that, by 1900, Baile Mhúirne was being jokingly described as the 'capital' of the Gaeltacht (*Príomh-Chathair na Gaeltachta*). The community there were led by the indefatigable Dr Lynch, who organised a 'parliament' every Sunday after mass, at which the Irish-language papers were eagerly scrutinised and discussed. The doctor had fought (on the French side) in the Franco-Prussian war of 1870, and been captured. He had also spent some time in the United States and in Mexico, before returning to study medicine at Queen's College, Cork. Besides being the community doctor, he also organised a cooperative and a small manufacturing business, as well as a market in Baile Mhúirne. His name figures regularly in the Irish-language newspapers of the time as an inveterate organiser of *feiseanna*, *aeríochtaí* and every other kind of social event.

Alongside the doctor in Baile Mhúirne were Mícheál Ó Briain and Donncha Ó Buachalla, both teachers in the local school. Donncha Ó Buachalla[4] became principal in 1924 and served there until his retirement in 1944. Long before that date, however, he was 'a well-known figure at Irish gatherings in Cork and Kerry in the early days of the Revival'.[5] Always extremely interested in the finer points of the language, he compiled a manuscript dictionary of Baile Mhúirne Irish which is now in the Royal Irish Academy, Dublin. In the 1950s he was a regular panellist on the

---

1 'The master's house' (as it was called) still stands, not far from 'The Top of Coombe', well-known to followers of traditional music and song as the highest pub in Ireland!
2 Tomás Ó hIarfhlaithe was married to a sister of Bess's mother.
3 Seán Ó Cróinín & Donncha Ó Cróinín, *Scéalaíocht Amhlaoibh Í Luínse* (Dublin 1971) viii–xiv.
4 For a brief biography, see Diarmuid Breathnach & Máire Ní Mhurchú, *Beathaisnéis 1882–1982*, 5 (Dublin 1997) 114–15.
5 Breathnach & Ní Mhurchú, *Beathaisnéis* 5, 114 (citing Peadar Ó hAnnracháin in the *Southern Star*, 1 May 1957).

Irish-language programme *Conas adéarfá?* ['How would you say?'], predecessor of the better-known *Fadhbanna Gaeilge* ['Irish problems'], on which my father was a regular contributor. He also organised a *Buíon Seanchais* (storytelling group), which comprised Diarmuid Ó Ceallaigh, Seán Ó Mainnín, Pats 'Lómánach' Ó Héalaí, Jer Ó Héalaí, Aindrias Ó Scanaill, Dónal Ó Mulláin, Pádraig Mac Suibhne, Dónal Ó Héalaí, and Amhlaoibh Ó Loingsigh, and which provided encouragement and practice for the would-be participants in the *Oireachtas* competitions.

Mícheál 'Máistir' Ó Briain was one of the 'Four Masters' of Baile Mhúirne (together with Tadhg Ó Ríordáin, Mícheál Ó Loingsigh, and Conchubhar Ó Deasmhumhna) and gathered stories and poems for publication in the newspapers,[6] as well as a valuable collection of rare and unusual Irish words,[7] and a collection of prayers in Irish.[8] Into this world came a series of collectors, both locals and outsiders, whose combined efforts have left us a treasure-trove of traditional songs and airs.

THE EARLY COLLECTORS IN BAILE MHÚIRNE

First among the song-collectors was Seán Ó Cuill (1882–1958),[9] born and reared in Cúil Aodha, whose mother was well-known as a repository of Irish poetry. Seán himself first showed evidence of an interest in such things with his *Músgraidhe Fileata*, a collection of 120 local songs, which was awarded first prize at the *Oireachtas* in 1901. The adjudicators of the competition, Tadhg Ó Donnchadha ('Tórna') and Pádraig Ó Siochfhradha ('An Seabhac') remarked that there were a lot of fine songs in the collection, but because the author was unwilling to cede copyright in their publication to the Minister for Education, it never appeared in print. However, his published editions of Irish songs did almost fill two volumes of the *Journal* of the Irish Folk Song Society (1923 and 1924).

With the establishment of the Free State he moved to Dublin, and became a civil servant, and there, in the mid-1920s, he founded and was first Secretary of a pioneer scheme called *Nua-Ghaeltacht*, whose purpose was to provide a housing-scheme in Drumcondra especially for Irish-speaking families. He also claimed to have devised the Irish 'average quota' electoral system of proportional representation.

Not long after Seán Ó Cuill came A. Martin Freeman (1878–1959),[10] whose 'Ballyvourney Collection' is perhaps the most famous of all collections of Irish traditional song. Born in Tooting in London, Freeman acquired a remarkable grasp of spoken Irish and was a fine scholar of the language as well. His editions of medieval Irish historical texts are still useful today,[11] but it is for

---

6   Many of their prize-winning efforts were published in the *Proceedings of the Oireachtas*, 1897–1901, *Measgán Músgraighe* (1907), *Madra na nOcht gCos* (1907), *Trí Scéalta* (1907), *Scéalta Triúir* (1919), and *Scéalta Andeas* (1920).

7   The collection was edited by Brian Ó Cuív, *Cnósach focal ó Bhaile Bhúirne* (Dublin 1947). Among the people consulted by Prof. Ó Cuív in the preparation of his text was Bess Cronin. Mícheál Ó Briain's list was used prior to the *Cnósach* by Pádraig Ó Duinnín, in the second, revised edition of his famous Irish-English dictionary. The Baile Mhúirne words are denoted by the abbreviation 'By'. It was Fr Dinneen (xi) who coined the term 'Four Masters' in reference to these four.

8   The manuscript of this collection, dated 26 Jan. 1913, is amongst my father's papers. The prayers were collected from Tadhg Ó Ríordáin, Conchubhar Ó Deasmhumhna (and his mother), Peig Ní Dhonnchadha (from whom A. Martin Freeman was subsequently to collect many of his songs), Séamus Ó Muimhneacháin ('An Pauper'), Cathair na Cátha, Donnchadh Ó Séaghdha, and Mícheál Ó Loingsigh. Several of these prayers were published in Searloit Ní Dhéisighe [Charlotte Deasy] (ed), *Paidreacha na ndaoine* (Baile Átha Cliath 1924).

9   For a brief biographical sketch, see Breathnach & Ní Mhurchú, *Beathaisnéis 3* (Dublin 1992) 89–90.

10 For a brief biographical sketch, see Breathnach & Ní Mhurchú, *Beathaisnéis 2* (Baile Átha Cliath 1990) 39–40.

11 See, e.g., 'The annals in Cotton MS Titus A XXV', *Revue Celtique* 41 (1924) 301–30; 42 (1925) 283–305; 43 (1926) 358–84; 44 (1927) 336–61, and *Annála Connacht: The Annals of Connacht* (A.D. 1224–1544) (Dublin 1944).

1. (l. to r.) Bess's mother ('Seana-Mheáig'),
her brother, Mícheál Ó Tuama, and his wife.

2. Family group behind the Plantation
(back row, l. to r.): Frank, Bess, Dan;
(front, l. to r.): Donncha, Séan, Mick, Jack.

3. Bess with her husband Jack Cronin at the Plantation
(behind: sons Séan and Donncha).

4. Young Bess.

his pioneering work in Baile Mhúirne in 1913 and 1914 that he is best known. Before even the great English collector Cecil Sharp undertook his well-known collecting trips to the Southern Appalachian region of the United States,[12] Freeman had noted down and published the words and airs of 172 songs ('filling seven notebooks of music and five of words') from a variety of Baile Mhúirne singers of the generation before Bess Cronin.[13] Freeman's informants were Conchubhar Ó Cochláin (Conny Coughlan), from Doire na Sagart; Máirín Ní Shuibhne, of Cúil Aodha; Peig Ní Dhonnchadha, of Baile Mhic Íre; Gobnait Ní Bharóid, Doire na Sagart (all but the last-named well into their 70s in 1914), and an additional group that Freeman called 'younger singers', among whom we may probably count Bess Cronin herself.

Freeman's description of his recording activities, and of the reaction they evoked in his circle of informants and their friends, is worth quoting at length, since it gives a good 'feel' for the spirit in which the work was undertaken by both the singers and the collector:

> The people I was living with and their numerous circle (who all manifested a lively interest in my quest) were amused at my industry and astonished at the result. But they told me that I had a mere remnant of the songs of the neighbourhood. 'For the Irish is gone, and the old people are gone, and the songs are gone. If you had come here twenty years ago, *then* you would have got songs!'[14]

Despite this pessimism amongst his informants, however, Freeman succeeded in rescuing a treasure-trove of songs in both Irish and English, for although the great majority of older people in Baile Mhúirne at the time would have been monoglot Irish speakers, there was, nevertheless, a significant number who could both read and speak English, and indeed there were some (like Mícheál Ó Tuama, alias George Curtin) who could turn their hand to composing songs in English as well as in Irish.[15]

Equally fascinating is Freeman's description of the singing style that he encountered in Baile Mhúirne:

> Collectors who have worked in other districts of Munster tell me of peculiarities which — as far as my experience goes — are happily unknown in Ballyvourney, such as a shrill harshness in the high notes, a straining loudness throughout the song, or a uniformly dull, nasal, lethargic delivery. Out of the great number of singers to whom I listened I can recall but one who sang rather too loud for his own comfort, and two or three whose tone was distinctly nasal, though their voices were light and agile. With these exceptions the singers of the neighbourhood must in justice be called singularly good vocalists. They are blessed with just the right amount of 'nasal resonance'; their voices are easy, clear and full and their tone pure; they never exert themselves to sing loud, or pitch their songs too high. Time is of course their slave, not their master, and rhythm is their triumph.[16]

---

12 Sharp's journeys in the Southern Appalachians took place in 1916, 1917, and 1918.
13 A. Martin Freeman, 'Irish folk songs', *Jnl of the Folk Song Society*, pt 6, No. 23 (Jan. 1920) iii–xxviii, 95–205; No. 24 (Jan. 1921) 205–66; No. 25 (Sept. 1921) [265]–342.
14 *JFSS* No. 25, 334.
15 Bess Cronin believed that her father was the author of at least one of the songs in English that she knew. See No. 150.
16 *JFSS*, No. 25, xx.

The singing tradition of Baile Mhúirne was the subject of another study, compiled just after Freeman's visit, apparently by a local collector (sadly unidentified), whose work was submitted for the degree of M.A. in the National University of Ireland in 1917.[17] There are sixty-four songs in this collection, and the author's informants included Máire Ní Loingsigh (Máirín Amhlaoibh) of Cúil Aodha; Neillí Ní Shíothcháin, Ceapacha; Domhnall Ua Fuartháin, Baile Mhic Íre; Mícheál Ó Tuama, Baile Mhúirne; Séamus Ua Cróinín, Guagán Barra; Tomás Ua Súiliobháin, Guagán Barra; Diarmuid Ua Súiliobháin, Guagán Barra, and Domhnall Ua hUallacháin, also of Guagán Barra.

Another similar collection of Munster songs, which included some material from Baile Mhúirne, was made by Cáit Ní Dhonnchadha in 1943; it too remains unpublished.[18]

Around the time of Freeman's first visit to Baile Mhúirne — and perhaps inspired by it — Mícheál Ó Briain (1866–1942) began the work of collecting material in Irish that led to the publication of his *Cnósach focal ó Bhaile Mhúirne*. Although not a native of the area, 'Máistir' Ó Briain, shortly after he took up his teaching duties in the local school, recognised the great richness of the Irish language still predominantly spoken in the area, and its reflection in song and story. In addition to his work as amanuensis for two of his fellow 'Four Masters', he also noted down the words of over a hundred songs known locally, a collection which unfortunately disappeared after his death (although it was known to and seen by Caitlín Ní Bhuachalla, Head-Mistress of the girls' national school at Coachford, Co. Cork).[19]

Conchubhar Ó Deasmhumhna (1871–1928), another of the 'Four Masters' of Baile Mhúirne, was undoubtedly the most gifted of the group.[20] Able to both read and write Irish, he published several small collections of very fine stories for which he won prizes at the *Oireachtas* in successive years, and was a prolific contributor to all the Irish-language journals and newspapers of the Revival period. In 1924 he won an award at the *Oireachtas* for a collection of songs from local oral tradition, but the collection was never published.

After Mícheál Ó Briain and Conchúr Ó Deasmhumhna came Proinsias Ó Ceallaigh, from Gort na Tobratan, who collected material in the Múscraí area of West Cork (Baile Mhúirne and Cill na Martra) for the Co. Cork Vocational Education Committee, 1933–35. He wrote some songs from Bess Cronin, but his principal monument was a collection of 125 songs in Irish noted down from the singing of Nóra Ní Chonaill, Bean Uí Uidhir (Norry Hoare), who was born at Ullanes, and who was around eighty years old at that time.[21]

A near contemporary collection of songs in Irish was also made by Máire Ní Loingsigh, daughter of Amhlaoibh Ó Loingsigh, generally regarded as the finest storyteller of his generation.[22] This collection won first prize in a competition sponsored by the *Oireachtas* in 1941, but was never published.

17 National University of Ireland, Galway, James Hardiman Library, Douglas Hyde MS. 49. A typescript of 111 pages, the author's name on the spine is damaged and cannot now be deciphered, but appears to be Mac Craith (there is no title-page); he uses the pen-name 'Mac Léighinn' ['Student']. Although the work was submitted for examination to the National University of Ireland, I have been unable to trace any record of the author. The typescript is dated 27 June 1917.

18 National University of Ireland, Galway, James Hardiman Library, Douglas Hyde MS. 57.

19 Caitlín Ní Bhuachalla sent the texts of some of these songs to my father in 1943, and these are amongst his notes. For the list of songs, see the Appendix below.

20 For a brief biographical sketch, see Breathnach & Ní Mhurchú, *Beathaisnéis* 4 (Baile Átha Cliath 1994) 108–109.

21 Some of the songs collected by Proinsias Ó Ceallaigh were edited and published by Fionán Mac Coluim in 'Amhráin ó Mhúscraighe', *Béaloideas* 7/1 (Meitheamh 1937) 19–44. Most of the material, however, is still unpublished.

22 See Seán Ó Cróinín & Donncha Ó Cróinín, *Scéalaíocht Amhlaoibh Í Luínse* (Dublin 1971) and *Seanachas Amhlaoibh Í Luínse* (Dublin 1980).

5. Bess photographed by Robin Roberts at the door of the Plantation, 1951

Not long after Máire Amhlaoibh's collection, another local man, Séamus Ó Céilleachair, included thirty songs in Irish in his collection of folklore materials from Baile Mhúirne submitted for a Masters degree of the National University in 1944. His two informants were Nóra Ní Chonaill, Bean Uí Uidhir (Norry Hoare) and Mícheál Ó Fuartháin. Like almost all the previous items in our list, this too remains unpublished.[23]

One final person should be mentioned: Liam de Noraidh (1888–1972), who, between 1940 and 1943, in the course of work carried out for the Irish Folklore Commission, collected songs and tunes in Baile Mhúirne, Béal Átha an Ghaorthaidh, and Cúil Aodha (though in fact his primary interest, and principal source of material, was his native area of Decies in Co. Waterford).[24]

In addition to all the above, of course, there was also the material collected by my father, Donncha Ó Cróinín, on his regular visits home from teacher-training college in Dublin, and by my uncle Seán Ó Cróinín, who, from 1939 to the year of his death, in 1965, was full-time collector for the Irish Folklore Commission in Co. Cork. Their work, however, is probably better included in the activities of the next group of collectors to be discussed.

THE COLLECTORS FROM BESS CRONIN

In 1946, Séamus Ó Duilearga (James Hamilton Delargy), Director of the Irish Folklore Commission, conceived a plan to send collectors to the various Gaeltacht areas of the country, in order to record (in written form and in sound) samples of the story-telling and folklore of those areas, in particular, where the Irish language was felt to be in danger. Beginning in 1947, under the supervision of Seamus Ennis, the first field trips for song-recording were undertaken. The pioneering nature of this scheme deserves to be emphasised: the BBC, for example, did not undertake extensive field operations until the advent of portable tape recorders in the early 1950s.[25] The 1947 'expedition', however, had been undertaken in cooperation with the BBC, whose Director of Recorded Programmes, R.V.A. (Brian) George — himself a Donegal-man and a singer — 'was largely responsible for persuading the BBC to take the initiative' of establishing its own archive of folksongs and folkmusic.[26] The results of the Irish trip were sufficiently successful to convince the authorities in London that much material still remained to be recorded and the result was a five-year project for systematic field recording throughout Britain and Ireland, which was undertaken between 1952 (when Seamus Ennis was recruited from Radio Éireann) and 1957. (Seamus was with the Commission from 1 June 1942 until 1 August 1947, when he went to Radio Éireann, where he was Outside Broadcast Officer.)

---

23   This thesis, entitled *Seanchus ó Bhaile Mhúirne*, is in the James Hardiman Library, Galway.
24   See Liam de Noraidh, *Ceol ón Mumhain* (Baile Átha Cliath 1965), and Dáithí Ó hÓgáin et al., *Binneas thar meon* 1 (Baile Átha Cliath 1994).
25   See Marie Slocombe, 'The BBC folk music collection', *Folklore & Folk Music Archivist* 7/1 (1964) 3–13.
26   Slocombe, 'BBC folk music collection', 4.

These CBÉ and BBC field trips recorded songs from Bess Cronin in May and August 1947 and at various dates subsequently, up to August, September and November 1952.[27] Something of the excitement of these recording sessions can be felt in the descriptions of them that Bess included in the letters she wrote to my father at the time:

'The Old Plantation',
Tuesday, 25th Nov., 1949.

… We were watching and waiting all the week, and no one coming. We were nearly after forgetting about them. We heard Seamus came to Macroom on Wednesday: tomorrow week. Mick was in town, and Johnny was gone with them, and the old Mrs Lynch came down with Jocey (as Seamus calls her). He couldn't ask questions, but they said the party were gone out to Keeffe's place.[28] We were waiting on.

At about 8:30 last night the noise came. John Twomey and Frank were sitting here talking; Mick was gone. You wouldn't half see the two making for the front door, as the van and car went up the yard! In they came: Seamus, Jim Mahon, and Johnny. All the hurry started then, to go and pick up John Connell from his own house and Mick from Dan's. The stranger stayed with me … He drives the van and manages the recording. When things would go any bit slow, he'd speak from the van to hurry up. He told me while they were out that Seamus slept the day, and himself went rabbiting, for want of anything to do … He didn't leave here until after 1 o'clock.

Seamus and John Connell and Johnny stayed for a long time after. I thought, as they were out there, that they had Keeffe and Murphy[29] done, but they hadn't. 'Tis some others they were after. Some Art O'Keeffe played a fife with Murphy, and they didn't meet the other Keeffe at all. But they met Ned Buckley. He is a fairly old man, having a shop in Knocknagree, a great poet — he recited a lot of his work, but he can't sing it. Some of his poetry and song are in print now. Seamus got some from him. Johnny thinks he is a gifted man. They got songs from others too.

Seamus wanted to know then would we allow him to bring Keeffe and Murphy down here, or could we keep them for a night, if it was wanted. We said yes, of course, and welcome. He was very pleased then. He fixed on Thursday night — he said they would come some part of the night, as there is to be a dance or a wedding in the vicinity, and he should round them up after a few hours and try and bring Keeffe … So he settled on that, but we don't believe, as before, that he will turn up punctual — but they'll come sometime!

John Connell sang four songs, and well too. Mick sang some, and I a few verses — it was too late by right when they started, and with the tea and tack, etc., it ran up very late …

27 Test recordings of Bess were made by Seamus Ennis in May 1947 (see the Index of Recordings below, 327–32). These are, in fact, the earliest known recordings made of her.
28 Padraig O'Keeffe († 1963) was the best-known traditional fiddler of the Slieve Luachra area.
29 Denis Murphy († 1974) was Padraig O'Keeffe's most famous pupil.

So, that's the way, so far. I'll tell you the rest of the story after the next 'invasion'. If we can keep the news from the neighbours now, things are O. K …[30]

The sequel followed two days later:

'The Old Plantation',
Monday, 31st Nov., 1949.

Well now so,

I can sit down at my ease and record for you the events of the last few days. I can't put it all on paper, but I'll do my best.

I'm sure I told you how they left us after an all-night sitting until 6 o'clock a.m. Seamus faced for Kerry and was going to come and bring Murphy and Keeffe, satisfied that they could stay for a night. We were waiting on to see when would they turn up. The engineer, Mr Mahon, and his van appeared on Friday at 2 o'clock, and said that he was ordered to come, as Seamus & Murphy & Keeffe would meet him here at 4 o'clock.

He was waiting and waiting, the poor man, until 10:30, and when no one came, he made off for Macroom again (he was staying at Ronan's) and he was very sore over it. I'm telling you, he knows Seamus as good as we do!

They were all out at Murphy's the evening before, Thursday, but Keeffe was not available. He was attending a dance very near his home on that night, and everyone knew it would be a hard job to pick him up. But wherever they went, or didn't, they didn't come — after Seamus ringing up his man from Killarney and telling him to come at such a time, and they would be here!

But anyway, he left at half-past-ten. Johnny was coming out with the man behind, who was in Cork, and they noticed the van passing them east at Jeremiah's. They went back to the house and made no delay, but came up, and they met John Connell going home from here, and he told them. They said: 'Come on up again', and they were in to us straight.

We were all talking — 'Where did they go?' 'What kept them?' 'When would they come now?', etc., etc. One said 'They'll come yet tonight', and one said 'No'.

About 12:00 we saw light, and there they were, fairly good and groggy, and you never heard such excuses as Seamus had (and asking what was Mr Mahon saying, and all that) … and I said he took no notice of they being so slow, as we could not know what trouble they'd meet … Seamus then said he was a good man for his business …

They all sat in, had tea, and played until 4 o'clock in the morning. Our two men went to bed and Seamus went to Macroom, and promised to be out at 12 p.m. in the morning. The van came at that time, but Jim didn't wait until about 3 o'clock, and then there was hurry. They did splendid; everyone said they couldn't play better. Another fellow[31] from Keeffe's place came about 7 o'clock

30 Cited from a collection of letters in my possession. Bess Cronin always wrote these letters in English.
31 This was Paddy Cronin, then aged twenty-one. The session described by Bess was his first recording. Seamus (in an interview recorded with Pádraig Ó Raghallaigh) has described how Paddy cycled over twenty miles on a wet and windy night, with his fiddle strapped to his bicycle, and on arrival at the Plantation made a flawless recording, which earned him another session in the Radio Éireann studio in Dublin, and on the proceeds of that session he was able to travel to the United States, where he spent most of his years after that. Paddy is now back living in Killarney, and still playing away.

and he too broadcast a few tunes, and good. Seamus drove them down home at
11 o'clock, and went to Macroom after (Saturday night), and left for Dublin
after mass, Sunday. He promised he'd come at Easter. Mick sang a song or two,
and John Connell sang four, and good he is for it.

   I can't say more, I must post (and I haven't last said …).

It would be hard to better these descriptions for the vivid impression they give of the atmosphere
and excitement that were generated by those first recording sessions. They are clear evidence also
of the warm relationship that had built up between Bess and Seamus Ennis, a respect that was
mutual. In several recorded interviews for Radio Éireann, Ennis remarked on the high regard he
had for her singing, and for the generosity with which she was always willing to pass on her songs
to anyone who was interested in them. In a recorded conversation with Pádraig Ó Raghallaigh,
for example, when asked what were the parts of Munster that he would single out as being rich
in the heritage, Seamus replied: 'Ballyvourney, Ballingeary, Muskerry in general, Coolea'. And
when asked to recall the names of particular individuals he replied:

> The chief one was Mrs Elizabeth Cronin of Ballymakeera, Ballyvourney. I can
> remember frequently visiting her, and one afternoon I went out to visit her, to
> write more songs from her. She had a sheaf of songs written for me, and I told
> her she shouldn't be putting herself to the trouble — 'Ah,' she said, she'd rather
> be chatting with me than dictating songs to me! And I can remember the first
> song that I ever heard her sing was in the form of a lullaby, *Cuir a chodladh*, etc.
> It was a kind of lullaby thing, based on the Christ Child Lullaby (*The Jealousy of
> St Joseph*) … That was the first one I ever wrote from her. And I remember
> another one — she was a jolly lady too — *Cold potatoes, cold potatoes* etc.[32]

In another radio programme he gave the following brief description of Bess:[33]

> *Bean bheag théagartha ab ea í, a raibh aoibh an gháire 'na héadan agus loinnir a' ghrinn
> ina súile aici agus binneas a' cheoil 'na béal agus í gan fuadar a' réiteach a' té agus a'
> leagadh an bhúird romhainn (bhí mac léi [Seán Ó Cróinín] im' theannta). 'Sé thugaimse
> uirthi 'na dhiaidh sin: Banríon amhrán Mhúscraí. Ní raibh aon teora leis na poirt bheaga
> agus leis na hamhráintí mhóra a bhí ar a toil aici.*

> She was a stocky little woman who radiated jollity in her face and had a glint
> of humour in her eyes and sweetness in her mouth as she unhurriedly prepared
> tea and laid the table for us (a son of hers was with me [Seán Ó Cróinín]). The
> name I had for her after that was: 'The Muskerry Queen of Song'. There was
> no limit to the little tunes and big songs that she had by heart. (my transl.)

When Seamus brought Brian George to the Plantation for the first time he introduced him to
Bess as 'Brian George from the BBC, London' — 'I don't care he's from the ABC', she remarked,
'welcome!'; and that was the way with all the collectors who came to the Plantation.[34] Brian

---

32 'The Long Note', broadcast 5 Oct. 1982.
33 Broadcast, 1947.
34 An entry in my father's diary for 16 Aug. 1945 records the visit of an Englishwoman (*'Sasanach'*) by name of Joan Callen,
     who took photographs. I have unfortunately been unable to trace this individual.

6. Bess being recorded at the Plantation by the BBC (background: Seamus Ennis).

George was especially taken with Bess and remarked to my father that she was 'a remarkable woman'. He had particular reason to be impressed because it was from Bess that he recorded *Lord Gregory* (No. **83**), which he regarded as the high-point of his collecting career. The BBC had apparently searched high and low throughout England and Scotland for the air to this song, but the only version with any kind of tune was a sort of recitative rendering that they had recorded from an old woman in Scotland. In a BBC radio programme broadcast after Bess's death in 1956, Brian George remarked: 'I must say that, in all my experience of folksong collecting, I have never found greater satisfaction nor such wide variety'.[35]

In 1951 the great American folksong collector, Alan Lomax, began the collecting that was to result in the publication of the Irish volume in his *Columbia World Library of Folk and Primitive Music* (New York 1955), which contained songs recorded from Bess, amongst many others. Lomax had been introduced to Bess by Seamus Ennis and he recorded songs from her in both English and Irish. He also had interesting conversations with her, snatches of which are reproduced on the recording. When asked, for example, where and when she sang, Bess replied:

> I sang here, there and everywhere: at weddings and parties and at home, and milking the cows in the stall, and washing the clothes, and sweeping the house, and stripping the cabbage for the cattle, and sticking the *sciollán's* [seed potatoes] abroad in the field, and doing *everything*.[36]

---

35 From a talk by my father on the RTÉ programme, 'The Long Note', broadcast 13 Feb. 1978. Despite the best efforts of the BBC Archives staff, and of others, I have been unable to establish the precise date of Brian George's talk.
36 From the Columbia World Library record, by kind permission.

7. Mamie Lynch singing in Lios Buí (background: Mamie's mother, Bess, Dinny Lynch
(now Mamie's husband) (photo: George Pickow).

It is interesting to note, however, that not every song appealed to her, and in fact she surprised one BBC collector (Marie Slocombe) by singing the opening verse of *Lord Randal* (No. **84**) and no more. When asked if she had the rest of the song, the following conversation ensued:

> MS — 'Do you remember any more, what happened (in the song)?'
> BC — 'No, no, no, I don't. I often heard it. I often heard it.'
> MS — 'Where?'
> BC — 'I often heard it.'
> MS — 'You haven't heard it all.'
> BC — 'I often heard it, but I never learned it, no. I don't know, I didn't care for it, or something. I didn't bother about learning it, but just that I had that much, now.'

At the same time, several of her songs came to her only after prompting, either by collectors or by what other singers around her had performed. This was how she recalled *Pussycat's Party*, for example (No. **120**), which came to her after she had heard her niece, Mamie Lynch, singing *Pussy got the Measles*. There were certainly songs that Jean Ritchie and George Pickow recorded from Bess, but that my father had never heard her sing. There is no telling, either, what were the songs that she had once known, but long forgotten, although it can be assumed with reasonable certainty that many well-known local songs (such as *Cath Chéim an Fhia*, or *Máire Ní Laoghaire*) were part of her repertoire but, for whatever reason, were never recorded from her or written down by collectors. The process of collecting was always a haphazard one at the best of times, with the emphasis sometimes on the 'big songs' (i.e., the Child ballads), and at other times on more local compositions. By far the greater number of songs recorded are in English, which is understandable enough, given that the principal collectors (besides the Irish Folklore Commission) were the BBC or the various American collectors, Alan Lomax, Jean Ritchie and George Pickow, and Diane Hamilton

Jean Ritchie and George Pickow came to Ireland as a result of Jean's interest in the origins of the many songs that she and her family ('The Singing Family of the Cumberlands') had grown up with in the Southern Appalachian region of Kentucky. Jean was awarded a scholarship from the Fulbright Commission to trace her many songs back to Britain and Ireland, and in November 1952 she and her husband George visited Bess in Lios Buí (parish of Cill na Martra), where Bess was staying at that time. Over a period of three weeks they recorded many songs and tunes from Bess and her neighbours, several of them not previously recorded. Jean and George had the additional advantage that they were able to use the very latest 'state-of-the art' recording equipment: the first portable reel-to-reel recording apparatus, then only recently available in the United States. This was far superior to anything the CBÉ — or even the BBC — was using at the time, and the difference is evident in the quality of their recordings.

Jean penned some vivid descriptions of her stay in Lios Buí in the letters that she wrote to her family back in Kentucky:

> Castle Hotel,
> Macroom, Co. Cork.
> 26 November 1952

> … We are having a fine time in Ireland. I'm seeing things I never saw before, and making a lot of new friends. The Irish people are the friendliest people outside of Kentucky I ever saw. When I go into a country cottage here in County Cork it feels just like home.

> Last night we went out over the wild moors some miles from Macroom to visit Mrs Cronin, who looks like Mom and who sings beautiful old songs — some of the same ones we sing at home … We recorded miles of tape of her singing …

> Mrs Cronin is staying with her sister, an elderly lady who still has four grown-up children at home, and they every last one of them are merry and full of fun as crickets. It is a real country farm with millions of chickens, pigs, turkeys, guineas, cows, horses, a big barn full and running over with hay right now. They cook over the open fire, on pots hung from cranes, carry all the water from the spring. They wouldn't let us go without having supper, and we had pork which they took from a big barrel in the corner, bread baked in a sort of Dutch oven on the hearth, homemade butter and jam, and cups of hot tea. Afterwards we sat around the turf fire, on seats inside the chimney, and told stories of fairies and h'ants, and sang songs until after twelve o'clock (nobody ever goes to bed early in Ireland). It was much like old times at home and made me homesick for my childhood.[37]

---

37 Letter cited by kind permission of Jean Ritchie.

8. Bess and Jean Ritchie in Lios Buí, 1952 (photo: George Pickow).

9. Bess at Lios Buí, 1952 (background: Jean Ritchie) (photo: George Pickow).

10. Julia Twomey, with her husband,
in Portland, Oregon.

Jean and George were also treated to a strawboy wedding and a pre-Christmas Christmas party ('The Irish are like that — any *small* excuse, or a look sideways, and they are having a party. It's wonderful!'). Fortunately, they not only recorded many of these events on tape, George — a professional magazine photographer — also captured much of the excitement in a wonderful series of photographs that are now (together with the tapes) in the Ritchie-Pickow Archive in the James Hardiman Library, NUI, Galway.

The last important collector to visit Bess was the American, Diane Hamilton (Guggenheim), who recorded from her in Macroom in 1955, not long before Bess died. Although the quality of the recordings is excellent, Bess's health was clearly in decline at the time, and the illness that was to carry her off in the following year (she died on 12 June 1956) was already having its effect on her voice, which is very weak. But even at that late date, Bess was still able to provide one song (*Do Thugas Grá Cléibh Duit*, No. **53**) that had not previously been recorded.[38]

HOW BESS LEARNED HER SONGS

In a recorded interview with Alan Lomax, Bess recalled how she had learned most of her songs:

> Well, I learned a lot of them from my mother; and then I learned more of them from … We had … Well, we used to have lots of servants, you know. There'd be servants at the time. You'd have one now for, say, five or six months, and so on; and maybe that one would leave and another one would come. There'd be some new person always coming or going. Or a girl, cousins and friends, coming along like that and all, you know anyway?[39]

One of these cousins, Julia Twomey (Síle Ní Thuama) was a constant singing companion of Bess's — in fact, Bess maintained that her cousin had the better voice! The earliest-known public performance by Bess was with Julia Twomey, at the Feis in Macroom (reported in *Fáinne an Lae*, 8 Jan. 1899):

> Miss Bessie Herlihy, of Ballyvourney, was introduced by her uncle, Mr. D. Twomey … Miss Herlihy … contributed two Irish songs[40] and a recitation, '*An duine bocht uasal*' (also in Irish),[41] which were much admired for their beauty and the naive simplicity with which they were rendered …[42]

---

38   The field trip undertaken in 1956–57 by another American collector, Sidney Robertson Cowell, and her husband, covered Connemara and the Aran Islands, but did not venture south.

39   See *Cuckanandy*, Folktracks FAC 60, A.5.

40   One of Bess's neighbours, Neil Ní Bhuachalla, Bean Uí Thuama (a daughter of Jer Rua), in 1947 remarked to my father that the first song Bess sang at that feis began 'Tá bó bhán ag Máire 'n Ghaorthaig,/ Is fearr le crúth í ná'n Chiúrach Bhléineann'. (I have not managed to identify the song).

41   *Duine bocht uasal ag lorg déirce* was composed by Conny Desmond (Conchubhar Ó Deasmhumhna), a next-door neighbour of Bess's subsequently in Baile Mhic Íre. See Appendix 1 below (303–4).

42   Julia Twomey emigrated subsequently to America, and settled in Portland, Oregon, where she married. Although she and

One of the servant girls that her uncle's family had at Ráth was a young woman called Nóra Ní Laoghaire, who was always singing songs, and who was particularly good at 'puss music' (*poirtíní béil*), and she could keep groups of dancers going forever with this kind of hummed music (*choinneóch sí rínceoirí ar siúl go brách*). It was from her too that Bess learned the milking-song callad *Raghad-sa ó thuaidh leat, a bhó* (No. **121**).

On another occasion, Bess recorded how she first came to learn the song called *Mo Mhúirnín Bán* (No. **90**): She was asleep in bed one night when she was woken by a strange noise, which she thought at first was the sound of ghosts! She hid under the bedclothes but poked her head out after a while and listened: the sound was that of the women below churning butter! Her mother had to attend a funeral the next day, and had to have the butter churned and ready for collection before she left the house. There was an elderly neighbour had come to the house that evening (unknownst to Bess) and she and the other women spent the night sewing and then churning, with the old woman singing songs all the time. Bess heard her singing:

> *Ní sa chnoc is aoirde a bhíonn mo bhuíon-sa*
> *Ach i ngleanntán aoibhinn abhfad ó láimh;*
> *Mar a labhrann a' chuach faoi chuan san oíche ann …*

She jumped out of bed, ran downstairs, and told the startled women what had been going through her head upstairs in the bed. She then insisted that the old woman teach her the song, which she duly did, there and then, 'since there's no better time for you to learn it [the old woman remarked] than right now, because it's said that a person will learn something better before breakfast than at any other time!' The old woman recited the song three or four times, and Bess had it before the breakfast, along with many more (*d'fhoghlamaíos seó acu uaithe an uair céanna*), but some of these she later forgot (*do chailleas 'na dhiaidh san cuid acu*).[43]

The fact that Bess's father was a teacher, and that her grandfather and uncle had such an interest in books, doubtless meant that she was more exposed to the influence of the written word than would normally have been the case in late-nineteenth-century rural Mid-Cork. But even then, the influence is not to be overstated: the transmission of poetry and songs in this part of the country continues right down to the present day as a predominantly oral phenomenon, and though the number of books published in Irish grew significantly with the rise of the Irish language movement in the period between the foundation of the Gaelic League in 1893 and the establishment of the Irish Free State in 1922 and after, the vast bulk of what appeared in print was actually collected from folk tradition.

Bess herself recalled the intense scholarly interest that her father and grandfather before her had in the Irish language, and especially in printed books.

> I well remember listening to my father — God rest him! — telling me how my
> grandfather and another man (one of the Buckleys) used to be steeped in Irish
> books after mass on Sunday, from then till nightfall, and they reading and writing
> and discussing them together, until it happened finally that they took an interest
> in the Protestant bible. And I suppose that wasn't right, but they meant no harm,

---

Bess corresponded for a while, the connection was broken somehow; Julia never returned to Ireland. A son, Clifford J. Burke, was a G.I. based in England before D-Day, and wrote once or twice to the Plantation.

43 CBÉ 536, 29–31. The passage is too long to cite here in the original Irish. Translations are mine in all cases.

I suppose, but just that they wanted to see if there was any difference between it and their own bible.

Anyway, someone told the priest about it and he was livid. He said they had no right to be reading the Protestant bible, and that they should abandon it; and he read them from the altar, so that there was great merriment about them and much poking of fun.[44]

She also recalled an uncle (perhaps the Tomás Ó hIarfhlaithe with whom she went to live) who had an insatiable interest in books, both in Irish and in English. When such a book came into his hands, he would leave aside everything else, and read it from end to end. He had a phenomenal memory as well, and could recall the exact details of everything he had read.[45]

Much more important, however, for the dissemination of songs was the influence of beggars, of whom there were many walking the roads in Bess's time:

> There were poor people going the roads those days — lots of them — old men and old women, and they used to stay with my uncle when they called at night (and it is many the time he gave a bed to the poor — may God grant him favour for it and the Lord have mercy on his soul!).[46]

In one notebook of my father's there is a list of no fewer than sixty *Bacaig na Contae* ('The Beggars of the County'), all of whom Bess knew by name. These included 'Brídín flit-fleait', 'Jack the Pup' (Ó Luasa), 'Jack the Sweep' (Quilligan), 'Mick the Duck', and Mick Butler and his wife, who were ballad-singers. Bess said of another, Nóra Phádraig (described as *seana-bhean siúil*, 'an old woman of the road') that she was a wonderful singer *(bhí sí go seoidh chun na n-amhrán)*.

The printed newspapers and Irish-language magazines that proliferated in the years following the foundation of *Connradh na Gaedhilge* (the Gaelic League) in 1897 encouraged the publication of many of the songs known to singers like Bess (though none noted down from Bess herself). At the same time, well-known and much-loved older collections, such as John O'Daly's *The poets and poetry of Munster*, and Edward Walsh's *Irish popular songs* — and perhaps the occasional broadside ballad — may have popularised some of the songs in English, particularly the patriotic ballads like *Pat O'Donnell* and *Sean O'Farrell*. Older collections of Irish music, such as Petrie's and P.W. Joyce's, are evidence for the fact that some songs in Bess's repertoire were in circulation long before the language revival, but the pamphlets and booklets of Irish songs published in the early years of this century, all at very low prices, doubtless fuelled the enthusiasm for such things in places like Baile Mhúirne. Norma Borthwick's *Ceól-sídhe*, Fionán Mac Coluim's *Cosa buidhe arda* (and his numerous other collections), An tAthair Pádraig Breathnach's *Ceól ár sinsear* and *Songs of*

---

44 CBÉ 476, 282–83: 'Is maith is cuimhin liom bheith ag éisteacht lem' athair — beannacht Dé len' anam — á insint conas a bhíodh mo sheanathair agus duine eile (fear eile de mhuintir Bhuachalla), go mbídís ropaithe i leabhraibh Gaoluinne t'réis Aifrinn Dé Domhnaigh, as san go dtí an oíche, agus iad a' lé' agus a' scrí agus ag insint dá chéile mar gheall orthu, i dtreo 's gur chuadar insa Bhíobla an tSasanaigh i ndeire bárra. Agus, go deimhin, is docha nár ceart é sin, ach ní chun aon díobhála, b'fhéidir, a dheineadar é, ach chun go mbeadh fhios acu an raibh puinn difríocht idir é sin agus a mBíobla féin. Ach, ar aon chuma, d'inis duine éigin don sagart é agus do bhí an sagart ar buile. Dúirt sé ná raibh ao' cheart acu aon fál in ao' chor a bheith acu i mBíobla an tSasanaig, ach é fhágaint 'na ndiaidh, agus do labhair se ón althóir orthu, agus do bhí ana-spórt agus ana-mhagadh fútha mar gheall air.'

45 CBÉ 476, 284: 'Do bhí ceann maith aige, mar gach aon rud a léighfeadh sé ní dhearúdfadh sé aon fhocal de agus d'fhéadfadh sé gach aon áit gur léig sé agus gach aon ainm agus gach aoinní a insint duit agus cadé an sórd baill é agus cad a fhásfadh ann, agus gach aoinní mar sin.'

46 CBÉ 476, 284: 'Ach do bhí daoine bochta a' gabháil a' tslí an uair sin — seó acu — seandaoine, seana-mhná agus seandaoine, agus d'fhanaidís aige istoíche nuair a gheobhaidís a' tslí, agus is mó uair a thug sé leabaig dosna boicht — go dtuga Dia a thoradh dho, agus go ndeinidh Dia trócaire air a anam!'

Mount Massy the flower of Macroom.

1st

How I long to remember those bright days of yore
So sweetly by pleasures beguiled
And the friends that frequented my old cabin home
And the comrades I loved when a child
Oft I fancied I roamed by Mount Massy's green groves
Or poached by the light of the moon
Where the lark sang aloud neath that golden fringed cloud
In Mount Massy the flower of Macroom.

2nd

In the sweet Summer time when the weather was fine
What fun there would be at the gate
When the gadget would ring out the dancers to please
And the lovers their love-tales relate
How the Colleens would smile as they'd sit on the stile
Thats facing Mount Massys demesne
And their lovers so fair by their side standing there
While the gadget its sweet notes would strain

[chorus after each verse]

So friends come with me & its there you will see
The apples & cherries in bloom
For its you Ill invite where I first saw the light
In that sweet sunny spot called Macroom.

'Mount Massy, the flower of Macroom' written in Bess's own hand (personal collection).

the Gael, and many others, all provided the words and airs for hundreds of Irish popular songs, and for anyone interested in the subject (as the community in Baile Mhúirne in Bess's time certainly was) the after-mass 'parliament' on Sunday mornings must have included discussion of such material.

Of course, many of Bess's songs were local compositions, by travelling poets such as Pead Buí Ó Loingsigh, Domhnall Ó Luasa ('The Poet of Lisbwee'), the Poet Ahern, and closer to home, Donnchadh Ó Laoghaire, whose composition *Baile Mhúirne* (No. **29**) won first prize at the *feis* in Baile Mhúirne in 1900 (and appeared subsequently in print). Many humorous compositions by Mícheál Ó Tuama ('George Curtin')[47] and Conchubhar Ó Deasmhumhna (Conny Desmond) circulated by word of mouth; Conny and George Curtin were first cousins. Conny Desmond was a next-door-neighbour of Bess's after she married into the Plantation, and they got on well. My father remembered him as a frequent visitor to the house when he was young. Bess had a great regard for his literary skills in both Irish and English, and he could turn his hand to prose or poetry with equal facility. Individuals such as these could produce a verse or song at the drop of a hat, and the occasion need not be particularly important. For example, a neighbour of Bess's and Conny Desmond's, Pádraig 'Mothall' Ó Murchú (so called because of the mane of hair on his head) met someone on the road one day who asked him how he would translate into Irish the words of the song *Girleen, don't be idle* (No. **62**) ('Girleen, don't be idle, gather your ducks and mind them'). Pádraig thought for moment and then said:

> *A chailín bhig ghleoite mheidhrig*
> *Bailigh do lachain is feighil iad.*

The same people could turn out something in English with equal ease. On one occasion when George Curtin was visiting Conny Desmond (it was St Stephen's Day), a group of children came to the door and sang the familiar verse:

> The wren, the wren, the king of all birds,
> St Stephen's Day he was caught in the furze.
> Up with the kettle and down with the pot,
> Give us our answer and leave us be off!

George, who had a liking for the drop, was hoping that Conny would produce a bottle of stout (that being the custom around Christmas, when anyone came visiting), but the drink was slow in coming. Once the boys had gone, however, he started up with his own verse:

> The crow, the crow, the farmer's curse,
> St Stephen's Day we choked him with spuds.
> Down with the bottle and off with the cork —
> If you haven't a corkscrew we'll do with a fork![48]

From neighbours and acquaintances such as these, and from family and relations, Bess learned many of her songs.

---

47 Bess was distantly related to Mícheál Ó Tuama through her mother.
48 CBÉ 912, 424–25.

11. Bess at *c.*70 years.

Some of the older people had a knowledge of the printed literature, as Liam de Noraidh remarked in the case of one of his informants, Síle Bean Uí Ríordáin, Doirín Álainn. Although eighty years old when he met her, in 1940, she pulled down a book of Eoghan Rua Ó Súilleabháin's compositions on one occasion and, instead of reading the poems, she sang them, from the book, giving to each its appropriate air.[49] But that should not be taken to imply that the songs had been actually *learned* from such printed sources. There is no evidence whatever that Bess ever learned a song from a book or a newspaper, and the fact that she could read and write English (but not Irish) was simply the result of her schooling. School-going children of Bess's generation were familiar with the reading-books produced by Alex Thom & Co. for the Commissioners of National Education, in which they read selections of English prose, such as Burke's *Reflections on the French Revolution* (the opening words of which: 'It is now sixteen or seventeen years since I saw the Queen of France …' my father remembered Bess reciting from memory), *The Impeachment of Warren Hastings*, *The Vision of Mirza* ('Lochiel, Lochiel, beware of the day!'), and Goldsmith's *Deserted Village*. All fine, upstanding stuff, but not the 'Hidden Ireland'. Bess came from a long line of poets in Irish, the Ó hIarfhlaithe's, and one of their number (Dáth 'ac Phádraig) presided over the *dámhscoil* ('poetry school') in Múscraí in the late eighteenth century. The poets and poetry of Munster were part of a vibrant tradition of song and story, and the older people of Baile Mhúirne and Múscraí in general recounted the doings of such men (and women as well) as though they had experienced them themselves. Bess Cronin, the 'Queen of Muskerry Song' was part of that living tradition.

THE COMMERCIAL RECORDINGS

A niece of Bess's, Maighréad Bean Uí Lionaird, has recalled how she and her husband, Mícheál, encountered an acquaintance of his while out walking one day, and on being introduced to Maighréad the acquaintance asked if she was related to Elizabeth Cronin. When asked how he

49 Liam de Noraidh, *Ceol ón Mumhain* (Baile Átha Cliath 1965) 10. Seán Ó Cróinín used to do likewise.

12. Bess making decorations for the wren-bush
(photo: George Pickow).

knew of her, the acquaintance recounted how he had frequently heard Bess on the radio when he served as a sailor with the British merchant navy plying the North Sea, and he added that there was usually a rush down from deck when the BBC Light Programme, 'As I Roved Out' came on air, in hopes that the sailors would get to hear Bess singing! The appearance in 1955 of Alan Lomax's Irish volume in the *Columbia World Library of Folk and Primitive Music*, and of Jean Ritchie's *Field Trip* (c. 1955) and *As I Roved Out* (1960) first brought her to the attention of an international public, and in the 1960s various recordings made by the BBC were reproduced in the thematic collections of the Caedmon/Topic series. It is mainly for that reason that Bess Cronin's voice is so well known outside Ireland, not just across the Irish Sea but as far away as Australia and the United States.

But no attempt to produce a complete or representative collection of Bess's songs was undertaken until, in 1972, my father was approached by David Bland, who at that time was working with Bill Leader at Leader Sound, then based in London.[50] Leader Records were a small record company devoted to recording and publishing the traditional music of Britain and Ireland, and besides several albums of songs by such as the Copper family of Rottingdean (*A song for every season*, LEAB 404), *Unto Brigg Fair* (recordings made in 1905 by the Australian pianist and folkmusic-collector, Percy Grainger, from Lincolnshire traditional singers; LEA 4050), and *Charlie Wills* (the great Somerset-Dorset singer; LEA 4041), they also published LPs of two well-known Sligo flute and whistle-players (*Seamus Tansey with Eddie Corcoran;* LEA 2005) and Hugh Shields's collection of *Old British ballads of Donegal and Derry* (LEA 4055), a predecessor of his better-known collection, *Shamrock, rose and thistle*, also produced by Leader (LED 2070). The Leader proposal was to make a selection of the BBC recordings, and my father wrote to the BBC in order to secure permission for Leader to publish.

Unfortunately, Leader Sound began to encounter difficulties, financial and otherwise, at precisely that time. Lack of funds was the reason for the cancellation of a planned trip to Ireland by David Bland, and a move from London to Yorkshire in 1973 exacerbated the problems. The final blow came with the oil crisis of that year, as a result of which vinyl supplies for the record industry all but dried up. For a small company with very limited resources, the situation proved impossible and Leader Sound finally folded in 1974. The company's tapes and equipment were all seized as part of the bankruptcy settlement.

Some years later, in 1978, another proposal to publish a Bess Cronin selection was made, this time by Tom Munnelly, then (as now) working in the Department of Irish Folklore at University College Dublin (the former Irish Folklore Commission). Tom had an agreement in principle with Topic Records to publish one or more LPs, but for a variety of reasons the project never came to fruition. There were other suggestions as well: Seán Ó Riada, for example, urged my father to raise the matter with Garech de Brún at Claddagh Records, but nothing appears to have come of the idea.

The current project took shape after my father's death in 1990. Having inherited his papers, I began to research the materials relating specifically to my grandmother, and accidentally — as the result of a visit to my cousin, Mrs Mamie Lynch, of Rennanaree — discovered the existence of the recordings and photographs of Bess Cronin made by Jean Ritchie and George Pickow (now part of the Ritchie-Pickow Archive in the University Library, Galway). This was the spur needed to get the project moving again, and due in large part to the extraordinary generosity of Jean and George, that renewed impetus has led to this Complete Collection. Through their kind cooperation, that of the BBC and the Department of Irish Folklore in University College Dublin, and of the late Diane Hamilton,[51] it has been possible to bring together in this book and CD-set not just a selection of Bess's songs, but a complete listing of all known recordings.

In addition, the unique collection of manuscript materials assembled by my father (including autograph texts of some songs) has also enabled me to offer the definitive text of all Bess's songs, not just the recorded ones. The result is a collection of two-hundred-or-so songs, in Irish and in English, in a range and variety never seen before in Irish traditional music. I hope that, with this publication, not only will Bess Cronin's unique voice and singing style become familiar to a new generation of traditional song-lovers, but that Bess's songs will become available, once again, to all who want to learn and sing them.

---

50 I am grateful to David Bland for giving me his account of this correspondence.
51 The Diane Hamilton recordings are now deposited in the Irish Traditional Music Archive. I am grateful to her musical executor, Donal Lunny, for permission to use them, and to the Director of the Archive, Nicholas Carolan, for granting access to them.

BROLLACH

'B'fhéidir go bhféadfaí tuairisc éigin a thabhairt ar ball ar Eibhlís Ní Iarfhlaithe agus ar a cuid amhrán', adúirt m'athair sa ghearrachúntas a scríobh sé ar shaol agus ar shaothar a dhearthár, Seán Ó Cróinín, i mbliain a 1965, go gairid tar éis bháis do Sheán.[1] Ceann dár ndeacraibh é go bhfuilimíd in uireasa an chúntais a fhéadfadh an bheirt úd a scríobh ar na daoine ba thréithiúla a casadh orthu 'na siúltaibh, go mór mór ar a máthair féin, Eibhlís Ní Iarfhlaithe, Bean Uí Chróinín (nó 'Bess Cronin', mar ab fhearr aithne uirthi). Bhí clú agus cáil ar Bhess amuigh agus i mbaile toisc a raibh aici de Ghaoluinn spártha agus den tseana-nós amhránaíochta. Is mó duine a ghlaoigh an treo chúithi go dtí an Plantation i mBaile Mhúirne, cuid acu ag lorg na Gaoluinne agus tuilleadh acu ar thóir sean-amhrán, agus ní miste a rá ná go raibh an dá rud i dteannta a chéile aici ar áilleacht.

Amhráin Bhéarla is mó a thóg na bailitheoirí síos uaithi, fóiríor, ach ina dhiaidh san is uile, ní miste tagairt a dhéanamh do rud adúirt Brian George, príomhbhailitheoir an B.B.C., mar gheall uirthi agus é ag trácht uirthi tar éis a báis: '*In all my experience of folk-music collecting, I must say that I have never found greater satisfaction, nor such wide variety.*'[2] Allúraigh a bhíodh anso ar thóir an cheoil dúchais – Alan Lomax agus Robin Roberts, Jean Ritchie agus George Pickow, Diane Hamilton agus Brian George – bhainidís amach an Plantation i dteannta Shéamuis Mhic Aonghusa, fear go raibh leathchos aige is gach aon tsaol den dá shaol a bhí riamh ina thimpeall sna ceantracha Gaeltachta .i. saol an tseanacheoil agus na seanachainte. Anabhreitheamh ar cheol agus ar cheoltóirí ab ea Séamus agus tá ráite aige ar an raidió gur ar Bhess Cronin ba thúisce a thug sé cuaird i gCúige Mumhan chun cúrsaí amhránaíochta a cheadú léi. Do bhí an bhreith bunaithe i gcónaí ar an eolas aige, agus ní lú ná san an meas a bhí ag Bess Cronin air siúd.

Dála gach aoinní, tá ceard san amhránaíocht, agus bhí an cheard go smidithe ag Bess, ní hamháin sa stíl Ghaelach (nách ionann é agus an 'sean-nós' úd go mbíonn an chaint ar fad ina thaobh!) ach sa stíl eile a bhain leis na 'beailití' agus leis na seanamhráin Bhéarla. Bhí ana-thóir i gcónaí riamh orthu san, leis, i mBaile Mhúirne, na cianta sara dtáinig an gal go léir orthu, agus bhí ana-chnósach díobh ag Bess, go mór mór desna cinn gurbh fhios cé chúm iad – Seán Ó Tuama ('Johnny Nóra Aodha'), Mícheál Ó Tuama ('George Curtin'), an 'Poet Ahern', Pead Buí Ó Loingsigh, agus mar sin. Ar ndóin, ní ón gcloich a fuair sí na hamhráin: bhí seó díobh agá máthair ('Seana-Mheáig'), cuid acu a bhí neamhchoitianta, ach bhí traidisiún na hamhránaíochta leis na cianta i mBaile Mhúirne agus a fhios san go maith ag daoine ar nós A. Martin Freeman, Sasanach as Londain, a thug 'cúrsa roim bás' ar an áit i mbliain a 1912 chun pé cnósach trá amhrán a bhí fágtha i ndiaidh rabhartaí na mblian a bhailiú ósna seandaoine. Dar le muintir na háite, áfach, b'amhlaidh ná raibh ann ach go bhfuair an Sasanach radharc ar an gcaoilte déanach solais ón tseanabhladhm a bhí ag dul in éag cheana féin! 'Á, fóiríor géar', ar siadsan leis, 'níl ach an chaolchuid den tseanathraidisiún fágtha anois! Cá beag dhuit go bhfuil an uile dhuine a bhí go maith chun amhráin a dhéanamh imithe ar shlí na fírinne, agus na hamhráin go léir ina dteannta.' Fóiríor nár tháinig sé ar thóir na n-amhrán cúpla bliain roimis sin – ansan do bheadh amhráin aige!

Tá a fhios ag cách an méid a dhein Corcaígh agus Múirnigh le chéile in obair na haith-bheochana ó thosach,[3] agus bhí muintir Bhaile Mhúirne i gcónaí mórálach as. 'Príomhchathair

---

1   *Béaloideas* 32 (1964 [1966]) 1–42: 5.
2   Ibid.
3   Feic Seán Ó Cróinín & Donncha Ó Cróinín, *Scéalaíocht Amhlaoibh Í Luínse* (Baile Átha Cliath 1971) x–xiii.

na Gaeltachta' a tugadh air imeasc lucht an Oireachtais, agus a chomhartha san lena chois, mar gurbh iad daoine ar nós Amhlaoibh Ó Loingsigh agus Conchubhar Ó Deasmhumhna is mó a thug na duaiseana leo sna comórtaisí seanchais agus scéalaíochta i dtús an chéid. Comharsa béal dorais ag Bess ab ea Conchubhar ('Conny Desmond') agus is minic a labhradh m'athair ar an saibhreas Gaoluinne a bhíiana cheann aige. Ghlaodh sé ag triall ar Bhess aon uair a bhíodh an chaothúlacht aige, agus deirimse leat go mbíodh an chaint acu! Bhí an seana-nós amhránaíochta aige, leis, agus ní raibh aoinní ab ansa leis ná bheith ag cumadh bhéarsaí ar eachtraithe nó bladar éigin a thit amach sa chomharsanacht, agus neamhmeon fonn breá le clos uaidh ag gabháil leo. Bhí dioscán maith acu san tugtha aige leis 'na cheann óna mhuintir, agus cuid acu ag Bess uaidh.

Do bhí aithne i gcéin is i gcóngar ar Chonchubhar mar dhuine de 'Cheithre Máistrí Bhaile Mhúirne', agus duine eile acu ab ea Mícheál Ó Briain, duine desna hoidí múinte a bhí i Scoil Bhaile Mhúirne ag tús na haoise seo. Bhí dúil na bhflaitheas aige siúd in aoinní a bhain le Gaoluinn agus is é a chuir le chéile an bailiúcháin focal gur dhein *Cnósach focal ó Bhaile Bhúirne* dhe ina dhiaidh san.[4] B'é Donncha Ó Buachalla an t-Árd-Mháistir a bhí ar an scoil an tráth úd, agus d'fhéadfaí a rá go raibh Gaoluinn spártha aige siúd – rud a chuir sé in iúil do phobal na Gaoluinne i ndeireadh a shaoil faid a bhí sé páirteach sa tsraith cláracha úd ar Raidió Éireann dár teideal '*Conas Adéarfá?*' B'é an Dochtúir Ó Loingsigh an tréanlaoch orthu go léir, agus é ina fhear cinn riain acu ó bhunú an Chonnartha.

B'shin an comhluadar a bhí ag Bess Cronin ón am gur phós sí Séan Ó Cróinín agus gur chuaigh sí chun cónaig i mBaile Mhúirne. Des na 'Pronnséisigh ón bPlantation' ab ea a fear céile, agus de Mhuintir Iarfhlaithe ab ea a máthair – treabhchas a bhí i gceannas ar Dhámhscoil Mhúscraí le dhá chéad bliain roimis sin agus a bhí ina n-airchinnigh ar theampall agus ar thearmainn Ghobnait Naofa le sinsireacht. Do bhí an fhilíocht ag rith iontu ó ghlúin go glúin agus b'é an dúchas san a bheir do Bhess an dúil go léir a bheith riamh aici sa bhfilíocht agus sna hamhráin. Cé go raibh Béarla a ndóthain agá lán desna seandaoine, bhí sé le tabhairt fé ndeara i gcónaí gur choinníodar an dá thaobh deighilte óna chéile, ach go raibh ar a gcumas ag an am gcéanna na hamhráin macarónacha a chumadh, agus a lán amhráin Bhéarla, leis. Ach i dtaobh amuigh den chumas a bhí iontu ar an gceapadóireacht, is deimhin go raibh níos mó den tseanfhilíocht 'na gceann ag an dream san. Is mór an chreach, i dteannta na coda eile, go bhfuil a bhformhór san imithe gan bith a dtuairisc. Céad bliain ó shoin ní raibh seanduine i mBaile Mhúirne ná go raibh amhráin agus ranna fáin aige, ach marach an gaisce a dhein Mícheál Ó Briain agus Donncha Ó Buachalla, Proinsias Ó Ceallaigh agus Séan Ó Cróinín, bheidís go léir imithe; sin mar a imíonn na gráinní ón scilligeadh.

Beidh sé 'na chathú go brách orm ná raibh sé de chaoi ag Séan Ó Cróinín, ná agem athair, cur síos ceart a dhéanamh ar an saol san agus ar a raibh de sheanachas agá máthair, mar gur bhain a cuid eolais agus a cuid cainte le saol atá imithe ar fad anois.[5] I dtaobh eolais de, ní raibh aoinne eile a fhéadfadh na láimhscríbhinní atá ag an Roinn Bhéaloideasa ó Sheán Ó Cróinín a chur in eagar mar ba cheart. Níl sa chur síos anso agam féin ach cuid den scéal. 'Sé atá sachnósach so ná iarracht ar an saibhreas san amhrán ag Bess Cronin a chur ar fáil airís dóibh siúd, in Éirinn agus thar lear, gur suím leo neithe den tsórd san. Mara mbeadh ann ach an méid sin beidh cuimhniú míos uirthi an fhaid a mhairfidh meas ar chine agus ar dhúchas 'nár measc.

---

4 Curtha in eagar ag an Oll. Brian Ó Cuív (Baile Átha Cliath 1947). B'é an tAthair Pádraig Ó Duinnín a thug na 'Ceithrí Máistrí' ar an mbuíon ar dtúis, agus tá a rian le feiscint ar fuaid an Fhoclóra aige, gach áit a bhfuil 'By' (=Ballyvourney) le léamh ann.

5 Tá ana-chúntas tugaithe agem athair ar an saol san sa réamhrá a chuir sé le *Seanchas Aomhlaoibh Í Luínse*, ach bhí bearthaithe aige cúram fé leith a dhéanamh dá mháthair nuair a bhí scothbhualadh déanta aige sna ráigiúin eile de chontae Chorcaí gur bhailigh Séan Ó Cróinín abhar iontu.

THE SONGS

The texts of the songs that follow are almost all taken either from Bess Cronin's own handwritten transcriptions, or from the sound recordings made of her singing, or from versions taken down by my father, Donncha Ó Cróinín, and his brother, Seán Ó Cróinín, by Seamus Ennis, or by some other collector. In the case of the songs for which there are sound-recorded versions, the printed text given here is that of the recording used for the CDs. In the notes I give alternative manuscript versions of the songs, for sake of comparison, since these often contain additional verses or versions that differ in some way from the printed text and the music. It was frequently the case that Bess remembered additional verses after — sometimes long after — she had first provided a song. These additional manuscript notes are usually identified as 'DÓC notebook' or 'SÓC notebook', indicating that they were noted down either by my father or my uncle. Other collectors are likewise identified by name.

In citing printed sources for the songs I do not mean to imply that Bess learned any of her songs or airs from printed books or pamphlets, but simply to indicate that many of the songs were in circulation both in Baile Mhúirne and in other Irish-speaking areas, where they were frequently noted down by field-collectors and published by the Irish-language newspapers and in early collections of Irish songs. Bess's own versions of songs are often identical to the printed versions; on occasions, however, they differ. In citing printed sources, therefore, I have tried to supply the reader with as much information as would enable meaningful comparison with the general body of Irish traditional song.

In a few instances, where the title of a Bess song has survived, but no known sound recording or transcription, I have given a text which I believe is what she would have sung, but which I have only from the singing of another family member or from a neighbour. In other instances, however, where I had no such source to guide me, I have noted only the title, and left it at that. The aim at all times has been to present as true a text as possible of Bess's songs.

In presenting the texts of songs in Irish I have, in most cases, used the standard spelling of the official *Caighdeán Oifigiúil* ('Official Standard'), but with minor variants (e.g., *roim ré*, for the standard *roimh ré*, etc.) to indicate, where necessary, the dialectal features of Bess Cronin's particular brand of Irish. The manuscript texts of Bess's songs, whether written down by Seamus Ennis, my father, or Seán Ó Cróinín, are generally written in the older, pre-simplified spelling of the Official Standard. I have standardised these for the main texts of the songs, but in the notes I have tried to give a flavour of the older system by retaining the original notebook orthography. In the case of those songs which were also noted down by A. Martin Freeman, I have rendered his quasi-phonetic spelling into a more regular orthography.

NOTE ON MUSIC NOTATIONS

The music notations are not an exact recreation of Bess Cronin's singing, but are instead intended as an aid to learning the songs. They may therefore be regarded as notations rather than transcriptions. Although every attempt has been made to represent the singing as faithfully as possible, the notations should in no way be regarded as a substitute for Bess Cronin's performance of the songs themselves. Instead, they give an outline of the melodic line and very little additional stylistic information such as ornamentation has been included. The songs have not been notated in the keys they were sung in, but rather, convenient keys for the purposes of notation. The beauty of a collection such as this is that the first point of reference is Bess Cronin's own performance of the songs. This keeps faith with the essential orality of the tradition itself and allows her singing to speak for itself.

SANDRA JOYCE,
Irish World Music Centre,
University of Limerick

Song-book

SONGS IN ALPHABETICAL ORDER

Superscript numbers throughout refer to CD and track numbers.

A Chaipín-ar-leathstuaic, a' bhfeacaís na caoire?[1/26]

1.   A Chaipín-ar-leathstuaic, a' bhfeacaís na caoire?
A Chaipín-ar-leathstuaic, a' bhfeacaís na caoire?
A Chaipín-ar-leathstuaic, a' bhfeacaís na caoire?
Ní fheaca 's níor chasas, is ní fheadar cá mbíd siad.

      Towdle-am diddle-am diddle-am dee-dee
      Towdle-am diddle-am diddle-am dee-dee
      Towdle-am diddle-am diddle-am dee-dee
      Towdle-am tally-rill tidle-am tee-dee

2.   A Chaipín-ar-leathstuaic, a' bhfeacaís na caoire?
A Chaipín-ar-leathstuaic, a' bhfeacaís na caoire?
A Chaipín-ar-leathstuaic, a' bhfeacaís na caoire?
Chonnac is do chasas, is chuireas i gcrích iad.

      Tidy-am diddly idy-am tee-dee
      Tidy-am diddly tidle-tee tee-dee
      Tidy-am diddly tidle-am tee-dee
      Owdle-tam tally-rill tidle-am tee-dee.

English Summary A female goaterd encounters a young man and asks him if he has seen her sheep. In the first verse he replies that he has not, and knows nothing about them. In the second he says that he has, and has turned them back homewards. A *double entendre* may be intended. The young man's nickname, *Caipín ar leathstuaic*, refers to his cap, which is perched at an angle on his head. **Recording** CBÉ 394b (1947). **Text** From the CBÉ recording. **Note** Title (twice) in one of Bess's song-lists (*A caipin erh leath stuaic*).

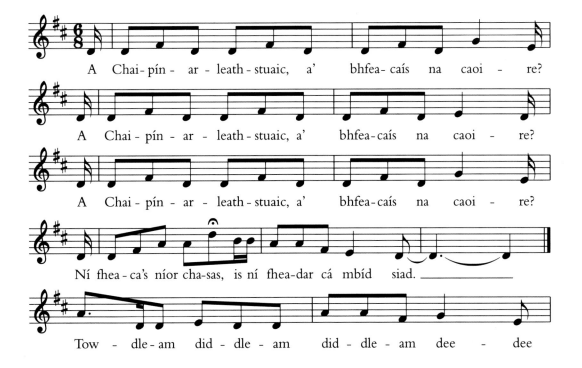

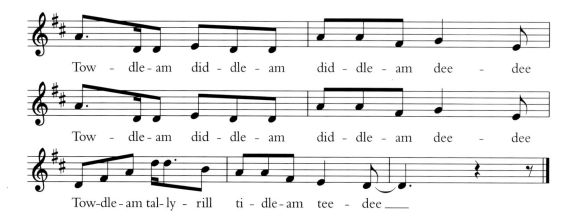

Tow – dle-am did – dle – am   did – dle – am   dee – dee

Tow – dle-am   did – dle – am   did – dle – am   dee – dee

Tow-dle-am tal-ly – rill   ti – dle-am   tee – dee

2

A farmer's wife I'll be

[… … …] farmer's son came whistling at the plough;
His field of corn and shining crown make music sweet for me,
And if ever I marry at all in my life, it's a farmer's wife I'll be.

Recording JR–GP (24 Nov. 1952).   **Notes** Bess had a snatch of a song, apparently with this title, sung to the same tune as *Bold Jack Donohue* [No. 33].

….. far – mer's song came whist – ling at the plough;—

His field of corn_ and shi-ning crown make mu – sic sweet for me,—

And if ev-er I mar-ry at all in my life, it's a far-mer's wife I'll be.

3

A Pheaid Bhuí na gcarad

1.   A Pheaid Bhuí na gcarad, is athtuirseach dúbhach do scéal!
      Mo cheol gur chailleas — ní scarfainn go brách lem' ghéim!
      An té thóg mo mhaide, go gcaillidh sé lúth na ngéag!
      An teinneas dá leagadh is an galar dá mhúchadh fé!

2. I nGúgán Barra bíonn fear ós gach áit ag glaoch;
   Do shuíos i gcuileachta do chaithfeadh go súgach braon;
   Do shuigh stróaire am' aice do bhradaigh a' liúit óm' thaobh.
   An caor dá leagadh nó an galar dá mhúchadh fé!

3. Is ar ór ná ar airgead ní scarfainn go brách lem' *fife*!
   An lá, faid a mhairfead-sa, malairt ab' fheárr ní bhfaghainn!
   Gach oíche dá dtagann ní mhothóchainn go lá dá seinnt;
   Tá ceol am' mhaide-se chasfadh dom' *hornpipe*.

4. Tá ceol am' mhaide do shroisfeadh an gleann go léir;
   Le gach oíche dá dtagann ní mhothóchainn a' siúl duibhré;
   Ba ghile ar a' lathaig í a' taitneamh ná lonnradh ón ngréin;
   Is gach tiúin dá gcasann do scaipeadh mo bhrón go léir!

English Summary The poet, a famous piper, was visiting Gougane Barra, near Macroom, Co. Cork, and while drinking in a pub, someone made off with his pipes. He grieves for his loss and curses the thief. **Text** From notes of DÓC's. **Printed Sources** Ó Ceallaigh & Mac Coluim, 'Amhráin ó Mhúsgraighe', *Béaloideas* 7/1 (1934) 19–44: 25 [sep. 9]. **Notes** Pead Buí Ó Loingsigh was a famous local piper around Baile Mhúirne. Born at Cúil near Gort na Tobradan c. 1830, he was widely regarded as the best musician in the Cork-Kerry region in his time, travelling around with his pipes and flute and returning occasionally to relatives who lived at Doirín Álainn. He composed several humorous and satirical songs about his neighbours, and there is a brief account of his life, with a list of his surviving compositions, by Seán Ó Cróinín, 'Pádruig Ó Loingsigh', *An Músgraigheach* 7 (Nollaig 1944) 6–7.

4

After the ball was over, Sally plucked out her glass eye

After the ball was over
Sally plucked out her glass eye;
Put her false teeth in a basin,
Hid all her bottles of dye;
Threw her cork leg in the corner,
Hung her false hair on the wall;
And then she stopped singing till morning
After the ball.

Text From a notebook of DÓC's (dated 23 July 1947). **Printed Sources** Cf. the alphabetical catalogue of songs contained in *Delaney's Song Book*, No. 1, Book 21 *After the ball*, and Book 4 *After the ball* (parodies). **Notes** Original words and music by Charles K. Harris. It is a parody of the kind common among children; cf. Opie & Opie, *The lore and language of schoolchildren*, 91 (a parody recorded from a group of 11-year-olds):

After the ball was over
She lay on the sofa and sighed.
She put her false teeth in soft water
And took out her lovely glass eye.
She kicked her cork leg in the corner
And hung up her wig on the wall,
The rest of her went to bye-byes,
After the ball.

5

Ag Lochán na Muinge

1. Ag Lochán na Muinge 'sea chonnac-sa an t-íontas
    Ná feicfidh mé airís faid a mhairfidh mé beo;
    Bhí Briainín ann sínte is é caite sa draoib,
    'Gus an rothar 'na phíosaí caite ar thóin an phoill mhóir.

2. Tráthnóna Dé Sathairn 'sea chuala mé an teagasc,
    Go raibh an rothar ceannaithe ar airgead mór;
    Tugadh abhaile é i lár fianaise geanúil
    Agus réitíodh amach é le go mbuailfear é ar bóthar.

3. Scread mhaidne ort, a Bhriainín, nách tú a dhein an smíochadh!
    Is nách tú a fágadh sínte ar leath-taoibh an bhóthair!
    Bhí t-easnaíocha briste is do chóta 'na phíosaí,
    Is do chnámh droma sníofa ag an lindéar, ar ndóin.

4. Cloiseadh i n-Ínse an fear bocht ag caoineadh
    Agus chruinnigh a ghaolta is iad brónach go leor;
    Nuair a chuireadar tarraing i gceart-lár na cíoc' air
    Dheineadar gníomh is an bríste thabhairt leo.

5. Ceanglaíodh le cáblaí i dtóin an phoill báite é;
    Bhí Nan ann ag gárthaíol, is Éamonn ag gleo;
    Nuair a tugadh go bruach é, cuireadh fios ar na Gardaí,
    Is gurb é deir an Sergeant, go n-éireóchaidh sé fós.

6. Nuair a tómhaiseadh an linn-ghort le slabhraí is cáblaí
    Céad is fiche bhí an doimhneacht ón mbóthar;
    Is nách trua san don chréatúir a cuireadh go bhásta ann,
    Is gurb ar an gcéad lá de Mhárta a d'éirigh sé dhó.

7. Nách mó san nuacht a bhí insna páipéir!
    Nách mó fear láidir a cuireadh fén bhfód!
    Gur chásaigh Rí Sasana an scéal le Nan bhreá,
    An cleas d'éirigh don deá-fhear ag seana-gharraí Póil.

8. Do ghoil Mussolíní go brónach is go cráite,
    Nuair a chuala sé trácht ar an ndúnmharú mór;
    Gurb é adeir Herr Hitler, dá gcloisfeadh sé i n-am é,
    Go mbeadh sé i láthair ag Bun an Chrainn Mhóir!

9. Brón ort, a Mhuircheartaigh, nách tú dhein an léirscrios!
    Is nách tú a fhág éagmais ar Éamonn go deo!
    Dá mbeifeá gan boc ar bheith istigh it' *agent*,
    Ní ghoilfeadh an scéal so ar an bPápa sa Róimh.

10.   Tá dochtúirí ag teacht ar an bhfarraige as Éigipt
    Le breathnú go géar air is leigheas a thabhairt dó;
    Tháinig scéala ar an mbaile ón Uachtarán Éamonn
    Gur masla don Ghaeltacht má théann sé fén bhfód.

11.   Beidh cuimhne ag mac Aindriais go dtiocfaidh lá an tSlábha
    Ar an gcontúirt chruinn géar gur chuaidh an fear san ann;
    Is a liachtaí lá fada a chaith sé 'na léine
    Ag obair go géar ag caith' suas lena shleán.

12.   Mo bhrón is mo mhairg nách úd é an scéal cráite,
    Má chrochann an bás chun bealaí uaighe thú;
    Beidh smúit ar an gcumann ag teacht ar Fhéil Phádraig
    Is níl bean óg dá bhreátha ná caillfear le cumha.

13.   Tháinig teachtaire anall ó cheann-phort na Státaí
    Agus dúirt go mba náireach an cleas é so tír;
    An leagan d'éirigh ar bhruach an Phoill Báite
    Is beidh seanchas cráite go deireadh an tsaoil.

14.   Is cosúil le mallacht an t-ímpire céadna
    Nó eascaine ghéar a dhéanfadh manach nó naomh;
    Nó a mheasann tú ar thuill sé droch-phaidir i n-aon chor,
    Nuair a stop sé a ghaolta as an gcasáinín caol.

15.   Bhí an casán sin acu ó aimsir Rí Seárlas,
    Chun gur tháinig na scréabars isteach insan áit;
    'S gur fhágaigh siad Briainín 'na luí sa dícéille,
    Nuair a rith sé ón soitheach a bhí ag gabháil dosna Stáit.

16.   Beidh cuimhne go h-éag ar an maidin breá céadna,
    Bhí an buinneán dá shéideadh ag an soitheach ar an gCuan;
    Bhí Briainín 'na chodladh is a chloigeann fén éadach,
    Is ar shaibhreas na Gréige ní thiocfadh sé anonn.

17.   Nuair a thiocfaidh an séasúr a chuirfidh toradh ar na géaga
    Beith raithneach is sméara agus féar ins gach gleann;
    Beidh cladhthacha na páirce dá leagadh as éadan
    Is fear cosanta an réimse — mo léir! — ní bheidh ann.

18.   Níl caora dá bhradaí ná gabhar insan taobh so
    Ná fuil cruinnithe ó Aoine ag ithe sa pháirc;
    Is an té a ruaigfeadh siar iad thar Chlochar-an-Léasa
    Mo léir! — tá sé claoite is i gcontúirt a bháis.

19.   Níor roinneadh a' talamh so amach ó lucht rialtais,
    Is níor tháinig aon díol — sin ní ná fuil cóir!
    Ach nuair a thiocfaidh an saol is go gcuirfear ar caoi
    Beidh Áine ag caoineadh faoi leath-trom go deo!

English Summary A mock epic on a bicycle accident suffered by a local brave. The event takes on international significance, with messages of condolence from President de Valera, Mussolini and Hitler, and from President Roosevelt of the United States! **Text** CBÉ 283, 380–87.   **Printed Sources** Ó Baoill & Ó Baoill, *Ceolta Gael*, 21 (a modern version).   **Note** I do not know the background to this song, but the language and length suggest a Connemara origin, rather than a local, West Cork one.

6

All ye that's pierced by Cupid's darts[1/8]

1. All ye that's pierced by Cupid's darts, of high and low degree,
    I hope you'll pay attention, yet an advice take from me!
    Don't leave behind the lass you love for the sake of self or gold,
    Or if you do, you'll rue the day before you will grow old!

2. When my love and I absconded, I'll remember ever more:
    On the 18th day of February, in the year of '84.
    To the sunny side of sweet Deshure, from my native home Lisbwee,
    In that very merry charming spot, reared since my infancy.

3. In fair Kilmichael parish, now, forever I must abide.
    Its praises too I did unfold when I was but a child.
    My ambition sure for living there, it's true, I did proclaim;
    So my lot is cast, my sentence passed, for life there to remain.

4. By Terelton's splendid station, built for the constabulary —
    My near and next-door neighbours, now, forever more they'll be.
    Their belts and bayonets dazzle me each sultry summer's day;
    When on duty for Her Majesty they are bound and must obey.

5. And sometimes I feel lonesome, my native home to part;
    For my near and dear relations from me are far apart.
    My brothers, and my sisters too, I seldom can them see;
    But my only consolation is *Cuisle Geal Mo Chroí*.

6. So farewell to famed Kilbarry and to famous Silvergrove!
    Likewise to Clannty Carthy and to Lisbwee Beg and More!
    And to each very merry, charming maid who had a dance with me;
    But the one I danced with after all was *Cuisle Geal Mo Chroí*.

7. It's once I had a paramour behind 'longside Gougane;
    And others not so far away I would not tell at all.
    And some have crossed the stormy main — may God there with them be!
    But the one I chose amongst them all was *Cuisle Geal Mo Chroí*.

8. So farewell to good old neighbours and to him who leads them on!
    Who came here of his own accord and recommended Dan.
    He saw me in my cradle and he watched me tenderly,
    Where I surely had no notion of *Cuisle Geal Mo Chroí*.

Recording BBC 19026 (21 Sept. 1952).   **Text** From the BBC recording; another in the collection of Bess's hand-written songs; a third, identical, text in a DÓC notebook; a fourth in CBÉ 283, 175–78 (in the order 1, 2, 4, 5, 3, 7, 6, 8).   **Notes** A heading in the notebook reads '(Poet of Lisbwee — Dan Lucey)', for whom see Nos **13** and **135**. See also CBÉ 1591, 361–64 (Cork 1960).

All— ye that's — pierced by— Cu-pid's darts, of— high and low deg-ree,

I hope you'll pay at - ten-tion yet and ad-vice   take   from   me!

Don't leave   be - hind   the   lass   you love for the sake — of self   or   gold,

Or— if   you —— do you'll— rue the day be - fore you — will grow old!

7

Amhrán an ghanndail

1.   Um thráthnóna inné 'sea chualas an scéal
Ar scafaire gléigeal ganndail,
D'imíodh thar caol i n-imeall móinfhéir
Is do thugadh roinnt féir 'na chabhail leis.
Tá duine ar an mbaile go gceilfidh mé a ainm
Is do ghéaraidh sé madra donn leis.
Ba thrua leat é dhearcadh nuair a síneadh é marbh,
'S is dóigh liom gur stracadh an ceann de.

2.   Isé dúirt Tomás, nuair airigh sé a thásg,
'Ciorrú air! Níor ghá dho an scannradh!
Mar i dtaobh aon tsaghas fáis, ní raibh sé le fáil,
Mura raghadh sé ag snámh nó a' damhas ann!
Ní raibh insan áit ach tuínneacha báite,
Ní stadfadh préachán ná seabhac ann.
Go ndeintear é bháthadh, é chrochadh nó lámhadh,
An té thug ana-bhás don ghanndal'.

3.   Do bhí sé scafánta, cumasach láidir,
Chuirfeadh sé bláth ar ghéanaibh!
An t-é a chífeadh gach lá é ag taisdeal na mbánta
Do chuirfeadh sé áthas cléibh air!

Osna mo chroí atá agam le h-ínsint,
Go bhfuil sé gan brí lag traochta.
Táim creachta gan puínn de shaibhreas an tsaoil
Is is baolach dá dhruím go n-éagfad.

4. Ó, gura madra i bpéin é, treascartha faon lag,
   Eascainí géana an domhain air!
   A theanga 'na bhéal go gcrapfaidh 'na chraos,
   Is san angaid go gcaochtar dall é!
   Mar bharr ar gach tubaist é titim sa tine,
   Go loisctear a uireas'a dhranndal!
   Gach cnámh leis a mhilleadh, go gcráfar é tuilleadh,
   'Gus bás chuige i n-uireasba an snamhaire!

English Summary A mock elegy on a wandering gander that strayed onto a neighbour's land. The neighbour set his dog on it and the dog killed the gander. The poet curses the dog and wishes every misfortune on it. **Text** CBÉ 283, 351–52. **Printed Sources** Breathnach, *Ar gceól féinig*, 32–33; cf. Ó Ceallaigh & Mac Coluim, 'Amhráin ó Mhúscraighe', *Béaloideas* 7/1 (1937) 19–44 32–33 [sep. 16–17]. **Notes** CBÉ 283 has the following note 'Amhrán an Ghanndail — do cheap Mícheál Ó Tuama, file, do mhair i mBaile Mhúirne deich mblian ó shoin' [*'Amhrán an Ghanndail', composed by Mícheál Ó Tuama, a poet who lived in Ballyvourney ten years ago'*]. Breathnach, *Ár gceól féinig*, 33, has the following 'Fear oibre Mícheál. Do bhíodh sé ag obair i dteannta muintire an Athar Pheadair Uí Laoghaire' [*'Mícheál was a labourer who used to work for Canon Peter O'Leary's family'*]. Note that eight lines of the song have been added in error to Neil Ní Uidhir's *Amhrán na nGabhar* in Ó Ceallaigh & Mac Coluim, 'Amhráin ó Mhúscraighe', *Béaloideas* 7/1 (1937) 19–44 [sep. 16–17].

8

Amhrán an tsagairt

1. Nuair a chuas go dtí'n coláiste mar a ndeintear na sagairt seo
   D'fhiafraíodar díom-sa a' raibh *sweetheart* ag baile agam.
   Do labhraíos-sa, is ba bhréag dom é, 'Riamh in aon chor níor bhacas iad',
   Is gurbh í brídeach na gclaonrosc a bhí t'réis mo chroí a chealg dom.

2. Is ar maidin Dé Domhnaig agus deabha orm chun Aifrinn
   'Sea do chonnac chúm a' chúilfhionn is do luíos súil uirthi i gan fhios dóibh.
   Nuair a chuirim orm an léine agus an éide bhreá bheannaithe,
   Is gur bhinne liom bheith á pógadh ná ag ól fíon na Gréige.

3. An té chífeadh mo riún-sa maidean dhrúchta a' gabháil a' bhóthair
   Do bhí *flounce* lena gúna agus búclaí 'na bróga.
   Is mó ógánach múinte thabharfadh súil ar mo stór-sa,
   Is ná faigheadh éinne acu súd í gan cúig mhíle i bpóca.

English Summary A priest recounts how he was asked, on entering the seminary, if he had a girlfriend. He denied it, though in fact he had (and still has) a sweetheart. He thinks of her constantly, even when saying Mass. **Recording** CBÉ 1063a (1947). **Text** From the CBÉ recording; there is another, 2–page manuscript copy by DÓC (dated 31 July 1947), which has 5 vv. and different readings in places. **Printed Sources** Freeman, 'Irish folk songs', *JFSS* 6/3, No. 23 (Jan. 1920) 169–70, No. 24 (5 vv.). For another version, recorded in Grange, Co. Waterford, in 1940, see Ó hÓgáin, *Binneas thar meon* 1, 206–7 (4 vv.). **Notes** The order in the DÓC MS. copy is A, 2, 1, 3, B. DÓC suggests the following order A, 2, 3, 1, B. There is a third text (vv. 1–3, much the same) in another DÓC notebook. The 5–verse manuscript version by DÓC is as follows:

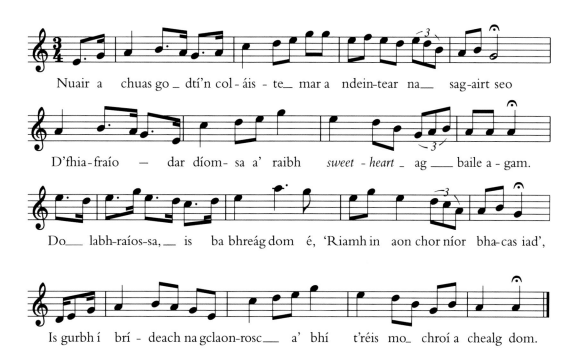

Nuair a chuas go _ dtí'n col-áis-te_ mar a ndein-tear na_ sag-airt seo

D'fhia-fraío — dar díom-sa a' raibh *sweet-heart* _ ag _ baile a-gam.

Do_ labh-raíos-sa, _ is ba bhreág dom é, 'Riamh in aon chor níor bha-cas iad',

Is gurbh í brí-deach na gclaon-rosc_ a' bhí t'réis mo_ chroí a chealg dom.

A.   Tráthnóinín saoire 's mé ar buidheachtaint na gréine
      'Sea do dhearcas-sa mo dhian-ghrá 's í ag amhrán 'na haonar.
      Do shuíos ar taobh cnocáin agus d'éisteas léi tréimhse
      Is ba mhísle liom bheith á pógadh ná ag ól fíon na Gréige.

B.   A shagairt na n-árann, druím lámha do-bheirim feasta leat,
      Ó thoghais-se mar chéile i dtúis do shaoil Muire Bheannaithe;
      Do dhearbhuís is do mhóidís ná beadh agat a h-atharrach,
      Agus cócól ní dhéanfainn ar a' saol do mhnaoi a h-ainme.

Freeman prints a text which he collected from Conny Coughlan of Doire na Sagart; it is very similar to the one above (I have normalised his spelling):

a.   Tráthnóinín saoire 's mé ar bhuíochtaint na gréine
      'Sea do chonnac-sa mo ghrian-ghrá 's í ag amhrán 'na h-aonar.
      Do shuíos ar thaobh cnocáin, agus d'éisteas léi tréimhse,
      'S ba mhísle liúm bheith á pógadh ná ag ól fíona na Gréige.

b.   'S nuair a théim-se sa choláiste, san áit go ndeintear sagart dinn,
      Fiarfaíod siad díom a' raibh aon sweetheart ag baile 'gam.
      Dúrt-sa, 's ba bhréag dom, riamh i n-aon chor ná feacas í,
      Agus rún-shearc mo chléibh-se tar mh'éis ag an baile 'gam.

c.   Ar maidin Dia Domhnaigh, agus fonn orm chun Aifrinn,
      Cuirim orm a' léine agus an éide bhreá bheannaithe;
      Nuair a chím chugham a' chúilionn, luím súil uirthi i ganfhios dóibh,
      'S ní h-ar Muire bím a' cuimhneamh, ach ar bhrídeach na mala-rosc.

d.   'S isé mo léan gan mé sínte leat síos go dtí amáireach,
      I mballín beag uaigneach 's gan a thuairisc agad' mháithrín!
      Do shínfinn-se síos le dian díogras grá dhuit,
      Agus mara mbeadh an éide ní thréigfinn go brách tu!

e.   'A shagairt na n-árann, druím lámha bheirim feasta leat,
      Agus gur thomhais-se mar chéile 'dtúis do shaol chughat Muire Bheannaithe!
      Do dhearbhaís 's do mhóidís ná déanfá-sa a h-atharrach,
      Agus cocól ní dhéanfainn ar a' saol de mhnaoi a h-ainme.'

Another copy, from Máire Bean Uí Chonaill, a neighbour of Bess's, in a notebook dated 30 July 1947, has 4 vv. (A, 1, 2, B); a note says it was sung to the air *Tá Gleann i níbh Laeire* [= *Na Gleannta*, No. **101**]. The text is more-or-less identical, but v. 2 reads as follows:

2.   Nuair a chuas insa choláiste, san áit go ndeintear sagairt díobh
      D'fhiafraíodar díom-sa a' raibh aon sweetheart sa bhaile 'gam;
      Dúrt-sa, 's ba bhréag dom, riamh in ao' chor nár bhacas iad,
      Agus gurb í Péarla an Chúil Chraobhaigh a bhí t'réis mo chroí 'chealgadh.

For an even more explicit song about a liaison between a woman and a priest, see J. J. Lyons, 'Nóra Óg Ní Cheallaighe', *An Gaodhal* 9/6 (Sept. 1892) 212–13.

9

Amhrán Pheaidí Bhig

1.   Lá is me a' dul go Drochad Banndan a' ceannach blúire ghamhnaig,
      Do chuireas-sa mo ghamhnaichín i gcabhlaichín go lá.
      Bhí ceol is rínce 's damhas ann, is do shuíomair síos 'na dteannta,
      Is ba ghairid dúinn go rabhamair gan mheabhair seal mar chách.

2.   Nuair oir sé dhómh-sa gluaiseacht ní rai' sí agam, ná a tuairisc,
      Agus dúrt-sa féin lem' bhuachaill an ghamhnaichín d'fháil.
      Go mbíodh *blackguardaí* na tuaithe á rá gur b'shiúd í suas í,
      'S gurbh é 'ndinidís de thrua dhom: 'A bhfuarais, a Sheáin?'

3.   Do shiúlaíos cnuic is sléibhte 'gus bóithre cumhanga caola
      Is abhfad amach óm' ghaolthaibh gan aon tuairisc d'fháil.
      Gurbh é deiridís lena chéile: 'Ní aithnímíd tu in ao' chor —
      Ciocu duine chuaigh ar strae tu, nó réice bocht fáin?'

4.   D'ínseas páirt dem' scéal dóibh 's an chuid ba mhó den éitheach:
      Gur duine chuaigh le céird me bhí saor glan gan cháim.
      Go rabhas a' dul go Béara 's gurbh ann a bhí mo *station*;
      Mara ngearrfaidís na 'Géannaig' an t-éadach dem' chnámhaibh.

5.   ('S) Níor crádhadh riamh an croí 'gam gur ghabhas trí Ínse Geimhleach,
      Mara a mbíodh cailíní insan oíche am' chíoradh 'gus am' chrá.
      An bhean do strac mo bhríste, is na gealasaí gur scaoil sí,
      Mara bhfuair sí siúd a sceimhle ní fíor pioc ó Sheán!

6.   Do chuireas lámh am' phóca, is ní raibh ann ach feoirling.
      Do thugas do mhnaoi an óil é a' díol a' cáirtín dí.
      Do chuir sí síos 'na phóca é is do shíl gur giní óir é;
      Do chuireas díom a' bóthar 's is módhmharach do bhíos.

English Summary The poet recounts his misadventures during a trip to Bandon (Co. Cork), to buy a calf at the market there. He tied up the calf and proceeded to enjoy the dancing, drinking, and carousing that was going on, but when it came time to leave, there was no sign of the calf. He wanders the highways and byways between Bandon, Castletownbere, Inchageela and home, searching for the animal. He abandons the search eventually in a pub in Inchageela and spends his last farthing on drink and consolation.   **Text** From DÓC notebook (dated 18 May 1946); another, single-page copy by SÓC (vv. 4, 5, 6 only).   **Notes** A slightly different text is printed in *An Múscraíoch* 3 (Samhain 1991) 8, from Eoiní Maidhcí [Ó Súilleabháin], of Cúil Aodha, whose father was a contemporary of Bess's.

10

An Béarla breá

1. Casadh amach mé go Ráth Maordha
    I dtúis na h-oíche is mo chroí go h-árd;
    Is cé ná raibh mo shúil le siamsa
    Níor fhágas é chun go bhfuair mé a lán.

2. Do bhí ann cruinn romham, scoth Gael na tíre;
    Ó Chathair Saidhbhín go h-Oileán Árann;
    Do bhí cigirí, oidí, is údair ghrinn ann,
    Faoi threabhsair caola is bónaí árd.

3. Do shuíos síos chun go gcuirtí suíochán
    Ar cheist 'tá spíonta is gan ceol dá bharr;
    Teanga na naomh atá ag dul i ndísc,
    Is an deis a chlaoifeadh an Béarla breá.

4. Do labhair an duine i nGaeilge líofa,
    Is ba mhaith leis milleán do chur ar chách;
    Bhí an Connradh millte ag daoine críonna,
    Is lena ngníomhartha ní raibh bun ná barr.

3. Bhí náire saolta ag Gaeil na Midhe
    Teanga a sinsear á labhairt ós árd;
    Mar bhí na seoiníní ag déanamh grinn díobh,
    Bhí orthu claoi le teanga an Ghall.

4. Níl brí ar bith chun gur labhair mo laoch
    Ar mhuintir Árainn is ar a gclann;
    Do bhí sa Ghaeltacht ar feadh míosa
    Is do scaip an Béarla abhfus is thall.

5. Do bhíothas ag preabadh le neart an díocais
    Is a cuid páistí ná raibh bun ná barr;
    Níor fhocal ba thúisce ráite ná scríofa,
    Do thosnaigh siorrthaíol gleo 'gus ár.

6. Is níl aon fhírinne sa méid a rinneabhair,
    Ní labharthar Béarla ar chnoc go h-árd;
    Is dearg-bhréag é, is éitheach mhíllteach,
    Do cuireadh thíos dhúinn go súghach sámh!

English Summary The poet describes a meeting he attended, where Irish-speakers from various Gaeltacht's, from Cahirciveen to the Aran islands, and Meath as well, were complaining about the degree of infiltration by English into their neighbours' dialects. It ends with one speaker getting particularly worked up and denying that any word of English is spoken where he's from.
Text CBÉ 283, 394–96.

I I

An bhfeaca sibh Cóil?

1. An bhfeaca sibh Cóil? An bhfeaca sibh Cóil?
   An bhfeaca sibh Cóilín Éamoinn?
   An bhfeaca sibh Cóil? Nách aige a bhí an sógh,
   An lá a fuair sé an bríste bréidín!

   Go mairidh tú, a Chóil, a Chóil, a Chóil,
   Go mairidh tú a Chóilín Éamoinn!
   Go mairidh tú, a Chóil, an chúig is sé scóir,
   Is go mairir do bhríste bréidín!

2. Raol ó Dhaidí, is raol ó Mhamaí,
   Is ganndal bán ó Shéamus.
   Pingin ó Cháit, is leath-phingin ó Phól,
   I bpóca an bhríste bréidín!

   Go mairidh tú, a Chóil, a Chóil, a Chóil!
   Go mairidh tú, a Chóilín Éamoinn!
   Go mairidh tú, a Chóil, an chúig is sé scóir,
   Is go mairir do bhríste bréidín!

English Summary A satirical song, mocking Coley and his new britches.   **Text** CBÉ 283, 391.

I2

An bínsín luachra²ᐟ⁷

1. *Go moch is mé go h-uaigneach ar bruach coille gluise lá,*
   A's mo choin agam a' gluaiseacht go h-uasal agus gunna am' láimh,
   Cé chífinn chúm ach stuaire an chúil dualgaig a's an mhiníl bháin,
   Agus abhar a bínsín ar a buim aice den luachair ba ghluise fás.

2. Alone as I went walking one morning by the green wood-side,
   With my gun and dogs commanded a fair maid by chance I spied;
   I instantly saluted her, her fair locks by chance did view;
   With her bunch of rushes making, as pl[e]asing as ever grew.

3. *Is do bheannaíos-sa don' chúilionn agus d'fhiarthaíos di cá raibh a gnó;*
   Nó dá dtabharfadh sí dhom póigín, go leigheasfadh sé dhá dtrian mo bhrón.
   'Sé dúirt sí: 'Ná dein díth dhíom, ó ráiníos-sa chomh moch at' threo,
   Is ná loit mo bhínsín luachra tar éis a bhfuaras-sa dhá thriobóid'.

4. As I stepped up to this fair maid and I asked her where was she inclined to go;
   Or that if I could embrace her, 'twould ease me from grief and woe.
   She said: 'Kind sir, don't tease me, as you met me in those woods alone;
   For these rushes cost some labour, and so spare them and leave me home'.

5. *'Is a chailín bhig na luachra, do thugas gean dod' leacain bháin;*
   A's go bhfuil mo chroí istigh buartha, suigh lem' ais agus t'rom do lámh'.
   'Sé dúirt sí: "Leog dod" ráite, tá'n luachair seo ró-ghlas go fóill,
   Is ar theacht mí na Bealthaine beidh bínse againn den luachair nóig'.

6. Said I: 'My pretty fair maid, have pity and don't be unkind;
   For it's here I am condoling, for you have my heart beguiled'.
   She says: 'Kind sir, take care, and don't me tantalise;
   For you seem to be a schemer, and also of a fickle mind'.

7. *Is nách buacach blasta bláthmhar d'fhásaid siad ar bruach na h-abhann!*
   Is gan de bheann acu ar bháistigh sa gheimhreadh, nó ar shneachta throm.
   Nílid siad níos breátha níos áille ar fuaid a' domhain;
   'S gurb é dúirt sí: 'Fan go lá againn: Tá a lán acu nár ghearras lom'.

Recordings ITMA SE (May 1947) — JR-GP (2 Nov. 1952). **Text** From the JR-GP recording. **Notes** Another version in a DÓC notebook has one more Irish and English verse:

A. *'S nách bríomhar tapaidh láidir go gheárrthainn-se beart le fonn!*
   Mar a mbíonn bric sa loich a' snámh ann a' pléireacht ar fuaid na h-abhann;
   Bíonn a' lon 's a' chuach 's a' smólach go ceolmhar ann ó chrann go crann;
   Is do shuíomair ar a'mbínsín go grámhar agus d'fhanas ann.

B. How handsome and transparent those rushes grow whilst in their prime!
   Their verdure is superior to those upon the river Nile.
   Those rushes grow spontaneous by nature through frost and snow;
   Through hills where crystal fountains so gazing do gently flow.

Verse B is clearly intended as a rendering of v. 7 in our text.

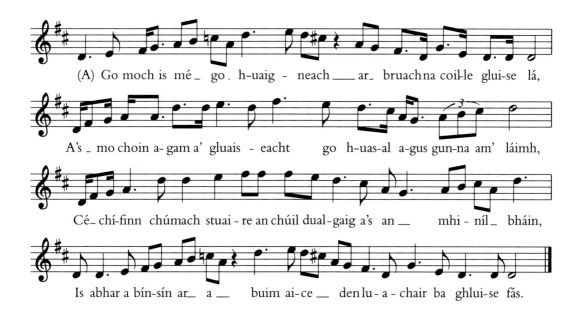

(A) Go moch is mé _ go . h-uaig - neach ___ ar_ bruach na coil-le glui-se lá,

A's _ mo choin a-gam a' gluais - eacht go h-uas-al a-gus gun-na am' láimh,

Cé_ chí-finn chúmach stuai - re an chúil dual-gaig a's an _ mhi - níl _ bháin,

Is abhar a bín-sín ar_ a _ buim ai-ce _ den lu - a - chair ba ghlui-se fás.

13

An botháinín íseal gan fálthas[1/9]

1.   'Sé Cnocán a' Bhóthair do scóladh 'gcomhair tí,
     Foundation ar fhíor-bharra anairde.
     B'é an fear críche ba mhó bhí ann an *Poet* ó Lios Buí,
     Nó an *foreman* do shíolraigh thar sáile.
     Cé go raibh beannacht Dé 'na bhóthar — agus fáraoir má bhí!
     Bhí riail dheas 'na phóca agus a thomhaiseanna cruinn.
     Anois cnósaig, a chomharsain, mar tá seó agaibh 'n bhúr saoir,
     Chun a' Bhotháinín Íseal gan Fálthas.

2.   Ní raibh fuiscí ná pórtar i gcóngar aon tí
     Do thabharfadh braon dí as a' sclábhaíocht
     Don ghasra óigfhear bhí ar a' mbóthar 'na suí,
     Is go deimhin díbh óm' chroí, bhíos a' gáirí.
     Nuair a tháinig suas Nóra a's í a' fógairt na dlí
     Ar aon fhear tí do romharfadh thar bóthar aníos,
     Agus go deimhin díbh-se, ar neomat, do bhí gleo ag fir tí
     Chun a' Bhotháinín Íseal gan Fálthas.

3.   Is is buachaill bocht óg mé tá im' chónaí ar Lios Buí
     Is ní cóir dom aon *treason* a rá leo,
     Ach go deimhin gurbh í Nóra bhain na nótaí so óm' chroí
     Bheith a' díospóireacht fíochmhar lem' mháithrín.
     Cé gur chuaidh súd go mór dom ní chnósfad mailís,
     Mar imíonn ceol ban 'na cheo leis a' ngaoith.
     Machnaím sa treo chím agus fáraoir dá druím
     Go bhfeicfear i dtíos í gan fálthas.

Recordings CBÉ 398a (1947) — BBC 19027 (21 Sept. 1952).   **Text** From the BBC recording. I have two other versions in DÓC notebooks (one dated 7 May 1946), and another transcript, by Seán Ó Cróinín, in CBÉ 822, 19–21. There is a text also in Seamus Ennis's CBÉ copybooks (7 May 1947).   **Notes** The BBC recording has v. 3 only. I have also used a manuscript collection of Ballyvourney songs formerly in the possession of Caitlín Ní Bhuachalla, Headmistress of Scoil na gCailíní, Achadh Cóiste (Coachford), Co. Cork, dated 1943; her text is identical with Bess's. Seamus Ennis, in a note to his CBÉ copybook transcription, has the following information about the poet: 'Domhnall Ó Luasa' ó Lios Buidhe, a cheap an t-amhrán so nuair a caitheadh seana-bhean des na córsain amach "ar an aoileach". Do chaith bean a mic amach í mar níor choinnibh sí aon teidiol 'sa tig. Do dhein na córsain botháinín ar chliatháin a' bhóthair di agus is ann a bhí sí chun gur cailleadh í. I gCill na Mairtire 'seadh bhíodar. Dob' é Domhnall Ó Luasa an 'Poet' ó Lios Buí — (féach an chéad bhéarsa.)' ['*Donal Lucey from Lisbwee composed this song when an elderly neighbour-woman was thrown out of her house "onto the dungheap". Her son's wife threw her out because she had kept no title in the house. The neighbours built her a little hut on the side of the road and that's where she lived until she died. That was in Kilnamartra. Donal Lucey was the "Poet of Lisbwee"— see the first verse*'.]

Seán Ó Cróinín has the following note (dated 30 May 1942) in CBÉ 822, 21 'Dómhnall Ó Luasa ab ainm don té dhein a t-amhrán so, agus dhein sé seó amhrán nách é — idir Bhéarla agus Gaoluinn. Ó Lios Buidhe (parróiste Chill na Martra) ab eadh é. Bhí driothár aige — Diarmuid ab ainm do. Bhí driofúr aca — Síle Ní Luasa. Phós sí Dómhnall Ó hAilíosa, Sliabh Riabhach (B. Mhúirne). Dónsal Shéamuis Uí Ailíosa a thugaidís air. Tá clann Dhónsail i mBaile Mhúirne fós. Tá oifig an phoist (ag an Muileann) ag Síle. D'imthigh an Poet (Dómhnall Ó Luasa) a Chill na Martra. Chuai sé go Tír Éilthín (i gCill Mhichíl). Tá sé marbh le tamall maith' ['*Donal Lucey was the name of the composer of this song, and he composed many more besides, both in English and in Irish. He was from Lisbwee (par. of Kilnamartyra). He had a brother named Diarmuid, and a sister, Síle. She married Donal Hallissy of Slieveree (Ballyvourney). They used to call him 'Dónsal Shéamuis Uí Ailíosa'; his family is in Ballyvourney still. Sile owns the post office at the Mills. The Poet went to Killnarmartyra, and to Tír Éilthín (in Kilmichil). He is a good while dead*'.] Cnocán a' Bhóthair lies midway between Lisbweemore and Lisbweebeg, facing the house owned by Parthalán Ó Conaill (al. Denny Denis); the Nóra of the song was his mother. He is possibly the 'D.D.' mentioned in the song *Sweet Lisbweemore* [No. **142**]. For Donal Ó Luasa see also *All Ye that's Pierced by Cupid's Darts* [No. **6**] and *She's at the Bar, Selling Soap, Soda and Blue* [No. **135**].

'Se_ Cno-cán _____ 'a Bhó - thair 'gcomh - air tí,

Foun - da - tion ar fhíor - bha-rra a - nair - de.

B'é an fear crí - che ba mhó bhí ann an Po- et ó Lios Buí, _____

Nó an fore - man do shíol - raigh thar (a) sá - ile.

Cé go raibh bean-nacht Dé 'na bhó-thar, a- gus fã - raoir má bhí! _____

Bhí _ riail dheas 'na phó - ca is a thomhai-sea - nna cruinn.

A - nois cnó-saig, _____ a chomhar-sain, mar tá seó a- gaibh'n bhúr saoir,

Chun a' Bho-thái - nín _ Í - seal gan _ Fál - thas. (m)

CBÉ 822 and Caitlín Ní Bhuachalla's manuscript collection are the only texts that have our v. 3, but they all have the following additional verses:

     A.   Do thabharfainn-se cómhairle don pharóiste ar a' taoibh
             Is go mór-mór do bhaintrigh fágtha;
             Nuair a cheapaidís pósadh a chur mar threó ar a gclainn,
             Gan scarúint símplí lena n-áitreabh.
             Nuair a scríobhaid siad a nótaí ag fear comhnaíoch dlí
             Ar deich bpúint, nó féar bó, é go deó leanúint díobh —
             Mara ndeinid siad mo chómhairle, beidh a lóistín gan moíll
             I mBotháinín Íseal gan Fálthas.

     B.   Machnaím im' mheóin, is is dócha gur fíor,
             Nach ionadh droch-chroí ag á lán dom;
             Is go mór-mór daoine óga 'tá le pósadh gan moíll
             Mar ceanglófar dílis dom' bhárr iad.
             Ach go bhfuil carthannacht mhór le bheith fós leis an aois —
             Sin soluíd gach ló agaibh 'n bhúr gcóngar sa tír —
             Siné sirriam na paróiste á ruagairt le dlí
             I mBotháinín Íseal gan Fálthas.

C.   Stadfad-sa nóimeat, 's ní cóir domh-sa maíomh,
      Chun go bhfeicfidh mé crích ar mo mháithrín;
      Mar is gearr go n-imeod-sa as a' cóngar thar tír
      Agus, a dhritheáir, bí dílis go brách di!
      Machnaimh gur thóg sí go h-óg tu ar a cíchín
      A' glanadh do chóta 'gus i n-aghaidh an nóimit á nígh,
      Is ná cuir-se go deó í d'aon óig-bhean 'sa tír
      I mBotháinín Íseal gan Fálthas.

14

An bóthar ó thuaidh

1.   *An bóthar ó thuaidh 's an bóthar ó thuaidh,*
     An bóthar ó thuaidh go Tráilí,
     An bóthar ó thuaidh 's geata 'n tí mhóir,
     Mar a bhfásann an ghruaig ar na páistí.

2.   *Cá bhfuil na húlla mísle cúmhra,*
     Cá bhfuil na húlla a Mháirín;
     Cá bhfuil na húlla mísle cúmhra
     Táid siad i gcúinne an gháirdín
     [Táid said sa chúinne ag Máirín].

3.   Mary, Mary, quite contrary,
     Red roses in the garden.
     I picked two plums as big as my thumbs,
     Red roses in the garden.

4.   Tidy womaneen, tidy womaneen,
     Tidy womaneen *sásta*,
     That would milk her cow in the tail of her gown
     And drink it out of a saucepan.

5.   Courting is a foolish trade,
     I mean to give it over;
     I'll go home and marry a wife,
     And be no more a rover!

6.   Monkey here and monkey there,
     And monkey all along;
     Now who's the fool to give me the pen
     To sing the monkey's song?

Text From a DÓC notebook.   **Printed Sources** Petrie & Stanford, *The complete collection of Irish music*, 331, No. 1318 [music only; cf. also ibid., 113, No. 448: *The northern road to Tralee*, with a variant of the same air]; *An Lóchrann* (Lughnasa 1916) 3 (4 vv.); Mac Coluim & Pléimionn, *Cosa buidhe árda* 1, 21–22; Ua Braoin, *An cuaichín ceoil.*, 19.   **Notes** The text in *An Lóchrann* is as follows:

A. Bóthar ó thuaidh is bóthar ó thuaidh,
    Is bóthar ó thuaidh chun Tráighlí;
    Bóthar ó thuaidh 's an cómhngar a dtuaidh
    Agus bóthar ó thuaidh chun Tráighlí.

B. Is maith le Nóra prátaí rósta,
    Is maith le Nóra ím leó
    Is maith le Nóra prátaí rósta
    Agus bainne na ngabhar istoidhche.

C. Do ghearra-chos dheas, do ghearra-chos dheas,
    Do ghearra-chos dheas, a Nóra,
    Do ghearra-chos dheas ót' ghlúin go dtí t'alt
    Is tá an ainnir ar fad go córach.

D. Cá bhfuil na h-ubhla gheallais-se dhomh-sa?
    Tá siad i gcúinne an gháirdín;
    Gheóbhair do dhóthain, lán dhá phóca
    Agus cúpla póg ó'n gcailín.

This text is reprinted in *An cuaichín ceoil;* the version in *Cosa buidhe árda* is more-or-less identical. See also *An Lóchrann* (Feabhra 1926) 32 'Poirtíní Béil':

Tidy 'omaneen, tidy 'omaneen,
Tidy 'omaneen *sásta,*
She milked the cow in the tail of her gown,
And brought it home to Seáinín.

A note adds that it was to be sung to the air 'Royal Charlie'. The 'tidy womaneen' verse is known as *Tighteen Girleen* in Clare, according to Tom Munnelly. See No. **60** below.

15

An brannda thiar

1. A dhalta dhil dár thugas-sa m'annsacht dian,
    Geallaim-se go raghainn-se, gidh fonn mo rian,
    Ad' fheiscint le carthannacht i n-am gach bliain
    Ach ar eagla bheith treascartha ag an mbrannda thiar.

2. Ní seasgaireacht fé ndeara dhom ná clampar fiach,
    Ná m'anmhuinn do chraipinneach mo cheann cia liath;
    Ná seachain dul thar gharbh-chnocaibh reamhra Liag
    Ar eagla bheith treascartha ag an mbrannda thiar.

3. Eascaraid don anam agus namhaid do Dhia
    Do leageas cuirp dá calmacht gach ball dá dtriall;
    Glaise stoic as aiste stilleadh bhrannda riamh,
    Athair nimhe ba mhinic thug mo chrann gan tiall.

4. Is cleachtadh leis an leanbh beag gann a thiall
    Nuair a satalas ar aithinne ná ar a shamhail de phian.
    'Sé seachnann an lasair ann gach ball dá dtriall,
    Ní taise dom roim ragairne an brannda thiar.

5. Glac-se sin ó'm theachtaire, cia gann liom iad,
   Mo scata bruinneall gan faice chruit, ná bean dá riar;
   Tabhair cuid dod' bhanaltra is ceannsa mian,
   As geobhaidh uile am' ainm-se clann ad' rian.

6. A shuairc-fhir ghroí do ghní an ghreann 'sa sult,
   Ní fuath dod' mhnaoi ná díbh tug mall mé a ndul;
   Ná fuath don tslí, cé chím gur reamhar na cnoic,
   Ach fuath mo chroí a bhíonn don bhrannda agam.

English Summary A drinking-song, singing the praises of brandy. **Text** CBÉ 283, 388–90. **Printed Sources** O'Daly, *The poets and poetry of Munster*, 4th ed., 282–85 (6 vv.). **Notes** The song was composed by Diarmaid Mac Domhnaill Mhic Fhinghín Chaoil Mhic Charrthaigh, an 18th-century Cork poet. The text in *Poets and poetry of Munster* is more-or-less identical with Bess's.

16

An chúil daigh-ré

1. Cois a' Ghaorthaidh is breátha in Éirinn is is áille ar abhainn
   Bíonn mil is céir-bheach is toradh ar ghéagaibh agus úlla ar chrann.
   Do chloisfeadh éinne cantainn éan ann a bheadh míle ó'n mball,
   Cnó buí 's caortha ar barraí géagaibh a' fás go Samhain.

2. Nach dubhach scíosmhar atá an Laoi seo a' gabháil eadarainn thiar!
   Na tulcaí ciardhubh ar barra línn ann gan ceo gan néamh.
   Níl ínse lena taoibh ann ná pór breá ar fhéar;
   Ach a' barra fraoigh ar charraig aoird ann, is mo thrua-sa bhúr dtriath!

3. Ag Tóim thoir bíonn ceoltha agus Aifireann Dé
   Ag fearaibh óga gurbh' eol dóibh i dtigh 'n tabhairne ag glaoch.
   Ach ní le mórtas don tsórd san do bheirid leo an sway,
   Ach a' déanamh bóithre le fórsa tríd an gCúil Daigh-Ré.

4. Bíonn Aifireann ag sagairt ann gach lá 'n aghaidh an sé.
   Tiarnaí tailimh ann go ceannasach faoi mhórán réim.
   An t-arm so na Sacsan ann faoi scárlóid dhaor.
   'Sé sin barra 'gat do bheirim feasta dhuit a Chúil Daigh-Ré.

5. Do shiúlaíos Cúige Uladh agus dútha' Uí Néill,
   Agus as san go Cairbre agus bruach Loch' Léin.
   Im' taistealaibh ní fheaca-sa ná im' shiúl go léir
   Aon bhaile 'cu is fearr a thaithnfeadh liom ná an Chúil Daigh-Ré.

English Summary The poet sings the praises of his native place, with the usual stock descriptions of its natural beauty. **Text** From Seamus Ennis's CBÉ copybooks (Sept. 1946). **Printed Sources** Freeman, 'Irish folk songs', *JFSS* 6/3 (Jan. 1920) 146–49, No. 18 (vv. 2, A, 1, 3, 4, 5). **Notes** I have also used the Ballyvourney collection in Caitlín Ní Bhuachalla's manuscript of 1943, whose text is identical to Bess's. According to Bess, the song was composed by Seán Máistir Ó Conaill of Cluain Drochad (as was *Faiche Bhreá Aerach an Cheoil* [No. **57**]), but this is denied by Pádraig Ó Crualaoi; see Ó Cróinín & Ó Cróinín, *Seanachas Phádraig Í Chrualaoi*, 69 (no text). Freeman's text, from Conny Coughlan of Derrynasagart, has the following additional verse after our v. 1:

A.   Nuair a ghabhann sí Drom a' Cara siar agus ón dteorainn riabhaig
Is taitneamhach gach caise 'ci le ceo glan néamh;
Bíonn barra-glas ar bhaiseannaibh agus pór breá ar fhéar,
Is canntainn suilth i mbarra coille ag ceol na n-éan.

17

An corn óir

1.   Ríocht geal thuas ar neamh is i n-árd-fhlaitheas Dé
Do gach fíor fear groí is gach spéirbhean!
Siúd eile dár muíntir dob' aoirde clú roim ré,
Seo mo mhíle, míle searc leo 'gus léir-ghean!

Ó, líon corn óir dom le fíon nó le beoir dom,
Go n-ólaimíd deoch na bhfiann Éireann!
Slán beo lenár muíntir de shíoradh clanna Gael
Agus sláinte, sláinte siar le seana-Éirinn!

2.   Faid saoil sógh 'gus neart do gach deoraí thar sáil,
'Sé mo bhrón gach ló 'gus mo dhólás!
Gan iad do bheith slán ar bhántaibh Ínse Fáil,
Agus solas geal na naomh bheith ag trághaidh leo!

Ó, líon corn óir dom le fíon nó le beoir dom, etc.

3.   Tá clann óg ag fás agus clann óg gan baol,
Fós ag teacht chughainn de shíor stuic na féile.
Líon suas copán cóir, líon doras deoch na nGael,
Agus taoscaimís an corn leo le chéile!

Ó líon corn óir dom le fíon nó le beoir dom,
Go n-ólaimíd deoch na bhfiann Éireann!
Slán beo lenár muíntir de shíoradh chlanna Gael,
Agus sláinte, sláinte siar le seana-Éirinn!

English Summary A drinking-song, in which the exiled poet toasts his native land and regrets that all his fellow-countrymen who are abroad cannot be back in Ireland. **Text** From CBÉ 283, 374–75. The title is in one of Bess's song-lists *(Líon corn óir)*.

18

An gamhain geal bán[1/13]

1.   Ar maidin Dé Luain is mé a' machnamh,
a's mé ag imeacht ar mh'abhar féin,
Ar bhruach Toinne móire 'sea dhearcas

an ainnir dob' áille scéimh.
Anuas díom gur luaigeas mo hata
agus d'fhiosraíos den rí-bhean shéimh.
'Sé dúirt sí: ''Fhir mhóir, ná bí id' sheasamh,
suidh farainn go dtrághaidh a' saol'.

2. 'Diúlthaig don phláig is don donas;
    a dhuine, suidh síos go lá.
    Tá an bháisteach go hard ar na cnocaibh
    agus tuile 'sna haibhní lán'.
    Níor chás díbh a lán acu 'fheiscint
    ba dheise ná í do mhnáibh,
    Tar éis éalú ó Bhearna na Toinne
    'na bruinnil go Dún na mBárc.

3. Dá mbeinn-se, airiú, 'mBeanntraí an bhile,
    i gCill Choinne, nó thall sa Spáinn,
    Is gan éinne beo in Éirinn am' ghoire
    ach an bhruinneal sa tsliabh go lá.
    Is fíor ach go n-ólainn a dtuillinn
    i gcuileachtain phrionnsa mná,
    Is nach aoibhinn do réicí na cruinne
    nuair imirid cúig thar láimh.

4. Nach aoibhinn iad Ínseacha 'n Fhiolair
    mar a bhfásann an féar um Shamhain,
    Mar a bhfásann an bláth ar an mbiolar,
    's mar a doirtear gach bliain an gamhain.
    Bíonn ceol bínn ag róntaibh cois imill
    a' lorg fothain' ar ghéagaibh crann.
    Agus gréithre na gcéir-mbeach a' sileadh,
    agus iomarca éisc ar abhainn.

5. Nach buacach iad cuacha na luiche
    ag titim go drúcht léi ar bán!
    Is nach uasal í a gruadh mar a' luisne
    ba ghile ná'n déis ar tráig!
    A claon-dearc ba réidh is ba ghliste
    dár thugas di bliain searc-ghrá.
    'S gur liom-sa 'gus léi-se nár mhiste
    dá mbeadh tuilleadh 'gus bliain 'sa lá.

6. Dá mbeadh agam cúig as gach cluiche
    agus cuireata 'gcúl mo lámha,
    Is go n-iompóchadh ao' chúig acu 'm' choinnibh,
    do chuirfeadh mise buin-is-cionn lem' ghrá,
    D'imeoinn is do shnáimhfinn an caise
    is ní fheithfinn le lúng ná bád,
    Is ní fhíllfinn go brách ar aon duine,
    mara bhfillfinn am' chubhar cois trá.

ó ⸢ Bean Céitin Uí Chróinín (67), Baile Mhac Íre,
Baile Mhúirne. Co. Chorcaighe

Meadhon-Fhóghmhair 1946.

An Gamhain Geal Bán

Ar maidin Dé Luain is mé 'm aonarán
'S mé 'g imtheacht ar m' adhbhar féin
Ar bhruach tuinne móire 'seadh dhearcas
An ainnir dob' áille féin.
Anuas díom gur luigheas mo hata
Agus d'fhiosruigh don phríomh-bhean féin
'Sé dúairt sí 'fir mhóir ná bí 't' fhearann'
Suidhe farainn go dtráigheadh an taol.   ('Sí 'feartainn?)

"Tuilteadh don pláig is don donas
A dhuine suidh síos go lá
Tá'n bháisteach go h-árd ór na cnocaibh
Agus uile 'r na h-aibhnní lán.
Níor cás díbh a lán acu fearscint
ba deise ná í do mhnáibh
Tréis éalú ó bhearna na tuinne
Mna bruinneal (?) go dún na mbárc
                    (sic)

'An gamhain geal bán' transcribed from Bess Cronin by Seamus Ennis (CBÉ, UCD).

7. Do ghluaisíos ar thuairisc na bruinnile
    ba bhinne 's dob' aeraí cáil,
    Ó Thuama go bruach Loch an Doire,
    is ó Inis go Sliabh don stáir.
    Am' chuardaibh, cé gur mhór iad mo shlite,
    níor thuigeas go raibh ao' bhean breá
    Go dtí stuaire na gruaige breá finne
    ar go dtugaid an Gamhain Geal Bán.

English Summary The poet sings the praises of his love, his 'bright white calf' of the title. He rhapsodises about her beauty and says that, were any misfortune to strike him, e.g., at card-playing, that would mean the loss of his love, he would throw himself in the gushing river and do away with himself. **Recordings** CBÉ 390a (1947) — Seamus Ennis (May 1947)[a private recording] — Diane Hamilton (1955). **Text** From the CBÉ recording. There is another in a DÓC notebook (dated 8 Aug. 1944), with 7 verses. Seamus Ennis transcribed from Bess another copy (Sept. 1946), now in the Dept of Irish Folklore, UCD, which also has seven verses; only vv. 1–2 are in his recording. Another text, written by SÓC on a single loose sheet, has vv. 1–2. **Printed Sources** Petrie & Stanford, *The complete collection of Irish music*, 292, No. 1155 (music only 'set from J. Buckley. Mr. Joyce'); cf. Joyce, *Old Irish folk music and songs*, 12, No. 18 (music only); Freeman, 'Irish folk songs', *JFSS* 6/4 (Jan. 1921) 246–49, No. 24; Breathnach, *Ceól ár sínsear*, 133–34 (6 vv.). **Notes** A note by Seamus Ennis in his CBÉ text says that this song was learned by Bess from the father of Seán Ó Muirthile [recte Seán Ó Muirithe, Ráth](later a primary-school principal in Co. Wexford) in Baile Mhúirne, *le linn di bheith 'na gearrachaile óg* ('when she was a youngster'). Ennis also says that the same air was used for the song 'A spéirbhean, ná bíodh ort aon mhairg' (= *Grá mo Chléibh*, No. **65**). The text in *Ceól ár sínsear* is very similar to ours. There is a tune with this title in Joyce, *Old Irish folk music and songs*, 12, No. 18. 5e ba ghliste cf. *Tá an t-amhrán go gliste aige*, in a note by SE from BC; cf. the song *Ar mh'aisling aréir* in Pádraig Ó Ceallaigh, 'Amhráin ó Mhúscraighe', *Béaloideas* 7/1 (1937) 19–44 39 [sep. 23] 'An tu Palas ban-dé go raibh Gaoluinn gliste aice?' The version of this song noted down by Freeman from Peig Ní Dhonnchú, Baile Mhic Íre, differs in interesting ways from Bess's; because she came from the same townland and parish, I give the full text here for comparison [I have normalised the quasi-phonetic text printed by Freeman]:

A. Ar maidin Dé Luain is mé a' machnamh,
    Ag imeacht ar m'ábhar féin,
    Ar bruach Toinne Móire 'sea dhearcas
    An ainnir ab' áille scéimh.
    Anuas díom do thógas mo hata,
    'S gur umhlaíos don stáid-mhnaoi shéimh.
    'Sé dúirt sí: 'Suidh suas, ná bí at' sheasamh,
    Suidh farainn go dtráthfaidh a' saol'.

B. 'A Sheáinín, a ghrá-ghil 's a chumainn,
    ''S a dhuine, suidh síos go lá.
    Tá an báisteach go h-árd ar na cnocaibh,
    Agus tuile sna h-aibhní lán'.
    Níor chás díobh a lán acu dh'fheiscint
    Ba dheise ná í do mhnáibh;
    Agus d'éala' sí liúm-sa thar tonnaibh —
    'Sí bruinneal na gciamhal mbán.

C. Is dóigh leó gurb óige 'gus mire
    D'fhúig mise faoi rial mar 'táim;
    Do chuir Éire 's Clár Fódla am' choinnibh,
    'S an tuineann de shíoraí ghnáth.
    Á shíor-rá go n-ólainn a dtuillinn
    I gcuideachta an phrionnsa mná.
    'S nách aoibhinn do réicí na cruinne,
    Nuair a imirid cúig thar láimh!

D. Dá n-imirínn cúig in aon chluiche,
    'S go bhfaghainn cuireata i gcúil mo lá';
    Go n-úntódh aon aon acu im' choinnibh
    'Chuirfeadh mise buiniscionn lem' ghrá.
    D'imeoinn is snámhfainn a' tuile,
    'S ní anfainn le luíng ná bád;
    'S ní fhillfinn go brách ar aon duine
    Go bhfillfinn am' chumhar cois trá.

Ar _____ mai-din Dé- Luain is mé a' mach-namh,

A's _ mé ag i-meacht ar mh'abh- - ar _ féin, _____

Ar bhruach Toi - nne_ Mói - re sea dhear-cas

An _ ain-nir dob' áil - - le scéimh.

A - nuas díom gur luai-geas mo ha - ta

A - gus d'fhios-raí- os den rí - - bhean _____ shéimh,_____

'Sé _____ dúirt sí: _____ 'Fhir mhóir ná bí id' shea - samh,

Sui - dh fa - rainn go dtrághaidh_____ a saol'. (a)

E.   'S is bog duallach a gruaig cinn léi a' tuitim,
Go truipeallach fionn cas breá.
Ó, bhuaileann sé a guaille go truithibh,
Is scriosann sé an drúcht den bhán.
A cúimín ba néata, ba ghile,
Dár thugas d'ao' mhnaoi riamh grá,
D'fhonn éalaithe ó Bhéal Átha 'Chuinne
Le bruinneal go Dún na mBárc.

F.   'S dá mbeinn-se i mBeanntraí an bhiolair,
I gCíll Choinne, nó thall sa Spáin,
'S gan éinne beó in ao' chor am' ghoire
Ach an ainnir sa bhfraoch go lá.
A caol-mhala néata ba ghloine,
Ba ghile ná'n drúcht ar bán —
('Gus) liúm-sa 'gus léi-se nár mhiste
'Á mbeadh tuilleadh 'gus bliain sa lá!

G.   'S nách aoibhinn ar ínsiní an mhuilinn,
Mar a gcastar a' fiadh gach Samhain!
Mar a bhfásann a' bláth ag gach bile
'S mar a n-oirthear gach bliain a' gamhain!

Bíonn ceol binn ag róintibh cois imill
'Gus binneas breá ag éan ar crann;
Céir-bheach i gcréithribh a' sileadh
Agus iomarca éisc ar abhainn.

The text in *Ceól ár sínsear*, 133–35, differs in various ways from ours; the order of verses is 1, 2, 3, 6, 7, 4. Verse 3 of Breathnach's edition reads as follows:

H.   Is dóigh leo gurb óige 'gus mire,
Chuir mise fí riaghail mar táim,
D'fhúig Éire 's Clár Fódhlacht um choinnibh,
'Gus a mhairean dom mhuíntir ghnáth.
'Ár bhfíor dóibh go n-ólfainn-se a dtuillfinn
I gcuideachtain phrionnsa mná,
A's nách aoibhinn de réicíbh na cruinne,
Nuair imiríd chúig thar lámhaibh.

19

An goirtín eórnan

1.   Is buachaillín fíor-óg mé, 's go bhfóire orm Rí na nGrást!
Do thug searc do chailín óg i dtigh an óil 'gus í 'na córú ghearr.
Ní raibh hata uirthi ná húda ná búcla bheadh déanta 'phrás,
Ach téip i gcluais a bróige, 'sí mo stór í go bhfaghaidh mé bás.

2.   Ní dod' ghoirtín eornan ba dhóigh liom go dtabharfainn grá;
Ná dod' chúpla cóifrín den ór bhuí dá mbeidís lán;
Do chapaill ná do bhólacht go deo, deo, ní chuirfinn i dtábhacht,
Ach blas do chúpla póigín ba dhóigh liom gurb iad ab fhearr.

English Summary A young man woos his love by telling her he has no interest in her 'little field of oats' or her wealth, her horse, cows or anything else, only the prospect of her kisses. **Recordings** CBÉ 398b (1947) — Diane Hamilton (1955). **Text** From the CBÉ recording. **Printed Sources** Borthwick, *Ceól-sídhe* 1, 76 (6 vv. 1, 2, 0, D, E, H); see also Joyce, *Old Irish folk music and songs*, 258 (music only); cf. Freeman's 'Irish folk songs', *JFSS* 6/3, No. 23 (Jan. 1920) 191–94 (9 vv.); cf. also *JIFSS* No. 18 (Dec. 1921) 11, No. 4 (1st v. and tune); Breathnach, *Cnuasachd bheag amhrán* 4, 21 (3 vv.); idem, *Ceól ár sínsear*, 117 [same as previous text]; Ní Annagáin & de Chlanndiolún, *Londubh an chairn*, No. 52 (4 vv.); cf. Petrie & Stanford, *The complete collection of Irish music*, 350, No. 1399. **Notes** Additional verses are given below from a DÓC notebook (dated Domhnach Cásga, 25 April 1943). I have compared NUI, Galway, James Hardiman Library, Douglas Hyde Collection, MS. 49, 50–51, No. 44 (from Dónal Ó Fuartháin, Baile Mhic Íre, c. 1917). Two versions are preserved in NUI, Galway, Hyde MS. 14, 70–71. There is another (garbled) version in NUI, Galway, Hyde MS. 57, 104–5. The verses in Bess's version are very similar to the first 2 verses in Conny Coughlan's text, published by Freeman; the verses in Freeman's text are in the order 1, 2, S, T, U, W, Z, M, V. I have also used the manuscript of Ballyvourney songs formerly in the possession of Caitlín Ní Bhuachalla, Coachford, Co. Cork, which has 3 verses (T, 2, U). The text in *Ceól ár sínsear*, 117, has the verses in the order 1, T, H. The air is the same as that for *An Buachaill Rua*. These additional verses are from a DÓC notebook:

A.   Buachaillín fíor-óg mé 's go bhfóiridh orm Rí na nGrást!
D'fhúig searc do chailín óg i dtigh an ósta le comhrádh geárr.
Ní raibh hata 'uirthe ná húda ná búcla buí bheadh déanta 'phrás,
Ach téip i gcluais a bróige: 'sí mo stór í chun go bhfaghaidh mé bás.

B.   Ní dod' ghoirtín eórnan, a stóirín, do thugas grá;
Dod' chapaill ná dod' bhólacht, cé gur mór iad súd re rá;
Ná don charn óir buí bhí i bpróicín aged' mhaimí lán,
Ach le blas dod' chúpla póigín, is dóigh liom gurb iad ab' fheárr.

C.   Is cosmhail mé nó an t-éinín bhéadh a léimrigh ó chrann go crann.
Dá n-eósfainn brí mo scéal duit go mb'fhéidir go ndéanfá rún;
Beir leitir uaim fi shéala go Cúil Chraobhach na bhFolt Fionn,
Go bhfuil mo chroí dh'á chéasa 'gus nách féidir dom codladh ciúin.

D.   Beir leitir uaim Dia Domhnaigh is tabharthas chun grá mo chléibh.
Le h-eagla í bheith le pósadh le h-óig-fhear ó chiúis an tsléibh'.
Níl sagart insa deoiseas do phósfadh í gan toil uaim féin,
Ná go mbainfinn de a chlóca, ba dhóigh liom gur mhaith mar scéal.

E.   Do raghainn insa Ghréig leat, mo chéad-searc is mo mhíle stór.
Is do raghainn airís it' fhéachaint ag éisteacht le fuaim do cheoil.
Ní éarfainn mór-chuid spré leat, ach céad a's dá mhíle póg;
A rúin mo chroí ná tréig ansa t-saol so do bhuachaill óg!

F.   A mhaighdean chlúvail mhánla, 'sé mo léan-chreach is mo mhíle brón.
A' dtiocfá liom lá gréine ar taobh cnuic nó ar Gleann na Smól?
Sheinnfinn ceolta bhréaga is do rinncfinn leat go preas ar bórd.
A rúin mo chroí ná tréig ansa t-saol so do bhuachaill óg!

G.   Do raghainn leat thar sáile, a bháb dheas na gcuacha óir;
      A's ní éarfainn púnt le n-áireamh ód' mháithrín dá dtígheach im' threó.
Is sáirfhear modhail gan cháim mé d'fhúig grá searc is gean dod' chló;
A rúin mo chroí ná tréig ansa t-saol so do bhuachaill óg!

H.   Tá gaoth andeas a's tóirneach a's mór-shruith ar abha na Laoi;
Sneachta ar na bóithre a's mór-sioc dá mheasca tríd.
Ní fhanann fuaim ag clocha mhuilinn ná ceol binn ag éan ar craobh;
Ó chailleas-sa mo stóirín, 'sí thógfadh an ceo dem' chroí!

I*a*.   Ba mhaith liom buidéal fíona bhéadh líonta agus puins ar bórd.
Ba mhaith liom málaí píbe bhéadh líonta le siollaí ceoil.
Ba mhaith liom log de'n oidhche thabhairt sínte le bruinneal óg;
Níor ghrádhas iad óg ná críonna ná claoidhfeadh le tamall spóirt.

I*b*.   Ba mhaith liom buidéal brannda a's gan amhras do bheinn fairseag fial
Ba mhaith liom cailín donn deas a's ba gheann liom í mhealladh siar.
Is deas do dhéanfainn púmpa 's is cúmtha bheadh a lasga im' dhiaidh.
Is fial go bhfuil an clampar gan amhras le seal am' thriall.

Another text (transcribed 26 April 1943 [= Luan Cásca]), entitled ''s bhéarsa ó É[ilís] Ní Ch[róinín]'

J.   Do raghainn anonn sa Ghréig leat a chéad-searc 's a mhíle stóir;
'S do thiocfainn anall am' aonar ag éisteacht le fuaim do cheoil.
Ní iarrfainn fén mar spré leat ach céad a's dá mhíle póg;
'Gus a phlúir na mban gan aon locht ná tréigse mo chroí faoi brón.

K.   Ba mhaith liom buidéal brannda a's gan amhras bheith fearúil fial
Ba mhaith liom cailín donn deas a's dob' fhonn liom í mhealladh siar
Is deas a dhéanfainn púmpa a's is cúmtha bheadh a lasg im' dhiaidh
Ach anois ó tháim i dteannta 'sé 'n clampar a leannas riamh.

L.   A's a *landlady* na n-Árann tá'n bás a' dul am' chroí le tart:
Tabhair aon cháirt amháin dom im' láimh sara ngabhad amach!
Coinnibh cúntas geárr ar a' gclár agus cuir síos cailc;
Agus tabhair faoi thuairim sláinte cúl fáinneach mo chailín deas.

M.   Ba mhaith liom buidéal fíona bheadh líonta agus puins ar bórd;
Ba mhaith liom málaí píbe bheadh líonta de shiollaíbh ceoil;
Ba mhaith liom seal den oíche bheith sínte le cailín óg;
Níor ghrádhas riamh óg ná críonna iad mar ná claoifidís liom go deo.

N.   Cadé sin díbh-se a dhaoine dá sínfinn-se ar barr an fhéir?
Nó a' dul don talamh íochtraigh le díogras do ghrá mo chléibh;
Nó dá seolfadh *push* den'n ghaoith mé sa tír úd go mbíonn sí féin;
Do gheobhainn mo shláinte airís a's is fíor go mbeinn sásta léi.

O. Móra dhuit-se 'éinín etc. *[see next entry]*

A third text (transcribed 27 April 1943):

P. Is buachaillín fíor-óg mé 's go bhfóiridh orm Rí na nGrást!
Thug searc do chailín óg i tigh an óil is í n-a córú dheas;
Ní raibh hata uirthe ná húda ná búcla buí bheadh déanta 'phrás;
Ach téip i gcluais a bróige 'sí mo stór í go bhfaghaidh mé bás.

Q. Ní dod' stáicín eórnan, a stóirín, a thugas grá;
Ná dod' chúpla cóithrín den ór bhuí dá mbeidís lán;
Do chapaill ná do bhólacht go deo ní chuirim i spás;
[Ach blas do chúpla póigín ba dhóigh liom gurb iad ab'fhearr.]

R. Do raghainn anonn don Ghréige le céad-searc dom mhíle stór;
Do thiocfainn anall am aonar ag éisteacht le fuaim do cheoil;
Ní iarfainn-se mar spré leat ach céad a's dá mhíle póg;
'S a phlúr na mban gan aon locht ná tréig feasta 'n buachaill óg!

S. Raghad thar n-ais 'am dhúthaigh mara bhfaghad piúnt a's gloine lán;
Tá grá ró-mhór ag triúr dom dá ndiúgann an tiarsa ar bráid;
Marab ineann a's a scrúille nár dhiúg a's nár ól riamh cárt;
Agus sidí sláinte an chiúin-fhir nár dhiúl riamh do phuins ar clár!

T. Móra dhuit-se 'éinín tá 'léimrigh ó chrann go crann!
Dá n-innsinn brí mo scéil duit níor bh'fhulaís nó do;
Beir leitir uaim fi shéala chun cúil chraobhach na bhfolta bhfionn,
Go bhfuil mo chroí dh'á chéasa a's nách féidir liom codladh ciúin.

U. 'S tiocfaidh ár a's tóirneach a's mór-uisce 'n-abhainn na Laoi;
Beidh sneachta a' stop' i ndóirse a's bólacht 'á dtreasgairt tríd;
Ní fhanfaidh guth ag smólaigh ná ceol binn ag éan ar craoibh;
Ó chailleas-sa mo stóirín, 'sí thógfadh a' ceo dem' chroí!

V. Míle fáilthe aduaidh rómhat, a bhuachaillín ó Chnoc na bhFiann!
Aithním ar a ród thu agus cóngar na coille 'niar;
Mo mhallacht ar a bpósadh go bhfuil mór-cheangal aige 'rm riamh!
Agus mo chúig céad slán leat a óige, mar is brónach atáim it' dhiaidh!.

W. A lanleaidí na n-árann tá'n bás a' dul im' chroí agen' dtart.
Líon ao' chárt amháin dom im' láimh sara ngabhad amach!
Dein-se cúntas geárr ar a' gclár a's cuir síos cailc;
Agus siúd fi thuairim sláinte cúil fáinneach mo chailín deas.

X. Beir leitir uaim Dé Domhnaigh a's tabharthas chun grá mo chléibh
Ar eagla go mbeadh sí pósta leis an óig-fhear ó bhárr a' t-sléibh'.
Níl sagart insa deoiseas do phósfadh í lem' balairt féin;
Ná go mbainfinn de a chóta 's ba dhóigh liom gur mhaith san féin.

Y. Ba mhaith liom buidéal fíona bheadh líonta 'gus *punch* ar bórd;
Ba mhaith liom málaí píbe bheadh líonta do shiollaíbh ceoil;
Ba mhaith liom seal den oíche thabhairt sínte le cailín óg;
Níor ghrádhas riamh óg ná críonna iad ná claoifeadh le tamall spóirt.

Z. Ba mhaith liom buidéal brannda 's do b'annsa liom bheith fearúil fial;
Ba mhaith liom cailín donn deas a's dob' fhonn liom í mhealladh siar;
Is deas mar dhéanfainn púmpa a's is cúmtha bheadh a lasg am' dhiaidh
As ó chuireas mó hóló i dteannta 'sé an clampar do leanas riamh.

A fourth text (1 v. + 1st line of another) in another DÓC notebook: '*An Goirtín Eórnan*: véarsa eile ó É[ilís Bean Uí] Ch[róinín].'

a. Is ba mhaith liom bheith a stróireacht lem' stóirín ar íntinn suilth;
Is ba mhaith liom bheith á pógadh i ndóchas go mbeadh sí agam;
Ba mhaith liom bheith ar tórramh gach mór-ghloine 'á líonfaí puins;
Is is mairg ná bainfeadh spórt as an óige nuair a bhíonn sí aige!

L: 'A *landlady* na nÁrann', etc. — cf. Petrie & Stanford, *The complete collection of Irish music*, 276, No. 1088, and 314, No. 1249: 'A bhean a' tíghe na páirte'. There are 6 vv. of this song in the Royal Irish Academy MS. 24 C 55 (19th c.) 232–33, incl. our vv. 2, 1, L. The other verses are:

b.   Mallachtaidhe na h-aoine d'an tír seo ina bhfuillim ann
       'S gur síadhe liom ló gon oidhche, 'ná bliadhain annsa mbaile úd thall
       Ann súd bhiodhach an reel aguinn ceól pípe 'gus punch ar clár
       Go leór den coper bhuidhe 'guinn, a's é líonta de'n lion d'bhfearr.

c.   Cad é sin díbhse a dhaoine da n-íthinnse barr an fhéir
       'S dá déithinn faoi'n dtallamh íochtrach le díograis do ghrádh mo chléibh
       Dá d-tigeadh siolladh an ghaoith o'n d-tír na bhfuil mo dhian-ghrádh féin
       Go bh-faighinn mo slainte 'rís, a's o'm intinn go m-beidhin sástadh lei

d.   Is mór an cursaidhe brón liom go deó 'gus an brise croidhe
       Mo chaillín deas d'á póga ag aen stróinse faoi bharr na craoibhe
       Fógraim díth na m-bróg air an og-bhean na 'r fhan mar bhí
       'As fheabhus do sheinnfinn ceól di la'n fhomhar is í buaint an lín.

The text in Caitlín Ní Bhuachalla's manuscript has our verses T, 2, and the following version of v. U:

e.   Tá gaoth andeas is tóirthneach is mór-shruth i n-abha na Laoi,
       Sneachtadh ar na bóithribh is mór-shioc dá mheascadh tríd.
       Ní fhanann fuaim ag róintibh ná ceól binn ag éan sa chraoibh,
       Ó chailleas mo stóirín, 'sí thógadh an cheó dem' chroidhe.

The placename Cnoc na bhFiann in verse V has been identified as Knocknaveen, townland Glen, Clareisland (Co. Mayo); see C. S. Boswell, 'Placenames from our older literature II,' *Irisleabhar na Gaedhilge* 14, Uimh. 169 (Deireadh Foghmhair 1904) 641–46: 642 (cited Freeman, 193).

20

An seanduine

1. Comhairle do fuaras-sa thíos ar a' mbóthar:
    Ón rógaire sagairt: an seanduine 'phósadh.
    Ba chuma leis siúd ach go méadóinn a phóca,
    Is me fhágaint 'n fhaid mhairfinn ag brath ar na comharsain!

    Is ó, mhuise, a sheanduine, leat-sa ní gheobhad-sa!
    Is ó, mhuise, a sheanduine, leat-sa ní gheobhad-sa!
    Is ó, mhuise, a sheanduine, leat-sa ní gheobhad-sa!
    Agus cúpla duig ionat 'dteannta bheith breoite!

2. Dá bhfaghainn-se mo sheanduine báite i bpoll móna,
    Do thabharfainn abhaile é 's do dhéanfainn é 'thórramh;
    Do cheanglóinn a chosa do chosaibh na comharsain,
    Is do roinnfinn-se puins ar na buachaillí óga!

    Is ó, mhuise, a sheanduine, leat-sa ní gheobhad-sa!
    Is ó, mhuise, a sheanduine, leat-sa ní gheobhad-sa!
    Is ó, mhuise, a sheanduine, leagadh 'gus leonadh ort!
    Agus cúpla duig ionat 'dteannta bheith breoite!

3. Chuas-sa go Corcaigh a' d'iarraidh gléas tórraimh:
    Píopaí 'gus tobac agus cláracha cómhrann.
    Thánag-sa abhaile go h-athtuirseach brónach —
    Cé gheobhainn ach mo sheanduine 'róstadh bruthóige!

    Is ó, mhuise, a sheanduine, leat-sa ní gheobhad-sa!
    Is ó, mhuise, a sheanduine, leat-sa ní gheobhad-sa!
    Is ó, mhuise, a sheanduine, leat-sa ní gheobhadsa!
    Agus nár bheire'n sagart ná tosach an fhómhair ort!

English Summary A woman laments having accepted the advice of her local priest, to marry an elderly neighbour. She knows the priest is only interested in the marriage-fee, while she will be left 'dependent on the neighbours'. The song moves between her not accepting the match and her having accepted it; i.e., in the first two verses the arrangement is hypothetical, but in verse 3 she describes going to Cork to buy things for the wake, only to find, on her return, her 'dead' husband roasting potatoes! **Text** From a DÓC notebook. **Printed Sources** See O'Daly, *The poets and poetry of Munster*, 4th ed., 24 and 120 n. (v. 1 only, and chorus); Borthwick, *Ceól-sídhe* 1, 55 (5 vv.); Mac Coluim, *Sean-amhráin na Mumhan* 3, 16; *An Lóchrann* (Iúl 1916) 7 (3 vv.); Freeman, 'Irish folk songs', *JFSS* 6/3, No. 23 (Jan. 1920) 104–7, No. 4 (5 vv.); Breathnach, *Sídh-cheól* 2, 136–37, No. 60 (5 vv.). **Notes** The song was composed by Aindrias Mac Craith, a famous Limerick poet of the 18th century, known by the nickname An Mangaire Súgach ('The Jovial Peddlar'), for the reason — as O'Daly remarked — that 'many of the productions of our poet were penned amid … bacchanalian revels, and are, indeed, redolent of the uisce beatha bottle'. The text in *An Lóchrann* (supplied by Fionán Mac Coluim) is similar to ours and has the same three verses. The version given by Freeman is from Peig Ní Dhonnchú of Ballymakeera, aged 78 in 1914; Ballymakeera was Bess Cronin's townland also. The tune called *An Seanduine Crom* in P.W. Joyce, *Old Irish folk music and songs*, 13, No. 20 is only distantly related to Peig Ní Dhonnchú's song; there is a second (unrelated) song called *An Seanduine* in Freeman's collection, No. 67. For the tune's supposed relation to the Scottish air *The Campbells are coming*, see the discussion in *JFSS* 6/3, No. 23, 106–7. In the notebook version, at line 3d *róstadh bruthóige*, an alternative is given *caitheamh a thóna*, from 'K' (= Domhnall P. Ó Céilleachair). The Freeman text from Ballymakeera is very similar to ours (as one would expect), but has the following additional verses at the beginning and end:

> Is triúr a bhí agam am' cheangal le h-iarlais,
> Mo mháthair is mh'athair 's a sagart chómh dian leo;
> Chuadar abhaile a's do chaitheadar féasta,

'S is annamh a thigeann mo charaid am' fhéachaint —
Is ó mhuise, a sheanduine, etc.
'S is mór a trua 'n chríonacht a' cloí leis an óige!

'S dá mbeadh súd agam-sa, capall is srian air
Iallait mhaith leathair, agus béalbhach iarainn,
Bhéarfainn mo sheanduine 'mach ansa tsliabh liom,
'Gus do thabharfainn a' faraire abhaile insan iallait.

Borthwick, *Ceól-sídhe*, 55 has the following additional two verses between vv. 1 and 2 of our text; otherwise the texts are more-or-less identical:

Phós mise an sean-duine, bhí orm dith chéille;
Rinne mé an méid sin ar chomhairle mo ghaolta;
Chuaidh mé abhaile leis, faraor an sgeul san!
A's d'eirigh mé ar maidin a's b'fhearr liom an t-éag dam.

Chuir mé mo shean-duine siar go Tír Iarail,
I n-áit a raibh míle 'gus fiche de shliabh ann;
Chrap a chuid iosgad a's thuit a chuid fiacal,
A's tháinig sé abhaile 'na bhromachán bliadhna.

Fionán Mac Coluim, *Sean-amhráin na Mumhan*, 16, has the following variant on v. 2:

Dá bhfaghainn-se mo sheanduine báidhte i bpoll móna,
A chosa bheith briste's a lámha a bheith leóinte,
Do thabharfainn abhaile é is dhéanfainn é thórramh,
Is do shiúbhlóighinn amach leis na buachallaíbh óga.

21

An spealadóir

1. I meán an fhómhair 'sea casadh mé, b'athtuirseach dúbhach mo scéal,
   Go breoite brónach athtuirseach, gan aiteas insa tsaol;
   Tá mo pháircín féir gan gearradh 'gam, 'na theasc ag ceann an eathlainn,
   Cuid na gcómharsan treascartha is é beárrtha go cré.

2. Do smaoiníos féin am' aigne istoíche tré'm néall,
   Go raibh beirt d'fhearaibh chalma ó thaoibh Uí Mhaol.
   Féna ngéin gur chuaidh mo theachtaire chun páircín féir do ghearradh dhom,
   'S is grámhar fáilteach freagarthach do thánadar araon.

3. Dá bhfaghainn-se speal ó Shasana 'gus crann ó Loch Léin
   Cloch is clár is gainimh air ó thaoibh Uí Mhaol.
   Do chuirfinn faobhar ar maidin suas do sheasóchadh ar feadh seachtaine
   'S nách beárrtha bheadh an t-acra le fáinnín a' lae.

English Summary A farm labourer, laid low by ill-health in mid-autumn, sings the praises of his friends, who came to his aid.
Text From CBÉ 737, 77–78. **Notes** A note by Seán Ó Cróinín reads 'Tá tuille dhen amhrán so ná fuil aice i n-aonchor. Fonn luaimneach a ghabhann leis' ['*There is more to this song that she doesn't have at all. There's a jaunty air to it*'].

22

Anonn's anall, is tríd an abhainn[1/28]

1. *Anonn 's anall is tríd an abhainn,*
   A chailleach, do mharaís me! A chailleach do mharaís me!
   Anonn 's anall is tríd an abhainn,
   A chailleach, do mharaís me! A chailleach do mharaís me!

2. *Anonn 's anall is tríd an abhainn,*
   Do bhainis mo chaipín díom! Bhainis mo chaipín díom!
   Anonn 's anall is tríd an abhainn,
   Do bhainis mo chaipín díom! Bhainis mo chaipín díom!

3. Over and hither and through the meadow,
   So, hag, you destroyed me! Hag, you destroyed me!
   Over and hither and through the meadow,
   So, hag, you annoyed me! Hag, you annoyed me!

4. *Anonn 's anall is tríd an abhainn,*
   A chailleach do mharaís me! A chailleach do mharaís me!
   Anonn 's anall is tríd an abhainn,
   Do bhainis mo bhaitín díom! Bhainis mo bhaitín díom!

5. *Anonn 's anall is tríd an abhainn,*
   A chailleach do mharaís me! A chailleach do mharaís me!
   Anonn 's anall is tríd an abhainn,
   Do bhainis mo chaipín díom! Bhainis mo chaipín díom!

5. Over and hither and through the meadow,
   So, hag, you annoyed me! Hag, you annoyed me!
   Over and hither and through the meadow,
   So, hag, you destroyed me!

Recording CBÉ 395b (1947). **Text** From the CBÉ recording. **Printed Sources** Petrie & Stanford, *The complete collection of Irish music*, 311, No. 1236 (music only); cf. Mac Coluim & Pléimion, *Cosa buidhe árda* 1, 39-40. **Notes** The title is in one of Bess's song-lists, as *Annon sa anall*. There is another copy of v. 1 in a DÓC notebook (dated Christmas 1944), where the song is described as a *Poirtín Béil* ('puss-music'). Followed by Rócán — *ar a' bhfonn gcéadna* ['A jingle — to the same air']:

> Togha, togha leinbhín,
> Togha-togha, togha-togha, togha-togha leinbhín.
> 'S maith a' gnó bliana é, 's maith a' gnó bliana é.

This is the refrain to another song, in 4 verses, called *Togha togha leinbh* ('Ní thabharfainn do Fhionn thu'), which is printed in *An Lóchrann* (Samhain 1920) 2 (supplied by Tomás Ó Criomhthainn, 'The Islandman'). Tom Munnelly refers me to Breandán Breathnach, *Ceol rínce na hÉireann* 2, 6, No. 8, and 161 n. *(Tiocfaidh tú abhaile liom)*, which Breathnach describes as 'gaolmhar le "A chailleach do mharaís mé"' ['related to *A chailleach do mharaís mé*'].

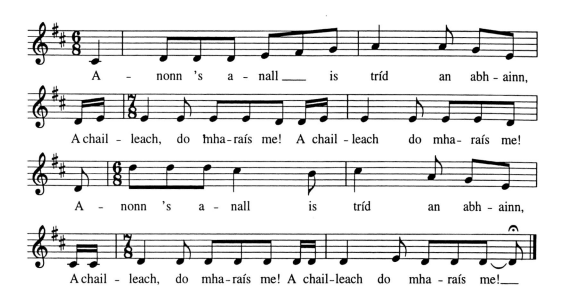

23

Ar bruach na Laoi

1. Ar bruach na Laoi insan oíche casag mé
    Gan buaireamh aigne — ba dhóigh liom féin —
    Chun go ndeagheas thar slí le díth mo mhearathail
    I gcuantaibh daingeana nárbh' fhearr de mé.
    Ní fheicinn an spéir le h-aon chorp mearathail,
    A's dá lasfadh an ré ní fhéadfainn amharc air.
    Ní raibh maitheas a' glaoch ná d'éinne freagairt dom
    Ag fuaim gach caise 'gus ag gárthaibh éan.

2. Do shuíos-sa síos go tríosmhar athtuirseach,
    Gan súil le casadh go brách sa tsaol.
    Faoi ard-toir droíghin go fíllthe taiscithe,
    Is gan de chlúdach leapa le fáil ach é.
    Do bhí éisc a' tíocht do dhruím gach caise acu,
    Géanna ar línn ann, míoltha is mara-phoic,
    Naosgaigh, faoilinn 'gus scíol do lachanaibh
    A' tíocht gan eagla a' trácht ón spéir.

3. Do chaitheas-sa suím don oíche mar sin dom,
    Go scíosmhar, athtuirseach cráite i bpéin,
    Is mé a' déanamh smaointe im' shuí cois abhainn dom,
    Is é a' síor-chur ceatha is a' cáthadh braon,
    Chun gur dhearcas-sa an ríog fá iadhadh na bratainne
    Do chealg mé im' chroí le saíghdaibh daingeana;
    A samhail 'sa tír lem' línn ní fheaca-sa,
    Is gurbh í d'fhúig scamaill ar mhnáibh an tsaoil.

4. Do leagas-sa dhíom gan mhoíll mo hata dhi
    Síos dom' bhathas le bárr mo mhéar;
    Is do chanas fá thrí dhi brí mo mhearathail
    Sa tír gur casadh nó gur túrladh mé.
    Fiosruím díot: 'An sídh-bhean t'ainm-se,
    Nó an tú Clíodhna ó thaoíbh na Carraige
    Lenar cailleadh dá druím na groí-fhir chalma,
    Sínte marbh ar lár a tsléibh'?'

5. Dob' iontach riamh liom triall 'na h-aice siúd,
    A' cliaraíocht sealad le h-áilleacht scéimh,
    Mara bhfaghainn-se bia go criartha taiscithe
    Agus ciall gan easpa le fáil sa réim.
    Do bhí na measa 'na slaoda ar ghéagaibh dara 'cu,
    Úlla 's caortha, sméara is áirní,
    Mil agus céir 'na slaoda á gcaitheamh ann
    Agus cnó buí, geallaim, ar bhárr na gcraobh.

6. Tá mórán Éireann éin ná feadar-sa
    A' déanamh neadacha i mbárr na gcraobh.
    Bíonn fiolair agus cuacha agus mórchuid eatorra
    Go suanmhar socair i ndán a' tsaoil.
    Bíonn an druid 'san seabhac ar chrann 'na n-aice siúd,
    An chiairseach shleamhain is an creabhar breá beathaithe.
    Cáig agus c'lúir 'na dtrúpaibh a' taisteal ann
    Agus smólaigh bhreaca 'na n-árus féin.

7. Tá tuilleadh ná dúrt-sa i gcuantaibh dorcha
    Don chuallacht shocair seo ar fán an tsaoil.
    Bíonn na sionnaigh go suairc ann i bpluaisibh dorcha
    Ar uair an bhrothaill 's i meán an lae.
    Gluaisíd faolchoin, eacha, is marcaigh ann
    Uaisle ag éamh lá gréine ar leacain chnuic
    Do choíll ní staonaid do chéim ná d'achrann
    Gur fúigeadh marbh é ar lár a' tsléibh'.

English Summary The poet takes an evening stroll by a bank of the river Lee and, in the course of describing his idyllic surroundings, he is surprised by a vision a woman of matchless beauty. There follows a lengthy description of her attributes. The song seems to end rather confusingly, apparently with the poet's death. **Recording** Seamus Ennis (May 1947) [a private recording]. **Text** From the Seamus Ennis recording; a second in CBÉ 822, 15–18 (dated 30 May 1942); another text in a notebook of SÓC's (?from Séamus Ó Liatháin, Cluain Drochad), which I have occasionally preferred to Ennis's. There is a separate copy in Seamus Ennis's CBÉ copybooks (Sept. 1946). **Printed Sources** Breathnach, *Cnuasachd bheag amhrán* 3, 3–4 (3 vv.); idem, *Ceól ár sínsear*, 67–68 [same as previous text]; Ó Caoimh, *Fáinne an Lae* (Meán Fómhair 1926) 3; Ní Annagáin & Clainndiolúin, *An londubh*, 25 = Ní Annagáin & de Chlanndiolún, *Londubh an chairn*, No. 40 (4 vv.); cf. Ó Cróinín & Ó Cróinín, *Seanachas Phádraig Í Chrualaoi*, 67–68 (4 vv.) and 238 [with references to earlier editions]; Ó Muirithe, *Cois an Ghaorthaidh*, 28–30, 59, No. 20 (8 vv.). **Notes** I have also used the collection of songs compiled by Caitlín Ní Bhuachalla, of Coachford, Co. Cork (dated 1943), who had access to a Ballyvourney collection made by Mícheál Máistir Ó Briain. The text is identical to Bess's, but breaks off at 5f due to the loss of a page in the manuscript. Breathnach, *Cnuasachd bheag amhrán*, 3–4, has our vv. 1, 2, 6. The text in *An Londubh*, has four verses in the order 1, 2, 3, 6 of our text. According to a note in Breathnach's edition, the author of this song was the Cork poet Seán Máistir Ó Conaill; Breathnach's version was collected from Pádraig Ó Crualaoi, of Macroom, Co. Cork; cf. Ó Cróinín & Ó Cróinín, *Seanachas Phádraig Í Chrualaoi*, 67f. The same attribution occurs in CBÉ 822, 18 (Seán Ó Cróinín).

24

Ar maidin inné cois Féile bhinn

1. Ar maidin inné cois Féile bhínn,
    Is mé ag amharc liom féin is gan aon am' ghaoír,
    Do dhearcas-sa an bhé fím' dhéin a' tíocht,
    Gur thiteas-sa gan moíll le grá di.
    Ba chamarsach, péarlach, dréimreach buí
    Ó bhathas go féar léi ar céabh a cinn,
    A mala ba chaol ná an ré gan aois,
    A caol-chúm caoin d'fhúig an saoghad so am' chroí!
        Is ar leacain mo laogh bhí caortha is lít,
        Is mar eala ar a linn a bán-chnis.

2. Do dhruideas-sa léi le h-éigean chaoin,
    Is d'fhiosraíos féin den bhé cé h-í:
    'An tusa d'fhúig léirscrios laogh na Traoi,
    Nó an ainnir gur thug Naois di lán-ghean?
    An tú an fhinne-bhean shéimh d'fhúig strae chun Fínn,
    Gur cailleadh Dailc Tréan is na céadta dá druim?
    An tusa le h-éad chuir an léine á ní
    Fí dhéin an té d'fhúig éag dá druim?'
        Tair feasta let' scéal a's saor a bhuíon,
        Nó talfaidh gan moíll chun báis mé'.

3. D'fhreagair an bhé go béasach síth:
    'Ní cleachta mé in aon chor don tréata mhaoidhis.
    Tá a maireann dem' ghaoltaibh in Éirinn síoch
    Go ceannasach buíonmhar láidir'.
    'Tair feasta led' scéal chun go saorfair sínn,
    Is dom' dheascaibh ní baol duit-se an saod so am' dhruím.
    Le taithneamh dhot' scéimh d'fhúig an saod so im' chroí
    D'éagfaidh sínn mar a réifir sí,
        Carthannach déin is is déirc dhuit í,
        A's ní scarfam chun go scaoilfidh an bás sínn'.

4. Nuair a fuaireas-sa gur ghéill an bhé lem' laoí,
    Do leathas-sa a géaga is ba ghléigeal í;
    Ba thaithneamhach léi mar a bhréagfainn í
    A's ar maidin do bhíomair grámhar.
    'Ba dheacair tú ghéilleadh aréir', dúirt sí,
    A's mar mheasaim, is faon tar éis ataoi.
    Sin agat toil-shaor is tréall aríst,
    Nó téanaimís chun go dtéam fá chuíng'.
        'Á! Níor gheallas-sa dhuit-se, is let' shaol ná bí
        Chomh baoth aríst a bháb bheag!'

5. An té chloisfeadh an bhé tar éis ag caoí
    Is í ag tarrac ó chéile céabh a cinn,
    D'fhúig Aifreann Dé gur thréigeas í,
    Á! geallaim óm' chroí nár ghá san!
    Ar a h-athair do ghlaoigh — i ngaor a bhí —
    Ghairm sé céadta am' dhéidh gan moíll,
    Is tapaidh mar do léimfinn féinig claí,
    Féith is díg dá réach im' shlí,
        A's sin mar a thréigeas laogh mo chroí,
        A's nár castar im' shlí go bráth í!

English Summary The poet encounters a beautiful woman and asks her if she is Helen of Troy, or one of a number of beautiful women in Irish mythology and legend. She says she is the epitome of Ireland. He professes undying love for her, if she will spend the night with him. She does so, but on the morrow he scoffs at her and makes off, with her father and friends in hot pursuit. **Text** From a DÓC notebook (dated 27 Aug. 1943). **Printed Sources** Freeman, 'Irish folk songs', *JFSS* 6, No. 24 (Jan. 1921) 255–56; Ó Cuill, *JIFSS* 21 (Dec. 1924) [1925] 29–30. **Notes** In Breathnach, *Sídh-cheól* 2, 154–56, No. 68 *Ar maidin indé 'gus mé am' shuan*, is ascribed to Seán Clárach Ó Domhnaill, and was taken down from Danny Warren of Macroom. There is a similar tune in Mac Coluim, *Fuinn na smól* 3, 30 and *JFSS* 6, 255. The version in *JIFSS* 21, 29–30, was taken down by Wilfrid Brown from Seán Ó Cuill, a Baile Mhúirne man who was a contemporary of Bess's; it reads as follows:

1. Ar maidin indé cois Féile bhíos,
    Ag machnamh liom fhéin agus gan aon im' ghaoir,
    'Seadh do dhearcas an bhé fím dhéin ag tigheacht,
    Is do thugas-sa gan mhoill searc gradh dhi.

2. Ba bhaclacha, péarlach, dréimireach buidhe
    A carn-fholt a craobh ach go féar ag tigheacht,
    A mala ba chaol ná'n rá gan aois,
    A claon-rosc caoin do chuir saeghaed trím chroidhe
    O! i leacain mo laogh do bhí caor a's lít,
    'Smar an eala ar an linn a bán-chneas.

For a song with a similar theme, see *Grá Mo Chléibh* [No. **65** below].

25

Ar maidin roim nóin

1. Ar maidin roim nóin is mé go breoite lag
    A' dul don chathair chun bróga nua thabhairt as,
    Do bhí ceathanna deor lem' leacain gan teorainn
        I gcionn flatha na Fódla chuir Seoirse ar n-aisc —
        Agus Ó, a bhean a' tí, cadí'n bhuairt sin ort?

2. Do bhuail umam óig-fhear gleoite deas
    'Gus i bhfochair a shórd ba mhéin liom stad;
    Do bhí 'ge 'na phóca ar meamram nó
        Na ranna a dhin Seán do Bhonaparte —
        Agus Ó, a bhean a tí, cadí'n bhuairt sin ort?

3. Do bhuaileas an ród go módhmharach mear;
    Bhí cuileachta ghleoite am' chóir 'na stad.
    'S i dti'n tabhairne an óil le h-aiteas ár sceoil

Do chaitheamair c'róinn nó dhó ar a' bhfear —
Agus Ó, a bhean a' tí, cadí'n bhuairt sin ort?

English Summary A young woman laments the Flight of the Earls from Ireland, but is comforted by verses in praise of Napoleon composed by an Irishman, which she hears from a young man whom she meets on the road. They retire to a hostelry where they carouse and sing.   **Text** From a DÓC notebook.   **Printed Sources** Borthwick, *Ceól-sídhe* 1, 89–90 *Ó'Bhean an Tíghe* (7 vv. 1, 2, A , 3, B, C, D); cf. Breathnach, *Sídh-cheól* 1, 114–15, No. 53 (7 vv., same as in *Ceól-sídhe*). See also Ó Cróinín & Ó Cróinín, *Seanachas Phádraig Í Chrualaoi*, 62–64.   **Notes** Composed by Donncha Caol Ó Súilleabháin, according to Pádraig Ó Crualaoi (Gaedheal na nGaedheal); cf. Ó Cróinín & Ó Cróinín, *Seanachas Phádraig Í Chrualaoi*, 62–64 62 (om. v. 2 but adds final v. E); see also 235–36 for additional references to previous editions. Borthwick, *Ceól-sídhe*, 89–90, has the following additional verses (A foll. 2; B, C, D foll. 3)

A. Nuair a dhearcas-sa códa Sheóin gan snas
    D'atharruigh mo shnódh a's mo bhrón do scaip
    Mo mhisneach do thóg agus tapa mo dhrólainn
    Le h-aiteas na sceólta nódh' do cheap

B. Nuair chaitheamair meón do phórthar mhaith
    Agus dramanna teó go leór le n' ais
    Talamh ár ndóthain béidh againn gan feóirling
    A's galla-phuic chróna ag romhar na gclas

C. Acht d'atharruigh ár spórt chun bróin gan stad
    Le *gazette* ó'n bpóist do sheól 'n-ár measc
    Ag aithris sceólta i bhfearannaibh Fódla
    Gur breabadh le h-ór ár mBónaipeart

D.   Seo feasta fé'n *yoke* 's is brón sinn seal
    'N-ár mbochtaineacht mhóir bíodh Job n-ár measc
    Is gairid mar lón dóibh fleadha agus póit
    Le caitheamh scoth glóire gheóbham-na ar neamh.

Seanachas Phádraig Í Chrualaoi, 64, has the following additional verse:

E. Níl mathas go deo i nglórthaibh ban,
    Ach tá taragaireacht mhór Naomh Seóin chun teacht.
    Bíodh úr bpaidir gach ló chun Athair na gCócht
    Atharrach Seoirse bheith i gc'róinn gan stad.

The text in Borthwick is from Tadhg Ó Cruadhlaoi (= Gaedheal na nGaedheal's brother). A heading in the notebook says 'Amhrán a bhíodh ag Dónailín Ó Riain' ['*A song that D. Ó R. used to have*']. At the end of the text 'ref. to *Ranna Phuic Cróna*, etc.' [v. B of Borthwick text].

26

Árdaig leat do shúsa!

1.   Árdaig leat do shúsa, do shúsa, 's do mhaide leat!
    Árdaig leat do shúsa chun siúil agus chun reatha leat!
    Tusa bheith it' phósa agus mise bheith ar meisce,
    Tusa leogaint dómh-sa agus mise leogaint duit-se!

English Summary A bawdy verse, in which a young woman urges her man to do his business.   **Text** From a notebook of DÓC's (dated 8 Aug. 1944), with the heading '*Rócán*' ('a ballad').   **Notes** The title of this song is in one of Bess's song-lists (*Aurdig leath the hoosthe*). A *súsa* is a blanket or rug; a *maide* is a stick (in this case, perhaps euphemistically, a walking-stick).

27

As Bacchus frequented his frolics

1.   As Bacchus frequented his frolics
      'Dti'n tabhairne, lá, insa Ghréig,
      'Tis there I beheld a fair damsel
      Do chealg me 'lár mo chléibh.

Text Fragment only from a DÓC notebook (dated 2 Jan. 1947).   **Printed Sources** Lyons, *An Gaodhal* 8/12 (Aug. 1891) 131; Norris, *An Gaodhal* 9/3 (Aibreán 1892) 171; *An Claidheamh Soluis* (2 Bealtaine 1914) 3 (5 vv.); 'Racaireacht ghrinn na tuaithe', *An Lóchrann* (Bealtaine 1925) 143–44; Ó Muirithe, *An tAmhrán macarónach*, 73–74, No. 30 (and 201) (7 vv.).   **Notes** Ó Muirithe, *An tAmhrán macarónach*, 73–74, prints from a broadside by Haly of Cork in the National Library of Ireland; he dates it early in the nineteenth century ('i dtús an 19ú haois'). It has the title *O'Sullivan's Frolicks* in the broadside (text ibid., 171–72), which is the title also in J. J. Lyons's text. According to Norris, Lyons made 'a proper mesh' of the text, and offers an improved version! Lyons's text was 'written in Philadelphia from the dictation of Mr John Connelly, a native of Rosscarberry, Co. Cork'. The version in *Racaireacht na tuaithe*, 143–44, is called *Frolic Uí Raghalla*, and a note says it was sung to the air of *An Gamhain Geal Bán* [No. **18**] or *Báb na gCraobh*. Ó Muirithe also had the song from the singing of his father, Seán Ó Muirithe, who knew Bess Cronin well. I give his text in full here (and have italicised the Irish).

1.   As Bacchus frequented his frolics
      I dtigh an tábhairne lá ins an nGréig,
      I espied a most beautiful damsel
      Do chealg mé i lár mo chléibh;
      Bereft of all reason and senses
      Do dhruideas go dána léi,
      I wish she was truly contented
      Gabháil liomsa thar mhnáibh an tsaoil.

2.   She answered and swore by all goodness,
      'Ní chreidim do ráitis bréig,
      Don't tease me with reasons insipid,
      Ach imigh is fág mé, a réic;
      It is now I am going to Cork City
      Ag tuiscint is ag foghlaim léinn,
      For a year I'll not come to this country,
      Nó b'fhéidir an uair sin féin.'

3.   'Believe me it's by you I'm tormented,
      A linbh is áille gné,
      Bemoaning a doleful condition
      Ó thiteas i ngrá led' scéimh.
      If God would grant my petition
      Mé a cheangal led' bhánchnis chaomh,
      All pleasures on earth would attend us

4.   'If you be in earnest,' ar sise,
      'Ní leanfad níos mó dem' léann.
      My parents do really insist on
      Go bhfuilim ró-óg go léir,
      But I am one-eighth of a century,
      Agus cuiream leis bliain uainn féin,
      And if they don't consent as we wish them,
      Go mbogfam an ród sinn féin'.

5.   Her tresses of hair were unravelled
      Ag titim go fáinneach léi,
      Her eyes were more curious in fancy
      Ná an plainéad ab áille gné;
      Her youth and her beautiful person,
      A mala, a srón, is a béal,
      Her cheeks like the roses called damask,
      Is go talamh gan cháim dá réir.

6. She neatly compares with fine images
    A déantar le snáthaid chaol:
    The phoenix, the lark and the linnet,
    An fiolar, an chuach is an naosc.
    She is elected by Venus and Sylvia,
    Olympus and Mithridates,
    She has gained from all living in Erin,
    Is dá n-áirínn an saol sa chraobh.

7. I instantly took her and kissed her,
    Ba bhinne ná flute a béal,
    And her speech so enlivened my spirits
    Gur chuma cá ngeobhadh a spré.
    And in sweet scented meadows and valleys
    Gur chaitheamar mí dár saol,
    Embracing and kissing each other
    Ar maidin, le faid an lae.

28

As I roved out one morning through Devonshire in England

1. As I roved out one morning through Devonshire in England
    We called to an ale-house, myself and my friends,
    It being on Saint Patrick's Day when we landed there quite merrily,
    We called for some porter, our thirst for to quench.

2. We drank to Garryowen and the ancient town of Limerick,
    To Erin's green fields and her daisy-clad hills,
    Where the boys do sing in chorus without spite or animosity,
    And the girls they do join them with a gravar jug of punch.

3. We drank away like topers, we passed no great apology.
    We drank without notation to adversaries or friends;
    Until a group there came that degraded our capacity,
    And swore by hocus-pocus that the papists they would kick.

4. We twigged them in a moment, we told them to conduct themselves.
    We told them to be partial, as we gave them no offence.
    But the more we were advising them, the more they were approaching us,
    And swearing every moment that the top-room we would quit.

5. They got so elated — they were ten to one approaching us —
    We got so irritated that we told them to resist.
    Then we commenced to flake them with our light shillelaghs,
    And we left them broken bones with our blackthorn sticks.

6. We left them to their surgeons' work, doctors came to visit them.
    They put plaster to their noppers, for we left them in their gore.
    We made them think of Paddy's land, where the boys are brisk and airy.
    Likewise the light shillelagh that grows in Erin's shore.

7.   Farewell unto old Erin, where the women fight courageously,
     That lovely fertile country where the milk and honey flows!
     Like the Promised Land of Egypt, when the Israelites obtained it,
     I hope I may survive for to see it free once more!

Text From the collection of Bess's hand-written songs; another (identical) copy in a DÓC notebook. A note of my father's says 'From Seana-Mheáig' (= Bess's mother); a second note reads 'Fonn *Stáicín Eórnán* (almost)' [Air *Stack of Barley* (almost)]. For another song, with the same charming sentiments, see Joyce, *Ancient Irish music*, 86–87, No. 84. See also CBÉ 912, 539–43 (collected by Seán Ó Cróinín in Co. Cork, 1960). **Notes** 2d *gravar* = *grámhar* 'loveable'; 3b *adversaries* spelt thus in both copies; 6b *noppers* cf. Eric Partridge, *A dictionary of slang and unconventional English* (New York 1937) s.v.

29

Baile Mhúirne[1/6]

1.   Tréimhse chaitheas le seal go h-aerach,
     i measg mo ghaoltha go soilbhir sámh,
     Gan suím i gcleasaibh ná i gcúrsaí an t-saoil seo,
     do chuirfeadh m'intinn ar seachrán.
     Thugas gean is urraim dom' bhaile dhúchais,
     fuair cion is clú ar fuaid Ínse Fáil.
     Is ní thréigfead feasta an grá ró-dhlúth soin
     do Bhaile Mhúirne go bhfaghaidh mé bás.

2.   Is breá é amharc a cnoc 'sa sléibhte,
     'sa gleannta féarmhara ar maidin cheóidh
     Is fuaim gach caise ag sníomh go héasca,
     go sroiseann béal na Mara móir',
     Is breá é a coillte 'na gcrannaibh díreacha,
     ag fás go líonmhar i measg gach gleann,
     Go bhfaigheann an sionnach sgáth is díon ann,
     an druí ciardubh, an broc 's an creabhair.

3.   Is ann do gheóbhaidh tú an t-údar léanta,
     do fhíor-fhuil Éibhir na mbéimeann óir
     Go bhfuil grá is urraim acu dá dteangaibh dhúchais,
     san Béarla brúite faoi scamall mhór.
     Ní staonfaid feasda do Sheán Ó Lúndain,
     ach leanfaid clú a sinsear sóghail
     Chun saoirse thabhairt dá dtír gan diúltha,
     mar bhí ar dtúis againn i nÉirinn óig.

4.   Is ann do gheófá an ainnir mhánla
     gur bh'fonn léi sár-fhear suí seal 'na treó
     Go bhfuil a mala ar dhath an áirne
     sa leaca áluinn ar sgáil an róis.
     Is binne fuaim a teangan Gaeilge,
     'ná Orpheus éachtach ag gléasadh ceóil
     Nó Dáire Duanach do chuirfeadh suan ort,
     bhí ag Fionn Mac Cumhaill i dTeamhair fadó.

5. Tá Baile Mhúirne go fairsing fáilteach,
ag riar ar tháintibh do ghabhann an treó,
Go bhfuil grá ar lasadh i gcroí gach aon ann,
rug bárr ar aon rud dá bhfeaca fós.
Bíonn triall na sluaite do'n Tiobraid naomhtha
tá le cian i gclú is i ngradam mhór,
Is impím feasta ar Ghobnait Naofa
bheith mar dhíon is scáth dúinn pé áit go ngeóbham.

English Summary This is a poem in praise of Ballyvourney (Co. Cork), particularly its scenery and the richness of its Irish-language tradition. **Recording** BBC 19026 (21 Sept. 1952). **Text** From the BBC recording. **Printed Sources** 'Dán-mholadh Bhaile Mhúirne', *An Claidheamh Soluis* (20 Aibreán 1901) 83. **Notes** Composed by Donnchadh Ó Laoghaire on the occasion of the feis at Baile Mhúirne in 1900, where it was awarded 1st prize. For a similar poem, by the same author, in praise of the river Sullane, which won 1st prize at the Ballyvourney feis in the year following, see Mícheál Ó Murchadha, 'Dán-mholadh an t-Suláin', *Irisleabhar na Gaedhilge* 12, No. 140 (Bealtaine 1902) 74–75. There is a brief account of the composer in Capt. Francis O'Neill, *Irish minstrels and musicians*, 337–40.

30

Barbara Allen[2/28]

1.   It was early, early in the summer-time,
     When the flowers were freshly springing;
     A young man came from the North Country
     Fell in love with Barbara Allen;
     Fell in love with Barbara Allen;
     A young man came from the North Country,
     Fell in love with Barbara Allen.

2.   He felt sick and very, very bad,
     And more inclined to die.
     He wrote a letter to the old house at home,
     To the place where she was dwelling,
     To the place where she was dwelling.
     He wrote a letter to the old house at home,
     To the place where she was dwelling.

3.   Very slowly she got up,
     And slowly she came to him.
     The first word she spoke when she came there
     Was 'Young man, I fear you're dying,
     Young man, I fear you're dying'.
     The first word she spoke when she came there
     Was 'Young man, I fear you're dying'.

4.   'Dying, dying, not at all,' he said —
     One kiss from you would cure me'.
     'One kiss from me you ne'er shall see,
     If I thought your heart was breaking,
     If I thought your heart was breaking,
     One kiss from me you ne'er shall see
     If I thought your heart was breaking'.

Child 84   **Recordings** CBÉ 430a (1947) — JR-GP (24 Nov. 1952) = *Jean Ritchie Field Trip. Field recordings in England, Scotland and Ireland by Jean Ritchie and George Pickow.* Collector Limited Editions CLE 1201 (Port Washington, New York 1955) No. 8 — Diane Hamilton (1955).   **Text** From the JR-GP tape, compared with Seamus Ennis's 1946 transcription in CBÉ 1591, 525–27. There is another copy in Ennis's CBÉ copybooks (Sept. 1946).   **Printed Sources** Child, *English and Scottish popular ballads* 2, 276–79; 3, 514 (No. 84); Sam Henry, 'Songs of the People', *Northern Constitution* (19 May 1928), No. 236 = Huntington & Hermann, *Sam Henry's Songs of the People*, 375–76.   **Notes** There is a gap in Ennis's text, as there is in all versions recorded from Bess. The text in his transcript has the following slight variants 2a 'He felt sick' 'He fell' sick' JR-GP; 2b 'dying' 'die' JR-GP; 4a 'Dying, dying, I am not at all —' (om.'he said').   He also has the following fragmentary additional verse:

       He turned his pale face towards the wall
       And his back side towards the window —
       […   …   …   …   …]
       […   …   … a red rose and a lily.

For a different Irish air to this song (not unlike *The Gypsy Laddie, O*) see Joyce, *Ancient Irish music,* 79, No. 78, and for the tunes in general, Bronson, *The traditional tunes of the Child ballads,* 4 vols (Princeton, New Jersey 1957–72). Recordings and discussions of this famous ballad are legion.

Barb'ra Allen

It was early, early in the Summer-time
when the flowers were freshly springing
A young man came from the north countree
Fell in love with Barb'ra Allen
Fell in love with Barb'ra Allen
A young man came from the north countree
Fell in love with Barb'ra Allen.

He fell sick and very very bad
And more inclined to dying
He wrote a letter to the old house at home
To the place where she was dwelling (*as in the last verse*)

Very slowly she got up
And slowly she came to him
The first word she spoke when she came there
Was "young man I fear you're dying"

"Dying, dying I am not at all —
One kiss from you might cure me."
"One kiss from me you ne'er shall see
If I thought your heart was breaking"
He turned his pale face towards the wall
And his back side towards the window ---
- - - - --- - : - a red rose and a lily.

'Barbara Allen' transcribed from Bess Cronin by Seamus Ennis (CBÉ, UCD).

It was ear - ly, ear - ly, in the sum - mer time,

When. the flowers were fresh - ly sprin - ging;

A _____ young man came from the north coun - try

Fell _ in love with Bar - bara Al - len;

Fell in love with Bar - bara Al - len,

A young man came from the north coun - try,

Fell _ in love with Bar - bara Al - len.

<h1 style="text-align:center">31</h1>

<h1 style="text-align:center">Beautiful and bold Trainer-O</h1>

Note Title only from one of Bess's song-lists. **Printed Sources** Royal Irish Academy, SR 3 C 37, No. 8; NLI General Coll., 4 copies. Another two copies in Cambridge University Library Ballads, vol. 3, 260 and 4, 113. **Notes** There is no recording of this song by Bess, so far as I know. The NLI broadsides that I have seen (4) are more-or-less identical to the Academy text. The following text is from a broadside in the Royal Irish Academy, Lord Moyne Collection:

1.   I am a young damsel that lies here in bondage,
     The same I can never deny,
     That I feel in love with a young collegian
     In Drogheda college now does lie.

2.   My eyes they grew dim and my spirits I did loose,
     When I heard of that sad heavenly news,
     That I for ever more my darling shall loose
     He is my beautiful bold Treanor O.

3.   I wrote a petition and sent it to my true love
     Still thinking it might stop his degrees,
     I knew his intention that he was determin'd
     The blessed robes to wear speedily.

4.   When the Bishop had read of the same,
     He said noble Trainor a statute of fame,
     In spite of the ladies you must be ordained
     And a priest unto Paris you must go.

5.   Now adieu sweet Balingrove where my love and I did wander,
     When drest in its mantle of green,
     No more shall it bloom since my true love is gone,
     Until he does return unto me.

6.   The small birds shall join and quit their melody,
     No more shall the cuckoo be heard on the tree,
     But straightway to Paris away they will flee
     With my beautiful bold Treanor O.

7.   My love being returned from his ordination
     The world might then have pitied me,
     On the ensuing Sunday near Balli[n]akill,
     O its there I first did him see.

8.   Standing on the altar his robes he did wear
     With his red rosy cheeks & coal black hair
     He won the ladies hearts and he left them in dispair,
     He is my beautiful bold Treanor O.

9.   The pagans do worship some gods of gold
     And some parents do worship the same,
     For thirty bright pieces our Saviour was sold,
     Blessed and praised be his holy name.

10. But my cruel parents for sake of the store
     They would have me sold out for ever more
     I would sooner beg my bread from door to door,
     With my beautiful bold Treanor O.

11. Now since my true-love has changed his mind,
     And turned his back to all female kind,
     To the way of religion myself I will incline,
     With my beautiful bold Treanor O.

The air is the same as that for *The Green Linnet*. 'Uileachan Dubh O' is the old name for the air; see Breandán Breathnach, 'The man and his music — Willie Clancy', *Ceol* 2/3 (1965) 70–77: 77, who remarks that the song was 'very popular in Munster many years ago'. See the recording in *Seoda Cheoil* (CCÉ CEF018).

32

Betsy of Ballindown Brae

1.   Young men and maidens, I pray, lend an ear,
     To hear the sad fate of two lovers so dear!
     Charming young Betsy of Ballindown Brae
     And the Lord of the Moorland that led her astray.

2.   One night as this young man lay down for to sleep,
     Young Betsy came to him and o'er him did weep.
     Saying, 'You are the young man that caused me to roam

Far, far away from my friends and my home.
My own blushing cheeks, alas! moulder away
Beneath the cold tomb in sweet Ballindown Brae'.

3.   He awoke from his slumber like one in surprise
'Yes! Yes!, It's the voice of my Betsy!', he cries;
'And if she be dead as the vision now say,
I'll lie by her side in sweet Ballindown Brae'.

4.   He called to his servant for to saddle his steed;
Over hills and high mountains he rode with great speed.
Until he arrived at the noon-time of day
At the cot of young Betsy of Ballindown Brae.

5.   Betsy's own father stood by his own gate,
Like a man quite forlorn, bewailing his fate.
The young man advanced to him and offered relief,
And begged him to tell him the cause of his grief.
'I had but one daughter', the old man did say,
'And now she lies low in sweet Ballindown Brae'.

6.   'Her skin was as fair as the lily or swan,
As bonny a lass as the sun e'er shone on.
Her heart it was broken, she died in despair,
Sometimes went frantic and tearing her hair.
And all through a young man that led her astray,
And left her far, far from sweet Ballindown Brae'.

7.   'Yes, I am that young man', the stranger replied.
'I constantly said that I'd make her my bride'.
And out from its scabbard a small sword he drew,
And with heart unrelenting he pierced his breast through.
And when he was dying those words he did say:
'Lay me down by young Betsy of Ballindown Brae'.

Laws P 28   **Text** From Bess's handwritten song collection.   **Printed Sources** National Library of Ireland, General Coll., 2 broadside versions, one by W. Birmingham, Thomas St, Dublin. Apparently not the same as Joyce, *Old Irish folk music and songs*, 150, No. 322 (1 v.); Sam Henry, 'Songs of the People', *Northern Constitution*, 4 Apr. 1925, No. 73 = Huntington & Hermann, *Sam Henry's Songs of the People*, 412–13. There are two ballad sheets entitled *Ballindown Brae* in Cambridge University Library Ballads, vol. 3, 263, and 4, 147.   **Notes** See Laws, *American balladry from British broadsides*, 262–63, P 28 *Bessie of Ballington Brae:* 'Come all you young men and maidens so fair,/Come list to a tale of two lovers so dear —/Charming young Bessie of Ballydubray/And the Lord of the Moorlands who led her astray'; see also Mackenzie, *Ballads and sea songs from Nova Scotia*, 101, No. 31. He refers to M. C. Dean, who printed a version of this song, entitled 'Ballentown Brae' in *The flying cloud*, 44–45 'It tells the story of the betrayal of Bessie by the Lord of Morelands, of her death, and of her appearance (or that of her ghost) before her betrayer during the night'. He refers also to an English broadside in the Harvard collection (without printer's imprint) entitled *Sweet Ballenden Braes* — a lament by a deserted maiden who is going back to Ballenden Braes to die. It is in the same measure and stanza as the song under discussion, and is (Mackenzie thinks) quite certainly to be connected with it. Mackenzie has only a few lines from our song (vv. 4, 7). The NLI broadside copies are identical to Bess's, but one has the following additional four lines at the end:

All things being read[y] the grave it was dug,
And with bonny Betsy the young lord was laid,
So all young maidens from your cot do not stray,
But think of young Betsy from Ballindown brae.

This verse is also found at the close of Sam Henry's text; he has the following opening verse as well:

Come all you young fair maids, I pray lend an ear
Unto the sad fate of two lovers so dear,
Concerning young Bessie of Ballindown Brae
And the laird of yon moorland that led her to stray
From Ballindown Brae, sweet Ballindown Brae,
He courted young Bessie from Ballindown Brae.

The title occurs in one of Bess's song-lists as *Young men and maidens, I pray*. The song is still very popular in Irish tradition.

33

Bold Jack Donohue[2/10]

1.   In Dublin town I was brought up, that city of great fame;
     My parents reared me tenderly and many that know the same;
     For being a bold United Boy they sent me across the main;
     For seven long years to New South Wales to wear the convict chain.

2.   I was no longer than six months upon the Australian shore;
     I turned out a Fenian Boy, which I often did before.
     There were McNamara and Andrew Ward, and Captain Mackey too;
     They were the chiefs and associates of Bold Jack Donohue.

3.   O'Donohue was taken all for a notorious crime;
     His sentence was to be hanged upon the gallows high;
     But when they went to Sydney Jail they missed him in the stew,
     And when they went to call the rolls they missed O'Donohue.

4.   O'Donohue made his escape, for the woods he did repair,
     Where tyrants never show their face, neither by night or day.
     Every week in the newspaper there's something published new
     Concerning that bold Fenian boy called Jack O'Donohue.

5.   O'Donohue was walking one summer afternoon —
     Little was his notion that his life would end so soon! —
     A sergeant of the horse police discharged his carbine,
     And loudly cried to O'Donohue to fight or to resign.

6.   'To resign to you, you cowardly dog, is something I ne'er shall do!
     I'd rather fight with all my might!', said famed Jack Donohue;
     'I'll range those woods and valleys like a wolf or a kangaroo,
     Before I'd work for governments!', said famed Jack Donohue.

7.   At once the horse police fired until a fatal ball
     Lodged in the breast of O'Donohue, which caused him for to fall.
     Before he closed his mournful eyes to this world he bid adieu:
     'Ye people all, both great and small, please pray for O'Donohue!'

Laws L 22.   **Recording** JR–GP (24 Nov. 1952) = *As I Roved Out*, Smithsonian Folkways Recordings (Washington, D. C., 1960); reissued by Ossian Publications (Cork 1990).   **Text** From the JR–GP recording.   **Printed Sources** Edwards, *The convict maid*, 77 ['The Adventures of Brave Jack O'Donough']; *Delaney's Irish song book*, No. 2, 21; Zimmermann, *Songs of Irish rebellion*, 269–71,

No. 76; Lomax, *The folk songs of North America in the English language*, 117–19, No. 59; Anderson, *The story of Australian song*, 118–22 (who reports the existence of a broadside ballad in Cambridge University Library entitled *The Adventures of Jack O'Donohoe*, said to date from 1867 approximately [? = CUL Ballads, vol. 3, 156 [?157]; vol. 4, 180]); Meredith & Anderson, *Folk songs of Australia and the men and women who sang them*, 63–64, 97; Jolliffe, *The third book of Irish ballads;* 40–47; Palmer, *Everyman book of British ballads*, 134–35 No. 59; Lomax, *Cowboy songs and other frontier ballads*, 64–65. See Laws, *American balladry from British broadsides*, 178. **Notes** This is perhaps the best-known Irish-Australian ballad after *The Wild Colonial Boy*, and the two are often inextricably mixed in transmission and frequently sung to the same tune *(The Wearing of the Green, Irish Molly-O, etc.)*. Jack Donohue was killed in a shoot-out with police near Sydney on 1 Sept. 1830. For details, Laws refers to G. C. Ingleton, *True patriots all* (Sydney 1952) 130, which contains a newspaper account of the bushranger's death, along with a text of the ballad ('Come all you gallant bushrangers', etc.). Laws remarks dryly 'Interestingly enough, none of the police were killed or injured when Donahue was slain'. Anderson, *The story of Australian folksong*, 118, gives the following two verses from a broadside ballad in Cambridge University Library dated c. 1867(?) entitled *The Adventures of Jack O'Donohoe*:

> 1.   Attend each valiant highwayman and outlaws of distain,
>   Who choose to live in slavery or wear the band of chains,
>   Attention pay to what I say, believe me if you do,
>   I will relate the wretched state of Jack O'Donohoe.
>
> 2.   This bold undaunted highwayman, as you shall understand,
>   Was banished for his natural life from Erin's happy land,
>   In Dublin town, of high renown, where his first breath he drew
>   The deeds of honour titled valiant Jack O'Donohoe.

The version he prints, 119–21 is close to ours, though there are slight differences in the details. The older version of the song is more detailed, and is often found with a refrain; there is a broadside copy in the Royal Irish Academy (Zimmermann, 270). Edwards, *Convict maid*, prints a text taken from a broadside in the University of Liverpool Library in an album entitled *Lyra Milesiana*, with no printer or date given. Zimmermann's text is printed from a broadside in Trinity College Dublin, c. 1870, 'by John McCarthy', described as a new version of an older ballad; this version is very close to Bess's. See Philip Butterss, '*Bold Jack Donahue* and the Irish outlaw tradition', *Australian Folklore* 3 (1989) 3–9 (with further references). The most authoritative discussion is in John Meredith, *The Wild Colonial Boy Bushranger Jack Donaghue, 1806–1830* (Ascot Vale, Victoria 1982). Anderson (121) states that the song was banned at one stage in Australia and it became an offence punishable with forfeiture of licence for it to be sung in public houses. Zimmermann, 271, points out that the reference in the song to Captain Mackey helps to date it; William Mackey was a Fenian commander in Co. Cork in the rising of 1867 and was sentenced to twelve years' penal servitude in March 1868. Released three years later, he blew himself up in an attempt to bomb London Bridge in 1884. According to Meredith, however, Captain Mackey was a later addition to the song. Palmer's version (recorded from Ned Costello of Bermingham (Mrs Costello's son), has a different air, but the words are very similar. The ballad migrated also to America, where it was collected by John Lomax and published in his *Cowboy songs*.

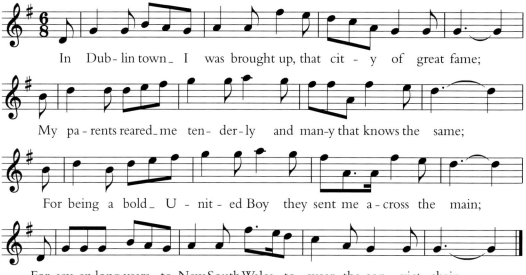

34

Buachaill na gruaige breá buí

1. As I went out walking one morning in Spring
   To hear the birds whistle and the nightingale sing,
   I espied a comely damsel sitting under a tree,
   And she lamenting her *Buachaill na gruaige breá buí*.

2. I stepped up to this fair maid and bade her good day:
   'Come, tell me your ailment, come, tell me, I pray.
   Dry up those tears which in torrents do flow,
   For the cause of your wailing I'd much like to know'.

3. 'Oh, young man don't tease me, but go on your way,
   For I am in trouble this many a day;
   For I once loved a young man near the town of Tralee,
   And I called him my *Buachaill na gruaige breá buí*'.

4. 'This young man was handsome and mild, to be sure.
   His lips they were red and his heart it was pure.
   I would give all the riches in North Germany
   For one kiss from my *Buachaill na gruaige breá buí*'.

5. 'Oh Molly, lovely Molly, you're no stranger to me.
   Don't you think of that night that we drove from Tralee?
   So get yourself ready and married we'll be,
   For I am your own *Buachaill na gruaige breá buí*'.

6. 'Oh Willie, lovely Willie, such a thing cannot be,
   Until better acquainted our parents will be.
   But I will get ready and married we'll be,
   For you are my *Buachaill na gruaige breá buí*'.

7. This couple got married, I hear people say,
   And off to Killarney they drove the next day.
   They are living now near the town of Tralee,
   And I hope they'll be blest with a large family.

Text From Bess's handwritten collection of songs.   **Notes** There is a version recorded by Alan Lomax in January 1951 from Michael Cronin, in BBC 21208; for other versions, see CBÉ 578, 487–88 (Kerry 1938); CBÉ 1592, 16–17 (Cork 1960).

35

Buachaillín donn

Note The title occurs in one of Bess's own handwritten song-lists *(Buachaillín Dhonn)*, but I have no text from her. **Printed Sources** Hughes, *Irish country songs* 4, 56–58; cf. CUL Ballads, vol. 3, 158 *Boughleen Dhoun*; there is another ballad in the same collection, vol. 5, 219, called *Boughil na Grouga Dhowna*, and another entitled *My Boughleen Dhoun*, vol. 3, 393. There is another again, entitled *Song called the Bouchleen Dhounin* vol. 6, 447. **Notes** Hughes, Irish country songs, has two verses and an air (attributed to John Keegan Casey [1845–78]); the first verse is as follows:

My true love he dwells in the mountains,
Like a war eagle fearless and free;
By the side of the low tuning fountains
That wander thro' wide Annalee.
His soul has more valour and honour
Than a king with a palace and crown;
For the blood of the race of O'Connor
Fills the feins of my buachaillín donn.

36

Buduran's Ball

1. You lads and gay lasses of every description
   Draw near and I'll give you a verse of a song
   Kindly relating our latest convention —
   It's not my intention to keep you too long.
   I know you are waiting with eager attention;
   Your names I shall mention at every call,
   Thinking to please and to gain your affection,
   I'll give a few sketches of Buduran's Ball.

2. On Saturday morning a party came prancing,
   Quickly advancing with hearts full of glee;
   Dressed up in good order, both charming and handsome —
   I'm sure they were anxious to get on the spree!
   They came from the borders, walking, galavanting,
   Well-formed for action, both lofty and tall.
   Just like an army when drawn out for action
   They came with their faction to Buduran's Ball.

3. They came from all quarters and swarmed together,
   In spite of the weather, through fog, mist and spray.
   Just as I saw them, I walked to them hither,
   I being at my leisure the very same day.
   In beholding their garments I did my endeavours
   I viewed their complexions and looked at them all.
   Well knowing that soon after we would be conversing
   In getting possession of Buduran's Ball.

4. They finished the yarn according to fashion —
   Indeed, you would fancy their work it was fine! —
   For Jamesy keeps cloth that is awfully handsome,
   In every mansion I hear it do shine.
   It's fit for the parlour and hall full of grandeur —
   Indeed, it's no wonder we'd give him a call! —
   Expecting a garment in all its attraction,
   And then we'd go dancing to Buduran's Ball.

5.   The night it was falling soon after the dinner,
And everything looking most cheerful and gay;
The girls' department was awfully busy
To get in a figure without much delay.
This noble commander was drawing down his whiskers,
Himself and Jack Sullivan blinking them all.
And from that until morning our party were drinking,
Dancing and singing at Buduran's Ball.

6.   I often took walks to where parties assembled
In spite of the weather in many a place;
Drinking according with all sorts of merriment,
Plenty of girls, as many as you please.
Our picnics were always regarded with pleasure,
Thundering welcomes whenever you call.
By the mock sticks of war, for to give them their merits,
I never saw better than Buduran's Ball.

7.   But now I'm striving this rhyme for to finish,
For dreary old Christmas is coming, you see;
Which makes us retire from our highest conventions
As more precious business is coming on me.
So now as we're inclined to combine through the winter —
Indeed, we will venture to give you a call!
Hoping to find you enticing and willing
To come with your shilling to Buduran's Ball.

Text From Bess's collection of handwritten songs.   **Notes** This song was composed by Johnny Nóra Aodha (for whom see also *Lackagh Bawn* [No. **79**] and *The Tailor Bawn* [No. **177**]. Note that Bess omits precisely that verse in which the neighbours are mentioned (as promised! — 'Your names I shall mention at every call', 1f). There is a recording of this song, from the singing of Dan Cronin (Bess's eldest son), made by his daughter, Máiréad Mulligan (née Cronin). It has only the first 3 verses, and the following one, which is not in Bess's handwritten copy:

A.   The Yankee she brought us an awful big faction,
Some that were handsome and some that were quare.
They came from Kilgarvan, Tom Wall and Tadhg Rodger,
And more of the Harringtons down from Kenmare.
Out from Iveleary came weavers and millers
And masons for mending and building up walls;
Other relations called Leahys and Finnegans
All of them running to Buduran's Ball.

There are other versions in CBÉ 283, 243–45 (Cork 1936) and CBÉ 1591, 358–61 (Cork 1960). The air is the same as for *Nice Little Jenny from Ballinasloe* [No. **103**].

37

Casam araon na géanna romhainn

1.   Tráthnóinín saoire ar bhuíochtaint na gréine
Do dhearcas-sa an spéir-bhean bhéasach óg

Ag taisteal im' choinnibh tré imeall na sléibhte —
Bhí lasadh na gcaor 'na gné 's 'na snódh.
Ba chamarsach, triopallach, fionna-chas, néata,
Ag casadh 's filleadh le h-iomradh a chéile.
A bearta 'na ndualaibh ag titim go féar léi,
'S í ag casadh na ngéanna ón ngaorthadh ar neóin.

2.   Do dhruideas 'na coinnibh go h-innealtha éasca,
      'S do bheannaíos go séimh don réilthin óig.
      D'fhiosras di-se an ngeóbhadh liom mar chéile,
      'Nó bhfuil ceangal na cléire ort le h-aon fhear beo?
      Má thigeann tú liom-sa gheóbhair fairsinge 's féile,
      Cion agus urraim thar a maireann de bhéithibh;
      Mise agus tusa ag súgradh le chéile,
      Agus casfam araon na géanna rómhainn'.

3.   'S é dúirt sí am' fhreagra: 'Ní oireann do scéal dom —
      Imigh, a réice, agus dein-se do ghnó;
      Níl eolas agam-sa ar do shaibhreas saoltha
      Is ní chreidfinn-se bréithre baotha ód' shórd.
      Dá n-imínn go dealbh gan talamh ná tréada
      Bheadh mo mháthair is m'athair ag caismirt 's ag plé liom;
      Triall-se ort abhaile chómh tapaidh is fhéadfair
      Agus casfaidh mé féin na géanna rómham'.

4.   'Béarfad eolas duit feasta ar mo shaibhreas saoltha —
      Suidh anso taobh liom féin go fóill!
      Beidh do bhólacht go fairsing is do bha bhoga ag géimrigh,
      Tithe deas aoltha déanta id' chómhair;
      Beidh do sheisreach capall ag branar 's ag réabadh,
      Gasra d'fhearaibh ag grafadh na sléibhte,
      Mise 'gus tusa ag bhálcaeracht le chéile,
      Agus casfam araon na géanna rómhainn'.

5.   Mar gurbh é siúd a thaithíos i dtigh mh'athar féinig —
      Screadach na ngéan agus géimreach na mbó;
      Cuigean dá cnagadh roim éirí na gréine,
      Agus casfam araon na géanna rómhainn.

English Summary The poet meets a beautiful young woman one evening, herding her geese on the mountain-side. He promises her wealth and affection, if she will agree to marry him. The song ends inconclusively in this version, but the additional verses in the notes indicate that the suit was successful.   **Text** From a single loose handwritten sheet, by DÓC, plus last verse from a notebook copy.   **Printed Sources** Ó Briain, *An Lóchrann* (Deire Fóghmhair 1916) 5 (6 vv.); Freeman, 'Irish folk songs', *JFSS* 6/3, No. 23 (Jan. 1920) 169–70, No. 24 (1st line only).   **Notes** A note in the DÓC notebook adds that the air to this song was the same as for *Gleann Cam*. The song in Freeman's Ballyvourney collection, No. 24, has the same opening line, but differs otherwise from our text. The text in *An Lóchrann* was collected by M[ícheál] Ó Briain, one of the 'Four Masters of Baile Mhúirne'; we can assume therefore, that his version represents something very close to the one that Bess was famliar with, and indeed the two are identical, as far as they go; Ó Briain, however, has two additional verses:

        A.   Ní slighe dhuit chun mhartha bheith ag racaireacht éithigh
              A's mé fhágaint at' dhéidh i léan 's i mbrón,
              A's gur bhaoghal duit na flaithis do dheasgaibh mé thréigion,
              Dá ndéanthá-sa bréag ar sgéal dá shórd;
              Do bheadh mallacht na n-easbol 's na n-aingeal go léir ort
              Mo mháthar is m'athar is na hEaglaise naomhtha

Dhom chlaonúghadh le cleasaibh chun peacaidh
Ag casadh araon na ngéanna rómhainn.

B.　　Ní slighe dhom chun martha bheith ag racaireacht éithigh
As go bhféadfaidh tu féinig feuchaint rómhat
Go ragham go dtí an sagart chun margadh dhéanamh
As ceangal ó'n gcléir bheith orrainn féin go deó;
Ní le súil go bhfaghainn rachmus ná ana-chuid spré leat,
Acht taithneann do phearsa, do mhaise a's do mhéinn liom,
Is ró gheárr a mhairfead, mo cheasna mara réidhfir —
Agus casfam araon na géanna rómhainn.

38

Ceó draíochta sheól oíche chun fáin mé

1.　　Ceó draíochta sheól oíche chun fáin mé,
Is ar mh'intinn gur thárluig chugham suan;
Am' shíor-chasadh i gcoilltibh gan áitreabh
Go dlaoi-chnoc na Blárnan 'sea chuas;
Do shíneas cois crainn go raibh bláth air,
Agus taoibh liom go dtáinig sí suas;
An chaoin mhaiseach mhíonla ba bhreátha
Dár shíolraigh ó Ádam anuas.

2.　　Bíogann mo chroí ionnam le h-áthas,
Dá gnaoi thugas lán-ghean go luath;
Dá braoithe, dá rinn-rosc, dá gáire,
Agus dá dlaoi-leacain álainn gan ghruaim;
Dá dlaoi-foltaibh buí casta fáinneach,
Is dá cíoch-cruinne bláthmhara cruaidh;
Dá shíor-fhaid í an oíche níor cás liom,
Bheith a' síor-amharc áilleacht a snuadh.

English Summary The poet describes a visionary encounter with a phantom woman, whose beauty he extols. She is, presumably, an epitome of Ireland (as is the case usually in such songs). **Text** From CBÉ 737, 75. **Printed Sources** *Irisleabhar na Gaedhilge* (Deireadh Foghmhair 1904) 570–71, 657 [facsimile 658] (5 vv.); Freeman, *JFSS* 6 (1921) 181–83; Ó Muirithe, *Cois an Ghaorthaidh*, 10–11, 48–50; cf. O'Daly, *Poets and poetry of Munster*, 6. **Notes** A note by Seán Ó Cróinín in CBÉ 737, 75, reads 'Bhí cúpla bhéarsa eile den amhrán so aice ach táid siad dearmhadta aice. Do bhí sé ráidhte gur sagart a cheap é. De réir *Irisleabhar na Gaedhilge* isé Pádruig Ó hIarfhlaithe do cheap é' [*'She had a couple more verses of this song, but she has them forgotten. It was said that a priest composed it. According to I. na G., it was P. Ó hI. composed it'*]. Bess was distantly related to Pádraig Ó hIarlaithe, a well-known 18th-century Muskerry poet, through her father. For a very interesting discussion of the song, and its close relationship to another famous 18th-century composition, *Úirchill an Chreagáin*, by the Armagh poet Art Mac Cumhthaigh, see Diarmuid Ó Muirithe, *Cois an Ghaorthaidh*, 48–50. Our song is not to be confused with another, of the same title, by the most famous 18th-century poet of all, Eoghan Rua Ó Súilleabháin, for which see Pádraig Ua Duinnín, *Amhráin Eoghain Ruaidh Uí Shúilleabháin* (Baile Átha Cliath 1901), 32–34. A handwritten copy of the poem by Seán Ó Cróinín has the following additional verses:

''Sa bhríghdeach na mín-ghlac ar fhásann
an tú Aoibhill ón mbán-chraig adtuaidh?
An tú Clíodhna nú Maoile nú Áine,
gan aimhreas fuair bárr ar gach sluagh?
Nú an fhaoileann thug Naois leis thar sáile
an fhíon-chrothach chráidhte rug buadh,
Nú an cubhaidh leat-sa ínnsint i dtráth dhom
Cadé an tír as a dtángaís ar chuaird?'

'D'fhíor-Chlanna Míleadh le rádh mé,
'n-ar dísceadh mo cháirde chun cuain;
Is thíos cois Banna aoibhinn go ghnáthaim,
is le díograis go dtánga annso ar ruaig.
Dá mhaoidheamh go mbeidh bíocun na Blárnann
'n-a aoil-bhrogaibh áitribh go luath;
'S an Stíobhart do bhí seal go fánach
'n-a rígh ar thrí áitribh go buan.'

Tá nídh eile ar m'intinn le rádh leat,
más binn leat mé thrácht air ná luadh;
Go bhfuil Laoiseach go buidheanmhar 'san Spáinneach
'Sa bpríomh-loingeas lánmhar i gcuan.
'N-a mbeidh díth againn ar críoch Inis Fáilbhe
Ná stríocfadh dá namhaid ar cuaird;
'S gur i bhfiosgaireacht fhíor-dheire an Mhárta
Is eadh mhaoidhfeam go háirighthe an buadh.'

Ó Muirithe, *Cois an Ghaorthaidh*, 11, has another three verses (from early manuscripts).

39

Cois abha Móire

1. Cois abha Móire is mé a spealadóireacht lá breá dom' shaol
   'Sea do dhearcas smólach do chailín ghleoite, is bhí a brághaid mar aol.
   Bhí dath an óir-bhuí ar a folth go féar léi, is a dá súil séimh,
   Is a dá chích ghleoite ar a boirlín ómair nár sháraigh aon.

2. Nuair a chonnac-sa an óig-bhean a' teacht am' thómas dob árd mo léim;
   Mo chroí le dóchas do phreab ar neómat chun bheith páirteach léi.
   'Sé dúirt sí: 'A stróire, cad is dóigh leat — ní h-áil liom é —
   Is gur cailín óg mé atá gan nóchar ag gabháil liom féin'.

3. 'Más cailín óg tu atá gan nóchar ar t'ábhar féin,
   Dein mo chomhairle agus beidh tú pósta thar mhnáibh a tsaoil;
   Cuirfead cóir ort — each ar seól fút, is bheith go brách led thaobh;
   Beidh rinnce is ceól agus puins ar bórd agat go fáinne an lae'.

4. 'Ní h-obair dómh-sa bheith a' dul thar m'eolas le fánaí maol,
   Ná chun bheith pósta le neach dod' shórd-sa, ná ag aon-fhear sa tsaol.
   Cé gur cheapais óg chughat bheith a' mealladh óig-bhan is á bhfáscadh led' thaobh,
   Tá cuid don chlóbhar le gearradh fós agat, 's is náireach é'.

5. 'Tá mo speal-sa nódh agam is mo chrann go gleoite, is mo lámh dá réir;
   Is go deimhin, a óig-bhean ná fuilim pósta le h-aon bháb sa tsaol!
   Níl agam bólacht ná, fóiríor, gnó dhíobh, ach mo phá 'n-aghaidh a' lae,
   Is ní h-aon stróire ná a shórd mé thug grá dhuit féin'.

Text CBÉ 912, 535–36. **Notes** A note after the text reads 'Sé mo thuairim go raibh bhéarsa nú dhó eile don amhrán san ann, ach ní fhéatainn cuímhneamh ar a thuille de. Is fadó riamh airigheas é don chéad uair — agus is dóigh liom gur ag bacach éigin a bhí sé. Is cuímhin liom beirt nú triúr acu agus bhíodar chómh binn le haon londubh' ['*I think there were one or two more verses in that siong, but I cannot remember any more of it. It's a long time since I heard it first, and I think it was some travelling man that had it. I remember two or three of them and they were as sweet as any blackbird'.*]

40

Cois abhainn na Séad[1/16]

1. Cois abhainn na Séad ar uair a' lae
    Is mé a' dul faoi dhéin mo ghrá deas,
    Mar a mbíd caortha agus cnó buí ar ghéagaibh,
    Is mil 'na slaod ar bhántaibh,
    Do labhradar na héin, do lasadar na spéartha
    Is bhí an fhairrge go tréanmhar lán suas;
    Do mhúsgail a' ghrian do bhí le sealad mór gan chiach
    Agus d'éirigh an t-iasc 'na thánrith.

2. Ansúd ar dtúis dom i n-imeall ciúmhaise
    Coille cúmhra thárlaig
    An fhinne-bhean fhionn gur bhinne í ar a tiúin
    Ná an *fiddle*, fliút, 's ná an chláirseach.
    Ba bhreá deas í a súil is a mala chaol fhionn,
    Is a leaca bhí mar chúbhar na trá 'muigh;
    Ba ghile í ar a píb ná an eala ar a' linn,
    Is do líon mo chroí le grá dhi.

3. Mo chreach agus mo chás gan mise agus mo ghrá
    Bheith tamall gach lá 'n-ár n-aonar;
    Go ciúin agus go tláth roim an Aifrinn do rá,
    Agus gan neart ag ár námhaid teacht taobh linn!
    A chiúin-bhean bhán na leabhair gromán,
    D'fhúigis mh'intinn buartha;
    Is is mór go mb'fheárr lem' chroí thú fháil
    Ná an ríocht is é fháil mar dhualgas.

4. Mo chreach agus mo chiach agus mh'athtuirse go dian,
    Tríos na dúthaíbh siar go brónach,
    Imeasc na gcliar bhí le sealad mór fí chiach
    Mh'athtuirse 's mé a d'iarraidh nóchar.
    A óig-bhean ghrianaig, a chogaraig 's a chiallaig,
    Is cliste mar a rianfá an brón díom;
    Is go bhfuilim féin at' dhiaidh le tuilleadh agus dhá bhliain
    Is ná coinibh i bpian níos mó mé.

5. Máirt 'sea a bhíos a' trácht na slí
    'Sea dhearcas aníos mo ghrá chugham;
    Is go mb'fheárr liom-sa í theacht slán chugham i dtír
    Ná an ríocht is é fháil 'na dhualgas.
    A phlúr na saighead agus na mbláth chómh mín-chrobh
    Nár fúigeadh riamh claoite i n-aon chath;
    Tabhair dómh-sa scríobh-pion ó bhárr do mhín-chrobh,
    An bhfágfaidh mé an tír nú an baol dom?

English Summary The poet rhapsodises about his *aisling*-like lover, whose physical beauty he extols. He has been pursuing her for over two years and asks plaintively if he should persist in his efforts or abandon them and leave the country.   **Recording** CBÉ 418 (1947).   **Text** From the CBÉ recording; there is another in CBÉ 737, 83–85.   **Notes** The last verse is clearly defective, as Seán Ó Cróinín noticed. He gives better readings from Diarmuid Ó Duinnín, another Baile Mhúirne *seanchaí*. There is a recording of the song, as sung by Máire Ní Cheocháin (Máire Keohane), from Coolea (near Baile Mhúirne) in Alan Lomax, *Columbia World Library of Folk and Primitive Music* 1 (New York 1955) [SL–204].

41

Cuckanandy[1/3]

1. *Hups!, a Sheáin, a bhráthair, fuair do mháthair bás!*
    Ó, ní bhfuair, ní bhfuair: do chuaigh sí suas sa tsráid!
    Hups!, a Sheáin, a bhráthair, fuair do mháthair bás!
    Ó, ní bhfuair i n-aon chor, chuaigh sí suas sa tsráid!

    Coc-a neaindí neaindí, coc-a-neaindí ó
    Coc-a-neaindí neaindí, coc-a-neaindí ó
    Coc-a-neaindí neaindí, coc-a-neaindí ó
    Poirtín Sheáin a' tSíoda is iníon Philib a' Cheoil.

    He didn't dance, dance, and he didn't dance today
    He didn't dance, dance — no, nor yesterday.
    He didn't dance, dance, and he didn't dance today,
    He didn't dance, dance, he won't till after tea.

    Throw him over, over, throw him oversea!
    Throw him over, over, he'll be hear today!
    Throw him over, over, throw him oversea!
    Throw him over, over, he'll be here for tea!

    Throw him up, up, throw him up high!
    Throw him up, up, and he'll come down by-and-by!
    Throw him up, up, throw him up high!
    Throw him up, up, and he'll come down by-and-by!

    Teabha-dí eigh-dí, eigh-dí, teabha-dí eigh-dí eam
    Teabha-dí eigh-dí, eigh-dí, eigh-dí eigh-dí eam
    Teabha-dí eigh-dí, deigh-dí, eigh-dí, eigh-dí eam
    Tidití eigh-dí, eigh-dí, deigh-dí, eigh-dí eam.

Recordings CBÉ 387b and 392b (1947, 1951) — BBC 12614 (7 Aug. 1947) = Kennedy, *Folktracks* F–60–160, A2 (1981) — Lomax, *Columbia World Library* SL–204 (1951), A7 — JR-GP (24 Nov. 1952) — Diane Hamilton (1955). **Text** From the BBC 12614 recording. There is another in Seamus Ennis's CBÉ copybooks (Sept. 1946)). **Printed Sources** Ritchie, *From fair to fair*, 68–69 (from Bess Cronin). **Notes** Seamus Ennis has the following note to the song in his CBÉ copybook 'Mar do bhíodh ag na seanamhná fadó a' déanamh grinn dosna páistí óga ar a nglúnaibh nó 'na mbaclainn' *['As the old women used to have when they were making sport for youngsters, dandling them on their knees or in their laps'].* The last part (lilted) is not in Lomax. Jean Ritchie, in a talk given at the Galway Arts Festival, 20 July 1991, remarked that Bess had another (unrecorded) verse of this song:

> Piper sell your pipes and buy your wife a gown!
> Piper sell your pipes and buy your wife a gown!
> Piper sell your pipes and buy your wife a gown —
> I wouldn't sell my pipes for all the wives in town!

See her *From fair to fair*, 68–69 (which has three additional verses). According to a note by 'Seán Saor' [= Seán Ó Cróinín], *Irish Press*, 13 Feb. 1953, p. 2, entitled 'An Béiceachán agus an Chaillichín', the tune of *Poirtín Sheáin a' Phíce* [sic] *is Rinnce Philib a' Cheoil* used to be sung by a pooka or ghost known as Caillichín na Glaoití, that supposedly haunted the hills around Cúil Aodha.

Hups! a Sheáin, a bhrá - thair, fuair do mháth - air bás!

Ó, ní bhfuair i n-aon chor, chuaigh sí suas sa tsráid!

Hups! a Sheáin, a bhrá - thair, fuair do mháth - air bás!

Ó, ní bhfuair i n-aon chor, chuaigh sí suas sa tsráid!

Coc - a - neain - dí neain - dí, coc - a - neain - dí ó

Coc - a - neain - dí neain - dí, coc - a - neain - dí ó

Coc - a - neain - dí neain - dí, coc - a - neain - dí ó

Poirt - ín Sheáin a' tSíod - a is in - íon Phi - lib a' Cheoil

42

Cu-Cúc, a chuaichín[1/7]

1. Cu-Cúc, a chuaichín, cá ndéanfam a' samhradh?
    Cu-Cúc, a chuaichín, déanfam isna gleannta é.
    Cu-Cúc, a chuaichín, cá ndéanfam a' samhradh?
    Cu-Cúc, a chuaichín, déanfam isna gleannta é.

English Summary 'Cuckoo, where will we spend the summer? Cuckoo, we'll spend it in the glenns' (repeated). **Recording** CBÉ 393b (1947). **Text** From the CBÉ recording; another text in a DÓC notebook (1st v. only). A third text in another DÓC notebook has four verses. **Printed Sources** Ó Tuama, *An chóisir cheoil* 1, 6 (4 vv.); Mac Coluim, *An saoghal Gaelach* [Vocational Education Supplement] 8 ('Um Fhéile Michíl 1953') 4 (6 vv., collected from Mícheál Ó Luasaigh, Baile Mhúirne); De Noraidh, *Ceol ón Mumhain*, 44–45. **Notes** The song is a lullaby. The additional verses in DÓC's notes read as follows:

A.   Cu-cúc, a chuaichín, cé gheobhaidh 'nár dteannta ann?
     Cu-cúc, a chuaichín, beidh an dreoilín 's a chlann ann.
     Cu-cúc, a chuaichín, cé gheobhaidh 'nár dteannta?
     Cu-cúc, a chuaichín, beidh an dreoilín 's a chlann ann.

B.   Cu-cúc, a chuaichín, cad a bheidh ann dúinn?
     Cu-cúc, a chuaichín, beidh mil agus leamhnacht.
     Cu-cúc, a chuaichín, cad a bheidh ann dúinn?
     Cu-cúc, a chuaichín, beidh mil agus leamhnacht.

C.   Cu-cúc, a chuaichín, an baol dúinn an seabhac ann?
     Cu-cúc, a chuaichín, éalóimíd fé chrann ann.
     Cu-cúc, a chuaichín, an baol dúinn an seabhac ann?
     Cu-cúc, a chuaichín, éalóimíd fé chrann ann.

This is the text that appears in Ó Tuama's *Cóisir cheoil* 1, 6. The version noted down by Fionán Mac Coluim from Mícheál Ó Luasaigh, Baile Mhúirne, in 1952, is more complete:

a.   Cucúín, a Chuaichín, cá ndéantham an Samhra?
     Cucúín, arsan cuaichín, déantham sa ghleann so, déantham so ghleann so.
     Thar magh 'gus míncheanntair sé'n gleann so mo roghasa,
     Tá 'gainn sa choill ann foithin is díon,
     Tá macha 'gus meall ann, muileann is mallshruth.

b.   Cucúín, a chuaichín, cad a bheidh ann dúinn, cad a bheidh ann dúinn?
     Cucúín, arsan cuaichín, beidh mil agus leamhnacht, bia 'gus annlan.
     Beidh sóluistí a bpáirc 's ar chlaidhe 'gainn, is feithidí reamhra, ní heagal dúinn ganntar
     Beidh caora mísle, dóthain ár gcroidhe 'cu,
     Ar thor is ar chrann ann, nár dtómus más call dúinn.

c.   Cucúín, a chuaichín, cé bheidh nár dteannt 'un, cé bheidh nár dteannt 'un?
     Cucúín, arsan cuaichín, beidh a dreoilín 'sa chlann ann ár rí beag's a chomplacht,
     Beidh ba's caoire 'un, uain is laoigh leó, a rith 's a damhas ann is siorraig a pramsaigh,
     Beidh cearca fraoigh ann 's an smóilín 's an Piotairisg bramhsach, is mion-éin a cannt'reacht.

d.   Cucúín, a chuaichín, 's an baoghal dúinn an seabhac ann, an baoghal dúinn an seabhac ann?
     Cucúín, arsan cuaichín, éalóimíd fé chrann uaidh.
     Má thugann sé fogha fúinn, beidh na mná tighe i bhfeighilt na sicíní,
     agus a bagairt go trom air, ag cur eagal is scannr' air,
     Beidh buachaillí ar a thí, is gach éinne 'na namhaid ann, ag foghluí an chamghuibh.

Cu - Cúc,   a chu-ai-chín, cá ndéan-fam a' samh - radh?
Cu - Cúc,   chu-ai-chín,___ déan-fam is-na gleann ___ ta é.
Cu - Cúc,   a chu-ai-cín, ___ cá ndéan-fam a' samh - radh?
Cu - Cúc,   a chu-ai-chín, ___ déan-fam is-na gleann-ta   é.

e.   Cucúín, a chuaichín, is a bhfantham go Samhain 'un a bhfantham go Samhain 'un
      Cucúín, arsan cuachín mise teachtaire 'n tSamhraidh, ní thaithiníonn an tSamhain liom,
      Tar éis tamall grinn dom, ins an ngleann aoibhinn seo, éalódsa le fonn cheart, thar bóchna na domhan mear
      Anonn go tírín is geal le mo chroidhe-si na mbíonn grian teas is greann 'un idir gheimhre 'gus Samhra.

f.   Ach taréis bhúr ngeimhre, fuar fada cóimhthigh, is Earrach na rabhartha,
      i mín-bhéal na Bealtaine, beadsa arís anso, ar ghéigín
      Is mé a fógairt a tSamhraidh, ar gharraithe is geamhartha.

A note in de Noraidh, 44, states that vv. A, B, C, e (which he gives) were composed by Ó Luasaigh. For a similar 'little Drachteen', see O'Daly, *Irish language miscellany*, 111–12

43

Cuir a chodladh[2/2]

1.   Cuir a chodladh, cuir a chodladh, cuir a chodladh an seanduine;
      Cuir a chodladh, nigh a chosa agus bog deoch don tseanduine.
      Cuir a chodladh, cuir a chodladh, cuir a chodladh an seanduine;
      Cuir a chodladh, nigh a chosa agus bog deoch don tseanduine.

2.   Feoil úr, feoil úr, feoil úr don tseanduine;
      Feoil úr, braon súip 's é thabhairt don tseanduine.
      Cuir a chodladh, cuir a chodladh, cuir a chodladh an seanduine;
      Cuir a chodladh, nigh a chosa agus bog deoch don tseanduine.

3.   Ubh circe, ubh circe, ubh circe don tseanduine;
      Ubh circe, blúire ime 's é thabhairt don tseanduine.
      Cuir a chodladh, cuir a chodladh, cuir a chodladh an seanduine;
      Cuir a chodladh, nigh a chosa agus bog deoch don tseanduine.

English Summary The song is a lullaby, in which the child is soothed to sleep by having its feet washed and being given something to drink. The *seanduine* ('old man') is the baby, and the *deoch* ('drop') is a drink of milk. The list continues with fresh meat, soup, a hen's egg and a pinch of butter!   **Recordings** CBÉ 390b (1947) — BBC 12614 (7 Aug. 1947) — JR-GP (2 Nov. 1952).   **Text** From the JR-GP recording; there is another in a DÓC notebook (dated 18 May 1946). The BBC 1947 recording omits the last 'Ubh circe' and 'Cuir a chodladh', while it has a short English introduction, in which Bess says that the person trying to lull the child to sleep was a poet. The JR-GP tape also has a brief discussion and explanation of the verses.   **Printed Sources** Mac Coluim, *Duanaireacht do leanbhaíbh*, 33; Mac Coluim & Pléimionn, *Cosa buidhe árda* 1, 11; Ó Tuama, *An chóisir cheoil*, 6 *Bog braon don tseanduine*. The text in Ó Tuama's *Cóisir cheoil* is identical to Bess's, save for the first verse:

        Bog braon, bog braon, bog braon don tseanduine;
        Bog braon, 's blais féin, bog braon don tseanduine;
        Cuir a chodladh, etc.

The texts in *Duanaireacht do leanbhaíbh* and *Cosa buidhe árda* have only the first two verses; otherwise they are much the same.

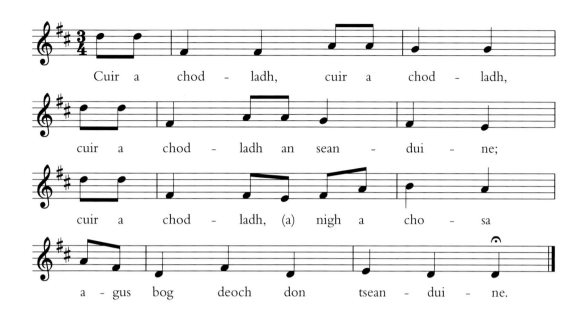

Cuir a chod - ladh, cuir a chod - ladh,

cuir a chod - ladh an sean - dui - ne;

cuir a chod - ladh, (a) nigh a cho - sa

a - gus bog deoch don tsean - dui - ne.

44

Dá bhfaghainn mo rogha dhe thriúr acu

1.   Dá bhfaghainn mo rogha dhe thriúr acu, 'thriúr acu, 'thriúr acu,
    Dá bhfaghainn mo ragha dhe thriúr acu, ceocu 'cu súd ab fhearr liom?
    Ó míle gile tu, grá mo chroí 'gus míle tu,
    Ó míle gile tu, ní a' magadh leat atáim-se.

2.   Ní phósfainn féin an táiliúirín, an táiliúirín, an táiliúirín,
    Ní phósfainn féin an táiliúirín, bíonn cailc de shíor ón gclár air.
    Ó míle gile tu, grá mo chroí 'gus míle tu,
    Ó míle gile tu, ní a' magadh leat atáim-se.

English Summary A woman asks jocosely which suitor she should marry, a tailor, [a blacksmith, or a fisherman], and gives reasons why each in turn would be unsuitable. **Recording** JR-GP (24 Nov. 1952). **Text** From the JR-GP recording. **Printed Sources** Mac Coluim, *Duanaireacht do leanbhaíbh*, 12; Mac Coluim & Pléimionn, *Cosa buidhe árda* 1, 30–31 (4 vv.) [ibid, 15–16 = *Is trua gan gáirdín úl agam*]. **Notes** The song repeats the formula with three suitors 1, the tailor; 2, the smith; 3, the shop-keeper; only the first verse is recorded. The air is the same as that used for *The Kerry Cow* [No. **167**] (= *Peata an Mhaoir*), and *Is Trua gan Gáirdín Úll Agam*. The texts in *Cosa buidhe árda*, 30–31, and *Duanaireacht do leanbhaíbh*, 12, have these extra verses:

A.   Ní phósfainn féin an t-iasgaire, an t-iasgaire, an t-iasgaire.
    Ní phósfainn féin an t-iasgaire, mar bíonn sé fliuch go bhásda.

B.   Ní phósfainn féin an gabha dubh, an gabha dubh, an gabha dubh.
    Ní phósfainn féin an gabha dubh, mar bíonn sé dubh sa cheárdchain.

In *Cosa buidhe árda* the verse about the tailor, instead of '*bíonn cailc de shíor ón gclár air*' reads '*Bíonn codla grífin ón gclár air*'; the verse about the fisherman has, instead of '*mar bíonn sé fliuch go bhásda*', the line '*mar raghadh sé dá bháthadh uaim*'. The version in *Duanaireacht do leanbhaíbh*, 12, has another alternative for the same line '*Phriocfadh sé me le n-a shnáthaid*'.

45

Dá mba liom-sa an ainnir[1/21]

1. 'S dá mba liom-sa an ainnir, ní thabharfainn d'aon réice í;
    b'fhearra liom faraire gasta, dea-shaothair
    Go mbeadh bólacht bhreá leathan maidean ar chaoltha,
    mar b'iad súd do chleachtas le hiníon a' déirí.
    'Ól ná caitheamh ní thaitneadh leo súd,
    ná cnósacht do scaipeadh ti' an leanna', 'sea dúrt.
    Insa Ghúagán go bhfeaca-sa go moch maidean Cuirlín ann,
    is is seolta a chasadh sé bata ar Chiarraíochaibh.

2. Ni bhfaighidh Eilic Óg í, a stóirín 's a bhuíonaigh —
    tá a mhalairt de ghnó aige is is córa dhó cloí leis.
    Tá a fhuip fhada i dtreo aige is a chóistí ar fuaimeat
    chun dul go tig a' Róistigh ar scór leis na buachaillí.
    Cuirfead-sa an ainnir, mar mheasaim, i gcrích;
    geoig Reddy, airiú, an ainnir 'tá cheana aige i dtíos.
    Tá an citeal 's a' *tea-pot* go gléasta sa chúinne
    agus cúimín deas aolta chun Mary do stiúrú.

[3. An beart nuair a hardaightí 'n-aird' ar a' mbuachaill,
    Go rithfeadh isna h-ardaibh 's ní cháisíodh a' t-ualach.]

Recording CBÉ 388b (1947). **Text** From the CBÉ recording. Cf. CBÉ 1591, 77–78 (Cork 1960). There is a separate copy also in Seamus Ennis's CBÉ copybooks (Sept. 1946). The Seamus Ennis transcript only has the last two lines; it appears to be from another song.

ná   cnó-sacht do scai-peadh ti' an   lean-na,' 'sea   dúrt.

In-sa   Ghú-gán   go bhfea-ca - sa   go moch mai-dean Cuir-lín   ann,

is is   seol-ta   a   cha-sadh sé   ba - ta ar Chiar - raío - chaibh.

46

Dá mbeadh mac an mhaoir agam

1. Dá mbeadh mac an mhaoir agam,
    Dá mbeadh mac an mhaoir agam,
    Dá mbeadh mac an mhaoir agam,
    'S na caoire beaga bána.

    Ó míle gile tu, grá mo chroí 'gus fiche tu,
    Ó míle gile tu, 's ní a' magadh leat atáim-se.
    Ó míle gile tu, isteach lem' chroí 'sea chuirim tu,
    Ó míle gile tu, 's tú peata geal do mháthar.

2. Is trua gan gáirdín úll agam,
    Is trua gan gáirdín úll agam,
    Is trua gan gáirdín úll agam,
    Is cúpla tor cabáiste.

    Ó míle gile tu, grá mo chroí 'gus fiche tu,
    Ó míle gile tu, 's ní a' magadh leat atáim-se.
    Ó míle gile tu, isteach lem' chroí 'sea chuirim tu,
    Ó míle gile tu, 's tú peata geal do mháthar.

3. Is trua gan bólacht bhainne agam,
    Is trua gan bólacht bhainne agam,
    Is trua gan bólacht bhainne agam,
    Is Cáitín óna máthair.

    Ó míle gile tu, grá mo chroí 'gus fiche tu,
    Ó míle gile tu, 's ní a' magadh leat atáim-se.
    Ó míle gile tu, isteach lem' chroí 'sea chuirim tu,
    Ó míle gile tu, 's tú peata geal do mháthar.

4.   Dá mbeadh *dandy cap* orm,
      Dá mbeadh *dandy cap* orm,
      Dá mbeadh *dandy cap* orm,
      'S é lán do chnaipí bána.

      Ó míle gile tu, grá mo chroí 'gus fiche tu,
      Ó míle gile tu, 's ní a' magadh leat atáim-se.
      Ó míle gile tu, isteach lem' chroí 'sea chuirim tu,
      Ó míle gile tu, 's tú peata geal mo mháthar.

Text From Seamus Ennis's CBÉ transcription (dated Sept. 1946). **Printed Sources** Petrie, *The Petrie collection of the ancient music of Ireland*, 42–43 (2 vv.); cf. Petrie & Stanford, *The complete collection of Irish music*, 375, No. 1501 (air only) [cf. 291, No. 1151]; Sigerson, *Bards of the Gael and Gall* , 347 [English only]; O'Daly, *Irish language miscellany*, 70; *Fáinne an Lae* (12 Márta 1898) 3; Mac Coluim, *Duanaireacht do leanbhaíbh*, 24–25; idem, *Cosa buidhe árda* 1, 15–16 (5 vv.); Breathnach, *Cnuasachd bheag amhrán* 1, 3 [3 vv. 'Is truagh gan peata 'n mhaoir agam']; idem, *Ceól ár sínsear*, 3 [same as previous text]; cf. Maguidhir, *Mo stóirín cheóil*, 4–5; Ua Braoin, *An cuaichín ceoil*, 23; Ní Ógáin, *Duanaire Gaedhilge*, 25. **Notes** Seamus Ennis, in his DIF transcript, gives the tune as D/ 44 B G G A | B Ch D D | E C D B | C$_h$ E D C$_h$ | etc. Another text in a DÓC notebook reads as follows

a.   Is trua gan peata an Mhaoir agam,
      Is trua gan peata an Mhaoir agam,
      Is trua gan peata an Mhaoir agam
      Is na caoire beaga bána.

      Is ó goirim, goirim thú,
      Is grá mo chroí gan cheilg thú,
      Is ó goirm, goirm thú,
      Is tú peata beag do mháthar.

b.   Is trua gan maoilín bán agam,
      Is trua gan maoilín bán agam,
      Is trua gan maoilín bán agam
      Is fáilthe ó mo ghrá geal.

      Is ó goirim, goirim thú, &c.

c.   Same as in our text.

Petrie, *Petrie collection*, 42–43, has verses a and 3 above; *Fáinne an Lae*, 1898, has verses 3, a and chorus. The text in *Duanaireacht do leanbhaíbh*, 24–25, has the verses in the order 2, 1, 3, b, 4. The text in *Cosa buidhe árda* 1, 15–16, has the verses in the order 1, 3, b, 4. Breathnach's text in *Cnuasachd bheag amhrán*, 3, and *Ceól ár sínsear*, 3, is the same as a, b, c above, as is that in Maguidhir, *Mo stóirín cheóil*, 4–5. Sigerson's English text is eclectic.

47

Dance for your Daddy-O!$^{2/11}$

1.   Dance to your Daddy-O!
      Dance to your Daddy-O!
      Dance for your Daddy-O,
      My pretty little child!

2.   Dance to your Daddy-O!
      Dance to your Daddy-O!
      Dance for your Daddy-O,
      My pretty little child!

3. I'll buy my child a saucepan,
    I'll buy my child a spoon-O!
    I'll buy my child a riding-horse
    And he will go to school!

4. Dance to your Daddy-O!
    Dance to your Daddy-O!
    Dance for your Daddy-O,
    My pretty little child!

Recordings Lomax, *Columbia World Library* SL–204 (1955) A6 — Kennedy, *Folktracks* F–60–160 (1981) A1. **Text** From the Lomax recording; another in a DÓC notebook. **Printed Sources** Ford, *Children's rhymes, children's games, children's songs, children's stories*, 129–30; Opie & Opie, *The Oxford dictionary of nursery rhymes*, 140–41; Meek, *Moon Penny*, 11. See Karpeles, *Cecil Sharp's collection of English folk songs* (2 vols), 2, No. 400 (2 vv.) [cf. Karpeles, *The crystal spring*, 135, No. 127]. **Notes** This is a dandling song. There is a very similar version in a DÓC notebook:

1. Dance and I'll play for you,
    Dance and I'll play for you,
    Dance and I'll play for you,
    Báillín of shnow!

2. Dance and I'll play for you,
    Dance and I'll play for you,
    Dance and I'll play for you,
    Báillín of shnow!

3. Oh! Won't you carry me,
    Oh! Won't you carry me,
    Oh! Won't you carry me,
    And carry me home!

4. Oh! Won't you marry me,
    Oh! Won't you marry me,
    Oh! Won't you marry me,
    And carry me home!

The Opies give the words of a five-verse ditty, *The Little Fishy*, attributed to one William Watson (*Fordyce's Newcastle Song Book* 1842), which is very like our song; cp. Karpeles, *Cecil Sharp's collection of English folk songs*, 2, No. 400 *Dance to Thee Daddy*:

Dance to thee daddy, my little laddy,
Dance to thee daddy, my little man.
Thou shalt have a fish, thou shalt have a fin,
Thou shalt have a haddock when the boat comes in.
Thou shalt have a codlin boiled in a pan,
Dance to thee daddy, my little man.

Dance to thee daddy, my bonny laddy,
Dance to thee daddy, my little lamb.
When thou art a woman fitter to be married
Thou shalt have a penny for to buy a man,
Thou shalt have a penny, thou shalt have a penny,
Dance to thee daddy, my little lamb.

The text in Karpeles, *A crystal spring* 135, No. 127 (collected in 1909), is more-or-less identical with the above, but has slightly different wording in v. 2:

Dance to thee daddy, my bonnie laddy,
Dance to thee daddy, my little lamb,
When thou art a man and fit to take a wife
Thou shalt wed a maid and love her all your life,
She shall be your lassie, thou shalt be her man,
Dance to thee daddy, my little lamb.

Compare Robert Ford, *Children's rhymes*, 129–30:

Dance to your daddie,
My bonnie laddie,
Dance to your daddie, my bonnie lamb;
And ye'll get a fishie,
In a little dishie,
Ye'll get a fishie when the boat comes hame!

Dance to your daddie,
My bonnie laddie,
Dance to your daddie, my bonnie lamb!
And ye'll get a coatie,
And a pair o' breekies —
Ye'll get a whippie and a supple Tam!

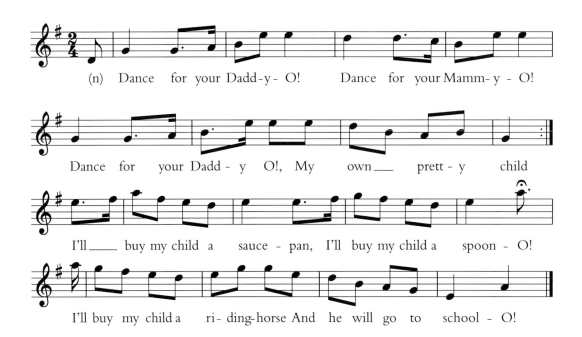

(n) Dance for your Dadd-y- O! Dance for your Mamm-y - O!

Dance for your Dadd - y O!, My own____ prett - y child

I'll____ buy my child a sauce - pan, I'll buy my child a spoon - O!

I'll buy my child a ri- ding-horse And he will go to school - O!

48

Derby ram[2/17]

1. As I went down to Derby, it being a market day,
    It's there I saw the finest ram that ever was fed upon hay
    O-me-rambo-rambo-riggedy, o-me-rambo-ray
    O-me-rambo-riggedy, sold on a market-day

2. The market grew up to the sky,
    And the eagle builds its rest and learneth him to fly
    O-me-rambo-rambo-riggedy, o-me-rambo-ray
    O-me-rambo-rambo-riggedy, sold on a market day

3.   The wool that grew on his belly, it grew down to the ground
     I sold a pound in Dublin for thirty-thousand pound
     O-me-rambo-rambo-riggedy, o-me-rambo-ray
     O-me-rambo-rambo-riggedy, sold on a market day

4.   The horns of this ram, they were thirty tons of coal,
     And twenty tons of oil were knocked out of his marrow bones
     O-me-rambo-rambo-riggedy, o-me-rambo-ray
     O-me-rambo-rambo-riggedy, sold on a market day

5.   The b- on this ram, they would reach across to Spain,
     And I heard the sailors say that they would run them back again
     O-me-rambo-rambo-riggedy, o-me-rambo-ray
     O-me-rambo-rambo-riggedy, sold on a market day

6.   All the boys in Derby were fighting for his eyes,
     To have them there as footballs, for they were much the size
     O-me-rambo-rambo-riggedy, rambo-rambo-ray
     O-me-rambo-rambo-riggedy, sold on a market day

7.   The man that blooded was up to his knees in blood,
     And the girl that held the basin, she was swept away with the flood
     O-me-rambo-rambo-riggedy, o-me-rambo-ray
     O-me-rambo-rambo-riggedy, sold on a market day

8.   Any of you that don't believe me — you think it is a sham —
     You may go down to Derby and see this wonderful ram
     O-me-rambo-rambo-riggedy, o-me-rambo-ray
     O-me-rambo-rambo-riggedy, sold on a market day.

Recording JR-GP (24 Nov. 1952).   **Text** From JR-GP recording.   **Printed Sources** Broadwood & Fuller Maitland, *English county songs*, 44–47 (3 versions); Greig, *Folk-song in Buchan and folk-song of the North-East*, No. xiv; Karpeles, *Cecil Sharp's collection of English folk songs*, vol. 2, 375–78, No. 325 (3 versions) [cf. Karpeles, *The crystal spring*, 128, No. 120]; Opie & Opie, *The Oxford dictionary of nursery rhymes*, 145–46, No. 129; Kennedy, *Folksongs of Britain and Ireland*, 660–61, and 679, No. 304 *The Ram Song*. **Notes** As the Opies remark (146), 'This extravagant chronicle, which has been current for certainly two centuries, is capable of infinite expansion, each new verse being an attempt to outdo the last'. The song was known in North America as well as in Britain and Ireland. The ram is incorporated in the Derby borough coat-of arms.

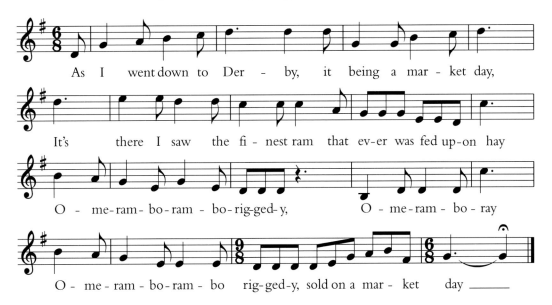

49

Did you see my man?[2/25]

1. Did you see my man? He was a fine man.
    Did you see my man looking for me?
    Did you see my man? He was a fine man.
    Did you see my man looking for me?

2. He wore a blue jacket, a pair of white stockings,
    A hump on his back and he blind in one eye.
    Did you see my man? He was a fine man.
    Did you see my man looking for me?

3. Did you see my man? He was a fine man.
    Did you see my man looking for me?
    He wore a blue jacket, a pair of white stockings.
    A hump on his back and he blind in one eye.

Recording JR–GP (2 Nov. 1952).   **Text** From the JR–GP recording.   **Note** Obviously a comical song for children, I have no printed text.

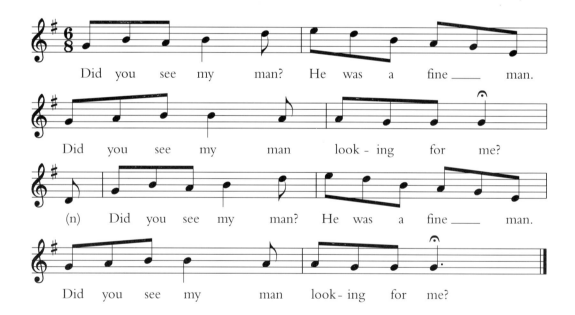

50

Did your wife go away?

1.   I'm as troubled a young man as any can be,
Since I married a damsel, her age it was scarce twenty-three;
I'm sorry to marry such a false-minded one,
She left me alone and went off with another young man.

2.   Three months we were wed when this damsel I took her to town;
Expenses I paid on the way, I gave her a crown;
On going through a street a friend took me in for a drain,
And while we were in, the pair made off in the train!

3.   So when I came out, I ran mad through the square,
Crying out 'Ochón!', and ready to tear off my hair;
A neighbour named Ned put out his head at a door,
Saying 'Did your wife go away; will she e'er come back any more?'

4.   I went to the priest, these words to him I did say
'You married me to a damsel who lately has led me astray;
I gave you five pounds on grounds you'd lead me through life;
If you'll loosen the knot, I'll ne'er again wed a wife'.

5.   He told me go home until more about that he would see,
But wherever I go, I'll ne'er be content where I'll be.
For when I go to town the neighbours come out to the door,
Saying: 'Did your wife go away; will she e'er come back any more?'

6.   I've an acre of land, a dandy fine pig, and a cow;
A duck and a drake, and no one to take care of them now;
I'll sell them all out, for now I am tired of my life,
And says each man to Dan: 'Go along and look for your wife!'

Text CBÉ 476, 55–57 (dated 1938); another in CBÉ 283, 446–47 (dated 1932). The two are almost identical.

51

Do bhíos-sa lá a' fiodóireacht

Note Title only from one of Bess's handwritten lists.

52

Do gheallais dómh-sa

1. Do gheallais dómh-sa, agus do gheallais bréag dom,
   Go mbeifeá rómham ag cró na gcaorach;
   Do leogas fead agus dhá chéad glaoch ort,
   Is ní bhfuaireas rómham ach na huain a' méilig.

2. Is dóigh lem' mhuíntir gur maighdean acu me,
   Nuair a bhím-se féinig am' chladhaire banarthlan;
   Bíonn mo laogh agam i bpluais na carraige
   Agus istoíche thriallaim leis a ngealaigh air.

3. Do gheallais dómh-sa, ach bhís a' magadh fúm,
   Go bhfaghainn lúng óir uait agus crann seóil airgid;
   Dhá bhaile déag agus baile margaidh,
   Agus baile cuain ar bruach na farraige.

4. A ógánaigh óig, bhís anuiridh am' mhealladh-sa,
   Agus tán tú i mbliana a d'iarraidh m'atharrach;
   Cuirim-se Dia go dian 'na sheasamh leat,
   A' leagadh do chlú agus a' dúchtaint t'aigne.

5. A ógánaigh óig, más a d'iarraidh mná thu
   Go seólaidh Dia i gcuan í fháil tu;
   Úrlár lom fé mhórán gárlach —
   A n-athair dall agus iad gan mháthair!

English Summary A young woman laments the promises of her lover which she believed. He has abandoned her, with child. **Text** From CBÉ 912, 659–60, headed 'Sean-amhrán' ['An old song']. **Printed Sources** Ó Donnchadha & Mac Piarais, *An tAithriseoir* 1, 7–8 *(Cumha chroidhe chailín)*; Ó Donnchadha, *Irish Review* (Aug. 1911) 296–97; Ó Duibhginn, *Dónall Óg. Taighde ar an amhrán*, esp. 69–81. **Notes** This is the song better known as *Dónal Óg*. See Seosamh Ó Duibhginn, *Dónall Óg. Taighde ar an amhrán* (Baile Átha Cliath 1960), esp. 69–81, for a very comprehensive treatment of all the recensions of the text. Tadhg Ó Donnchadha & Pádraig Mac Piarais (eds), *An tAithriseoir* 1 (Baile Átha Cliath 1900) 7–8 *(Cumha chroidhe chailín)* is the same as Ó Duibhginn, 74–76. CBÉ 47, 43–44 is a version in 8 verses collected by Proinsias Ó Ceallaigh of Baile Mhúirne from Nóra Ní Chonaill, Bean Uí Uidhir ('Norry Hoare'). It has the same initial verse as our song; vv. 4 and 7 are our vv. 4 and 2 (with minor variations in the wording). Among the songs collected by Freeman in Baile Mhúirne is one entitled *Dá mbeinn-se féin i gcé Phort Láirge* (noted down from the singing of Conny Coughlan), which has our vv. 2, 3, 4 (in that order) embedded in it. See Freeman, JFS 25 (Sept. 1921) 270–71. Freeman recognised the verses as misplaced.

53

Do thugas grá cléibh duit[2/24]

1. 'Do thugas grá cléibh duit, a spéirbhean, ar dtúis,
   Do leogas mo shúil ar do bhán-chnis;
   'S gur bh'fhearr liom ná mórchuid den' ór athá am' thrúnc,
   Go mbeifeá sa chúinne 'gem mháithrín.
   Do leaba romhat cóirithe ó ló 'gat sa rúm,

'S do mhachaí breá bó do bheidh romhat ann le crú;
Chuirfinn búclaí id' bhrógaibh, luach coróineach is púint —
'S a stóirín, ná tabharfá do lámh dom?'

2.   'Ní thabharfainn mo lámh duit go brách le h-aon fhonn,
Go gcuirfead scéala ar dtúis chun mo mháithrín;
Mar go bhfuair sí do thuairisc go suarach 'na cluas
Ná go n-ólfá do chrúsc i dtigh'n tabhairne.
Níorbh aon ní leat a ól luach coróin nó trí púint,
A' caitheamh do stór ar mhná óga is ar lionn;
'S dá dtriallfadh leat fear ceoil ní bheadh feoirling id' thrúnc,
'S a stróire, cé thabharfadh bean bhreá duit?'

3.   'Ná creid-se na bréithre ná na bréaga so ar siúl,
Mar is annamh mo dhul go tigh'n tabhairne;
Tá airgead am' póca agus mórchuid im' thrúnc,
A's níor ólas riamh púnt ar aon láthair.
Beidh a mhalairt 'e ghnó agam sa bhfómhar atá chughainn
Baint garraithe prátaí 's cur stácaí ar a móin;
Mo mhachaí atá lán de bhóaibh bána 'gus dubha,
'S gan éinne á gcrú ach mo mháithrín.'

4.   'S cár ghaibh na stácaí bhí timpeall do thí,
'S cá bhfuil na caoire le n-áireamh?
Nó cá bhfuil an eórna bhí in Eochaill dá díol,
'S cár chuiris na ba cíordhubha is bána?
Má bhíos-sa chómh baoth a's gur ghéilleas dod' shlí,
Imeoidh an méid sin sa spéir leis a' ngaoith;
Ní phósfainn lem' shaol tu dá dtéinn ar a bh*fleet*,
A's mairfead-sa choíche ar mo shnáthaid!'

English Summary A young man asks a woman's hand in marriage, but she has heard her mother disparaging him. He denies the mother's charges of excessive drinking and music-making in pubs, and promises to change his ways and settle down, but she is not persuaded. **Recording** Diane Hamilton (1955). **Text** From the Diane Hamilton recording. **Printed Sources** Mac Coluim, *Fuinn na smól*, 6 and 32; Freeman, 'Irish folk songs', *JFSS* 6/5, No. 25 (Sept. 1921) 295–99, No. 70 (8 vv.). **Notes** The title is in one of Bess's handwritten lists of songs (*The hugus gra cleiv duth*). This is one of the songs noted down by A. Martin Freeman from Conny Coughlan of Derrynasagart, and from Elly Lynch, of Cúm na Cloiche (another townland in the parish of Baile Mhúirne). He has our first three verses followed by four more, then our v. 4 as final verse; the additional verses are as follows (I have normalised the spelling):

A.   'Tá fear siopa in Eochaill do gheobhainn-se go h-umhal,
'S is dócha gurb é siúd ab fhearr liom;
Tá díol as mo mháistir an rátha athá chughainn,
'S gan dabhat is ansúd bhead am' scoláire.
Do thógas ar láimh í go lána bheag chumhang,
Ba ghairid 'na dhiaidh sin go raibh daor-phuins á tabhairt,
Do b'fhearr í chun glaoite ná éinne sa riúm,
Is do ghol sí go h-umhal as a dtáinig.

B.   Ar maidin amáireach nuair a éirigh a drúcht,
Do liúigh sí 's do bhéic ar a máithrín;
Do fhliuch sí a cuid éadaig le braonacha súl,
Is do léig sí go dtabharfainn an fáin di.
Dúrt-sa léi éisteacht is déanamh go ciúin,
Go raghainn-se a' díol eórnan go hEochall na long,
Chuirfinn scataí breá caorach ar an aonach so chughainn,
Is go bpósfainn am' riúm í gan spleáchas.

C.   Do ghearras a' bóthar 's a' comhgar anonn,
        'S ní fheaca ar aon chúinne den tsráid é;
        Do ghluaiseas go suarach fé thuairim a' tí,
        'S bhí íonadh ar na daoine cá dtánag;
        Dá fhaid a bhí an bóthar ní dúirt sé liom suí,
        Ná 'Bain díot do chlóca go n-ólfair braon dí';
        Sé dúirt na comharsain nár bhfónta é mo shlí,
        'S ná raibh aon-bhall go luífinn go lá aige.

D.   Bhí seanduine stuacach ar fhuarma 'na shuí,
        'S gan aon-phioc 'na phíopa ach é cnáireac;
        Seana-bhean thúirseach sa chúinne 'na luí,
        Mar a mheasaim, gurbh í siúd a mháthair;
        Dá mhéid é a chuid cruatain ní bhfuair sí braon dí —
        Bhí caitín a's úil aige a' cuardach a' tí,
        Bairilín beag suarach anuas uirthi ón síon,
        'S gan aon-phioc den díon air ón mbáistig.

Freeman has a lacuna in v. 2e–h, which can be supplied from our text. I have also compared NUI, Galway, Hardiman Library, Hyde MS. 14, 30–32, which has 8 verses in the order 1, 2, 3, A, B, C, D, 4.

54

Down by the groves of Tullig^{1/30}

1.   Down by the groves of Tullig, near Millstreet's pretty borders,
    As I roved out one morning, as Phoebus arose,
    To view the pretty scenery, so pleasing and so charming,
    Enlivened by those warblers that tune on each grove,
    When a maiden fair accosted me, whose beauty bright attracted me,
    With Cupid's lights distracted me, I really do own.
    Her carriage was most graceful and gaily she accosted me,
    Full banishing all reason in a neat and winning tone.

2.   I paused in deep astonishment, absorbed in meditation,
    Enraptured with this fair one in a most angelic tone.
    Her dress quite loose and freely o'er the green grass it was trailing,
    And her hair in ringlets waving most gracefully was thown.
    There was beauty in her symmetry, in her features fair civility.
    Her teeth were like the ivory and her countenance far more.
    A maiden fair more graceful in stateliness and dignity
    In the course of all my ranges I never saw before.

3.   I thought in her no mortal, I was so infatuated.
    I asked her was she Venus, that queen of great note,
    Or whether she was Ceres of the ditties of exuberance,
    Or that sparkling queen of beauty which wounded me full sore.
    Or if she was Diana-kin that ruined that huntsman bold-a-kin,
    Or Phoebus bright, that sparkling queen of celebrated lore.
    She says with great perplexity 'Young man, you are mistaken,
    No connection with those deities I really do own'.

4.   She said 'I am a ruined damsel that is sorrowfully ailing,
    Which causes me so early to wander all alone.
    My friends they are neglecting me and sweethearts are forgetting me,
    And poets of late are rejecting me, I really do own.
    But coming on next season I will sail to California,
    And I'll bid adieu to Erin, my acquaintances and home'.

5.   'For such a scheme, projectible, my pretty gentle maiden,
    Dame Fortune my soon smile on you, for all that you know.
    The morning might be frowning and the clouds being dull and rainy,
    But at noon gentle Phoenix might brilliantly glow.
    There's many a handsome swain that would have you to obtain,
    As you stand in fortune fame with a plain suit of clothes.
    Whilst others, if they had the property of Damer,
    The truth I will explain, no scheming I propose'.

6.   She says I am a novice of those naturalist engagements,
    Exerting since creation in the youth of my course.
    I will avoid all flattery, or any misdemeanour,

For love is operating and I'm longing for some sport.
She smiled and cast one glance at me,
Next moment she was gone from me.
She uttered out ''Tis vanity,
We're not leading one course'.
Pity such a gentle heiress,
That she was not more fond of me,
So now I am forsaken and I mean to say no more.

Recording BBC 11991 (7 Aug. 1947).   **Text** From the BBC recording; another in Bess's own hand-written collection of songs. A third copy (also in Bess's hand) in a DÓC notebook (text identical). Another text in CBÉ 476, 119–20 (omits vv. 5 and 6).   **Notes** The title is in one of Bess's song-lists (Down by the groves of Tullig). 3c Ceres: most manuscripts have 'serious' and the like, but CBÉ 476, 120 has Caerus; 5d Phoenix: Phoebus text 2; cf. 1st line of Sweet Killydysart [No. **141**]; 5g Damer: A 17th-century millionaire-miser much talked about in Irish tradition.

1st Verse.

Down by the groves of Tullig
Near Millstreets pretty borders.
As I roved out one Morning
As Phœbus arose
To view the pretty Scenery
So pleasing & so charming
Enlivened by those warblers
that tune on each grove
When a Maiden fair accosted me
Whose beauty bright attracted me
With Cupids lights distracted me
I really do own
Her carriage was most Graceful
And gaily she accosted me.
Full banishing all reasons
  in a neat & Winning tones
            2

I paused in deep astonishment
absorbed in Meditation.
Enraptured with this fair None.
in a most angelic tone.
Her dress quiet loose & freely
  oer the green grass it was trailing.

'Down by the groves of Tullig' in Bess's own hand (private collection, DÓC).

55

Down the green fields[2/3]

1. Down the green fields we'll jig it, we'll jig it,
    and down the green fields we'll jig it along.
    Down the green fields we'll jig it, we'll jig it,
    and down the green fields we'll jig it along.

2. When you'll go mowing you'll get her, you'll get her,
    and when you'll go mowing you'll get a young lass.
    When you'll go mowing you'll get her, you'll get her,
    and when you'll go mowing you'll get a young lass.

3. Under the stairs you'll get her, you'll get her,
    and under the stairs you'll get a young lass.
    Under the stairs you'll get her, you'll get her,
    and under the stairs you'll get a young lass.

Recordings CBÉ 388c (1947) — JR-GP (2 Nov. 1952). **Text** From the JR-GP recording. **Printed Sources** See Ritchie, *From fair to fair: folk songs of the British Isles*, 55–56. **Notes** There is another text in a DÓC notebook, which has the order 1, 3, 2. A (partial) third text is preserved in Bess's handwritten collection of songs (1st two lines of v. 1 only). Jean Ritchie's text is from Bess's singing, but she has the following two additional verses (the first a variant of our v. 3):

> Out in the kitchen you'll find her, you'll find her,
> Out in the kitchen you'll find a young lass;
> Out in the kitchen you'll find her, you'll find her,
> And out in the kitchen you'll find a young lass.
>
> Come from the cooking we'll step it, we'll step it,
> Come from the cooking we'll step it along.
> Come from the cooking we'll step it, we'll step it,
> And come from the cooking we'll step it along.

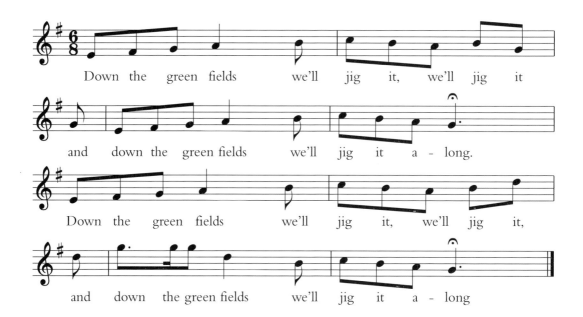

56

Erin's green shore

1.   One evening of late as I rambled
     By the banks of a clear purling stream,
     I sat down on a bank of primroses
     And I gently commenced for to dream.
     I dreamt I beheld a fair female,
     Her equals I ne'er saw before;
     As she sighed for the wrongs of her country,
     As she strayed along Erin's green shore.

2.   I quickly approached this fair female,
     Saying, 'My jewel, come tell me your name.
     In this country I know you're a stranger,
     Or I wouldn't have asked you the same'.
     She resembled the goddess of Liberty,
     And green was the mantle she wore;
     Bound round with the shamrock and roses
     That grow along Erin's green shore.

3.   'I can know you're a true son of Gráinne;
     My secrets to you I'll unfold.
     I'm here in the midst of all danger,
     Where I know not my friends from my foes.
     I'm a daughter to Daniel O'Connell,
     I came to awaken my brothers
     That slumber in Erin's green shore'.

4.   Her eyes were like two sparkling diamonds,
     Or the stars on a cold frosty night.
     Her cheeks were like two blooming roses,
     And her teeth of that ivory so white.
     She resembled the goddess of Freedom,
     And green was the mantle she wore;
     Bound round with the shamrock and roses
     That grow along Erin's green shore.

5.   Transported with joy, I awakened,
     For I knew I had been in a dream.
     Since this beautiful damsel has left me,
     I long to be slumbered again.
     May the heavens above be her guardian!
     For I know I shall ne'er see her more.
     May the sunbeams of glory shine o'er her!
     As she strayed along Erin's green shore.

Laws Q 27   **Text** From Bess's handwritten songs; there is another text in CBÉ 283, 168–69. The two are basically identical.
Printed Sources *Delaney's Irish song book*, No. 1, 7 (5 vv.); Ó Lochlainn, *More Irish street ballads*, 262–63 (5 vv.); Zimmermann,
Songs of Irish rebellion, 178–80, No. 27 (6 vv.); Wright, *Irish emigrant ballads and songs*, 355–56; Milner, *The bonnie bunch of roses*, 129–30

(5 vv., adapted from a broadside printed by A. Jackson of Moore St, Birmingham); Laws, *British broadside ballads*, 286. **Notes** Zimmermann, *Songs of Irish rebellion*, 178–80, has a text from a Haly broadside in Cambridge University Library which is similar to ours. Wright, *Irish emigrant ballads and songs*, 356–57, has two versions, very similar to Bess's, recorded from a Mrs Jane Hentaberry, aged 77, of Devil's Island, and from a Mrs John Fogarty, of Joe Batt's Arm (recorded July 1952). According to Tom Munnelly, *The Mount Callan Garland: songs from the repertoire of Tom Lenihan of Knockbrack, Milltown Malbay, County Clare* (Dublin 1994) 83, this song 'has had a huge popularity throughout the English-speaking world … because of its inherent poetic appeal and not merely because of the patriotic sentiments in the song'. He reports that Tom Lenihan (and most Irish singers) sang the song to a variant of the air to *Cailín deas crúite na mbó* (ibid., 82).

57

Faiche bhreá aerach an cheoil[2/27]

1. Mo shlán thar lear chun mná 'gus fear is gach áitreabh le chéile,
          ó fhágann sé an Gaorthaidh go Bríd;
    Is mo shlán chun na háite úd ná feicim féin i n-aonchor,
          mo shlán chun an méid úd sa chíll!
    Mo shlán chun na habhann gan cham, gan chuise!
    Is mo shlán chun na Banndan — is mó leabhair-bhreac inti!
    Mo shlán chun an teampaill úd Ard na Cuilce!
    Mo shlán chun gach stáid-bhruinneal óg!

2. A impire na páirte, tabhair slán mise ón méid seo,
          ó tharlag i gcéin seal sa bhall!
    Bíonn rás ann gach lá 'rm a's mná liom go taodmhar,
          gan fáilthe, gan féile, gan greann.
    Ní stadfaidh mé den stáir sin go Clár geal na Mumhan,
    Mar a labhraidís na mná liom is a' gáire liom le fonn.
    Cead síneadh síos lem' chairde gaoil go brách insan úir
          atá ar faiche bhreá aerach an cheoil.

3. A's is breátha an áit ná Phoebus nuair a théann sí chun síoraigh,
          bíonn lonnradh na soilse 'na chló.
    Mar shaothar na naomh gheal do deineadh insan oíche,
          gan stáitse, gan bíoma, gan bórd.
    Gach n-aon dá dtigid chun a gcurtha bíonn a bpeacaí scurtha in am,
    Agus daíll go bhficid fruig do phiocadh tar éis a dturais ann.
    Lucht maidí croise brúite briste is ró-bhreá a rithid stang
          ar faiche bhreá aerach an cheoil.

4. Bíonn a' pluma dubh 's a' t-áirne go h-ard ar na craobhachaibh
          agus úlla ar bharr géaga na gcrann.
    An chuaichín ba shuairc bhinn a' labhairt insa Ghaorthaidh,
          is fuaim 'ci go h-aerach sa bhall.
    Bíonn fiolar ann 's an chuach ar barr gach bile;
    An druide agus an seabhac ar a' gcrann thall 'na gcoinnibh;
    An smóilín bhinn a' labhairt ann gach am lena binneas,
          ar faiche bhreá aerach an cheoil.

5. Bíonn na gadhair ann chun fiadhaigh agus an fiadh rómpa ar saothar,
    agus marcaigh 'na ndiaidh siúd ar seol
Trí chnocaibh, trí choillthibh, trí ghleanntaibh gan staonadh,
    chun gur síneadh é ar taobh Leacain Mhóir.
Bíonn ceol agus rinnce ann, bíonn aoibhneas is spórt,
Agus imríd poc báire go sásta ar a' gcóir.
Is mó bruinneall mhodhail mhúinte agus ógánach óg
    atá ar faiche bhreá aerach an cheoil.

English Summary The poet rhapsodises about the beauties of his native place (Kinneigh, near Bandon, Co. Cork), where in the local church the infirm are healed and the lame are miraculously cured. He recounts a long list of its scenic merits. **Recordings** CBÉ 391 and 417 (1947) — BBC 18758 (29 Aug. 1952) — Seamus Ennis (May 1947) — Diane Hamilton (1955). **Text** From the Diane Hamilton recording. The CBÉ version cuts off at v. 4, line 5. The BBC '52 version is livelier & better, but differs in v. 2. There is another text noted down by Seamus Ennis in a CBÉ copybook (Sept. 1946); it has 5 vv. (1, 3, 2, 4, 5). **Printed Sources** Mac Coluim, *Fuinn na smól* 5, 16 (5 vv.); Ó Buachalla, 'Sean-amhrán ó'n Mumhain', 21–22 (5 vv.); Freeman, 'Irish folk songs', *JFSS* 6/5, No. 24 (Sept. 1921) 324–27, No. 81 (3 vv.); Breathnach, *Ceól ár sínsear*, 144–46 (5 vv.); Laoide, *An cúigeadh leabhar*, 43–44 (5 vv.) [an identical collection of texts, also edited by Seosamh Laoide, appeared with the title *Réalta de'n spéir* (Baile Átha Cliath 1915), with the same pagination.] This is a reprint of the text in Ó Buachalla's *Irisleabhar na Gaedhilge* article. **Notes** Bess Cronin thought that Seán Máistir Ó Conaill wrote this song (along with *An Chúil Daigh-Ré* [No. **16**]), but this is denied by Pádraig Ó Crualaoi in *Seanachas Phádraig Í Chrualaoi* 69. Mícheál Ó Buachalla, in *Irisleabhar na Gaedhilge* 12, 21–22, did not know who composed the song (which he published from memory); but he remarks that in local tradition it was said to have been made for a little sacred tower in the churchyard of Kinneigh, about nine miles from Bandon. Angels built the tower by night, but a certain woman saw the work in progress, whereupon it was stopped. Freeman's version was collected from Conny Coughlan of Derrynasagart. Freeman's text has our vv. 1, 3, 2, but with some differences in the words; verse 2, e.g., begins as follows:

A.   'S a Rí ghil na nGrás ngeal, tabhair slán sinn ón méid seo,
      Ó rángamair i téacht seal sa bhall —
      Rás ar geach ard-chnoic is mná linn go téadach
      Gan fáilthe, gan féile, ná greann, etc.

The text in *Irisleabhar na Gaedhilge* has the following version of our verse 2 at the beginning:

B.   Mac Mhuire geal na ngrás d'ár dtabhairt slán ins an méid sin,
      Ó thárlamair i gcéin seal 'sa bhall,
      Mar a mbíonn rás as gach áit orainn 's na mná linn go taodmhar
      Gan faesamh, gan daonnacht, gan ghreann;
      Rachamaoid do'n stáir sin go Clár geal na Mumhan
      Mar a labharthaidh na mná linn, is gáirfid le fonn
      'S cead comhráidh lem' cháirde gaoil nuair thráchtam 'san úr-ghlais
      Ar faithche bhreágh aorach a' cheoil.

It has the following additional verse after our v. 4:

C.   Bíonn an rás ann 's an fiadhach ann, 's an fiadh buidhe ar saothar,
      Is sínid go tréanmhar 'na dheóidh,
      Tré choillte, tré dhroigheanta, tré aibhne 's tré shléibhte,
      Go bhfúigid é ar thaobh cnuic go fann;
      Is aoibhinn fear a' rinnce go hintinneach leó,
      Agus imrid báire go sásta ar a gcóir,
      Is taithneamhach liom gach cúilfhionn deas óg,
      Ar faithche bhreágh aorach a' cheóil.

I have also compared the text in NUI, Galway, James Hardiman Library, Hyde MS. 57, 1–4, which has 5 verses in the order 3, 4, 1, C, 2. The air is the same as for *Sweet Boney, will I e'er see you more?* [No. **140**].

Mo shlán thar lear chunmn á a'gus fear____ is __ gach áit-reabh. le chéi- le,

Ó fhág-ann sé an Gaor - thaidh go Bríd;

Is mo shlán chunna há-ite____ úd ná feic-im_ féin i n-aon- chor

Mo shlán chun an méid úd sa chíll!

Mo_ shlán_ chun na habh-ann _ gan _ cham,_____ gan chuis- e!

Is mo shlán chun na Bann - dan is mó leabhair bhreac in - ti!

Mo_ shlán chun an teamp-aill- úd_ Ar - d na Cuil-ce!____

Mo shlán chun gach stáid - bhruinn-eal óg!

58

Famed Killabane

1.   Blest be the homesteads and scenes I hold dear,
By Saint Gobnait's fine borders and valleys so fair.
Where the majestic river by yon flowery vale
Flows down by the woodland and home of the Gael.
In past days of childhood and sweet happy hours
I roamed through that wild wood and sainted old bowers,
To gather the wild rose and fair *ceanabhán*
That grows in abundance by famed Killabane.

2.   It's often I roamed the wild mountain crest,
     Through glades and green valleys with those I loved best;
     But the comrades of boyhood and friends I have met
     By famed Ballyvourney I cannot forget.
     As memory glides over that pleasant old time
     The war-pipers call and the maidens divine,
     While dancing a jigtime from midnight till dawn,
     Or sing loud the praises of famed Killabane.

3.   Far over the billows my thoughts fondly roam
     Through the States of Columbia, that land o'er the foam,
     Or to long-lost companions, the fairest and best,
     In that fair town of Chester, that home of the West.
     Never more shall we join in that wild tally-ho,
     Resounding the depths of the valleys below,
     Whilst chasing the wild hare at Autumn's grey dawn
     From the furze-brakes and hillsides of famed Killabane.

4.   Then farewell companions afar o'er the tide,
     Of Atlantic's blue waters which cannot divide
     Or unbind the fond memories which shall ever remain
     In the hearts that would yearn to meet you again.
     Where the winter wind blows o'er the heather-clad hills
     Through woodland recesses and steep mountain rills
     Comes down in the murmur of a proud swelling Sullane,
     That glides by the arbour of famed Killabane.

5.   O, famed Ballyvourney, there's no place on earth
     Your equals for manhood or friendship or mirth!
     For long-vanquished Erin bright hopes e'er remain
     In the stout-hearted sons of the old Clann na nGael.
     Adieu to each landscape and cairn and mien!
     Thy pure winding clusters are grand to be seen!
     Adieu to each mountain and dew-spangled lawn!
     To the clear crystal fountain of famed Killabane!

Text From Bess's own handwritten collection of songs.   **Note** There is another very fine version of this song recorded by Diane Hamilton from Bess's near neighbour, the late John O'Connell. I have no printed version.

59

First I married a fiddler

Notes Title only, from one of Bess's handwritten song-lists. See the song entitled *Dá bhfaighinn mo rogha dhe thriúr acu* [No. **44**].

60

Foxy Davy

1. Going for water, going for water,
    First I met with her, first I met with her.
    Going for water, going for water,
    First I met with her, Kitty McHugh.

2. Foxy Davy, Foxy Davy,
    Won't you marry me, won't you marry me?
    Foxy Davy, Foxy Davy,
    Won't you marry me? — Indeed then I won't!

3. Cold potatoes, cold potatoes,
    Salt and dip with them, salt and dip with them.
    Cold potatoes, cold potatoes,
    Salt and dip with them, milk with them too.

4. Foxy Davy, Foxy Davy,
    Won't you marry me, won't you marry me?
    Foxy Davy, Foxy Davy,
    Won't you marry me 'nd carry me home?

Text From a notebook of DÓC's. An appended note suggests that the whole was repeated.   **Notes** A brother-in-law of Bess's, D. J. Cronin, made the following extempore verses for Sonny Right, a neighbour who had won buttons from him:

> Old John Healy, Old John Healy,
> Starch to stiffen him, starch to stiffen him,
> Old John Haley, Old John Haley,
> Starch to stiffen him, graze for his shoes!'

In a recorded interview with Pádraig Ó Raghallaigh of RTÉ (2 March 1978), Seamus Ennis sings a slightly different version of v. 3, which he said he learnt from Bess. See also *An Lóchrann* (Feabhra 1926) 32: 'Poirtíní Béil':

> Tidy 'omaneen, tidy 'omaneen,
> Tidy 'omaneen *sásta*,
> She milked the cow in the tail of her gown,
> And brought it home to Seáinín.

A note adds that it was to be sung to the air 'Royal Charlie'. The song is in one of Bess's own lists with the title *Fancy* (sic) *Davy won't you marry me.*

61

Gallant Tipp' boys

Note Title only, from one of Bess's handwritten song-lists.

62

Girleen, don't be idle[2/19]

1. *A chailín bhig ghleoite mheidhrigh,*
   A chailín bhig ghleoite mheidhrigh,
   A chailín bhig ghleoite mheidhrigh,
   Bailigh do lachain is feighil iad!

   A chailín bhig ghleoite mheidhrigh,
   A chailín bhig ghleoite mheidhrigh
   A chailín bhig ghleoite mheidhrigh,
   Bailigh do lachain is feighil!

   A chailín bhig ghleoite mheidhrigh,
   Bailigh do lachain is feighil iad!
   A chailín bhig ghleoite mheidhrigh,
   Bailigh do lachain is feighil iad!

2. Girleen don't be idle, girleen don't be idle,
   Girleen don't be idle, gather your ducks and mind 'em!
   Girleen don't be idle, girleen don't be idle,
   Girleen don't be idle, gather your ducks and mind 'em!

   Girleen don't be idle, gather your ducks and mind 'em!
   Girleen don't be idle, gather your ducks and mind 'em!

Recordings CBÉ 396b (1947) — JR–GP (24 Oct. 1952). **Text** From the JR–GP recording; another in CBÉ 912, 415. **Notes** Bess remarks (CBÉ 912, 415) that the Irish part of this jingle was composed extempore by Pádraig 'Mothall' Ó Murchú, a near neighbour of hers, when someone asked him to 'put Irish' on the English jingle.

63

God be with you, Davy!

1.   God be with you, Davy!
      I had you for Christmas, and I had you for Easter,
      And now I haven't your ould breeches
      Thrown up in the tayster!

Text From a DÓC notebook (dated 31 Dec. 1946).

64

Good night, Molly darling, good night

1.   I've come for to bid you good night, Molly dear,
      And a message to leave at your door.
      For I see there's a light in your window
      And I know you are wakened, *a stór.*

2.   The snow is fast falling around me
      And making the green fields look white.
      But, oh! if it snows ten times harder,
      I'll bid you, my darling, good night.
          Good night, good night,
          Good night, Molly darling, good night.

3.   And if from your slumber you waken,
      Look down from your window above;
      And you'll see the footprints I have been making
      Which tell of the boy that you love.

4.   I'll wrap my cloak closely around me
      With my heart full of joy and delight.
      And I'll fly away alone to my cottage,
      But I'll bid you, my darling, good night.
          Good night, good night,
          Good night, Molly darling, good night.

Recording BBC 19021 (8 Sept. 1952).   **Text** From the BBC recording.   **Printed Sources** *Walton's treasury of Irish songs and ballads* (Dublin n. d.) 163.   **Notes** According to *Walton's treasury of Irish songs and ballads*, 163, the song was composed by Samuel Lover, although I have seen another edition of the same publication in which the ascription was to Joseph Crofts. I have not been able to locate a printed text.

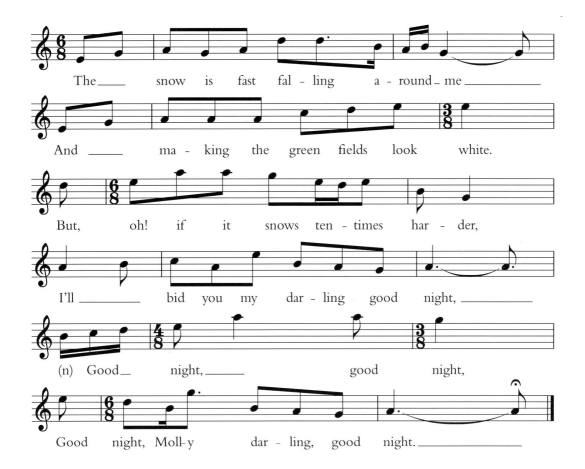

The___ snow is fast fal - ling a - round_ me___
And ___ ma - king the green fields look white.
But, oh! if it snows ten - times har - der,
I'll ___ bid you my dar - ling good night, ___
(n) Good_ night, ___ good night,
Good night, Moll- y dar - ling, good night. ___

65

Grá mo chléibh

1. [...   ...   .]
   [...   ...   .]
   'Sé dúirt sí: 'Dá sciúrdfadh chugham mh'athair
   Bheinn marbh go brách lem' shaol!'

2. 'S a spéirbhean ná bíodh ort ao' mhairg
   I dtaobh t'athar — ní gá dhuit é;
   Mar má thíonn tusa liúm-sa anso 'bhaile,
   Gach maidean geóbhair 'rán is té.

3. Thúrfainn bróga breá nua chughat ón gcathair,
   Is a mhalairt más fearr leat é.
   Sin snaídhmthe gan moíll sinn ag ceangal
   Ná scarfaidh go brách let' shaol.

              * * *

4. Mo bhríste breá cíordhubh gur stracadh,
   Is gur bascadh mo chnámha go léir;
   Sin ínsithe dhíbh-se i dtapa
   Conas a scaras le grá mo chléibh.

English Summary The poet encounters a beautiful young woman and sings her praises. There appears to be at least one verse missing at the beginning, and another in the body of the song, but the last verse implies that our hero was obliged to run for his life from the girl's father.   **Text** From a DÓC notebook (v. 1) and CBÉ 737, 74. Verses 2, 3 and 4 are in Seamus Ennis's transcript, CBÉ 912, 660, and in handwritten notes of SÓC's.   **Printed Sources** cf. Petrie and Stanford, *The complete collection of Irish music*, 293, No. 1156.   **Notes** In a note to his transcript of *An Gamhain Geal Bán* [No. **18**], Ennis remarks that the same tune was used also for this song. For another song with a similar theme, see *Ar Maidin Inné Cois Féile Bhinn* [No. **24** above].

66

Green grows the rushes-o

Note Title only, from one of Bess's handwritten song-lists.   **Printed Sources** *Delaney's Scottish song book*, 19.   **Notes** This song is one of Robbie Burns's most famous compositions. The text in *Delaney's Scottish song book* is as follows:

1.   There's nought but care on ev'ry han', in ev'ry hour that passes, o!
      What signifies the life o' man, an' 'twere na' for the lasses, o!

                         Chorus

      Green grow the rashes, Green grow the rashes, o!
      The sweetest hours that e'er I spent were spent among the lasses, o!

2.   The wordly race may riches chase, an' riches still may fly them, o!
      An' tho' at last they catch them fast, their hearts can ne'er enjoy them, o!

3.   Gi'e me a cantrie hour at e'en, my arms about my dearie, o!;
      An wordly cares an wordly men may a' gae tapsalteerie, o.

4.   And you sae douce wha swear at this, ye're nought but senseless asses, o.
      The wisest man the wald e'er saw, he dearly lo'ed the lasses, o.

5.   Auld nature swears the lovely dears her noblest works she classes, o;
      Her 'prentice han' she tried an man, an then she made the lasses, o!

67

Hang it up, boys, for sale!

Note Title only, from one of Bess's handwritten song-lists.

68

High Germany

1.   In this low meandering valley, who should I chance to see
      But my own dear lovely Willie and he waiting there for me;
      With his golden [chain?] all round his neck and sword unto his knee,
      And he bound for the wars that's in High Germany.

2.   'Oh, Willie, lovely Willie, le me gang along with thee,
Where the drums do sweetly rattle and we must be away!
I'll dress myself all in my best and gang along with thee,
And we're bound for the wars that's in High Germany'.

3.   'Your feet they are too tender and your fingers are too small,
And I fear you would not answer when on you I would call.
Your delicate constitution would not bear the unwholesome clime,
For there are hot and sandy deserts on the banks of the Nile'.

4.   'And Willie, lovely Willie, will you gang me your right hand
That you'll never wed another till you'll come back to Ireland;
That you'll never have no fair one, no one alive but me,
Till the wars they are all over that's in High Germany?'.

5.   Oh, Molly, dearest Molly, I will give you right my hand
That I'll never wed another till I'll come back to Ireland;
That I'll never have no fair one, no one alive but thee,
Till the wars are all over that's in High Germany'.

6.   'My curse attend the war and the how it first began,
For it has robbed old Ireland of many a clever man.
It took from me my own true love, besides my brothers three,
Laid cold in the mounds that's in High Germany'.

Laws N 9   **Recordings** BBC 19025 (8 Sept. 1952) = Kennedy, *Folktracks* F–60–160 (1981) B8.   **Text** From the BBC recording. **Printed Sources** Cf. *A much admir'd love song call'd the* BANKS OF THE NILE, No. 147 in the Gilbert Coll. Dublin (P. Brereton, 7 vv.) and Sam Henry, 'Songs of the People', *Northern Constitution* (2 June 1928), No. 238a (*The Banks of the Nile*, 7 vv.) = Huntington & Hermann, *Sam Henry's Songs of the People*, 296–97; Milner, *The bonnie bunch of roses*, 84 (6 vv.), from a broadside by Fortey of Bloomsbury entitled *The Banks of the Nile*; Cambridge University Library, vol. 1, 44, vol. 3, 73, and 4, 108 entitled *Much admir'd love song call'd the Banks of the Nile* is presumably identical with ours. See also Karpeles, *The crystal spring*, 79, No. 72; Laws, *American balladry from British broadsides*, 206–7.   **Notes** This is not, in fact, the version of *High Germany* commonly printed, but the song usually entitled *The Banks of the Nile* (see verse 3d). The ballad sheet texts and Sam Henry's version have our vv. 3 and 6 preceded by the following four (in the Sam Henry edition):

A.   'Oh hark, the drums are beating, love, no longer can I stay,
I hear the bugles sounding, that call we must obey,
We are ordered out from Portsmouth — it's many a long mile —
To join the British Army on the banks of the Nile.'

B.   'Oh Willie, dearest Willie, do not leave me here to mourn,
You'll make me curse and rue the day that ever I was born,
For the parting with you, my love, is the parting of my life,
So stay at home, dear Willie, and I will be your wife.'

C.   'Oh Nancy, lovely Nancy, that's a thing that can't be so,
Our colonel he gave orders, no women there can go,
We must forsake our old sweethearts, likewise our native soil,
And fight the blacks and negroes on the banks of the Nile.'

D.   'Then I'll cut off my yellow locks and go along with you;
I'll dress myself in velvet gold, go see the captain, too,
I'll fight and bear your banner while fortune will on us smile,
And we'll comfort one another on the banks of the Nile.'

These are followed in his text by our vv. 3 and 6, and his text then ends with this verse:

E.   'But when the war is over, it's home we'll all return
        Unto our wives and sweethearts we left behind to mourn,
        We will embrace them in our arms until the end of time,
        And we'll go no more to battle on the banks of the Nile.'

Milner's text, from a London broadside, is identical with Henry's, but lacks the last verse above. The tune is a variant of that to
The Bonny Blue-eyed Lassie [No. **148**].

In this low me - and - ering val-ley, who ——— should I chance to   see

But my own dear love - ly Wil - lie   and   he wai- ting there _ for me;

With his gol - den chain all a- round his neck and sword   un-to his   knee,

And he bound   for the wars _ that's in   High _ Ger - man - y.

69

I am a maid that sleeps in love[2/13]

1.   I am a maid that sleeps in love and cannot tell my pain;
     For once I had a sweetheart, and Johnny was his name.
     And if I cannot find him, I'll mourn both night and day,
     And for the sake of Johnny I'll cross the stormy sea.

2.   I'll cut off my yellow locks; men's clothing I'll wear on.
     And like a gallant sailor this road I'll gang along.
     Enquiring for a captain a passage to get free,
     And to be his chief companion on the Banks of Liberty.

3.   The very first night the Captain lay down in his bed to sleep.
     Those very words he says to me: 'I wish you were a maid;
     For your cherry cheeks and ruby lips do often entice me.
     I wish to God and to my heart a maid you were to me!"

4.   'Oh, hold your tongue, dear Captain, and do not speak so strange;
     For if the sailors heard of it, they'd laugh and make great game!
     Sure, when we land on shore, brave boys, some pretty girls we'll find.
     We'll roll and sport along with them, for so we are inclined'.

5.   It was in three weeks after when we did land on shore —
      'Adieu, adieu, dear Captain, adieu forever more!
      For a sailor I was on ship by you, but a maid I am on shore!
      Adieu, adieu, dear Captain, adieu forever more!'

6.   'Come back, come back, my blooming girl, come back and marry me!
      For I have a good fortune and I'll give it all to thee,
      Besides five hundred guineas I promise will be thine,
      If you come back and marry me and say you will be mine!'

7.   'For to marry you, dear Captain, it's more than I can do.
      For once I had a sweetheart and he wore the jacket blue;
      And if I cannot find him I'll mourn both night and day,
      And it's for the sake of Johnny I'll live and die a maid'.

Laws N 12   **Recording** JR-GP (24 Nov. 1952).   **Text** From JR-GP recording; another in Bess's handwritten collection of songs.   **Printed Sources** Milner, *The bonnie bunch of roses*, 102–3 [from Bess's singing]; Palmer, *Songs of the Midlands*, 36; Laws, *American balladry from British broadsides*, 208–9.   **Notes** The song should possibly be *I am a Maid that's Deep in Love*, which is the title in Palmer's *Songs of the Midlands*, 36. His version is as follows:

'For I am a maid that's deep in love, and I dare not once complain,
For I'm in search of my true love and Johnny is his name,
Enquiring for the captain my passage to go free,
That I might find the lad I love while crossing the deep blue sea.

Well the ship it went on gaily and the wind it did blow fair,
And when I reached Columbia's shore no danger did I fear.
It is once I was a man on sea but a maid I am on shore,
So adieu, adieu, sea captain bold, adieu for ever more.'

'O come back, come back my pretty Mollie, won't you marry me?
I have a handsome fortune and all I'll give to thee,'
'Oh it's once I had my own true love and Johnny was his name
And until I find that lad I love I'll live and die a maid.'

Palmer's version was collected from Mrs Cecilia Costello of Bermingham in 1951, published by Marie Slocombe and Patrick Shuldham-Shaw in the *Jnl of the Engl. Folk-Dance Soc.* 7/2 (1953) 96–105 99–100, and described there by A. L. Lloyd as 'something of a find'. Laws gives the song the generic title *The maid in sorrow*.

I ___ am a maid that sleeps in love and _ can-not_tell my _ pain

For _ once I had_ a _ sweet_ heart and_ Joh-nny was his name

and_ if I can-not_ find ____ him, I'll mourn both night and_ day

And it's for the sake_ of _ Joh - nny I'll _ cross the- stor - my sea.

70

I have a bonnet trimmed with blue[2/6]

1. I have a bonnet trimmed with blue;
    Why don't you wear it? So I do.
    I have a bonnet trimmed with blue;
    Why don't you wear it? So I do.

2. I will wear it when I can;
    When I'll go away with my fair-haired man.
    I will wear it when I can;
    When I'll go away with my fair-haired man.

3. Open the window, do love, do!
    Listen to the music playing for you!
    Open the window, do love, do!
    Listen to the music playing for you!

4. I have a bonnet trimmed with blue;
    Why don't you wear it? So I do.
    I have a bonnet trimmed with blue;
    Why don't you wear it? So I do.

Recording JR-GP (24 Nov. 1952).   **Text** From the JR-GP recording; a second in a DÓC notebook (vv. 2, 3, 1); a third in another DÓC notebook (vv. 1, 2, 3), and a fourth in Bess's handwritten collection of songs (1st two lines of v. 3 only).   **Printed Sources** Opie & Opie, *The singing game*, 442. See also Hughes, *Irish country songs*, vol. 4, 18–19 ('a polka fragment').   **Notes** The Opies have the following version of the song:

> 'I have a bonnet trimmed with blue.'
> 'Why don't you wear it?' 'So I do.'
> 'When do you wear it?' 'When I can —
> When I go out with my young man.
> My young man's away at sea,
> When he comes back he'll marry me;
> Buy me a biscuit, buy a tart,
> What do you think of my sweetheart?'

— from Orpington, 1906. Sung to *King Pippen Polka*, and known from c.1850 to the 1930s. Hughes, *Irish country songs* 4, 18–19, has 'When he comes back he'll play for me, Tip to the heel and tip to the toe, And that's the way the polky goes'.

71

I'll tell you a comical story

1.   I'll tell you a comical story,
'Tis wonderful droll, I declare.
And for fear I might bother or bore you
I'll give it a sort of an air.
How Mary gave Neilus a pounding,
And Thady got a trouncing from Liz.
So the case in detail I'm expounding,
Kind neighbours draw round, here it is.

2.   How Neilus bought Thady's young jennet,
And Thady purchased Naily's old ass.
'Pray', said Mary, 'what gain is there in it? —
By Jaysus, not a hap'orth, but loss!
You had a fine stately young donkey,
You cast him away for two quid.
You made a queer deal with the Yankee,
Now, didn't you, Thady, sure you did!'

3.   'Oh!' said Thady, 'pray have patience a moment,
And don't get so woefully cross!
Very soon I'll procure you a motor,
Which will need neither hay, oats, nor grass.
It will glide o'er the road like a swallow,
Up and down hill it will fly.
We'll be home after scaring through Mallow,
Ere those socks on the rack will be dry'.

4.   Then who should jump in at that moment
But Liz, as she gripped a big stick,
Saying 'Thady, though I daresay you're busy,
Hop east for your jennet right quick!
Make haste, don't be lazy, don't linger,
Or my temper, I think, shall break loose'.
She kept aiming at Thady with her finger,
And giving him tinker's abuse.

5.   Then to add to this dreadful commotion
Con stood before them right grim.
Well, boys, I'd a kind of a notion
He'd fracture the most of poor Jim!
'That poisonous firebrand you sold me
Has smashed the stall door into *brus*.

He's not quite as mild as you told me —
I'm telling you so to your puss!'

6.   'You're a cheat, a *cábóg* and a rascal;
Of conscience you don't own a bit.
And with the *ciotóg* he made for him
And such a *falltóg* as he hit!
He tumbled him over the table,
Knocking sliggers of ware in his fall;
And Mary gave Con with a cable
A dig, and the same made him squall.

7.   There was hair of all shades flying in bunches.
Old Jemmy said — 'Send for the police!'
It was like a day in the trenches,
And none of them looking for peace.
The row being by now complicated
And I can't well relate how it went;
For I got a stray knock in the pate
And right under the grate I was sent.

Text From Bess's handwritten collection of songs (2 copies); another handwritten copy by SÓC (v. 7 only).   **Printed Sources**
Ó Súilleabháin, 'Abair Amhrán', *An Múscraíoch* (Bealtaine 1994) 8.   **Notes** This song was composed by George Curtin, alias
Mícheál Ó Tuama. Seán Ua Súilleabháin, in his (unpublished) account of the poet and his compositions, 40 ff. (which he kindly
allowed me to use), has the following background to the story 'Another of George's compositions, *The Two Donkeys*, is about two
drinking companions who, to relieve financial embarrassment during a drinking bout in Babe Murphy's establishment in
Macroom, exchanged a young and an old donkey in a type of trade-in arrangement. All was well until the bargain was vetoed
by their wives, and one of the donkeys didn't live up to the advertising that preceded the sale'. Seán Ua Súilleabhán points out that
the reference to trench warfare implies that the song was composed during or after the First World War. His version has a *Rye
tooril aye* refrain after every verse. The version in *An Múscraíoch* was learned from Eoin Ó Súilleabháin, a younger contemporary
of Bess's. The following words may require explanation 5 *brus* 'smithereens'; 6c *ciotóg* 'left hand'; 6d *falltóg* al. *palltóg*, 'a thump or
heavy blow'; 6f sliggers presumably from Irish *sliogán* 'shell, fragment'.

72

If I was a fair maid

1.   If I was a fair maid and fairer than any, O!
I'd marry a tailor before I'd marry any, O!
He'd sew, and I'd sew, 'n' we'd all sew together, O!
What a jolly time we'd have sewing for each other, O!

2.   If I was a fair maid and fairer than any, O!
I'd marry a sailor before I'd marry any, O!
He'd sail and I'd sail 'n' we'd all sail together, O!
What a jolly time we'd have sailing with each other, O!

3.   If I was a fair maid and fairer than any, O!
I'd marry a shoe-maker before I'd marry any, O!
He'd sew and I'd sew 'n' we'd all sew together, O!
What a jolly time we'd have sewing for each other, O!

Text From a Seamus Ennis transcript now in the Dept of Irish Folklore, UCD (Sept. 1946). The title only is in one of Bess's song-lists *(If I was a Fair Maid, fairer than)*, perhaps to be identified with the song known as *First I'd marry a sailor.* **Printed Sources** Milligan Fox, 'Twelve Ulster folk songs from the neighbourhood of Coleraine', *JIFSS* 9 (Jan.-June 1910) 10–18: 16. **Notes** Seamus Ennis, in his CBÉ copybook version, gives the continuation as follows:

> He'd (1) sew and I'd (1) sew 'n' we'd sew all together–o
> *(repeated three times)*
> What a jolly time we'd have (1) sewing for each other–o
> (2) sailing with, etc., (3) sewing for, etc.

The version printed by Milligan Fox, (with air, described as 'Step Dance'), goes as follows:

> 1. If I were a fair one, fairer than any, O!
>   I'd marry a carpenter before I'd marry any, O!
>   For he'd chip and I'd chip, and we'd chip together, O!
>   And what a jolly time we'd have chipping one another, O!

She adds that the verses are filled out by reference in succession to a soldier, tinker, tailor, shoemaker, nailer, boatman, and mason, who would respectively shoot, block, stitch, work, hammer, row and build.

73

In Kerry long ago

1. Oh! God be with you, Kerry, where in childhood I made merry,
    When I'd hear the fiddler tuning up and rosining his bow.
    At the crossroads we were dancing and our colleens shyly glancing,
    Just like their dark-haired mothers did in Kerry long ago.

2. Now my heart is sad and weary, in my dreams I see my Mary,
    And her golden tresses flying and her cheeks are all a-glow.
    In my ear I hear her singing, with harp and fiddle ringing,
    As she played the Stack of Barley in old Kerry long ago.

3. We drove down to Mary's dairy and our hearts so light and airy,
    At the churn we'd take our turn till the butter would overflow.
    Then to the kitchen we'd retire and pick out the biggest liar
    For to tell us fairy stories of Kerry long ago.

4. Then we'd stroll home by the moonlight and our colleens' waists we'd hug tight,
    For to save them from the fairies in the ratheen down below.
    We'd say 'Good night!' and kiss them, we'd go home and pray 'God bless them!'
    The sweethearts of our boyhood in Kerry long ago.

Recording CBÉ 395a (1947). **Text** From the CBÉ recording. **Note** I have no printed version.

Oh!___ God be with you Ker-ry, where in child - hood I made mer - ry,

When I'd__ hear the fid - dler tu - ning up and ro - si - ning his bow.

At the cross-roads we were dan-cing and our col-leens shy - ly glan-cing,

Just like their dark-haired mot - hers did in Ker-ry long a - go.

Now my heart is sad and wea - ry, in my dreams I see my Mar - y,

And__ her gol - den tres - ses fly - ing and her cheeks are all a - glow.

In my ear I hear her sin-ging, with___ harp and fidd- le __ rin- ging,

As she played the Stack of Bar - ley in old Ker- ry long a - go.

74

Insa Ghaorthaidh thuit

1.   Insa Ghaorthaidh thuit, 's a' ghaoth anoir,
         'Sa Ghaorthaidh thuit an oíche 'rainn.

English Summary The full text (for which, see below) indicates that this is a love song, in which the poet laments his single status, and wishes for female company.   **Text** Just the refrain from a DÓC notebook.   **Printed Sources** See Ó Lochlainn, *An Claisceadal*, Duilleachán 18.   **Notes** There is an interesting conversation about this song and its tune, with Seán Ó Cróinín and the piper Willie Clancy, in Ciarán Mac Mathúna's radio programme *Donnybrook Fair*. Clancy had the well-known air and Seán Ó Cróinín had the less-well-known words. Ó Lochlainn's text is as follows:

> 'Sa nGaortha thuit, 'sa nGaortha thuit,
> 'Sa nGaortha thuit an oidhche 'rum;
> 'Sa nGaortha d'éisteas le n-a guth;
> Is truagh mo thoisc gan Síle 'gam.
>
> Is buachaill aerach éadtrom mé,
> Sonaí, séanmhar fíor-ghasta.
> Comhnuím liom féin le tréimhse 'dtigh,
> 'S gan éinne 'r bith 'san oidhche liom.
>
> Dá dtagthá féin le h-aontoil liom,
> 'S an chléir a chuirtheadh snaidhm orainn,
> Dhiún áit sa tsaoghal nach mbréagthainn thú
> 'S níor bhaoghal duit glór do mhuintir-e
>
> 'Sa nGaortha thuit, etc.

75

It was early, early in the month of spring

Text Title only in one of Bess's song-lists.   **Printed Sources** Greig, *Folk-song of the North-East*, No. cxxviii; Kidson, *A garland of English folk-songs*, 92–93; cf. Ó Lochlainn, *Irish street ballads*, 112–13, No. 56 (*My Boy Willie*); Healy, *Ballads from the pubs of Ireland*, 91–92, No. 38.   **Notes** Kidson's text in *A garland of English folk-songs*, 92–93, is as follows:

A.   'Twas early, early all in the Spring,
         My love was pressed to serve the King;
         The wind blew high and the wind blew low,
         Which parted me from my young sailor boy.

B.   Oh father, father, build me a boat,
         That on the ocean I may go float;
         And each King's ship that I pass by,
         I will enquire for my young sailor boy.

C.   She'd not sailed far across the deep,
         Before a King's ship she did meet;
         'Come jolly sailors tell me true,
         Does my love sail along with you?'

D.   'What jacket does your true love wear?
         What colour is your true love's hair?'
         'A blue silk jacket bound with twine,
         His hair is just the colour of mine'.

E.   'Oh no fair maid, your love's not here,
      He has got drowned I greatly fear,
      For on the ocean as we passed by,
      'Twas there we lost a young sailor boy'.

Gavin Greig's text, *Folk-song of the North-East*, No. CXXVIII, has 10 verses. He knew the song in several versions and believed it to derive from a printed broadside, and referred to Logan's *Pedlar's Pack of Ballads* under the title *The Disappointed Sailor*. He related the tune to that of *The Sailor Boy* and *The Oxfordshire Tragedy* in William Chappell's *Popular music of the olden time* (where it is traced to an operatic source of 1729). John Moulden has suggested to me that the song is to be identified with *My Boy Willie*, which is more-or-less identical with Greig's song. There is a version in Colm Ó Lochlainn's *Irish street ballads*, 112–13, No. 56 (9 vv., recorded from Verner, F.J. Bigger's chauffeur, in Belfast, 1912). There is also the possibility that the song intended by Bess in her list of titles is the one better known as *The Croppy Boy* ('It was early, early in the Spring'), which Bess has [No. **155**] — though one would expect such a well-known song to be listed under that title. The two songs are given one after the other in Healy, *Ballads from the pubs of Ireland*, 91–92 and 93–94.

76

Johnny get your hair cut!

Note Title only in one of Bess's song-lists.

77

Just like the ivy

1.   Grandad sat at evenfall
      'Neath the dear old garden wall,
      Where the ivy was clinging all around;
      And a maiden young and fair,
      With blue eyes and golden hair
      Was nestling there beside him on the ground.
      'Some day you'll be leaving me for a sweetheart',
      The old man said,
      'Some day you'll be forgetting me'.
      With a smile the maid replied:
      'Just watch the ivy on the old garden wall,
      Clinging so tightly whate'er may befall.
      When you'll grow older I'll be constant and true,
      Just like the ivy, I'll cling to you'.

2.   'Now the ivy years ago', said the maid,
      'Began to grow, and the old wall supported it with pride.
      Now the old wall's in decay and is crumbling fast away,
      But the ivy clings more tightly to its side.
      Loving you I have always been,
      You have cared for me day by day.
      Loving I will always be, and at your side I'll always stay.

Gran - dad sat at ev – en – fall

'Neath the dear old gar - den wall

Where the iv – y was cling-ing all a - round

And a maid-en young and fair, with blue eyes and gold-en hair

Was ____ nest-ling there be - side him on the ground

'Some day you'll be leav - ing me for a sweet-heart' the old man said

'Some day you'll be for - get - ting me'.

With a smile the maid rep-lied:

'Just watch the iv – y on the old gar- den wall,

cling - ing so tight - ly __ what'- er may - be - fall

when you'll grow old - er I'll be cons - tant and true

Just like the iv – y, I'll cling to you

Just like the ivy on the old garden wall,
Clinging so tightly, whate'er may befall.
When you grow older I'll be constant and true;
Just like the ivy, I'll cling to you'.

Recording JR–GP (24 Nov. 1952). **Text** From the JR–GP recording. There is another copy in Bess's handwritten collection of songs. **Notes** This is a music-hall song, sung by Marie Kendall. I have not located a printed text.

78

Kitty got a clinking coming from the races

Note Title only, from Bess's song-lists. **Notes** Willie Clancy, *The pipering of Willie Clancy*, Claddagh CC32 (Dublin 1980), has this as 'Kitty … coming from the fair (single jig)'. Seamus Ennis, in his notes to the record, says 'Clinking is slang for an intimate act of warm admiration'! In the notes to *The drones and the chanters: Irish piping*, Claddagh SIF 1000 (Dublin 1971) it is described as a 'fling'. Breandán Breathnach, *Ceol rince na hÉireann* 2 (Baile Átha Cliath 1976) 177 n. 208, lists it as the name of a reel.

79

Lackagh Bawn

1. One pleasant morning in the month of August,
    As I chanced to walk by the Raughty-side,
    The birds were warbling, their notes were charming,
    And the sun was warm and very fine.
    The pleasant gardens and fields of corn
    Before the storm were getting ripe.
    In every form, I being so charmed,
    I gave up walking and sat awhile.

2. Thus contemplating the gifts of nature
    And every feature around the lawn,
    Where generations of true Milesians
    Had been a-feasting from night till dawn,
    I heard a wailing of lamentations,
    Poor Dan complaining to old Dearmawn,
    That he was forsaken by lovely Katie,
    She's going up lately to Lackagh Bawn.

3. To hear him calling, crying and bawling,
    Tears were falling down from his eyes,
    Saying that both father and bouncing daughter
    Were full of p'laver and very sly.
    'When the days were warm we cut the corn,
    To please and charm this beauty bright.

I am now rewarded, my heart is scalded,
And the neighbours talking — they served me right'.

4.   I being a creature of that very nature,
That have met some failures all in my life,
I told him plainly: 'They often tease me,
And left me dreaming long winter nights'.
That they were schemers would beggar Damer,
To try to please them you should be wise.
That they were hateful and never faithful,
But always preaching and telling lies.

5.   To see them prancing, his heart was panting,
His eyes were dancing and very bright,
Saying, 'This young damsel is neat and handsome,
And I'd like her tandem each winter's night'.
Or should he fancy my sister Nancy,
Who is now advancing and getting fine,
I'll tell you one thing, the money's wanting,
Sure, I hope it's granted in coming time!

6.   I asked my neighbour, this little farmer,
To tell me plainly, or if he knew,
If this young Gaelic from stout Iveleary
Was coming lately for mending shoes.
But if it should please him, we'd hunt and chase him,
And make him stay down by Lackagh Bawn;
To dig his praties and drop his capers
Of sending papers to Kate Dearmawn.

7.   To my intention he paid attention
When I did mention what should I do.
To hunt those spakers of young shoe-makers,
And make them stay by their wax and tools;
That they were strangers and mountain rangers
And 'twould be dangerous to let them spawn.
You bet a wager he is a stager
And a long time reigning by Lackagh Bawn.

8.   I'd fish the Shannon for trout and salmon
And send it back for to let them see
That I was for them, if they would have me,
The devil blast them! They beggared me!
I gave her dandies of punch and brandy,
Or if she wanted, my very life.
Sure, it's now I'm watching, my head I'm scratching,
And I hope to Providence I'll get a wife!

9.   With Patsy Cronin I won't be joking.
I'm long controlling this heavy spite.
For to hunt and rattle and kill his cattle

I cut a wattle the other night.
With sticks and flogging I'll put them begging,
They won't be laughing, I'll let them see;
For when I was sparking, sure they were larking,
And very fond of remarking me.

Text From Bess's collection of handwritten songs.   **Notes** The song was composed by Johnny Nóra Aodha (for whom see also the songs entitled *Buduran's Ball* [No. **36**] and *The Tailor Bawn* [No. **177**]); cf. CBÉ 325, 139–40 (Cork 1936); CBÉ 862, 362–63 (Cork 1942).

80

Lanigan's Ball

1.   I married a wife and got no good of her —
        Nice and handy I got rid of her!
        When she died I closed the lid on her,
        Just in time for Lanigan's Ball!

        Six long months I spent in Dublin,
        Six long months doing nothing at all;
        Six long months I spent in Dublin
        Learning dance for Lanigan's Ball.

2.   She stepped out and I stepped in again;
        I stepped out and she stepped in again;
        She stepped out and I stepped in again,
        Learning dance for Lanigan's Ball.

Recordings Alan Lomax (1951) — JR-GP (24 Nov. 1952) — Kennedy, *Folktracks* F–60–160, A4 (1981).   **Text** From the JR-GP recording. There is another in Bess's hand-written collection of songs.   **Printed Sources** Milner, *The bonnie bunch of roses*, 213–14; Henry, 'Songs of the People', *Northern Constitution* (2 Oct. 1926), No. 151 = Huntington & Hermann, *Sam Henry's Songs of the People*, 534; Healy, *The Mercier book of old Irish street ballads* 4, 136–37 *The Death of Mrs O'Rafferty* (no source cited, but presumably from a broadside).   **Notes** There are four copies of a ballad called *Much admired song entitled Lannigan's ball* in Cambridge University Library Ballads, vol. 1, 17; vol. 2, 53; vol. 3, 128; vol. 4, 13. This is presumably identical with No. 160 in the Gilbert Collection, Dublin. Note that Bess's is not the version of the song commonly printed; e.g., by Colm Ó Lochlainn, *Irish street ballads*, 104–5 + 211, No. 52 ("In the town of Athy, one Jeremy Lanigan"). See, however, the query attached by Sam Henry to the song *James Raeburn's Farewell*, which reads as follows: 'Can any reader supply the song of which the following is a verse? —

Calm and easy I got rid of her, nice and easy 'deed I got rid of her,
Calm and easy I got rid of her, just in time for Lanigan's Ball,
She stepped out and I stepped in again, I stepped out and said nothing at all,
Five long weeks I lay at Magilligan learning the steps for Lanigan's Ball.'

See Huntington & Hermann, *Sam Henry's Songs of the People*, 534. Milner, *The bonnie bunch of roses*, 213, says 'The tune has a distinct second part courtesy of Jean Ritchie and George Pickow, who recorded it from the famed Cork singer Mrs. Elizabeth Cronin in the early 1950s'. Milner, however, does not reproduce the words of Bess's version above. Christie Moore's *Songbook* has a version which combines Bess's song and the ballad-sheet versions.

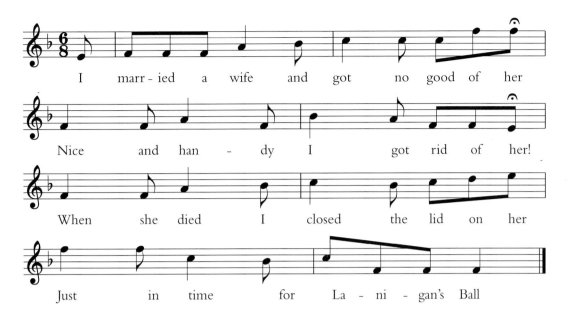

I marr-ied a wife and got no good of her
Nice and han-dy I got rid of her!
When she died I closed the lid on her
Just in time for La - ni - gan's Ball

81

Last night being windy

1. Last night being windy, I slept unsound.
   I dreamt my true love could not be found.
   I searched those green fields and mountains high
   For the lad I love is a sailor-boy.

2. Johnny, Johnny, I love you well.
   I love you better than my lips can tell.
   I love you better than my parents too.
   I'd forsake them all and I'd go with you.

3. There is an alehouse all in this town,
   And there my love he goes in and out.
   He takes his lassie upon his knee,
   Right well you know that it vexes me.

4. The reason he takes her, I'll tell you why,
   For she has got more gold than I.
   That her gold may melt and her riches fly,
   And that she may be as poor as I!

5. I wish, I wish that I got my wish!
   I wish my love was a little fish,
   And I to be fishing along the brook
   I would catch my love with a line and hook!

6.   I wish, I wish, and I wish again!
      I wish I was a maid again!
      A maid I am and a maid I'll be
      Until an apple grows on a laurel tree.

Recording BBC 19023 (14 Sept. 1952) = Kennedy & Lomax, *Sailormen and servingmaids* [= The folk songs of Britain 6], Topic Records 12T194 (1961) A 5.   **Text** From the BBC recording.   **Printed Sources** Petrie & Stanford, *The complete collection of Irish music*, 202, No. 811 *I wish, I wish, but I wish in vain* (music only); Palmer, *Songs of the Midlands*, 39 (vv. 3, 4); Vaughan Williams & Lloyd, *The Penguin book of English folksongs*, 53, 116. See Reeves, *The idiom of the people*, 90–92, with discussion at 43–45.   **Notes** This song is also known under the title of *The Alehouse* (see the Topic recording above). Seamus Ennis's BBC note reads as follows 'A version of the very widely known song which is the lament of a girl who has been abandoned by her lover in favour of another, "Who has more gold than I". Most full versions end with a stanza about her tombstone which is to tell the world she died of love, whence the title [*Died of Love*, an alternative title for this song]. This, however, is a 'commonplace' stanza common to this and a number of other songs and ballads involving hopeless love, and the present song is sometimes known by other titles such as *The Bold (or Brisk) Young Sailor* or *The Alehouse*. A modern burlesque version is *There is a Tavern in the Town*. The present recording is a very good variation with an unusual opening; it ends 'I wish, I wish, I wish in vain …' and the 'deep in love' stanza does not occur. Mrs Cronin does not know where she got it but knows it from childhood'. The 'I wish, I wish' motif is common in ballads; see Reeves, *Idiom*, 44. Ennis also pointed out that the tune is known in Ireland in association with another love-song in the same vein ('a very old one'), known as *Tiocfaidh an Samhradh*. Vaughan Williams & Lloyd, *Penguin book of English folksongs*, 53, have a version called *I wish, I wish*, from the singing of Mrs Costello of Bermingham, with four verses as follows:

A.   I wish, I wish, but it's all in vain,
      I wish I were a maid again;
      But a maid again I never shall be
      Till apples grow on an orange tree.

B.   I wish my baby it was born,
      And smiling on its papa's knee,
      And I to be in yon churchyard,
      With long green grass growing over me.

C.   When my apron-strings hung low,
      He followed me through fost and snow.
      But now my apron's to my chin,
      He passes by and says nothing.

D.   Oh grief, oh grief, I'll tell you why —
      That girl has more gold than I;
      More gold than I and beauty and fame,
      Bu she will come like me again.

See also Slocombe & Shuldham-Shaw, *Jnl of the Engl. Folk Dance & Song Soc.* 7/2 (1953) 96–105: 103. Palmer, *Songs of the Midlands*, 39 has a song called *A Brisk Young Man He Courted Me*, which has the following final 2 verses:

E.   There is a house in yonder town
      Where my love he goes and sits him down.
      He takes another girl on his knee;
      Why don't you think it's hard grief to me?

F.   Hard grief to me I will tell you for why:
      Because she's got more gold than I.
      Her gold it will waste and her beauty will pass;
      She'll come like me a poor girl at last.

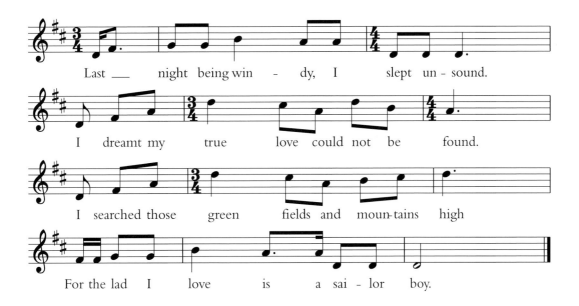

Last __ night being win - dy, I slept un - sound.

I dreamt my true love could not be found.

I searched those green fields and moun-tains high

For the lad I love is a sai - lor boy.

82

Little girleen with the curling poll, would you buy brooms?

Note Title only from one of Bess's song-lists.   **Printed Sources** Cf. the song *Green Brooms*, in Kennedy, *Folksongs of Britain and Ireland*, 504–5, No. 223 (with notes at 530).   **Notes** This is presumably the well-known song *Cutting down brooms*, given here from a manuscript version (in DÓC's possession) written down by Seamus Ennis from Seán 'ac Donnchadha (Sean MacDonagh), of Carna, Connemara, Co. Galway, in 1947:

1.   There was a man and he lived in the East,
     Where his trade it was cutting down brooms, green brooms.
     He had a son and his name it was John,
     And he stayed in bed until noon-day-noon,
     And he stayed in bed until noon.

2.   The father rose and up to John goes,
     And swore he would burn his room, gay room,
     If he didn't rise and sharpen his knives
     And go down to the woods to cut brooms, green brooms,
     And go down to the woods to cut brooms.

3.   Now Johnny went on till he came to a gate,
     The gate of a castle of fame, fame, fame.
     He saw a fair maid and stood at the gate,
     Saying: 'Fair maid, do you want any brooms, green brooms?'
     Saying: 'Fair maid, do you want any brooms?'

4.   The lady being up in her window so high
     She spied this young man so terrible neat, neat, neat.
     She said to her maid: 'Go down to the gate,
     And call in this young man with his brooms, green brooms,
     And call in this young man with his brooms'.

5.   And Johnny went into this castle so great,
     And entered this lady's room, gay room.
     She gave him a chair and bade him sit down,
     Saying: 'You're welcome, young man, with your brooms, green brooms,'
     Saying: 'You're welcome, young man, with your brooms'.

6.   They sent for the priest and married they were,
      All in the lady's room, gay room.
      So, boys, let us drink — or what do you think? —
      There is nothing like cutting down brooms, green brooms!
      There is nothing like cutting down brooms!

For another version, recorded by the BBC from Patrick Green of Ballinalee (Co. Longford), see Paul Clayton, *British broadside ballads in popular tradition*, Folkways Records FW 8708 (text, p. 7). Clayton points out that the song goes back to Thomas Durfey's *Pills to purge melancholy* 6 (London 1719).

83

Lord Gregory[2/1]

1.   I am a king's daughter that strayed from Cappoquin
      In search of Lord Gregory, may God I'll find him in!
      The rain beats at my yellow locks, the dew wets me still,
      The babe is cold in my arms, Lord Gregory let me in!

2.   Lord Gregory is not here and henceforth can't be seen,
      He is gone to bonny Scotland to bring home his new queen.
      Leave now those windows, and likewise this hall,
      For it's deep in the sea you should hide your downfall!

3.   Who'll shoe my babe's little feet, who'll put gloves on her hands,
      And who'll tie my babe's middle with a long and green band?
      Who'll comb my babe's yellow locks with an ivory comb,
      And who'll be my babe's father till Lord Gregory comes home?

4.   I'll shoe your babe's little feet, I'll put gloves on her hands,
      And I'll tie your babe's middle with a long and green band.
      I'll comb your babe's yellow locks with an ivory comb,
      And I'll be your babe's father till Lord Gregory comes home.

      Leave now those windows, and likewise this hall,
      For it's deep in the sea you should hide your downfall!

5.   Do you remember, Lord Gregory, that night at Cappoquin,
      When we both changed pocket handkerchiefs, and that against my will?
      Yours was pure linen, love, and mine was coarse cloth;
      Yours cost one guinea, love, and mine but one groat.

6.   Do you remember, Lord Gregory, that night at Cappoquin,
      When we both changed rings of our fingers, and that against my will?
      Yours was pure silver, love, and mine was block tin;
      Yours cost one guinea and mine but one cent.

7.   Do you remember, Lord Gregory, that night in my father's hall,
      When you stole away my fond heart, and that was worse than all?
      Leave now those windows, and likewise this hall,
      For it's deep in the sea you should hide your downfall!

8.   My curse on you mother, and my curse it being sore,
    For I dreamt the lass of arms came knocking to my door!
    Lie down, you foolish son, and lie down and sleep,
    For it's long ago her weary locks are waving in the deep!

9.   Come, saddle me the black horse, the brown or the bay!
    Come, saddle me the best horse in my stable this day!
    Till I'll range over valleys, over mountains so wide
    Until I find the lass of arms and lie by her side.

Child 76   **Recordings** BBC 18759 (29 Aug. 1952) = Kennedy, *Folktracks* F–60–160 (1981) A11 = Kennedy & Lomax, *The Child ballads 1 'The English and Scottish popular ballads'* Nos 2–95 [= The folk songs of Britain 4] Topic Records 12T160 (London 1961) B 6 — JR-GP (24 Nov. 1952) — .   **Text** From the JR-GP recording. There is a copy also in Bess's handwritten collection of songs.   **Printed Sources** Child, *The English and Scottish popular ballads*, 2, 213–26; 3, 510–12; 4, 471–74; 5, 225, No. 76 *The Lass of Roch Royal*; Walton, *Keltische Folksongs*, 107–8 (from Bess's recording).   **Notes** Child, *The English and Scottish popular ballads*, 2, 224, prints a version of this song called *The Lass of Aughrim*, which he acquired from an Irish emigrant, Mr G. C. Mahon, in Ann Arbor, Michigan, USA. Mahon had learned the song from a labourer at Tyrrelspass, Co. Westmeath, c. 1830. The song is perhaps best known from its inclusion (with the title *The Lass of Aughrim*) in James Joyce's short-story 'The Dead', in his collection *Dubliners*, and in John Huston's film of that story. (The 'loss of arms' in vv. 8b and 9d of Bess's version is a garbled rendering of 'the lass of Aughrim'.) For an excellent study of the song, see Hugh Shields, 'A history of *The Lass of Aughrim*', in Gerard Gillen & Harry White (eds), *Musical Studies* 1 Musicology in Ireland (Dublin 1990) 58–73. See also George I. Geckle, 'The "Dead Lass of Aughrim"', *Éire-Ireland* 9/3 (Autumn 1974) 86–96, who has an interesting discussion of Joyce's use of the song (though he is not quite accurate about Bess's version). The song occurs in one of Bess's own handwritten lists as *I am a King's daughter*.

84

Lord Randal

1.   What did you have for your breakfast, my own darling boy?
    What did you have for your breakfast, my comfort and joy?
    A cup of cold poison, mother dress my bed soon,
    For there's a pain through my heart and I'd want to lie down.

Recording BBC 21996 (29 Aug. 1954) = Kennedy & Lomax, *The Child Ballads* 1 [*The Folk Songs of Britain* 4], Topic Records (1961) A5.   **Text** From the BBC recording.   **Printed Sources** Child, *The English and Scottish popular ballads*, 1, 151–66; 498–501; 2, 498–99; 3, 499; 4, 449; 5, 208–209 and 413 (air); Joyce, *Old Irish folk music and songs*, 394–95, No. 812 (4 vv.); Henry, 'Songs of the People', *Northern Constitution* (1 July 1939), No. 814 = Huntington & Hermann, *Sam Henry's Songs of the People*, 415.   **Notes** Child, 1, 162, prints a version which was recorded from the recitation of a woman named Ellen Healy 'as repeated to her by a young girl at Lackabairn, Kerry, Ireland, about 1868'; this has our verse as v. 2. The text is identical with Bess's. A version of the ballad with two verses in English and one in Irish was recorded from Bess's brother-in-law, Michael Cronin of Lisbwee, by Jean Ritchie and George Pickow. There is a tune for this song in Petrie's *Complete collection*, 83, No. 330 (given to him by P. W. Joyce), with the title *Where were you all the day, my own pretty boy?*, but it is not Bess's tune. A version of the song in Irish was also very popular in Ireland; see Douglas Hyde, *Ériu* 2 (1910) 70–81. It is worth pointing out that this is one of the very few classic ballads that crossed the language divide into Irish; cf. Mac Coluim, *Smóilín na rann*, 17–18. Joyce, 394–95, has good discussion. Bess has some interesting remarks about this song in her conversation with the BBC collectors; see *infra*, **19**.

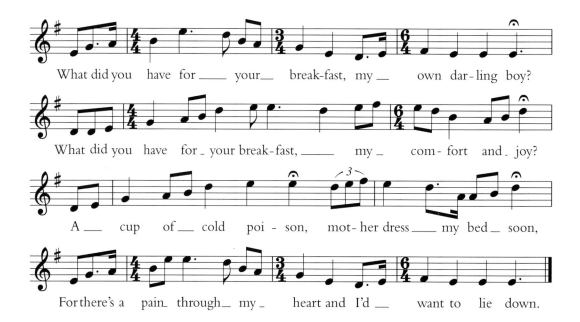

85

Lovely Molly

1. One evening as Johnny went out for a walk
    He met lovely Molly and to her did talk
    'Your limbs they are nimble, your ewe-lambs milk free,
    And we'll drive the ewes o'er with lovely Molly.
    And we'll drive the ewes o'er with lovely Molly.'

2. 'If my father was here, he'd talk about that;
    He's down in yon meadow, minding his flock.
    He's down in yon meadow, waiting for me',
    And we'll drive the ewes o'er with lovely Molly,
    And we'll drive the ewes o'er with lovely Molly.

3. 'Good morrow, old man, you are minding your flock,
    And I want a ewe-lamb, to get her in stock'.

'A ewe-lamb you'll get, and your choice out of three',
And we'll drive the ewes o'er with lovely Molly,
And we'll drive the ewes o'er with lovely Molly.

4. Johnny took Molly by the lily-white hand,
And opposite the old man this couple did stand,
Saying 'This is the ewe-lamb that you promised me,
And we'll drive the ewes o'er with lovely Molly,
And we'll drive the ewes o'er with lovely Molly'.

5. Johnny and Molly went out for a walk;
'Tis all about love the couple did talk.
They're going to get married, I hope they'll agree,
And we'll drive the ewes o'er with lovely Molly.
And we'll drive the ewes o'er with lovely Molly.

Recording CBÉ 1064a (1947). **Text** From the CBÉ recording; another (partial) text in a DÓC notebook. **Printed Sources** Kennedy, *Folksongs of Britain and Ireland*, 300, VII, No. 124 'Ca the yowes to the knowes'; see also 324, for references. **Notes** The title is in one of Bess's song-lists: *One Evening as Johnny Went Out For A Walk*.

One eve - ning as Joh - nny went out for a walk

He met love - ly Moll - y and to her did talk:

'Your limbs they are nim - ble, your ewe - lambs milk free

And we'll drive the ewes o' - er with love - ly Moll - y,

And we'll drive the ewes o' - er with love - ly Moll - y'

Lovely Mollie

One evg. as Johnnie went out for a wolk.
He met lovely M. & to her did tolk.
Your limbs they are nimble, your ewe-lambs milk free
{ & we'll drive the ewes o'er with lovely eyollee,
{ Repeat.

2.

If my father was here he'd tolk about that.
He's down in yon meadows minding his flock.
                                                    waiting for me.
and   .   .   .   .

3.

Good-morrow, old man, you are minding your flock.
and I want a ewe-lamb to get ies in stock.
a ewe-lamb you'll get a your choice out of 3
and -   .   .   .   .

4.

J. took up. by the lily-white hand.
& opposite to old man this couple did stand.
Saying this is the ewe-lamb that you promised me
and

5

'Lovely Mollie' from a notebook of Donncha Ó Cróinín's (private collection).

86

Maidean álainn ghréine

1. Maidean álainn ghréine is me'r thaobh Chnuic na Buaile
   'Sea dhearcas chúm an spéirbhean a's a bréad fliuch ón luachair;
   Do bhí gile is finne in éineacht go gléineach 'na gruadhnaibh,
       Agus d'fhúig sí mh'intinn lé-lag is is baolach nách buan a bheam!
   A's geobham airís a' crúiscín, a's bíodh sé lán!

English Summary The poet has an encounter with a vision (*spéirbhean*), whom he engages in conversation. She turns out to be the spirit of Ireland, wishing to be free of English rule.   **Text** From a DÓC notebook.   **Printed Sources** Ua Braoin, *An cuaichín ceoil*, 94 (3 vv.).   **Notes** In one of Bess's handwritten song-lists as *Maidean auling greine*. The DÓC notebook has only this first verse, with note 'ní críoch' [*'not finished'*]; there is an alternative given for the refrain 'A's geobham airís a' crúiscín, a's é lán, lán!'. See NUI, Galway, Hardiman Library, Douglas Hyde Collection, MS. 49, No. 23 *Maidean aoibhinn ghréine* (?). The text in Ua Braoin, *An cuaichín ceoil*, 94, is as follows:

> A. Maidin áluinn gréine 's mé'r thaobh cnuic na buaile
>   Seadh dhearcas cúilfhion mhaordha 'sa bréidín fliuch ó'n luachair
>   Bhí gile's finne'n éinfheacht go ghreineach 'na gruaidhnibh
>   A's d'fhúig sí m'inntinn leunmhar 'sis baoghlach nach buan a bhead
>   A's gheóbham airís an crúiscín lán lán lán.

> B. D'fhiafruigheas-sa go beusach de'n spéir-bhruinneal stuamdha
>   'Cá bhfuil do ghaolta nú cad é an taobh as gur ghluaisis
>   An bean ar fán an tsaoghail tú gan céile ar a thuairisc
>   Nú'n fíor gur tusa Cearnait chuir treun-mhuilte'r fuaimint?'
>   A's gheóbham airís an crúiscín lán lán lán.

> C. 'Sa óigfhir chlúmhail léigheanta ní h'aoinne mé d'ár ndubhráis
>   Ach bean do mhaithibh Gaodhal me tá leunuighthe ag cruadhtan
>   M'ainm cheart-sa Éire 'smac Searlleás ghá luadh liom
>   'Sbhur mbailte puirt ag béaraibh an éitigh a's an fhuadaigh
>   A's gheóbham airís an crúiscín lán lán lán.

87

Maidean bhog aoibhinn

1. Maidean bhog aoibhinn ar íoghair a' ghleanna
   Lem' thaoíbh gur thaisteal óig-bhean,
   Ba thaitneamhach braoíthe dlaoíthe is dearca
   Is a píp mar shneachta ar mhór-chnoc.
   Do gheal mo chroí dá clí mar eala,
   Le díogras searc dá cló ghlan;
   'Sé labhair sí liúm: 'Imigh uaim, a ghaige!' —
   Nuair a shíleas bheith dá pógadh.

2. 'Ní gaige anois mé, ná straeire magaidh,
   Ná réice ar easpa eolais;
   Is fiosraím féin díot féinig t'ainm

Sula léigfead mo hata ad' dhóid duit.
An tu an ainnir-bhean Hélen do thraoch na dragain
Go léir i gcaismirt chómhraic;
Do thréig an Ghréig is a céile leapan
Le h–aon-toil searc don óig-fhear?'

3.   'Ní duine don tréad san mé do chanais
I dtaobh gur dheas do ghlórtha;
Is cuma sa tsaol cá ndéanfair taisteal
Ach léig dod' bhladar beóil dom!'
Is eagal gach bé do ghéill dod' chleasaibh
Bheith ag imeacht seal gan sóchas;
Go dealbh i gcéin gan téarnamh abhaile
Tar éis bréag a chanadh leó san.'

4.   'A thaisge mo chléibh, ní baol dhuit feasta,
Sin bréag do cheap na comharsain;
Dar a leabhar úd inné do léigheadar na sagairt,
Níor chuireas-sa bean gan nóchar.
Mara bpógfainn féin a béal tais meala
Nó go raghainn léi seal a' stróireacht;
A chogair mo chléibh, tá an t-éag am' ghlaoidh!
Téanam abhaile is pósfam!'

5.   'Ó mhuise, fanfad-sa gan pósadh, is dócha, anois,
Ó stróaire buile 'ad' shórd-sa;
Gur thairrigís óg chughat ól agus imirt
Póit is clis is móide;
Ad' bhladaireacht beoil níl speóis agam
Mar do chomharsain dom gur chomhairlig;
Tabhair ort do bhóthar, a rógaire duine,
Do shórd ní dheaghaidh ar fónamh!'

6.   'Ó, a ainnir na lúb, ná diúlthaigh me,
Is go dtabharfainn cion is cóir duit!
Thar mhnáibh na Mumhan is tú mo chuid,
Is go siúlóchainn leat an Eóraip.
Chuirfinn bróg chaol chúmtha ort is búcla inte,
Gúna, *silk* agus clóca;
Agus each mear lúthmhar fút a' rith —
Thabharfainn súd is puins ar bórd duit'.

7.   'A fharaire shúgaig an úrla bhoig,
Is a phlúir tar fearaibh óga,
Gur glaise ar do shúil ná drúcht ar luibh
Is gur bhinne do ghuth ná smólach.
Dá léigfinn chughat mo rún anois —
Agus súil agam ná neósfá —
Do hata fím chúl, a rúin ghil, cuir,
Ar a ndrúcht sara bhfliuchadh an féar sinn'.

8. 'Do dhruideas anonn lem' rún ansan
    Is a béilín tais do phógas;
    Is is gairid gan mhoíll gur éirig linn
    Ár scéal airís d'athnóchaint.
    Mo chúilfhionn tsuilth níor dhiúlthaigh me,
    Is do bhréagas í go cóir cruinn;
    Do thréigeas ansan mo mhaighre grod
    Is ba séimhe mé ná Seóirse'.

English Summary The poet encounters a beautiful young woman and sings her praises. She resists for a while, but he persists and is eventually successful. They consummate their love but it is not altogether clear whether he abandons the young woman or his previous companion (*mo mhaighre grod*). **Text** CBÉ 912, 444–47 (dated 20 May 1943). A note by Seán Ó Cróinín reads 'Ní fheadar cé dhein an t-amhrán san. Seana-amhrán 'seadh é (E Ní Ch)' [*'I don't know who composed that song, but it's an old one (Bess Cronin)'*].

88

Marrowbones

1. There was a woman in this town — the truth to you I'll tell;
    She loved her husband dearly and another twice as well.
    To me fol-the-dol-ah rull-ah
    To me fol-the-dol-ah rull-ee
    To me fol-the-dol-ah rull-ah rull-ah
    And the blind man then could see.

2. She went unto the doctor, some medicine for to find:
    'Anything at all that would make an old man blind!'
    To me fol-the-dol-ah rull-ah
    To me fol-the-dol-ah rull-ee
    To me fol-the-dol-ah rull-ah rull-ah
    And the blind man he could see.

3. He gave her two long marrowbones and he told her 'Suck them all',
    And before he'd have the last one sucked he could not see at all.
    To me fol-the-dol-ah rull-ah
    To me fol-the-dol-ah rull-ee
    To me fol-the-dol-ah rull-ah rull-ah
    And the blind man then could see.

4. The doctor wrote a letter and he sealed it with his hand.
    He gave it to the old man that he might understand.
    To me fol-the-dol-ah rull-ah
    To me fol-the-dol-ah rull-ee
    To me fol-the-dol-ah rull-ah rull-ah
    The blind man then could see.

5. Now I am blind and helpless, in this world I can't stay.
    I'd rather go and drown myself, if I only knew the way.
    To me fol-the-dol-ah rull-ah
    To me fol-the-dol-ah rull-ee
    To me-fol-the-dol-ah rull-ah rull-ah
    The blind man then could see.

6. 'Now you're blind and helpless, in this world you can't stay:
    If you'd rather go and drown yourself I'll go and show the way'.
    To me fol-the-dol-ah rull-ah
    To me fol-the-dol-ah rull-ee
    To me fol-the-dol-ah rull-ah rull-ah
    The blind man then could see.

Laws Q 2 **Recordings** BBC 19022 (11 Sept. 1952) = Kennedy, *Folktracks* F–60–160 (1981) B11. **Text** From the BBC recording. **Printed Sources** Hughes, *Irish country songs* 4, 66–71 (with title *Tigaree torum orum*); full text Shields, 'Four songs from Glendalough', 4–14: 8–9 (5 vv.). See also Sedley, *The seeds of love*, 220–21, *The blind man he could see:* 'The tune and text given here are from Irish oral tradition, collated with a copy in the Sam Henry Collection' (p. 221); see Huntington & Hermann, *Sam Henry's Songs of the People*, 507 *(The Auld Man and the Churnstaff)*; Kennedy, *Folksongs of Britain and Ireland*, 465, No. 208 *(The Old Woman of Blighter Town)* (and notes, 482); Laws, *American balladry from British broadsides*, 274 *(The Old Woman of Slapsadam)*. **Notes** According to Seamus Ennis, in his BBC note, 'Mrs. Cronin couldn't recall the final verses', which, in fact, provide the punchline to the song: the woman leads the 'blind' husband down to the river, whereupon he throws *her* in, and she drowns! Ennis also refers to another version (BBC 19027) sung by Bess's neighbour, John Connell of Danganasillagh. Hugh Shields suggests that the song is a burlesque of the international ballad of a tragic poisoning (*Lord Randal, Donna Lombarda, Schlangenkochin*, etc.) 'in which the faithless wife or mistress uses dishes ranging in the different accounts from "roasted eel" to "fish caught in the stable with a dung-fork"'.

89

Mo leastar beag^{1/4}

1. Do thógas mo láir dhonn liom a's 'na drom a bhí mo leastar beag,
   chun gur chuas don chathair leis, síos go bun,
   Mar chúnamh chun a' chíosa do dhíol agus na *tax*anna,
   agus bróga a thabhairt abhaile liom do chuirfinn ar mo chois.
   Ach is amhlaidh a bhí mh'arthach lán den smearadh agam,
   agus do thug sé náire go brách agus aithis dom.
   A's ní cheadóinn éinne 'm' chairde bheith láithreach a tharraicthe,
   ag iomarca 'esna dathannaibh do bhí 'na chorp.

2. Is siúd chugham a *Taster*'s a thráthar ar a bhaclainn;
   do riug ar bhaitheas air is do sháidh é go bun.
   Do thairrig sé aníos é is do bhuail ar a theangain é
   is dúirt sé, ambasa, go raibh sé go h-olc.
   Do thugas-sa súil-fhéachaint de thaobh mo leacan air —
   'Puililiú, a *Thaster* — ní hé go gcreachfair mé?
   Mar má thugann tú-sa an *title* dom go nglaoid siad "An t-Easpag" air,
   imireod mh'anam leat sara ngabhad uait amach!'

English Summary The poet takes his newly-churned butter for sale at the market, but the 'Taster' declares it impure. The song laments the poet's misfortune. **Recording** CBÉ 388a (1947). **Text** From the CBÉ recording. Another text (4 vv.) in a DÓC notebook (dated 8 Aug. 1944). A third text, noted down by SÓC from Séamus Ó Liatháin, of Cluain Drochad, has 4 verses, identical with Bess's. Another text in another DÓC notebook has vv. 1–2 and the following 2 verses also:

> Ar mo ghabháil tríd a' *weigh-house* is me bhí go h-athtuirseach
> mar gheall ar mo leastar beag a bhí go holc;
> Agus iad a' síor-cháineadh na mná chuir ar salann é —
> nár fhág sa bhaile é 's gan é thabhairt anso!
> Ach ní raibh bean mo thí le trí mhí sa bhaile 'gam,
> ach seana-bheainín chríonna bhí líonta 'dhathachaibh.
> Gurbh í an cailín beag óg is mó chuir ar salann é,
> agus d'fhág sí an cheanfhinn ann a dhein é lot.
>
> Ar mo ghabháil amach ón *weigh-house* nách me bhí go h-athtuirseach,
> a' triall ar mo bhaile beag siar go Gleann na nGealth!
> Mar a raibh mo stoc beag bó tógtha le trí seachtaine
> ag Liam Ó Bhreachallainn aniar ó Ghleann na dTor.
> Níor leig bean mo thí dhom suí ná seasamh
> nuair 'fhiafraigh sí dhíom cadé'n praghas a chuaidh an leastar beag.
> 'Á, don diabhal a bheirim thíos iad! Níor dhein sé a' t-airgead,
> 's ná creidfhinn ón eaglais ná go raibh sé *first*!'

90

Mo mhúirnín bán

1. Do bhíos-sa oíche Lae Féile Bríde
   I dtigh'n tabhairne thíos ar an mbealach ard.
   Do chonnac-sa an rí-bhean, d'fhúig sí 'mo chroí me;
   Do bhí sí aoibhinn deas álainn óg.
   D'fhúig sí teinn me 's do léig sí mh'intinn,
   Is Oileán na Múmhan-so, ní leigheasfadh mé.
   Mar go bhfuil mo chroí 'stigh 'na chúig céad píosa,
   Nuair ná faghainn cead suí síos lem' mhúirnín bhán.

2.   Mo ghrá 's mo stór tú, 'cé gurb eol duit
    Go bhfaghainn togha an eolais chun éalú leat.
    Mar ná fuil tráthnóna ná maidean ró-mhoch
    Ná go silim deoir bhog nuair a bhím liom fhéin.
    Ach a' siúl na mbóithre is na gcoíllthe clómhair
    Is go deo, deo ní scarfainn leat!
    D'fhonn bheith at' phógadh le bláth na h-óige
    Is me bhéadh go módhmharach im' shuí let' ais.

3.   Ní sa chnoc is aoírde a bhíonn mo bhuíon-sa,
    Ach i nGleanntán aoibhinn abhfad ó láimh.
    Mar a labhrann a' chuach ann faoi shuan san oíche;
    Bíonn cruithneacht bhuí ann is coirce bán.
    Bíonn ba, bíonn laoígh ann, bíonn bric 'na sluíod ann,
    Is an eala is míne ar a' loich a' snámh;
    Na beacha críonna is a n-árthaí líonta,
    Agus mil dá taoísgadh dom' mhúirnín bhán.

4.   Isé mo bhuaidhreamh ná faghaim cead cuardaigh
    Insa tír úd thuaidh mar a mbíonn mo ghrá.
    Bíonn mil ar chraobhachaibh agus ím ar uachtar,
    A's i dtuís an fhuachta bíonn na crainn fé bhláth.
    Níl gaoth aduaidh ann, ná fearthainn fhuar-fhliuch;
    Is ró-bhreá an cuan é ar loíng ná ar bhád.
    Agus sin a n-iarfainn, is é fháil mar dhualgas:
    Cead suí go suairc ann lem' mhúirnín bhán.

5.   Duine 's fiche 'cu bhí síorraí i ngrá liom,
    Is ar lár na sráide níor chuireas suas.
    Nuair a chonnac-sa am' choinnibh an mhaighdean mhánla
    Agus tríd a' bhfáinne go ngeobhadh a cúm.
    Do bhí go talamh léi síodaí is cáimbric,
    Agus míl dá fásgadh trí ghruaig a cinn.
    Nuair iarras freagra, 'sé dúirt sí: '*Grant pardon*,
    Ach táim-se in áirithe ag an dTiarna Cínn'.

English Summary The poet laments his absence from his loved one. He describes his locality in idyllic terms (with references to worker bees *(beacha críonna)* and every other kind of natural beauty. He claims to have had twenty-one suitors already, but they all pale into insignificance beside this beauty. Alas! She is already betrothed to Lord Keane. **Text** From a DÓC notebook (dated 24 May 1946). **Printed Sources** Ó Laoghaire, *An Gaodhal* 8/10 (Sept. 1891) 120 (4 vv.); Ó Máille & Ó Máille, *Amráin chlainne Gaedheal*, 35–36; Breathnach, *Ár gceól féinig*, 164–66 (5 vv); De Noraidh, *Ceol ón Mumhain*, 37 (2 vv.). **Notes** The Ó Máille's, *Amhráin chlainne Gaedheal*, 35–36, and Breathnach, *Ár gceól féinig*, 164–66, have 5 verses, beginning with our v. 4 and followed by these four (Breathnach):

A.   Ní ar sliabh ná'r mínleach tá stór mo chroidhe-se,
    Ach ar thaltaibh aoibhinn a dtig torthaí ar chrann;
    Bíonn an chuach go haoibhinn ar bharr na craoibhe ann,
    Tá'n chruithneacht maol ann a's an coirce bán.
    Bíonn an fiadh's a laogh ann, tá bric 'n-a sgaoth ann;
    Tá'n eala go haoibhinn ar an loch 's í ag snámh;
    Tá'n mheach lághach chríonna 'n-a nead go díonmhar;
    Tá'n coileach fraoigh ann, an chearc a's a hál.

B.   Is ar sliabh go cinnte tá stór mo chroidhe-se,
    'S ní chodluighmim oidhche, ach ag déanamh bróin;

'Sí cum an síoda í, 'sí méara mín í;
Béal tanaidhe dílis a's meall sí a lán.
Ba bhinne liom uaim í 's na gleanntaibh 's uaigneas
Ná ceileabhar cuaiche 's ná ceól na n-éan;
'S go mb'fhearr liom ón uair sin, dá mbudh liom an stuaidh-bhean,
Ná lámh i n-uachtar ar Chlainne Gaedheal.

C.   Shíl mé, a stóirín, mar bhí tú óg deas,
Go ndéanfá foghluim ar éalódh liom;
'S nach bhfuil tráthnóna ná maidin fóghmhair,
Nach tú'n réalt eólais a bhí ag gabháil rómham.
Ag siubhal na móinte 's na gcoillte clódhmhar,
Ní bheadh orm brón ná duibhthin croidhe;
Ach mé bheith pósta lem' mhíle stóirín,
'S mo lámh bheith bródamhail ar a brollach mín.

D.   'S a riúin 's a chéad-shearc, a bhfuil tú ag éisteacht
Le gach éin-nidh dá bhfuil mé rádh?
'S dá mbeinn mo chléireach chomh maith le Faelean
Ar leath do thréartha ní fhéadfainn trácht.
Bhreoidh tú mo chroidhe 'stig de ló a's d'oidhche —
Ó, a Dhia dhílis, nach cladhartha táim?
Mé bheith i ngrádh le plúr na mban mánla,
'S mo chroidhe dhá rádh liom nach bhfuil maith dhom ann.

A note in the DÓC notebook reads 'Fonn *Lá le Pádraig*. Same air as preceding song (= *One pleasant evening, as pinks and daisies*)[No. **114**]'. De Noraidh gives an air which he noted down from Tadhg Ó Murchú, An Coirreán, Co. Kerry in 1942. Two other copies in CBÉ 737, 78–80, and CBÉ 912, 661–63 (dated 2 July 1943); they are not identical. There is a third copy in an SÓC notebook. A note in CBÉ 912, 661 reads 'Seo seana-amhrán a airíghinn fadó. Níl aon eólas agam i dtaobh cé dhein é ná éinnídh mar gheall air' *['This is an old song that I used to hear long ago. I know nothing about who composed it, nor anything about it'].* The song is entitled *'Sé fáth mo bhuadhartha* in *Amhráin chlainne Gaedheal.* The following explanations of some words were given by Bess herself: 1e *mh'intinn* pronounced *mh'aidhntinn* (i.e. with the vowel sound usually found in the Irish of the Déisi area of Co. Waterford); 2e *clómhair* pronounced *clóvair*; = 'clover'?; 2h *módhmharach* 'gladsome, happy' (BC); cf. *Amhrán Pheaidí Bhig* [No. **9**] (6 (d)) and **133** (F (b)); 3b *abhfad ó láimh* 'from being near' (BC); 3g *beacha críonna* 'working bees' (BC); 4c *ar chraobhachaibh* pronounced *ar chraoíchaibh*; 4d *taoís =túis*; 5h *Cínn* = 'Keane'?

91

Mo theaghlach

1.   Siúd thall thar an eas, mar a bhfásann gach craobh,
An both*á*inín beag aoibhinn do gealadh le h-aol.
Siúd agaibh mo theaghlach, is teaghlach mo ghaol,
Mar a chaithim mo shaol go sásta.

Seinn híra bhá, húra bhá, húgaibh ó hí,
Siúd agaibh an obair d'fhág meidhreach mé im' chroí;
Nuair a sheolaim mo chos chun mo theaghlach beag grinn,
Ar chríochnú ar shaothar mo lae dhom!

2.   Tá maise san áit úd agus breáthacht ró-mhór,
Tá biolar is neóinín is seamróg na dtrí gcluas;
Tá foithin sa gheimhreadh ó ghaoith an taoibh thuaidh —
Sin moladh 'gus tuairisc ar áilneacht!

Seinn híra bhá, húra bhá, húgaibh ó hí,
Siúd agaibh an obair d'fhág meidhreach mé im' chroí;
Nuair a sheolaim mo chos chun mo theaghlach beag grinn,
Ar chríochnú ar shaothar mo lae dhom!

3. Tá nádúr san áit úd agus éanlaith chun ceoil,
    Tá duilliúr is sméara 's an chéirseach 's an smól;
    Tá scáth ann is fuarthan ó bhrothall um neoin,
    Agus Móirín ag crónán don pháiste!

    Seinn híra bhá, húra bhá, húgaibh ó hí,
    Siúd agaibh an obair d'fhág meidhreach mé im' chroí;
    Nuair a sheolaim mo chos chun mo theaglach beag grinn,
    Ar chríochnú ar shaothar mo lae dhom!

Text CBÉ 283, 376–77. **Printed Sources** Breathnach, *Ár gceól féinig*, 58–59 (4 vv.). **Note** This song was composed by the well-known *seanchaí*, Diarmaid 'ac Coitir, of Sliabh Riabhach, Baile Mhúirne. Breathnach, *Ár gceól féinig*, 59, has the following additional verse:

> Guidhim sonas 's ádh ort, 'bhotháinín, gach am
> Mar ar thógas gan gábhtar mór-áireamh dom' chlann
> A gcroidhe 's a nádúr go brách go raibh teann,
> A's aoibhneas choidhche 'nbúr mbláth-shúl!

92

Molly Bawn[2/26]

1. Jimmy went out fowling with his gun in his hand,
    Fowling all day, as you may understand.
    His sweetheart being out walking, he took her for a swan,
    And he shot his Molly Bawn at the setting of the sun.

2. Jimmy went home with his gun in his hand,
    Sad and broken-hearted, as you may understand,
    Saying: 'Father, dearest father, you know what I have done?
    I have shot my Molly Bawn at the setting of the sun'.

3. Then up and spoke his father, although his locks were grey,
    Saying: 'Son, dearest son, do you not think of going away.
    Stay in this country until your trial is on,
    And you never will be hanged for the shooting of a swan'.

4. Molly, dearest Molly, you're my joy and heart's delight,
    And if you had lived, my dear, I'd make of you my bride;
    But now, as you are gone to me, I'll sail away and mourn,
    And soon I will be following you, my own Molly Bawn.

5. It was in three weeks after, to her father she appeared,
    Saying: 'Father, dearest father, don't think to shoot my dear.
    My white apron being around me, he took me for a swan,
    And he shot his Molly Bawn at the setting of the sun'.

Laws O 36   **Recording** JR-GP (24 Nov. 1952).   **Text** From the JR-GP recording.   **Printed Sources** Royal Irish Academy, SR 3 C 38, No. 8 (8 vv.), Haly, Printer, Hanover-Street, Cork; NLI General Coll. (6 vv.); Joyce, *Old Irish folk music and songs*, 220, No. 409 (who cites earlier editions); cf. Baring-Gould, Sheppard & Bussell, *Songs of the West: folk songs of Devon & Cornwall*, 18, 128–29, No. 62 *(At the setting of the sun)*; Sharp & Manson, *Folk-songs of Somerset*, No. 16 [which I've not seen]; this is presumably the same text as in Karpeles, *Cecil Sharp's collection of English folk songs*, 1, 235–36, No. 51 *(Shooting of his Dear)*. See also the fragment in the *JIFSS* 3/3–4 (1905–06) 25; Ó Lochlainn, *Irish street ballads*, 58–59, No. 29; Laws, *American balladry from British broadsides*, 243–44. There are four ballad sheets entitled *Young Molly Bawn* in the Cambridge University Library Coll., vol. 3, 250; vol. 4, 55, 330; vol. 6, 283. [The song of this title in Howe, *Songs of Ireland*, 100–1, is not our song.]   **Notes** The broadside version in the Royal Irish Academy, SR 3 C 38, No. 8, printed by Haly of Cork, has 8 verses, the last four being very similar to the text in our version. The first 4 verses in the broadside read as follows:

> A.   A story, a story, to you I will relate,
>   Of a young female, whose fortune was great,
>   She walked out one evening, she walked all alone,
>   And she stopped under a bower a shower to shun.

> B.   Young jemmy being coming with a gun in his hand,
>   He was fowling all day, until the evening came on
>   Her apron being about her, he took her for a swan,
>   But alas, to his grief, it was his own Molly Bawn.

> C.   Come all you young heroes that handle the gun,
>   Beware of late shooting when evening comes on,
>   Her apron was about her, he took her for a swan,
>   But alas, for my grief it was fair Molly Bawn.

> D.   When he came near her, and found it was she,
>   His limbs grew feeble, and his eyes could not see:
>   He took her in his arms, and found she was dead,
>   And a fountain of tears from his eyes down he shed.

The NLI broadside text has the above v. C as opening verse, followed by these 5:

> E.   He ran to his uncle with the gun in his hand
>   Saying Uncle, dear Uncle I am not able to stand.
>   I've a story to tell you which happened of late
>   I have [shot?] lovely Molly Bawn and her beauty was great.

> F.   Up comes his father and his locks they were gray
>   Stay in your own country and don't run away,
>   Stay in your country till your trial comes on
>   And I'll see you free by the laws of the land.

> G.   My curse on you TOBY that lent me your gun
>   To go a state shooting by the setting of the sun,
>   I robbed her fair temples and found she was dead
>   A fountain of tears for my Molly I shed.

> H.   I shot my own true lover — alas! I'm undone
>   While she was in the shade by the setting of the sun
>   Ah, if I thought she was there I'd caress her tenderly,
>   And soon I'd get marr[i]ed to my own dear Molly.

> I.   Young women don't be jesting when your lover is sincere,
>   For if you do they can't love you or e'er as you care,
>   You'll know by a young man's conduct, when he's gentle and bland
>   [T]hat he'll give you his heart and also hi[s] hand.

This last verse appears to bear no relation to the ones preceding it. The English version is significantly different from the Irish *Molly Bawn*, though the underlying story is clearly the same. For example, one verse in the version recorded by Cecil Sharp in his *Folk-songs from Somerset* (No. 16), and reported by Baring-Gould et al., reads:

> In six weeks' time when the 'sizes came on,
> Young Polly appeared in the form of a swan,
> Crying Jimmy, young Jimmy, young Jimmy is clear,
> He never shall be hung for the shooting of his dear.

[This is apparently the same text as in Karpeles, *Cecil Sharp's collection of English folk songs*, 1, 235, where the above verse is v. 5]. The version in Joyce's *Old Irish folk music and songs*, 220, has been touched up by someone with literary pretensions. For discussion, see Hugh Shields, 'Some songs and ballads in use in the province of Ulster … 1845', *Ulster Folklife* 17 (1971) 3–24. Palmer, *Everyman book of British ballads*, 55–56 No. 21 has a version from the Donegal singer Packie Byrne, and refers to his *Songs of a Donegal Man*, Topic 12TS257 (London 1975) [Our song is not to be confused with another of the same title composed by Samuel Lover].

(A) Jim-my went out fowl-ing with his gun in his hand,
(A) fow-ling all day, as you ___ may ___ un-der-stand.
His sweet-heart being out walk-ing, he___ took her for a swan,
And he shot his Moll-y Bawn ___ at the set-ting of the sun.

93

Mount Massey, the flower of Macroom

1. How I long to remember those bright days of yore,
    So sweetly by pleasures beguiled,
    And the friends that frequented my old cabin home,
    And the comrades I loved when a child!
    Oft I fancied I roamed by Mount Massey's green groves,
    Or poached by the light of the moon,
    Where the lark sang aloud 'neath that golden-fringed cloud,
    In Mount Massey, the flower of Macroom.

    So friends, come with me, and it's there you will see
    The apples and cherries in bloom;
    For it's you I'll invite where I first saw the light
    In that sweet sunny spot called Macroom.

2. In the sweet summer time, when the heather was fine,
    What fun there would be at the gate!
    When the gadget would ring out, the dancers to please,
    And the lovers their love-tales relate!
    How the colleens would smile, as they'd sit on the stile
    That's facing Mount Massey's demesne,

And their lovers so fair by their side standing there,
While the gadget its sweet notes would strain!

So friends, come with me, and it's there you will see
The apples and cherries in bloom;
For it's you I'll invite where I first saw the light,
In that sweet sunny spot called Macroom.

3.   Oft I danced on the green with my blue-eyed colleen,
As handsome a lass as stood there;
And I as light-hearted as any young lad,
I then knew no sorrow or care.
When the dancing was o'er we went straight through the groves,
Each lad with his lassie in bloom.
That spot of my birth — there's none sweeter on earth —
Than Mount Massey, the flower of Macroom.

So friends, come with me, and it's there you will see
The apples and cherries in bloom;
For it's you I'll invite where I first saw the light
In that sweet sunny spot called Macroom.

4.   So now I must roam far away from my home
And sail o'er the wide raging sea;
And leave friends behind that were loving and kind,
And that colleen that dearly loves me.
So farewell to the groves where so often I roamed
And plucked the sweet violets in bloom!
And I hope once again for to see that demesne
In Mount Massey, the flower of Macroom.

So friends, come with me, and it's there you will see
The apples and cherries in bloom;
For it's you I'll invite where I first saw the light
In that sweet sunny spot called Macroom.

Text From Bess's handwritten collection of songs.   **Printed Sources** Healy, *Ballads from an Irish fireside*, 21–22, No.10 (3 vv., no source given).   **Notes** This song was composed by Tom Kelleher, of Masseytown, Macroom. I have seen another version in an undated copy of *Ireland's Own* — 'the bane of every folklore collector's life', in the words of Séamus Ó Catháin, *The bedside book of Irish folklore* (Cork 1980) 11; it differs in places, and lacks our v. 3.

94

Mrs Mulligan, the pride of the Coombe

1.   I'm a thumping fine widow, I live in a spot
In Dublin, they call it the Coombe.
My shop and my stall are both out on the street,

And my palace consists of one room.
At Patrick St Corner, for forty-six years,
I've stood there — I'm telling no lie —
And while I stood there nobody would dare
To say black was the white of my eye.

You may travel from Clare to the County Kildare,
From Drogheda right up to Macroom;
And where would you see a fine widow like me? —
Mrs Mulligan, the Pride of the Coombe.

2.   I sell apples and oranges, nuts and split peas,
Bananas and sugar-stick sweet.
I sell second-hand clothes on a Saturday night,
And my stall's on the floor of the street.
I sell fish on a Friday, laid out on a board,
Cod fish and some beautiful ray;
I sell mackerel and herrings — o! herrings so sweet! —
That once lived in dear Dublin Bay.

You may travel from Clare to the County Kildare,
From Drogheda right up to Macroom;
And where would you see a fine widow like me? —
Mrs Mulligan, the Pride of the Coombe.

3.   I have a son, Mick, who plays on the fife,
He belongs to the Longford St Band.
It would do your heart good to see him march out
When the band goes to Dolly Mount strand.
In the Park on a Sunday I cut quite a dash,
All the neighbours look on in surprise
At my new Paisley shawl and my bonnet so tall,
Sure I'd dazzle the sight of your eyes!

You may travel from Clare to the County Kildare,
From Drogheda right up to Macroom.
And where would you see a fine widow like me? —
Mrs Mulligan, the Pride of the Coombe.

Text From Bess's handwritten collection of songs; another in a DÓC notebook (also written by Bess). **Printed Sources**
Dublin Academy of Music pamphlet; Ó Lochlainn, *Irish street ballads*, 230–31. See Ward's *Collection of Irish comic songs*, 43–44 *Biddy Mulligan, the Pride of the Coombe* (identical text); *Walton's new treasury of Irish songs and ballads*, 2, 23 (different arrangement).
Notes The song was supposedly written and composed by Seamus Kavanagh, but for reservations concerning such attributions, see Tom Munnelly, *Mount Callan Garland*, 121.

1st Mairisheen went to Bonane.

Good people I crave your attention
I'll sing you a verse of a song
And indeed it is not my intention
To keep you a-waiting too long
You know since that game went against me
I never can sleep until dawn
My spirits completely have left me
Since Mairisheen went to Bonane.

2nd

For a long time we both were acquainted
Exactly the space was two years
I took up the matter quite easy
Thinking that there was no fear
But suspecting that it was a schemer
That wanted my favours withdrawn
So to rack + to whack + to tease me
She got this young swain from Bonane.

3rd

Tis many an evening I rambled
And facing the West I was prone
To see me both racing + prancing
Tho very much wanted at home
Tis many the garden I trampled

'Muirisheen went to Bonane' written by Bess Cronin (private Collection).

95

Muirisheen went to Bonane

1. Good people I crave your attention;
   I'll sing you a verse of a song.
   And indeed it is not my intention
   To keep you a-waiting too long.
   You know since that game went against me
   I never can sleep until dawn;
   My spirits completely have left me,
   Since Muirisheen went to Bonane.

2. For a long time we both were acquainted;
   Exactly the space was two years.
   I took up the matter quite easy,
   Thinking that there was no fear.
   But suspecting that I was a schemer
   That wanted my favours withdrawn,
   So to sack and to whack and to tease me
   She got this young swain from Bonane.

3. 'Tis many an evening I rambled
   And facing the west I was prone
   To see me both racing and prancing,
   Though very much wanted at home.
   'Tis many the garden I trampled
   And the fences I knocked on Deasmawn,
   But I'll give up my p'laver with Yankees,
   Since Muirisheen went to Bonane.

4. How often in deep conversation
   Our language was plain and discreet!
   I was building on a sandy foundation
   That soon slipped away from my feet.
   For knowing that some drops I was taking,
   And oftentimes staying out till dawn,
   She packed up her boxes quite hasty
   And went for a freke to Bonane.

5. 'Tis often I drank with her father
   Full many a saucepan of beer
   Each fair-day in Kenmare and Kilgarvan —
   Sure nothing could part us, my dear!
   He used to be praising his daughters
   And saying they were handsome and calm.
   But how queer and severe it comes after,
   When Muirisheen went to Bonane!

6. So now that she's gone to forsake us
    And has run this big race in full speed;
    And because we were always good neighbours
    I hope this young dame will succeed.
    For Nancy and the Yankee were decent —
    'Tis often they stayed up till dawn —
    Sure it was in a fit of vexation
    That Muirisheen went to Bonane.

Text From Bess's handwritten collection of songs.   **Notes** Composed by Johnny Nóra Aodha [= Seán Ó Tuama], of Killgarvan (c. 1886–1928). For another of his songs see *The Tailor Bawn* [No. **177**]. There is a private recording of this song, sung by Dan Cronin, Bess's eldest son, made by Máire Mulligan (Ní Chróinín), c. 1980. For other copies, noted down by Seán Ó Cróinín, see CBÉ 1591, 355–57 (Cork 1960); CBÉ 1682, 503 [1 v.] (Cork 1964). I have heard the late Micho Russell, of Doolin, Co. Clare, singing the song, which was learned by him from Séamus Mac Mathúna, who in turn recorded it from Pádraig Ó Tuama (Peaití Thaidhg Pheig) of Coolea. In line 4h *freke* = Irish *fréic* (English 'freak'); cf. also *True Friends and Relations* [No. **189**] (3 (g)). A handwritten scrap in Bess's own collection of songs may be part of this song:

> There was one from a chap that's convenient,
> And one from our neat tailor bawn;
> Sure, that sent her prancing and dancing
> And hastened her back to Bonane!

96

Mullach na ré

1. A bhfeacabhair-se a dhaoine an tine le h-aoirde
       bhí ar thitim na h-oíche i Mullach na ré?
    B'é cruach Dhónail Uí Ríordáin bhí go taiscithe líonmhar
       i dtosach an gheimhridh roim shneachta nó gaoth.

2. Tá an Inid gan mhoill ann is d'oirfeadh bean tí dho,
       níl tine ná gríosach a bheireóchadh an tae;
    Sé dúirt Dónal Ó Cuill — is maith an fear críche é —
       go dtabharfadh crib líonta is go ndéanfadh sé déirc.

3. 'Peaid Buí, is fear ceóil é, is glaoidh chun tigh an óil é;
       tabhair gloine nó dhó dho is cuardóidh sé é'.
    Is i dtosach an tráthnóinín dúirt duine des na comharsain
       gur ghaibh Dónal Eoghain síos treasna na ré.

4. Tá capall mear groí aige go mbéarfar a mhuíng de,
       is insint go cruinn díbh go raibh sé san aos;
    Mar gur b'é Seán Ó Cuill do casadh sa tslí air,
       bhí meaisín is cíor aige — is ceárdaí glan é!

5. 'Sé dúirt Máire Charthaigh go raghadh sí thar sáile
       go bhfuil sí trí ráithe is ná pósfadh sí é;
    Beidh síneadh gan sásamh — is ní bagairt ar mhnáibh é —
       mar ní bheadh aige páiste i gcaitheamh a shaoil.

6.   An *sergeant* 's a *peeler* ná déanfadh aoinní dho,
        an sagart á ínsint i bhforas don tsaol;
       Is más fíor iad mo dhánta go bhfuil air aon mháchail
        ná feicim go bráth tu i bpobal Chúil Ao!

English Summary A local song, about a rick of turf that went up in flames. A mock match-making is discussed and local personalities gently lampooned.   **Text** From CBÉ 737, 82–83; another text in DÓC's loose-leaf notes.   **Notes** There is another local text, noted down from Conchubhar Ó Buachalla, in CBÉ 1542, 331–32.

97

My father and mother are minding sheep

Notes Title only from one of Bess's song-lists. Tom Munnelly suggests tentatively that it might be the song known as *One evening as Johnny.*

98

My name is Bold Hewson the Cobbler

1.   My name is Bold Hewson the Cobbler
     And many's the good pair I have made.
     I'll pack up my ends and my awls
     And go home back again to my trade.

     With my wax-fol-dally-fol-dally
     With my wax-fol-dally-fol-dee
     With my rubby-dub-dubby-dub-dubby
     With my rubby-dub-dubby-dub-dee.

2.   I put up a side-piece for Miss Fanny
     Expecting to keep out the drop.
     If I'd be piecing and patching forever
     'Twould leak in the very same spot.

Text From Seamus Ennis's CBÉ transcription (Sept. 1946); another text in a notebook of DÓC's (dated 23 July 1949), where a note states that Bess learned it from 'Peaidí Thomáis' (presumably a neighbour of hers).   **Printed Sources** Chappell, *The ballad literature and popular music of the olden time*, 450–51.   **Notes** In his *Ballad literature … of the olden time*, Chappell reads 'This is one of the tunes introduced in the ballad-operas, *The Jovial Crew*, and *The Grub Street Opera*, both printed in 1731. *The Jovial Crew* of 1731 was an alteration of Richard Brome's comedy of the same name. The words of the song have not been recovered; but there appears little doubt of their having been a political squib upon Colonel Hewson, who was one of Charles the First's judges, and of those who signed his death-warrant. John Hewson was originally a cobbler, and had but one eye. He took up arms on the side of the Parliament, and being a man of courage and resolution, soon rose to be a colonel in their army. He was knighted by Cromwell, and afterwards made one of his Lords. He quitted England immediately before the Restoration, and died at Amsterdam in 1662.' Chappell quotes from two songs, *A hymn to the gentle craft; or Hewson's lamentation*, and *The cobbler's last will and testament; Or the Lord Hewson's Translation*. He then gives the first line 'My name is Old Hewson the Cobbler' with tune. This song is probably identical with the one in Bess's song-lists entitled *To me wax fol dally fol de*. It is perhaps best-known under the title *Dick Darby, the Cobbler*, popularised by Tommy Makem and the Clancy Brothers. See also the song called *Dick Darlin*, in *Wehman's 617 Irish songs* (New York, n. d., but c. 1900) 43. The song is in one of Bess's lists as *My name is bold Hughson the Cobbler.*

99

My true love's face is as bright

Notes Title only from one of Bess's song-lists. Tom Munnelly writes: 'Perhaps from the English-language version of *An Droighneán Donn*. On the other hand, it could be anything!' Alternatively, it could perhaps be the song called *The Cailín Deas* ("My true love's eyes are as bright") published in *JIFSS* 19 (Dec. 1922) 44–45:

> My true love's eyes are as clear and bright
> As the sky on a summer's day.
> Her golden locks and flaxen curls
> O'er her neck and shoulders gay.
> No land nor title does she own,
> She's a simple Irish lass;
> She was born near the walls of Garryowen,
> And they call her the Cailín Deas.
>
> There are maidens fair by the Shannon's side,
> And more by the Suir and Nore,
> Like pretty little shamrocks smiling all around
> Old Erin's lovely shore.
> But tripping o'er the mountains here.
> On a Sunday going to mass,
> The prettiest little girl amongst them all
> Is my own dear Cailín Deas.
>
> Of the green hill side where the rebels died
> And our Sires went fown to rest,
> Of Ninety Eight when our pikes sank deep
> In the Saxon foeman's breast,
> She'd love to hear of those gallant bands
> That fought in the mountain pass
> Each love-borne bride to adorn the heart
> Of my loved Cailín Deas.
>
> My true love's eyes have an angel form
> And dear was her love to me,
> She often told me to watch and wait
> And Old Ireland would be free.
> She told me watch and wait awhile
> And that day would come to pass.
> I wish to God every Irish girl
> Had a heart like the Cailín Deas.

See No. **113** below.

100

Na Conairigh

1.   A chúthaigh mhallaithe — ár is eascaine ort agus gráin Mhic Dé!
   Agus ar an ngasra dhíot ceangailthe go dlúth led' thaobh!
   Do dhearbhaigh i láthair Sasanaigh ar a' dtriúr i mbréig,
   'S do chuir na farairí thar na farraigí go dtísna *New South Wales*.

2.   An té bheadh 'na sheasamh is do dhéanfadh machnamh ar a' gcúis dá plé,
   Gur sheasaimh sí óna seacht ar maidin go dtí tar éis a naoi.

Le neart a ndearbhaithe gur chrith a' talamh a's iad thabhairt i mbréig,
Is mo thrua-sa an t-anam bocht, mar tá sé damanta, más fíor don chléir.

3.   Tá'n chroch 'na seasamh is an chnáib dá casadh dhúinn le bliain roim-ré.
Gur i ndiaidh na ndearbhaithe éist i gan fhios dúinn an dream gan séan.
Mar a bheadh feabhas ár gcaraid bhí ár muineál casta go doimhin san aol;
Chun gur casadh sinn chun ár dtéarma chaitheamh insna *New South Wales*.

4.   Tá casóg ghairid ghlas déanta ó mhaidin dúinn agus triús dá réir;
Culaith mhaith farraige, rud nár thaithíomair 'nár ndúthaigh féin.
Le linn an Aifrinn beidh na sagairt a' guí chun Dé
Sinn a theacht abhaile chun an eaglais ósna *New South Wales*.

5.   A Rí na n-Aingeal is a Mhuire Bheannaithe nach dubhach ár scéal!
An bhean do bheathaigh sinn is do thál bainne orainn bheith go dubhach 'ár ndéidh!
An téarma fada so go mbeidh sé caithte againn i mbliain a naoi;
Is go mbeidh orainn teacht abhaile ósna *New South Wales*.

English Summary The song curses the people who gave false witness against the Connery brothers, indicted and condemned to exile in New South Wales. **Text** From Seamus Ennis's CBÉ copybook transcript of Bess songs (Sept. 1946); another version in CBÉ 737, 72–74. The two are more-or-less identical. **Printed Sources** *Proceedings of the Oireachtas 1899*, 163–64 (5 vv.); Breathnach, *Ár gceól féinig.*, 144–45 (4 vv.); Ní Annagáin & De Chlanndiolún, *Londubh an chairn*, No. 33 (8 vv); Ó Baoill & Ó Baoill, *Ceolta Gael*, 36. **Notes** This song celebrates the dramatic events surrounding the trial and conviction of three Waterford brothers, John, Seamus, and Patrick Connery, who were sentenced to be transported to Australia. John Connery was tried in 1834 on separate charges of murder and manslaughter on the same day, but managed to escape conviction on both counts. His two brothers, convicted at another trial on a separate charge, made a spectacular escape from jail and were on the run for almost eight months, before being recaptured on 27 March 1838. They were transported on 8 September of that year and spent the rest of their lives in Australia. It should be noted, however, that this is not the best-known version of the song. The version published in the Oireachtas *Proceedings* of 1899 was recorded from Timothy Scannell (Tadhg Ó Scanaill) of Tureenglanahee, Kingwilliamstown, Co. Cork; a note attached to the title states that the song was composed in 1799. For an account of the trio, see Tomás de Bhaldraithe, 'Na Connerys', in Seamus Grimes & Gearóid Ó Tuathaigh (eds), *The Irish-Australian connection/An Caidreamh Gael-Astrálach* (Worcester 1989) 25–42; see also Diarmuid Ó Gráda, 'Na Connerys', *Comhar* 44/3 (Márta 1985) 22–25, and Breandán Mac Giolla Choille, 'Na Connerys sa bhaile', *Comhar* 44/4 (Aibreán 1985) 20–21. There is a full-length account in Brendan Kiely, *The Connerys: the origins of a Waterford legend* (Dungarvan 1989). Some of the readings in Scannell's version are preferable to those given by Ennis, e.g. 1c *i láthair Sasanaigh* (BC) vs *i láthair Sasanach*; 3b *Gur i ndiaidh na ndearbhaithe éist* (BC) vs. *Go ndeaghaidh na dearbhuighthe isteach*; 3b *ag an dream* vs. *an dream* (BC); 3c *Mar a bheadh feabhas ár gcaraid* (BC) vs. *Mura mbeadh feabhas ár gcarad*; 5a *nach dubhach* (BC) vs *nach truaighe*. The texts in Breathnach, *Ár gceól féinig*, 144–45, and Ní Annagáin & De Chlanndiolún, *Londubh an chairn*, are better again, preserving as they do the correct forms of the names (Comyn, the Connerys, etc.); Ní Annagáin & De Chlanndiolún, however, omit our v. 2, while Breathnach has run together parts of our vv. 3 and 4.

101

Na gleannta^{1/19}

1.   Tá gleanntáinín aoibhinn 'dir Laoi theas agus Banndan
Is do riug sé an barra aoibhneas ó choillthibh na mball so.
Do gheofaí adhmad chun tí ann dá aoirde bheadh ceann air,
'Dir shlata agus bíoma do bheadh fuíollach i gcrann de.

2.   Is tá gleann i Magh Chromtha is níor labhramair fós air,
Go mbíonn úird ann Dé Domhnaigh agus foghlaim ón Róimh ann.
Bíonn an breac geal ar scabhat ann, bíonn a' seabhac ann 's a' smóilín.
Bíonn a' míol buí cois na habhann ann le fonn um thráthnóna.

3. Is tá gleann in Íbh Laoire, Guagán Naofa an aoibhnis;
   Bíonn na haingil go léir ann, Barra Naofa dá gcoínleacht.
   Tá ínse fhada ghléigeal a' fás taobh le loch an aon-chnis
   Is an té go mbíonn an phéin air faigheann faoiseamh ó Íosa.

4. Bíonn a' ghealach ann, bíonn an ghrian ann, bíonn Dia ann 's a Mháthair,
   Bíonn an dá Aspal déag ann a' riarú na Páise.
   Bíonn na haingil 'na ndiaidh ann cé gur ró-mhór é a ngá leo,
   Agus trócaire ó Dhia dúinn nuair a thriallfam 'na láthair.

English Summary These are verses which were sung extempore by guests at a wedding, each in praise of his own locality. **Recording** BBC 19026 (21 Sept. 1952). **Text** From the BBC recording. I have also used the manuscript of Ballyvourney songs collected by Caitlín Ní Bhuachalla, dated 1943. **Printed Sources** Ó Foghludha [= Feargus Finnbéil], *Banba* (Nollaig 1902) 103; Laoide, *An cúigeadh leabhar*, 20–21. **Notes** The text published in *Banba* is a fuller and more accurate version of this song; Ó Foghludha explains that the verses were sung extempore by guests at a wedding, each in praise of his own locality; hence there were limitless opportunities for adding new verses. See also NUI, Galway, James Hardiman Library, Douglas Hyde MS. 49, 64–65, No. 55 *Guagán Barra* (from Dónal Ó hUallacháin, Guagán Barra). This version from Diarmuid Ó Foghludha, in *Banba* (Nollaig 1902) 103:

1. Tá gleann ag an Múrach ar chúlaibh Chnoic Bréandain
   Go mbíonn a chuid éisg ann i gcumhangroch fé chúl leacaibh daora.
   Bíonn a shioraigh ag súgradh 's-a bhuaibh bána ag géimrigh
   Is fíon agus lionn ann ag plúr na bhfear léigheanta.

2. Ta gleann ag an hÓrach isé is cóir dhuinn a mholadh,
   Is ní h-é an gleann so Ó Domhnaill cé gur mór iad a thortha.
   Bíonn airgead is ór ann, is fóireann sé ar bhochtaibh,
   Bíonn laoigh ag buaibh óga ann ar an bhfeorthain cois locha.

3. Tá gleann ag an mBrianach go mbíonn Dia ann 's a Mháthair,
   'S an dá Aspal déag ann ag déanamh na Cásga.
   Bíonn na haingil n-a ndiaidh ann 's is dian bhreágh é a gcáile,
   'S an trócaire ó Dhia dho'n té a thriallfadh chun a fhághaltha.

4. Tá gleann ag an Ríseach 'dir Laoi theas is Bannduin
   Go bhfuil adhmad chun tighe ann is fuighleach i gcrann de.
   'Dir lochda agus bhíoma is dá aoirde bheadh an ceann air,
   Is do sgiob sé an barr tímcheall ó choillthibh na ngleannta.

5. Tá gleann i Mághchromdha nár labhramair fós air,
   Go bhfuil úird ann gach Domhnach ag fir foghlumanta óga.
   An míol buidhe fé sgout ann, breac, seabhac agus smólach,
   Is gur thug sé an barr foghlum' ó gleanntaibh Chláir Fodhla.

6. Tá gleann annso i nInnse gur b'aoibhinn bheith sa tsamhradh ann,
   Go mbíonn an chuach i mbarr craoibhe ann, an coinín 's an ramhar-bhreac[.]
   Bíonn an lacha 's an faoilean sa taoide gach am ann,
   Is na luingeas dá aoirde ag teacht le fíon agus brannda ann.

The version in NUI, Galway, Douglas Hyde MS. 49, 64–65, has the verses in the order 1, a, b, 2, 3, 4, with the following two verses after v. 1:

a. Tá gleann ag an Major a's is féidir é mholadh;
   Tá tighthe breaghtha glégeala déanta d'aol is de chloich ann;
   An nóinín breagh craorach 'sa bhféar ann go glúineach,
   Agus ceol binn na n-éan ann gach aon mhaidin drúchta.

b. Níl caora maidin drúchta ná go mbíonn cúpla aici théinig
   Ná bó maidin shamhraidh gan ghamhain agus laogh aici;
   An searrach ag an láir is í ag tál ar a laoch mear,
   Níl abhall fiadhain gan ubhall ann ná cárthain gan chaora.

The Ballyvourney collection made by Caitlín Ní Bhuachalla has the same two additional verses in the same order. The version in Laoide, *An cúigeadh leabhar*, 20–21, entitled *Duthaigh bhreagh an Phaoraigh*, has 7 verses. (v. 5 is the same as our v. 4):

A. Cois na Leamhna mar a ghnáthuigheann ba, caoirigh agus gamhna,
Caisí boga uachtair agus mór-chuid de leamhnacht;
Ó's trom na slaoda, agus féar glas go glúinibh;
Agus ceól binn bhreagh ag éanaibh gach aon mhaidin drúchta.

B. Ní'l caora maidin, etc.

Note that the air is the same as that for *Amhrán an tSagairt* [No. **8**].

102

Ní thaithneann liom fear a bhíonn sásta

1. Ní thaitneann liom fear a bhíonn sásta,
  is ná h-athróchadh stád a mheon;
Ach a ghean ar ar chleachtaigh 'na pháiste,
  is ná feadair sé fáth a sceoil.
Dob' ait liom-sa fanúint mar fhásas,
  gan taisteal go h-áitreamh nua,
Óir cá fios do neoch ná go mb'fhearr leis
  an baile nár ghnáthaigh fós?

2. Ní maith liom ar fhear bheith ag cásamh,
  go mairgeach tráth na sógh,
An aicme bhí i mBanba Phádraig,
  's an t-aiteas fuair bás fadó.
Ba sheasc liom dá bhfanfadh gach ársacht,
  is go mairfeadh sean-ghnás go deo;

        Óir cá fios do neoch ná go mb'fhearr leis
          an cleas úd nár dhearna fós?

3.   Ní abraim leat ná go mb'fhearr liom
        seana-chara nó cairdeas nua;
    Óir tagann an caidreamh le h-ársacht,
        fíor-ghlan mar bhiotáile cóir.
    Ach cad fá go gcaithfinn bheith dána
        im' sheachaint ar chairdeas nua,
    Óir cá fios do neoch ná go mb'fhearr leis
        an cara nár ghrádhaigh sé fós?

4.   An garsún nuair thagann an grá air,
        is ainnis a chás gan 'gó;
    Mar a mheasann ná maireann de mhnáibh ann
        aon bhean mar a mhánlacht seoid.
    Ach an fhaid is tá an talamh so lán díobh,
        'gus gearra-chuid breá go leor,
    Uch! cá fios don aimid nár bh'fhearr leis
        an cailín nár ghrádhaigh sé fós?

English Summary The poet deplores the idea of staying in a rut, carrying on with old ways, when there are new experiences to be had. He likewise disapproves of any man tying himself down with his first love, without having tried other women!
Text CBÉ 283, 378–79.

103

Nice little Jenny from Ballinasloe[2/23]

1.   You lads that are funny and call maids your honey,
    Give ear for a moment, 'twill not keep you long:
    I'm wounded by Cupid — he has made me stupid —
    I'll tell you the truth, now, my brain's nearly wrong;
    For a nice little posie, who's really quite cosy
    Has kept me unable to walk to and fro.
    Each day I'm declining, in love I'm repining,
    For nice little Jenny from Ballinasloe.

2.   It being in September, I'll ever remember,
    I went out to walk by a clear river-side
    For sweet recreation, and to my vexation,
    This wonder of Nature I quickly espied.
    I stood for to view her an hour, I'm sure,
    The earth couldn't show such a damsel, I know;
    As that little girl — the pride of the world —
    My nice little Jenny from Ballinasloe.

3.   I said to her: 'Darling, this is a fine morning,
    The birds sing enchanting, it charms the groves;
    Their hearts do delight me, but you do invite me
    Along this kind water, 'tis time for to roam.
    Your beauty has won me and surely undone me,
    If you'll not agree for to cure my sad woe;
    So great is my sorrow, I'll ne'er see tomorrow,
    My nice little Jenny from Ballinasloe'.

4.   'Sir, I did not invite you, nor yet dare not slight you,
    You're at your own option to act as you please.
    I am not ambitious, nor e'er efficacious,
    I'm never inclined to disdain nor to tease.
    I like conversation, likewise recreation,
    I'm free with a friend and I'm cold with a foe;
    But virtue's my glory — will be till I'm hoary' —
    Said nice little Jenny from Ballinasloe.

5.   'Sir, yonder's my lover, if he should discover,
    Or ever take notice you've spoken to me,
    He'd close your existence, in spite of resistance,
    Be pleased to withdraw, then, lest he you might see.
    You see he's approaching, then don't be encroaching,
    He has his large dog and his gun there also;
    And although you're a stranger, I'd wish you from danger',
    Said nice little Jenny from Ballinasloe.

6.   I bowed then genteely, and thanked her quite freely,
    I bade her adieu and took to the road.
    So great was my trouble, my pace I had doubled,
    My heart was oppressed and sank down by the load.
    Wherever I'll mourn for beauteous Jane Curran,
    And I'll ramble about in affliction and woe;
    And I'll think on the hour I saw that sweet flower,
    My nice little Jenny from Ballinasloe.

Recordings BBC 19025 (8 Sept. 1952) = Kennedy, *Folktracks* F–60–160 (1981) — B12 JR-GP ER 4 (24 Nov. 1952). **Text** From the JR-GP recording. **Printed Sources** Sparling, *Irish minstrelsy*, 243–45 (7 vv. 'from a Waterford chap-book of 1835'); Ó Lochlainn, *More Irish street ballads*, 182–83 + 193, No. 92 (7 vv.) [from Sparling's *Irish minstrelsy*]; Healy, *Ballads from an Irish fireside*, 65–66, No. 40 (no source given, but probably taken from Sparling). **Notes** The air is the same as that for *Sweet Killydysart* [No. **141**]. Ó Lochlainn stated that he had not seen the song in print elsewhere. The version in Sparling's *Irish minstrelsy*, 243–45, is identical with ours, save that it has the following additional verse after our v. 4:

A.   'Most lovely of creatures! your beautiful features
    Have sorely attracted and captured my heart;
    If you won't relieve me, in truth you may believe me,
    Bewildered in sorrow till death I must smart;
    I'm at your election, so grant me protection,
    And feel for a creature that's tortured in woe;
    One smile it will heal me; one frown it will kill me;
    Sweet nice little Jenny from Ballinasloe!'

You lads that are fun-ny and call maids your ho-ney

Give ear for a mo-ment, 'twill not keep you long

I'm woun-ded by cu-pid, he has made me stu-pid

I'll tell you the truth, now, my brain's near-ly wrong

For a nice litt-le po-sie, who's real-ly quite co-sy

Has kept me un-ab-le to walk to and fro

Each day I'm de-cli-ning, in love I'm re-pin-ning

For nice litt-le Je-nny from Bal-li-na-sloe

104

Níl mo shláinte ar fónamh[1/1]

1.   Níl mo shláinte ar fónamh ó scaras leis an ól so,
      Tá casachtach agus ceo agus achrann mór im' chroí.
      Gurb é deirid na mná óga gur chúngaigh suas mo scórnach,
      Is ná seinfinn port ná ceol dóibh go rinncfidís dom ríl.
      Ach éirigh-se go ro-mhaith is cuir-se dhíot a' bóthar,
      A's ná hinnis páirt dod' ghnó dá maireann beo 'ed bhuín.
      Beidh a' coc 's a tiarsa romhat ann a's gloiní líonta ar bord ann,
      Is dá gcuirtí fút a' córda go gcaithfeá briseadh tríd.

2. Agus cuir-se uait na feánna agus éirigh go dtí an bráthair,
    Tógfaidh sé ar láimh tu agus stopfaidh sé thu ar ól.
    Tabarfaidh duit-se coráiste chun scarúint leis an áirseoir,
    Mar is minic leat é páirteach nó in éineacht leat sa ród.
    Tánn tú anois id' stráire, níl ór agat ná pláta,
    Níl bean agat ná páiste ach do phíopaí lán de cheol.
    Agus tiocfaidh, airiú, an bás ort i lúib a' chlaí nó i mbearnainn
    Agus beidh t'anam-sa go brách in Ifreann 'á dhó.

3. A's tá mo chroí chomh dubh le háirne nó le gual a buailfí i gceartain
    Ó airíos iad á rá go raibh Ifreann am' chóir.
    An sagart, an bráthair, an t-easpag a's an Pápa,
    Ní thógfaidís mo pháirt-se dá leanfainn-se dom' ól;
    Ach a' *landlady*, 'sí chráigh me nuair a thug sí an leabhar im' láthair
    Go n-ólfainn féin a sláinte is go suífinn síos go fóill.
    D'fhanas ar a' stáid sin go maidean lárnamháireach,
    Mo mheidilí a's mo chártaí gur fhágas-sa fén mbord.

4. Agus stadfad feasta 'em dhántaibh, ní dhéanfad a thuilleadh a rá libh,
    Ach go bhfuil Clanna Gael gan fálthas is gurb amhla' bheidh go fóill.
    Mar táid amuigh faoi'n mbáistigh a' grafadh agus a' tárlamh,
    Sagairt agus bráithre, reamhar-chuirp ag feoil.
    Dá n-oirfeadh ola bháis duit ní chuirfidís í ort láithreach
    Gan airgead nó pláta nó braonacha le n-ól.
    Ifreann tá lán díobh, idir shagairt agus bráthair,
    Is lucht meidilí agus cártaí anairde as a gcómhair.

English Summary The poet complains about having been driven to give up drinking by the clergy. He was successful for a while, but the landlady of a hostelry persuaded him to drink her health, and he relapsed into his old ways! He finishes with a blast against the clergy. **Recordings** CBÉ 379 (Aug. 1947) — CBÉ 419 (test recording, Aug. 1947) — BBC 11988 (7 Aug. 1947) — BBC 18760 (29 Aug. 1952) — Kennedy, *Folktracks* F–60–160 (1981) A9. **Text** From BBC 11988; there is another in DÓC's notes. A third text is in CBÉ 737, 80–82. There is a copy also in Seamus Ennis's CBÉ copybooks (Sept. 1946). The BBC 1947 version is fuller, with vv. 2, 3 and an introduction (in English); cf. CBÉ 1595, 71–72 (Cork 1961). **Notes** The song was composed by Pead Buí Ó Luínse, concerning whom Seamus Ennis has the following in his CBÉ copybook notes 'Amhrán Pheaid Buí — Composed by Pead Buí Ó Loínse. Born in Ballyvourney and buried 45 years now; was a "character" locally; had cures — being born on Good Friday and baptised on Easter Sunday. A dark, thickly made man, wore a black felt hat at all times; a gifted singer and composer; lived to an old age — not known, but said to be about 80; charmed all Mrs. Cronin's teeth when she was a young girl, so that she never suffered from tooth-ache until three days after his death; was really "a bad case for drink"; a piper and fifer; used play coming along the road to a house to advertise his arrival & collect a crowd for a dance in that house; had some "misunderstanding" with the local clergy a propos of taking the pledge & composed the following. "Had kind o' *cat-shúil*-s, you know, but he wasn't blind". — Mrs Cronin (1946)'. For further biographical information, see Pádraig Ó Tuathaigh, *Filí an tSuláin*, 94–97. The following variants may be of interest: 1e *ró-mhaith* Ennis has *ró-mhoch*; 2a *Agus* not in Ennis; *an bráthair* Ennis has *an máistir*; 2b *ar láimh* Ennis has *i láimh*; *stopfaidh* Ennis has *stadtha*; 2c *Túrtha sé dhuit* Ennis; 2g *Agus* not in Ennis; 3a *A's* not in Ennis; 3c *is an bráthair* Ennis; 3d *mo pháirt* Ennis; 3e *an leabhar an* not in Ennis; 3g *stáid stáir* Ennis; 3h *Mo chuid medalaí* Ennis; 4a *Agus* not in Ennis; 4c *Mar* not in Ennis; 4e *ola an bháis* Ennis.

Níl mo shláin-te ar fó - namh ó_ sca-ras leis_ an ól_ so;

Tá ca-sach-tach a - gus ceo a - gus ach-rann mór_ im' chroí.

Gur- b' é dei-rid na mná _ ó - ga_ gur chún-gaigh su-as mo scór - nach,

Is ná sein-finn port_ ná ceol dóibh go rinnc- fi - dís _ dom ríl.

Ach éi-righ-sé go ró _ mhaith is cuir - se dhíot_ a bó-thar,

A's ná hin-nis páirt dod' ghnó dá mai-reann beo 'ed bhuín.

Beidh a' coc sa tiar-sa romhatann_a's gloin í líon-ta ar bord _ ann,

Is dá gcuir-tí fút_ a' cór-da go gcaith-feá bri - seadh tríd.

105

Níl sé 'na lá [1/25]

1.   Éiri' it' shuí, 'fhir a tí,
Cuir umat do bhríste agus do hata,
Tá giní óir ar a' mbórd
Agus bean á ól go dtigig maidean.

Níl sé 'na lá ná 'na lá,
Níl 'na lá ná 'na mhaidin,
Níl 'na lá ná 'na lá,
Ach bean dhá rá agus í mar mhagadh.

2. Tá mo stocaí i dtigh an óil,
    Tá mo bhróga i dtigh a' leanna,
    Tá mo thiníl aoil gan dó
    Is is mór go mb'fhearr liom bheith sa bhaile.

    Níl sé 'na lá ná 'na lá,
    Níl 'na lá ná 'na mhaidin,
    Níl 'na lá ná 'na lá,
    Ach bean dhá rá agus í mar mhagadh.

3. Tá na caoire ag ithe an gheamhair,
    Tá na gamhna ag ól an bhainne,
    Tá na ba a' dul sa bhóna
    'S gan éinne beo 'gam chun a gcasta.

    Níl sé 'na lá ná 'na lá,
    Níl 'na lá ná 'na mhaidin,
    Níl 'na lá ná 'na lá,
    Ach bean dhá rá agus í mar mhagadh.

4. [...   ...   .]
    [...   ...   .]
    Tá na coilig go léir a' glaoch
    'S ba mhithid d'éinne bheith sa bhaile.

    Níl sé 'na lá ná 'na lá
    Níl 'na lá ná 'na mhaidin,
    Níl 'na lá ná 'na lá,
    Ach bean dhá rá agus í mar mhagadh.

English Summary A drinking-song, in which the the poet hears the landlady of a pub telling him to get up and dress himself, and at the same time a woman's mocking voice saying 'Not yet, it's not morning'. He then recounts the various duties he has neglected: herding sheep, calves at their mothers' milk, cows loose in the pound with no one to drive them, dogs all barking. He knows he should be at home, but his socks are in the ale-house and his shoes in the pub! **Recordings** BBC 18760 (29 Aug. 1952) — Diane Hamilton (1955). **Text** From the BBC recording. **Printed Sources** Ó Cadhlaigh, *An Lóchrann* 1 (Abrán 1916) 1 (5 vv.); Freeman, 'Irish folk songs', *JFSS* 6/4, No. 24 (Jan. 1921) 257–59 (5 vv.); Breathnach, *Sídh-cheól* 1, 18–19, No. 9 (4 vv.); cf. text in *The Kerryman* (n.d., but probably c. 1952); based apparently on Breathnach's edition; Ó Lochlainn, *An Claisceadal*, Duilleachán 23; cf. Petrie & Stanford, *The complete collection of Irish music*, 353, Nos 1411, 1412, 1413, and Joyce, *Ancient Irish music*, 57–58 (music with words of refrain only); Ó Baoill & Ó Baoill, *Ceolta Gael*, 71 (4 vv.). **Notes** There is another text in a DÓC notebook. Verse 2 is one of several such verses *(rócáin* or *poirtíní béil)* printed by Diarmuid Ó Muirithe, *An t-amhrán macarónach* (Baile Átha Cliath 1980) 141–42, from the singing of Fionán Mac Coluim on Radio Teilifís Éireann:

> Tá mo stocaí i dtigh an óil,
> Is mo bhróga i dtigh an leanna,
> Mo bha ag dul don phóna
> Is gan aoinne chun a gcasadh.

The version in Ó Lochlainn, *An Claisceadal* 23 (Dublin 1930) appears to be based on Mac Coluim's. The version in Ní Annagáin & De Chlanndiolún, *Londubh an chairn*, No. 68, differs from ours in almost everything but the refrain, and I have not included it amongst the possible sources for that reason. There is a version of this song in Freeman's Ballyvourney collection, *JFSS* 6/4, No. 24 (Jan. 1921) 257–59 (from Conny Coughlan of Doire na Sagart, Baile Mhúirne). I give it here for purposes of comparison [with spelling normalised from his quasi-phonetic orthography]:

> Níl sé 'na lá, ná 'na lá,
> Níl sé 'na lá, ná 'na mhaidin.
> Níl sé 'na lá, bhog ná bhreá,
> Ach bean dá rá 'gus í mar mhagadh.

A.   Éirigh a'fhir a' tí,
      Agus cuir umat do bhríste agus do hata,
      Chun go gcoimeádam cuideachta shuairc
      D'fhear a' chroí mhóir go maidin.

B.   Ná h-éirigh, a fhir a' tí,
      'S ná cuir umat do bhríste ná do hata!
      Mar den d'fheabhas braon dom chuid dí
      A raghaidh id' chroí go maidin!

C.   Buaileam síos is buaileam suas,
      Agus buaileam claon ar bhean a' leanna;
      Agus nuair ná gabhann sí liúm
      Beam a' siúl abhaile!

D.   Tá mo caoire ag ithe an gheamhair,
      'S tá mo ghamhna ag ól a' bhainne,
      'S tá fear a' chíosa i ndiaidh mo bhó,
      'S go deimhin, is cóir 'om trial abhaile!

E.   Tá lionn ar a' mbaile seo thiar,
      'S is lionn gan chiall gan chuimhne é;
      Tugann sé a radharc do dhallaibh
      Agus cuireann sé na bacaig a' rínce.

      Tá sé 'na lá bhog agus bhreá,
      Tá sé 'na lá 'gus 'na mhaidin.
      Tá sé 'na lá, bhog agus bhreá,
      'S go deimhin, is cóir 'om trial abhaile.

The text published anonymously in the *The Kerryman* (n.d. 1952?) appears to derive from Breathnach's *Sídh-cheól* version:

1.   Chodlas féin i dtigh aréir,
      Is tuirseach tréith do bhí mo chuisle,
      'Sé comhrádh béil bhí 'cu go léir:
      Ach mh'inghíon féin 's a boc ar buile.

      Tá 'n-a lá, níl 'n-a lá,
      Tá 'n-a lá 'gus ní'l 'n-a mhaidin,
      Tá 'n-a lá, níl 'n-a lá
      Ach solus ard atá sa ghealaigh.

2.   'Éiri' at' shuidhe a fhir an tighe,
      Cuir do bhríste 'mat go tapaidh,
      Coinnig suas cuideachta shuairc
      Do'n chroidhe mhaith mhuar go dtiocfa an mhaidin.'

      Curfã.
      Agus hucstaoraí dhomh stracadh ó n-a chéile.

3.   'N'éireó'd am' shuidhe,' ar fear an tighe,
      'S ní chuirfead bríste 'mum ná hata,
      'S blas ná braoin dem' chuid-se dighe,
      Ná raghaidh ad' chroidhe go dtiocfa an mhaidean.'

      Curfã.

4.   'Tá do bharaille ar a cheann,
      'S ní fheicim ann ach dríodar deasga,
      Tá mo ghiní ar an mbórd
      A's bím ag ól go dtiocfa an mhaidean.'

      Curfã.

There is a very similar version in *An Lóchrann* 1 (Abrán 1916) 1 (5 vv.), collected by Cormac Ó Cadhlaigh in Kinsale, Co. Cork. The song is listed in one of Bess's song-lists as 'Eirig at heue a irh a teue'.

Éiri' it' shuí, _____ 'fhir a tí,

Cuir u-mat do _____ bhrí - ste is __ do ha - ta,

Tá _____ gi - ní óir _____ ar __ a' mbórd

A - gus bean á ól go __ dti-gig mai-dean _____ (a).

Níl sé' na lá _____ ná 'na lá,

Níl __ 'na lá _____ ná _____ 'na mhai - din,

Níl __ 'na lá _____ ná _____ 'na lá,

Ach bean dhá rá a - gus í mar mha-gadh. __

106

No one to welcome me home

1. Dim in the twilight I wandered alone,
Far from the old house of yore,
Fatherless, motherless, sadly I roam —
There's no one to welcome me home.
There'll be no one to welcome me home far away,
There'll be no one to welcome me home.
And when e'er I'll return to the land of my birth,
There'll be no one to welcome me home.

2.   My old mother she stood on the quay all alone,
        With a handkerchief up to her eye;
        And just as the big ship sailed out with the tide,
        'Twas then she commenced for to cry,
        Saying 'My son, take this locket, it's a gift now from me',
        And inside it a photo was shown
        And these were the words that were engraved on the lid:
        'There'll be no one to welcome you home'.
        There'll be no one to welcome me home far away,
        There'll be no one to welcome me home.
        And when e'er I'll return to the land of my birth,
        There'll be no one to welcome me home.

Recordings BBC 19025 (8 Sept. 1952) = Kennedy, *Folktracks* F–60–160 (1981) B9.   **Text** From the BBC recording.   **Note** According to Seamus Ennis's BBC note, this is 'a late 19th century song but interesting for the singer's treatment of the tune, which is of some vintage'.

107

Old Donoughmore

1.   Oh! dark was the night, and weary the road,
       poor Pat had to travel alone;
   To keep his heart up and to shorten the way,
       he lifted a bit of a song.
   But nature at last compelled him to rest,
       his poor limbs so jaded and sore;
   A green mossy back he chose for a bed,
       convenient to Old Donoughmore.

2.   Soon in his dreams he was playing again,
       turf-sods flying high in the air;
   A weasel incautiously coming too close
       was quickly sent back to his lair.
   But Brown's frisky mule came trotting the way,
       and thinking the game should be o'er,
   He hit Pat a whack that left him outside
       his home in Old Donoughmore!

Text From CBÉ 476, 57–58. I have no printed version.

108

On a cold and stormy winter's night

Notes Title only from one of Bess's song-lists. It is perhaps identical with *The Faithful Sailor Boy* (**Laws** K 13), which begins:

'Twas on a dark and stormy night,
The snow lay on the ground;
A sailor boy stood on the deck;
The ship was outward bound.

His sweetheart standing by his side
Shed many a bitter tear;
At last he pressed her to his heart,
And whispered in her ear.

See Laws, *American balladry from British broadside ballads*, 147.

109

On board the *Kangaroo*[1/5]

1. At first I was a waiter-man that lived at home at ease,
   But now I am a mariner that ploughs the angry seas.
   I always liked sea-faring life and bid my love adieu;
   I shipped as steward and cook, my boys, on board the *Kangaroo*.

   Oh! I never thought she would prove false, or either prove untrue,
   As we sailed away through Milford Bay on board the *Kangaroo*.

2. 'Oh, think of me! Oh, think of me!', she mournfully did say,
   'When you are in a foreign land and I am far away.
   Now take this lucky thrupenny bit, 'twill make you bear in mind
   The loving, trusting, faithful heart you've left in tears behind'.

   Oh! I never thought she would prove false, or either prove untrue,
   As we sailed away through Milford Bay on board the *Kangaroo*.

3. 'Cheer up! Cheer up! my own true love, don't weep so bitterly!'
   She sobbed, she sighed, she choked, she cried, and could not say goodbye.
   'As I won't be gone so very long, 'tis but a month or two;
   And when I will return again, of course I'll marry you'.

   Oh! I never thought she would prove false, or either prove untrue,
   As we sailed away through Milford Bay on board the *Kangaroo*.

4. Our vessel she was homeward-bound from many a foreign shore,
   And many a foreign present unto my love I bore.
   I brought tortoises from Tenerife and toys from Timbucktoo;
   A China rat, a Bengal cat, and a Bombay cockatoo.

   But I never thought she would prove false, or either prove untrue,
   As we sailed away through Milford Bay on board the *Kangaroo*.

5. Paid off I sought her dwelling in a suburb of the town,
   Where an ancient dame upon the line was hanging out her gown.
   'Where is my love?' — 'She's married, sir, about six months ago,
   To a smart young man that drives the van for Chaplin, Son & Co.'.

   Oh! I never thought she would prove false, or either prove untrue,
   As we sailed away through Milford Bay on board the *Kangaroo*.

6. Here's a health to dreams of married life, to soap, to suds and blue,
   Heart's true lovers, patent starch, and washing-soda too.
   I'll go unto some distant shore, no longer can I stay,
   And on some China Hottentot I'll throw myself away.

For I never thought she would prove false, or either prove untrue,
As we sailed away through Milford Bay on board the *Kangaroo.*

7.   My love she's not a foolish girl, her age it is two score;
My love she's not a spinster, she's been married twice before.
They cannot say it was her wealth that stole my heart away:
She's a starcher and a laundress for eighteen pence a day.

But I never thought she would prove false, or either prove untrue,
As we sailed away through Milford Bay on board the *Kangaroo.*

Recordings BBC 18760 (29 Aug. 1952) = Kennedy, *Folktracks* F–60–160 (1981) B7.   **Text** From the BBC recording.   **Printed Sources** *Harding's Dublin songster* 3, No. 29, 696; see also Meredith & Anderson, *Folk songs of Australia, and the men and women who sang them*, 60 (1 v. and refrain only); Connolly, *The Christy Moore songbook*, 57 ('from the singing of Elizabeth Cronin'); words and music from the singing of Seamus Ennis (who learned the song from Bess) in Hugill, *Shanties from the seven seas*, 475–76; Edwards, *Australian Folklore Soc. Jnl* 23 (Oct. 1993) 444–45 (with music); Loesberg, *Favourite Irish ballads* 5, 12–13.   **Notes** The full text is printed in Edwards, 'On Board of the Kangaroo', *Austr. Folklore Soc. Jnl* 23 (Oct. 1993); it is more-or-less identical with Bess's version. In a private communication, Philip Butterss points out that there is another version (which I have not seen) printed in *A collection of Australian folk songs and ballads*, published by the Folk Lore Council of Australia in 1967; there is apparently no source cited. Meredith and Anderson, *Folk songs of Australia*, 60, have only v. 3 and the chorus; they say that 'Burl Ives has recorded another version on a disc devoted to Irish folk songs', but I have been unable to trace this recording. In his BBC notes, Ennis reads 'Chapping, Son & Co.' in line 5d; the *Australian Folklore Jnl* text has 'Chaplin, Horne and Co.'. The text in John Loesberg, *Favourite Irish ballads* 5 (Cork 1989) 12–13, is taken, via Christy Moore's version, from Bess's recording (with full acknowledgement, 97).

At first I was a wai-ter-man that lived at home at ease,

But now I am a mar-in-er that ploughs the an-gry seas,

I _____ al-ways liked sea-far-ing life and bid my love a-dieu;

I shipped as steward and cook, my boys, on board the Kan-ga-roo.

Oh! I ne-ver thought she would prove false, or ei-ther prove un-true,

As we sailed a-way through Mil-ford Bay on board the Kan-ga-roo.

110

On the 11th of March in the year '92

Note Title only from one of Bess's song-lists.   **Notes** Tom Munnelly suggests comparison with the song called *On the eleventh of January, in the year '96*; cf. CBÉ 219, 403–5 (Cork 1936). Alternatively, it may be a song like *On the 8th day of August, in the year '69*, for which see Bill Wanman (ed), *The wearing of the green. The lore, literature, legend and balladry of the Irish in Australia* (London 1965; NEL ed. 1968) 330–32. The song is about the bushranger, Harry Power (active in the 1850s). Alternatively, if we take the title given here as an error for *On the 11th of October in the year of '99*, it might possibly be a song that records the outbreak of the Boer War, which began on that date. Sean Ó Cróinín has the following notebook version of that song (noted down from Jerry Buckley, of Cnoc Raithín, in 1961):

> On the 11th of October in the year of '99
> This cruel war it did begin, which left many a mother crying;
> The shot and shell it flew like hail, you could hear the moans and cries
> Of the dying and the wounded, while on the field they lie.
>
> In the month of October this war did begin;
> When Ireland was deprived of some brave Irishmen.
> Married or single, to the war they must go;
> To die upon the field or to conquer the foe.
> We know there's no fear of the crowned heads at all,
> The men who have to face the powder and ball.
> Each poor mother's rearing to the battle must go,
> To die on the field or to conquer their foe.
>
> Chorus
>
> The Boers they are coming, oh dear, oh dear,
> Such roaring of cannons you never did hear,
> Since the days of old Boney, I'll tell you quite plain,
> There was never such slaughter by land or by main.

111

One day for recreation

1.   One day for recreation and silent meditation
      Down by a sweet plantation I carelessly did stray,
      Where Flora's decoration enriched each situation
      And rural habitation, that day, along the way.
      I was bent in admiration in viewing the Creation,
      Its grand illustrations I meant for to extol;
      When to my admiration I saw a constellation
      Whose proper appellation was 'The Phoenix of the Hall'.
      [....]

Text: This much (fragment only) from a DÓC notebook (dated 2 Jan. 1947).   **Notes:** Usually known as *The Phoenix of the Hall*, this song was composed by Dómhnall Ó Súilleabháin (Danny O'Sullivan); see CBÉ 692, 369-73 (Kerry 1940) and CBÉ 789, 58-60 (Kerry 1941).

112

One day to Adare, I being weary from travelling

Note: Title only from one of Bess's song-lists.

113

One evening fair for to take the air

Note Title only, from one of Bess's song-lists.   **Notes** Most likely it is *The Cailín Deas*, recorded from Michael Cronin ('Mike Lisbwee') on 7 May 1954 (BBC 20216):

1.   One evening fair for to take the air, as the summer sun went down,
       The moon in all her beauties rare the stars began to crown.
       By Dublin's Bay I chanced to stray, where a female form did pass,
       More brighter by far than the evening star, and they call her the *Cailín Deas*.

Compare the song entitled *Sweet Beaulieu Grove* ('One evening fair, to take the air') printed in *JIFSS* 10 (Dec. 1911) 19–20. Not to be confused with *The Star of Donegal*, e. g., in Sam Henry, 'Songs of the People', *Northern Constitution* (21 July 1934), No. 555 = Huntington & Hermann, *Sam Henry's Songs of the People*, 463, which has the opening line 'One evening fair to take the air'; cf. Colm Ó Lochlainn, *Irish street ballads*, 164–65 *(The Star of Donegal)*. Not to be confused with the Cailín Deas in No. 99 above.

114

One pleasant evening as pinks and daisies

1.   One pleasant evening, as pinks and daisies
       Closed in their bosom one drop of dew,
       The feathered warblers of every species
       Together chanted their notes so true.
       As I did stray, wrapped in meditation,
       It charmed my ears for to hear them sing.
       Night's silent arbours were just arising.
       The air in concert did sweetly sing.

2.   With joy transported each light I courted,
       While gazing around me with inspective eye,
       Two youthful lovers in conversation,
       Closely engaging, I chanced to spy.
       This couple spoke with such force of reason,
       Their sentiments they expressed so clear,
       That for to listen to their conversation
       My inclination was to draw near.

3. He pressed her hand and said, 'My darling,
    Tell me the reason you changed your mind;
    Or have I loved you to be degraded
    When youth and innocence are in their prime?
    For I was slighted and ill-requited
    For all the favours I did bestow.
    You shall surely tell me before I leave you
    Why you're inclined for to treat me so'.

4. With great acuteness she made him answer,
    Saying, 'It's on your favours I don't rely.
    You might contrive for to blast my glory;
    Our marriage-day you might never see.
    Young men in general are fickle-minded
    And for to trust you I was afraid.
    If for your favours I am indebted,
    Both stock and interest you will be paid'.

5. 'To blast your glory, love, I ne'er intended,
    Nor fickle-minded will I ever be.
    As for my debts, you could never pay them,
    Except through love and loyalty.
    Remember, darling, our first engagement,
    When childish pastime was all we knew?
    Be true and constant, I'm thine forever;
    I'd brave all dangers and go with you'.

6. 'You profess, good sir, I thank you for it;
    But yet your offers I can't receive:
    By soft persuasion and mild entreatment
    The wily serpent beguiled Eve.
    There are other reasons might be assigned —
    The highest tide, love, might ebb and fall —
    Another female might fit you better,
    Therefore I cannot obey your call'.

7. 'Yes, I admit that the tide's in motion
    And always moving from shore to shore;
    But still the substance is never changing,
    And never will until time's no more.
    I'd sound your fame with all loyal lovers,
    To fix their love on whose mind is pure,
    Where no existence can ever change it,
    Or no physician prescribe a cure'.

8. She says: 'Young man, for to tell you plainly,
    For to refrain you I am inclined.
    Another young man of birth and fortune
    Have gained my favour and changed my mind.
    Our future welfare I have considered,
    On fickle footing will I never stand.

> Besides, my parents would be offended
> To see you walking by my right hand'.

9. 'What had you, my darling, when once were born?
   What nature gave you, love, so had I.
   Your haughty parents, I do disdain them;
   Your ill got riches I do deny.
   An honest heart, love, is far superior,
   For gold and riches will soon decay.
   Sure, it's naked we came into this world,
   And it's much the same we will go away.

Text From a DÓC notebook. **Printed Sources** Royal Irish Academy, RR 66 H 17 (Lord Moyne Coll.) 113 (18 vv.); NLI General Coll.; four other copies in Cambridge University Library Ballads, vol. 2, 119; vol. 3, 272; vol. 4, 48 and vol. 6, 502. See Sam Henry, 'Songs of the People', *Northern Constitution* (1 Jan. 1927), No. 164 = Huntington & Hermann, *Sam Henry's Songs of the People*, 462–64; *Wehman's 617 Irish songs*, 5; *Delaney's Irish song book*, No. 4, 26 (18 vv.). **Notes** Learned by Bess from the singing of her mother, Maighréad Ní Thuama [= 'Seana-Mheáig'], this song is perhaps better known as *The True Lovers' Discussion*, which is the usual title in the broadsides and songbooks, and in Sam Henry's collection. It is, according to Tom Munnelly, the longest song common in current oral tradition; see his article, 'The long song singer Martin Reidy of Tullaghboy, 1901–1985', *Dál gCais* 8 (1986) 69–73. The broadside version entitled *The True Lover's Discussion* in the Royal Irish Academy Moyne Collection, and in the NLI, has a further 9 verses:

A. You're false when you say you fear,
   And slight my parents whom I love dear,
   I think it's justice for to slight you,
   If that's the course you mean to steer,
   By wealth or feature, or act of nature,
   You're not my equal in any line,
   Since I conjure you insist no further,
   It's to your wishes I'll not incline.

B. To falsify, love, I do deny it,
   Your imputation is wrong I swear,
   Like Eve, I find you're a real deceiver,
   Your heart's as foul as your face is fair.
   For the want of riches you meanly slight me,
   And my complexion you do disdain,
   Our skin may differ, but true affection,
   In black or white it's all the same.

C. Oh, curb your passion, sir! she did exclaim
   It was not to quarrel I met you here,
   But to discourse in moderation,
   And a real intention to make appear.
   I speak with candour, I will surrender,
   To what is proper in every way,
   If you submit to a fair discussion,
   And reasons dictate you will obey.

D. It's now too late to ask that question,
   When you despise me before my friends,
   Lebanons plains if you could command them,
   It's not sufficent to make amends,
   There's not a tree in the Persian forest,
   Retains its colour excepting one,
   And that is Laurel, which I will cherish,
   And always hold in my right hand.

E. The blooming Laurel, sir, you may admire,
   Because its verdure is always new
   But there's another you can't deny it,
   It's just as bright in the gardner's view.

It's wisely resting thro' the winter,
And blooms again when the Spring draws near
The pen of Homer has wrote its praises,
In June and July it does appear.

F.   You speak exceedingly, but not correctly,
With words supported your cause is vain,
Had you the tongue of the Siren goddess
Your exultation I would disdain.
It was your love that I did require,
But since you placed it on golden store,
I'll strike the string and my harp shall murmur,
Farewell, my love, for evermore.

G.   She seemed effected with eyes distracted,
With loud exclaiming she thus gave way
Sir, my denial was but a trial,
You gods be witness to what I say.
She says my darling if you don't forgive me,
And quite forget my incredulity,
A single virgin for your sake I'll wander,
While a green leaf grows on a laurel tree.

H.   So all young maidens I pray take a warning,
Let love and virtue be still your aim,
No worldly treasure should yield you pleasure,
But those whose persons you do disdain
All loyal lovers do then respect you,
And to your memory will heave a sigh,
The blooming rose and the evergreen,
Will mark the spot where your body lies.

I.   From Ballinahinch about two miles distance,
Where blackbirds whistle and thrushes sing,
With hills surrounded and valleys bounded
A charming prospect in the evening.
Where female's beauty is never wanting,
The lonely strangers a refuge find,
Near Mara Tenpenny, if you require,
You'll find the author of those simple lines.

Sam Henry had the same full text, but his final verse reveals the place of composition as Magheratimpan, which is near Ballinahinch, Co. Down. The author was a schoolteacher by the name of M'Kittrick, probably mid-nineteenth century.

115

Our good man

1.   Miles I have travelled, hundreds and more,
And whiskers on babies I never saw before.

Child 274   **Recording** BBC 21996–7 (Aug. 1954).   **Printed Sources** Child, *The English and Scottish popular ballads*, 5, 88–95, No. 274; cf. Huntington & Hermann, *Sam Henry's Songs of the People*, 508–9 *(The Blin' Auld Man, The Covered Cavalier)*; Reeves, *The idiom of the people*, 167–69.   **Notes** Only this much survives in the BBC recording. Bess explains how a man was puzzled, after years' of absence, when he found his own son had a beard. He suspected his wife had another husband. Sam Henry's statement (5 April 1924) that this was 'a song of a Jacobite in hiding when a household was divided against itself after the rebellion of 1715 or 1745 (first printed in 1776)' seems misplaced. It is generally interpreted as a cuckold's song and is popular in several languages; see James Reeves, *The idiom of the people*, 167–69. The verse with our two lines goes as follows (Reeves, 168, from a manuscript of Cecil Sharp):

> Now it's my old man came home one night
> Came home one night to me
> A strange man in the bed he found
> What stranger can this be?
> What stranger can this be, my love
> What stranger can this be?
> It's a baby his wife replied
> My mother she sent to me
> Many thousand miles I've travelled
> Ten thousand miles or more
> But whiskers on a baby's face
> I never saw before.

The song has crossed over into Irish as *Peigín is Peadar*. Bess speaks the lines in the recording, but has no tune.

116

Paddle your own canoe

Note Title only from one of Bess's song-lists. **Printed Sources** City of Dublin Library, Gilbert Collection (printed by Brereton, Lr Exchange St), and three copies in Cambridge University Library Ballads, vol. 1, 5; vol. 3, 95; vol. 4, 284. There is a 'New Version' also in the Gilbert Collection, and in the CUL Ballads, vol. 1, 194. See also McClaskey, *200 favourite songs & hymns for schools & homes, nursery & fireside*, No. 3 (New York 1885) 91 (more-or-less identical, but lacks our vv. 3 and 4). **Notes** The song was written by Harry Clifton, author of at least 500 songs, mainly set to waltz tunes composed by Charles Coote (proprietor of Hapwood & Crew, music publishers). It was first published in 1866 and was sung by Clifton in the early music-halls; see Peter Davison, *Songs of the British music-hall* (New York 1977) 28. The following version is from the Gilbert Collection (No. 33). I give the text 'warts and all':

[1.]   I'v travelled about a bit in my time,
And of trobles I've seen a lew,
But found it better in every clime,
To paddle your own canoe,

CHORUS —

My wants are small I care not all,
If my debts are paid when due.
I drive away strife in the ocen of life
While I paddle my own canoe,

[2.]   Then love your neighbour as yourself,
As the worl you go travelling through
And never sit down with a tear or a frown,
But paddle your own canoe,

[3.]   I have no wife to bother my life
No lover to prove true,
But the whole day long with a laugh & a song,
I paddle my own canoe,

[4.]   I rise with the lark & from daylight til dark,
I do what I have to do,
I'm careless of wealth if I've only the health,
To paddle my own canoe,

[5.]   It's all very well th dpend on a friend
That is if yau've prov'd him true,
But you'll find it better by far in the end,
To paddle your own canoe.

[6.]   To borrow is dearer by far than ta by,
        A maxim though old still true,
        You never will siSh [*recte* sigh]if you only will try
        To paddle your own canoe,

[7.]   If a hurricane rise in the mid-day skie
        And the sun is lost to view
        Move steadily by with a steadfast eye,
        And paddle your own canoe,

[8.]   The daisies that grew in the bright green fields,
        Are blooming so sweet for you,
        So never sit down with a tear or a frown,
        But paddle your own canoe,

117

Pat O'Donnell

1. My name is Pat O'Donnell, from the county Donegal,
    I am, you know, a deadly foe to traitors one and all;
    For the shooting of James Carey I was tried in London Tower,
    And on the accursed gallows there my life will be thrown down.

2. As I sailed on board the ship *Melrose* in August '83
    On our voyage to Cape Town he was made known to me;
    When I knew that he was Carey we had angry words and blows,
    Until he swore he'd take my life on board the ship *Melrose*.

3. I stood upon my own defence to fight before I'd die,
    A pocket pistol I drew forth and at him I let fly;
    I fired at him a second time and pierced him through the heart,
    Then I gave him a third volley, which made him soon depart.

4. Mrs Carey, running forth into the cabin where he lay,
    When she saw him in a pool of gore, it filled her with dismay —
    'Why did you shoot my husband?', now Mrs Carey cried —
    'I shot, and in my own defence, kind madam,' I replied.

5. The Captain got me arrested, in strong irons I was bound;
    He handed me as a prisoner when we landed in Capetown;
    I was brought back to England, my trial there to stand,
    The prosecutors of the Crown for Carey's wife and son.

6. As I was standing at the bar, and guilty found at last,
    The jury found me guilty and the judge my sentence passed;
    'For the shooting of James Carey,' the solemn judge replied,
    'On the 14th of September, Pat O'Donnell, you must die'.

7. So now farewell to Donegal, that spot where I was born!
    And not forgetting the United States, where I sailed round with scorn;
    Likewise Erin's lovely isle, her woods and valleys green;
    For never more around Erin's shore O'Donnell will be seen.

8. If were a freeman and to live another year,
    Then traitors and informers, I'd make them shake with fear;
    As St Patrick drove the serpents from this saintly Irish ground,
    I'd make them fly before me like a hare before the hound.

9. Now to finish and conclude, I have no more to say;
    I hear the death-bells tolling, now good Christians for me pray;
    And ask the Blessed Virgin, when on bended knees you fall,
    To pray for Pat O'Donnell from the county Donegal.

Text From CBÉ 283, 161–64. **Printed Sources** Ó Lochlainn, *Irish street ballads*, 210–11, No. 44a (9 vv.); Zimmermann, *Songs of Irish rebellion*, 284–86, No. 86 (7 vv.). **Notes** There is a version recorded by Alan Lomax from Michael Cronin, January 1951, in BBC 21209. Zimmermann published seven verses from a song-sheet in the P. J. McCall collection in the National Library of Ireland; it wants our verses 5 and 6. Colm Ó Lochlainn learnt the song from a maidservant, Ms. E. Gilshenan, from Virginia, Co. Cavan; he refers also to a broadside version, but without bibliographical details. The song is about the murder of James Carey, who turned state's evidence in the trial of the Invincible Society members who were arrested and tried for the murder of the British Chief Secretary for Ireland, Lord Frederic Cavendish, and his secretary, Thomas Henry Burke, on 6 May, 1882 in Phoenix Park, Dublin. Carey was secreted out of the country after the trial but encountered O'Donnell on board ship; they had a disagreement (one version being that they quarrelled over a game of cards) and came to blows; O'Donnell claimed that he defended himself by shooting Carey (29 July 1883). Another version of the story has it that O'Donnell recognised Carey from a newspaper picture of him and resolved to kill him. Needless to say, the song is popular still in Co. Donegal, and the singers' sympathies are usually with O'Donnell.

118

Paudeen O'Rafferty

Note Title only from one of Bess's song-lists. **Printed Sources** There are two ballad sheets of this song in Cambridge University Library Ballads, vol. 5, 592 and 770. See also Healy, *The Mercier book of Irish street ballads* 4, 134–35 *Paddy O' Rafferty*. **Notes** Healy cites no source, but presumably he obtained the song from a ballad-sheet in some Cork library. He gives the following text:

> I'm just going to sing to you, Paddy O'Rafferty —
> Sure you all heard of Miss Judy O'Doherty,
> Of late she became just a part of my property,
> Och, the devil may take such a comical tragedy.
> Och, when I think of the day she has got of me,
> I'll ever remember while there's a drop of me;
> She's spun me so clean, she'a almost made a rope of me,
> Show'ring the stones and the mortar on top of me.
>
> Och, when the creature first ran away with me,
> Her parents they said she thought a great deal of me;
> But soon she began for to scold and to rail with me.
> Och, but myself had but fairly got shut of her,
> Devil a ha'porth of good's to be got of her;
> If she was dead, I'd dance at the foot of her,
> And, with pleasure I'd pay for a neat wooden suit for her.

When first we got married I thought all was right with me,
There's a hole in the ballad, she was too long quiet with me,
But with her tongue and the tongs she would fight day and night with me,
Swearing and tearing, and squaring to fight with me.
Och, that myself had but fairly got rid of her,
If she were dead I would nail down the lid of her,
I'd pay half-a-crown to the boy that would dig for her
A hole wide and deep, and every way big for her.

I went to the bog just a cutting some turf with her,
Tried with good humour, and got nothing but scoff from her;
She slipp'd in a hole as I went over the moss with her,
By the powers then says I, there's an Irish divorce for you.
Now she is dead, and I fairly got shut of her,
The last sight I had was the best sight I got of her,
My jewel then, says I, there's a illegant spot for you,
But it's rather soft for to dance at the foot of ye.

119

Poirtín Sheáin a' tsíoda

Note Title only from one of Bess-s song-lists.   **Printed Sources** Mac Coluim & Pléimionn, *Cosa buidhe árda* 1, 23–24 = *Cosa buidhe árda* 2, 21. This is reprinted (as *Rínce Philib a' Cheoil*) in Ó Tuama's *Cóisir cheoil* 4, 2. The same version is also in E. Maguidhir, *Mo stóirín cheóil*, 14–15, and in the same author's *Pilib an cheóil*, 2–3; cf. also Ní Annagáin & De Chlanndiolún, *Londubh an chairn*, No. 59; The text in *Cosa buidhe árda* 2 (longer than the earlier version in *Cosa buidhe árda* 1) is as follows:

> Poirtín Sheáin a' tsíoda,
> Is rinnce Philib a' cheóil:
> 'Dein-si dhómhsa an rinnce!
> Is seinnfeadsa dhuitse an ceól!
> Ó 'se! a bhean! nach deas í!
> Ó 'se! a bhean! nach seóig!
> Ó 'se! a bhean! nach deas í!
> Rinnce Philib an cheoil.
>
> Poirtín Sheáin a' tsíoda,
> Is rinnce Philib a' cheóil;
> 'Mar sin bhíomair riamh
> 'S is amhla' bheam go deó!'
> Ó 'se! a bhean! nach deas í!, etc.

120

Pussycat's party[2/4]

1.   One evening a white pussy-cat
        Had such a nice party to tea;
        And she and her kittens, so frisky and fat,
        Were as happy, as happy as could be.

Oh my! 'Twas a wonderful sight!
Oh my! 'Twas a wonderful sight!
Oh my! 'Twas a wonderful sight —
Old Pussy-Cat's party that night!

2.   They had to sit round the floor in a ring,
Without any tables or chairs;
And then, in the midst of the fun,
There came a loud knock at the door.
And weren't they frightened, and didn't they run,
And never came back any more!

Oh my! 'Twas a wonderful sight!
Oh my! 'Twas a wonderful sight!
Oh my! 'Twas a wonderful sight —
Old Pussy-Cat's party that night!

Recording: JR-GP (2 Nov. 1952).   **Text:** From the JR-GP recording. I have no printed version.

121

Raghad-sa ó thuaidh leat, a bhó[1/11]

1.   Raghad-sa ó thuaidh leat, a bhó,
      Agus tiocfad aduaidh leat, a bhó,
      Cois Abha Móire, a bhó,
      Mar a bhfaghaidh tú seamróg,
      Neoinín barra-ghlas,
      A chuirfidh ag cneadaigh tu,
      Agus ó, mo chara thu!

2.   Is ó, mo chara mo bhó,
      Is ó, mo chara mo bhó!
      Is nár bhuailidh aon mhasla thu,
      Poll ná madra,
      Céim cruaidh carraige,
      Bearna bhascaithe,
      Do bhainfeadh aon leagadh astut,
      Agus ó, mo chara thu!

English Summary A milking-woman sings to her cow, wishing it safe from any harm.   **Recordings** CBÉ 387a, 392a (1947) — BBC 12614 (7 Aug. 1947) = Kennedy, *Folktracks* F–60–160 (1981) A10.   **Text** From the BBC recording. There is another text in a DÓC notebook (dated 8 July 1949).   **Printed Sources** 'Amhrán chrúidhte na Bó', *Timthiridh an Chroidhe Naomhtha* 6/3 (1916) 15.   **Notes** A note following the text reads 'Nóra Ní Laoire, cailín aimsire a bhí againn ar a' Ráth, a bhíodh ag gabháil don rócán so. Bhí sí thar barr chun poirtíní béil — puss music — choinneóch sí ringceoirí ar siúl go brách' *[N. Ní L., a servant girl we had in Ráth, used to sing this song. She was exceptionally good at 'puss music', and could keep dancers going forever'.]* The BBC 1947 take is slightly better; but it repeats v. 1 at the end. The text in *Timthiridh an Chroidhe Naomhtha* 6/3 (1916) 15, collected from Siobhán Ní Chróinín [= 'Siobhán an tSagairt'] from Ballingeary, Co. Cork, is called *Amhrán Chrúidhte na Bó* ['The Milking Song'].

          Mo chroidhe mo chaithiseach!
          Mo chroidhe mo phaidir thú!
          Aghaidh do lachta leat.
          Cúl do sheasgais leat.
          Go bhfaghair do thairbhe
          A bhanaltra an bhainne seo.
          Éireóchad ar maidin leat.
          Siubhlóchad cois Fleasga leat;
          Mara bhfaighead duit fairsinge,
          Fear mín fada duit
          Poll ná madra
          Ná aon ní basguitheach
          Do bhainfeadh iomard asat
          Ar linn an eadarshuth!

Ragh- ad - - sa ó thua- idh leat, a bhó, _____

Ag - us tioc- fad ad- uaidh leat, a bhó, _____

Cois Ab - ha Móir - e, a bhó,

Mar a bhfaghaidh tú _____ seam- (a) - róg, _____ (a) _____

Neoi - nín _____ barr- a - ghlas, _____

A chuir - fidh _____ ag cnead - aigh _____ tu,

A - gus ó, _____ mo chara thu!

122

Ré-chnoc mná duibhe

1. Nách aoibhinn dos na h-éiníní d'éiríonn go h-árd!
   Is do luíonn lena chéile ar aon chraoíbhín amháin!
   Ní mar sin dom féin ná dom' chéad míle grá,
   Mar is fada óna chéile orainn d'éiríonn gach lá!

2. A's ní crích is ní léan dom mo ghaoltha rith síos,
   Ach a' seachaint na bréige sara ndéanfadh aon díth.
   Gurbh iad slua sídhe na Gréine do ráinig lem' thaoíbh,
   Is do luaig mise óm' ghaolthaibh go ré-chnoc mná duibhe.

3. Tá cailín donn deas ar a' mbaile go mbím,
   Is gile í ná'n sneachta is ná'n eala ar a' línn.
   Dá mbeadh an oíche a' cuir sheaca níor ró-fhada liom í,
   Bheith ag éalú thar Caisil le grá geal mo chroí.

31·7·47.

Ré-Chnoc Mná Duibhe

I

Nác aoibinn dos na héiníní d'éiríonn go h-árd
Is do luíonn le na chéile ar aon chraoibín amáin
Ní mar sin dom féin ná dom chéad míle grá
Ach is fada ó na chéile orainn d'éiríonn gach lá.

II

Ar ní críoc is ní léan dom mo shaolta pré píor
Ac a feacaint na bhréige ropa ndéanfac aon níc
Gur b'iad grua ríor na gréine do ráinig lem taoib
Is do luaig mise óm shaoltaib go Ré-chnoc mná duí.

III

Tá cailín dom deos ar a' mbaile go mbím
Is gile í ná'n sneachta is ná'n eala ar a' linn
Dá mbeadh an óige ag cur sneachta, níor ró-fhada líom í,
Beidh ag éalú tar cnoic le grá ghil mo chroí.

(tá tuille de seo ion, ar lár.)

6.

J. & M. went out for a walk,
'Tis all about love this couple dis talk,
There going to get married, I hope they'll agree
+ well .

'Ré-chnoc mná duibhe' from a notebook of Donncha Ó Cróinín (private collection).

English Summary The poet bemoans the absence of his lover, which his relatives attribute to her having been taken by the fairies (doubtless to discourage the match). **Text** From a DÓC notebook. **Printed Sources** O'Daly & Mangan, *The poets and poetry of Munster*, 4th ed., 216–19 (8 vv.); Petrie & Stanford, *The complete collection of Irish music*, 363, No. 1451; Comyn, "'Fa'n gcaoill ghlais'", *Fáinne an Lae* (12 Márta 1898) 3 (2 vv.); Mac Coluim, *Bolg an t-soláthair. Cnuasach sean-rócán*, 28–29 (4 vv.); see also Borthwick, *Ceól-sídhe* 2, 85 *Nach aoibhinn do na h-éiníníbh* (v. 1 of our text + another, not in our text); Freeman, 'Irish folk songs', *JFSS* 6/3, No. 23 (Jan. 1920) 154–59, No. 20 (11 vv.); Mac Coluim, *Amhráin na ngleann* 1, 37–38; Breathnach, *Ceól ár sínsear*, 152 (5 vv.); idem, *Ár gceól féinig*, 161; Ní Annagáin & De Chlanndiolún, *Londubh an chairn*, No. 19; Ó Lochlainn, *An Claisceadal*, Duilleachán 9; Ní Ógáin, *Duanaire Gaedhilge* 1, 27; cf. Petrie, *Complete collection*, 363 No. 1451 ("Is aíbhinn do(s)na héiníníbh', air only). **Notes** A note at the end of the text in the DÓC notebook says 'Tá tuille dhe seo ion, dar léi' *['There's more of this, she thinks']*. Freeman's Ballyvourney version in *JFSS*, No. 23, has 11 verses. That in *Poets and poetry of Munster*, 4th ed., 216–19, has 8 verses, attributed to George Roberts, otherwise unknown. An English translation (Mangan's?) of Roberts's text is given in William G. Wood-Martin, *Traces of the elder faiths of Ireland* (Dublin 1902) 2, 12, entitled *The Dark Fairy Rath*, to illustrate the belief in fairies and their supposed practice of carrying off adults as well as children. The older version of the song in *Poets and poetry of Munster* preserves the placenames in their original form e.g., in verse (a) *Glaise na Tuaithe* (the Finglas river), which has become *geataí na tuaithe; slua sídhe na Gréine* (Knockgreany); *bruach na Máighe* (the river Maigue), which became *bruach geal na trá*; these are all in Co. Limerick. In verse (c) below the word *tír* has been altered to *Laoi*, to suit the new setting of the song in Co. Cork. Five verses of our song (vv. f, 3, e, b and 1) occur also in another song called *Tá Culaith Bhreagh Mo Phósta*, which is in NUI, Galway, Hardiman Library, Hyde MS. 57, 48–51, a collection of Munster songs written by Cáit Ní Dhonnchú. The text published by Freeman, *JFSS*, No. 23, from Conny Coughlan of Derrynagart (two versions, and a third, with different tune, from Peig Ní Dhonnchú of Ballymakeera) has eleven verses, including our three; I give his text, with orthography normalised:

a.   Is fada dhom ar buaireamh a cur tuairisc' mo ghrá
      I ngleanntaibh dubha uaigneacha am' ruagairt chun fáin;
      A shamhail ní bhfuaireas, 's do chuardaíos mórán,
      Ó gheataíbh na tuaithe go bruach geal na trá.

b.   Dá gcastaí mo ghrá 'rm ba nár dhom gan suí
      Go leogfainn mo lámh ar a brághaid nú ar a cinn;
      'Sé dúirt sí: 'A riúin, fág mé, ní h-ámhar duit sínn,
      'S gur bean dubhach ar fán me ó thárlag ad' línn'.

c.   'Ní bean dubhach i n-aonchor mé féin', adúirt sí,
      'Ach cailín ciúin tréitheach ón dtaobh thall de Laoi,
      Nár shín a taobh riamh le haon fhear sa ríocht,
      Agus bog díom suas do ghéaga, táim déanach óm' buíon'.

d.   Tá cailín donn deas ar an mbaile go mbím,
      Is gile í ná an sneachta 's ná an eala ar a' línn;
      'Á mbeadh an oíche cur sheaca níorbh fhada liom í
      Ag éaló thar caise le grá geal mo chroí.

e.   'Sí cara-gheal mo chroí istig, mo chiúin-chailín mná;
      Mo dhá láimh 'na tímpeall, 's do b'aoibhinn dár gcás;
      Ba bhreá deas a bríathra 's a cliabh ghlan gan cháim,
      Le h-áilleacht a gníomhartha, 's gan í 'gam dá bhárr.

f.   'S tá mo stocaí 's mo bhróga 'na stróicíbh liom síos,
      Níl pingin im póca ná feóirling, fóiríor!
      Tháinig próiseas nó dhó chugham lenar ólas den fhíon,
      'S is é mo lá leóin gan mé óg seal airís!

g.   'S ní críoch is ní léir dhom mo scéal a chur síos,
      A sheachain na bréige do dhéanamh a n-aon tslí,
      Go b'iad slua-sídhe na gréine do ráinig liom buíon
      Agus d'fhuadaig chun slé' uaim í i Ré-Chnoc Mná Duibhe.

h.   Do casadh de ruaig me a gCnoc uasal Mná Duibhe,
      Mar a ghnáthadh a' stuaire go stuama 'na suí;
      Ba chas cíortha dualach a bhí a cuacha léi síos
      Ar leath-taoíbh a gualann á luascadh le gaoith.

i.   Nach aoibhinn do na héiníníbh d'éiríonn go h-ard
      Agus luíonn lena chéile ar aon chraoíbhín amháin!
      Ní mar sin dom féin ná dom chéad míle grá,
      Mar is fada óna chéile orainn d'éiríonn a' lá.

j.   'S ní phósfainn bean chlóca, ní bheadh gnó aici bheith im' dhiaidh;
           Ní phósfainn na lóma de chrón-chaille riabhaig;
           Mar táim-se ar na móidibh 's mó gheobhadh bean le bliain
           Do shiúlfadh gan bhróga ar dhruim(?) Eóraip im' dhiaidh.

k.   ''S dá bhfaghainn-se fíon craorach i ndaor-chupaíbh óir,
           Agus banríon do dhéanamh díom fhéin ar a' gcoróinn(?),
           Ní shínfinn mo thaobh deas le h-aon fhear chun spóirt
           Chun go bhficfinn mo chéile a' teacht marbh nú beó'.

Freeman has a variant for v. (h) above:

(h)*   'A ógánaig uasail na gruaige breá buí,
           Druid anso anuas liom ar chomhgar na dí;
           Go dtógfainn an brón as a' ceo suas ded' chroí,
           Mar éiríonn an lóchán den choirce le gaoith'.

Borthwick, *Ceól-sídhe* 2, 85 has our v. 1, followed by this verse:

B.   Is báine í ná 'n lile, is deise í 'ná 'n sgéimh,
           Is binne í 'ná 'n bheidhlinn 's is soillsighe í 'ná 'n ghréin;
           Is fearr 'ná sin uile a h-uaisleacht 's a méinn,
           'S a Dhia 'tá is na flaithis, fuasgail do m' phéinn!

Breathnach, *Ár gceól féinig*, 161, has the same two verses, both probably taken from *Fáinne an Lae* (12 Márta 1898). Ní Ógáin, *Duanaire Gaedhilge*, 27, has 2 verses, v. (i) above and the verse just cited. Another text in DÓC's notes has two verses our v. 3, preceded by v. (a) in Freeman's text. The text in *Bolg an t-soláthair*, 28–29, opens with v. (a) above, followed by these three verses;

A.   'S is fada dhom ar buaidhreamh ag cur tuairisg mná duibhe
           Chun go bhfeaca uaim suas í ar an mór-chnoc 'na suidhe,
           Budh crothánach tiugh bacach a cuacha léi síos
           As gach taoibh d'á guailnibh dh'á luasgadh le gaoith.

B.   ''S cá tír nó cá háit duit i gClár Luirc do bhír?
           Má's ar buaidhirt taoi, suidh láimh liom 's tabhair slán fé gach buidhean,
           An tú maighdean na mbán-ghlac thug grádh ceart do Naois,
           Nó an stuaire chiúin ghrádhmhar sgiob Páris ó'n dTraoi?'

C.   'Ní héinne mé i n-ao' chor de'n méid sin d'áirighis,
           Acht chailín caoin Gaedhlach ó'n dtaobh eile 'n tír';
           'Sé dubhairt sí liom, 'Fág mé; ní hádhbhar duit mé',
           Agus uaim-se do léim sí mar éan ar an gcraoibh.

The text in *Amhráin na ngleann*, 37–38, is identical with this. That in Ó Lochlainn, *An Claisceadal* 9, is based on a, A, B above. Breathnach's text in *Ceól ár sínsear*, 152, opens with our v. (a), and ends with v. 1; it has the following as vv. 2, 3, 4;

D.   A's do casadh mo ghrádh 'rm is ba náir' liom gan suidhe,
           Do leogas mo lámh ar a brághaid is ar a croidhe;
           Is é dubhairt sí 'nois fág mé ní h-ádhbhar duit sínn,
           Is bean dúbhach ar fán mé do thárla it líon.

E.   Tá cailín donn deas ar a' mbaile go mbím;
           Is gile í ná sneachta 's ná eala ar línn.
           Dá mbeadh an oidhche a' cur sneachta níor bhfada liom í
           Bheith ag éalódh thar caise le cara mo choidhe.

F.   Dá gcastí do ruaig mé 'r Chnoc uasal Mná Dhuibhe,
           Mar a mbíon an cailín ciúin stuamtha go módhmharach 'n-a suidhe,
           Ba chas cíortha buacach a cuacha léi síos,
           Ar gach taobh dá guailnibh á luascadh le gaoith.

There is another version of the song, in five verses, in National University of Ireland, Galway, James Hardiman Library, Douglas Hyde MS. 49, 35–36, No. 28. The order of verses is a, b, B, C, and the following final verse:

G.   Do chruaidheas-sa mo ghéaga ar a caoil-chneas bhí mín,
           Mar shaoil mé í bhréagadh is gur chéile dhom í.

Is uaim-se do léim sí mar éan beag ó'n gcraoibh
Is seo buaidheartha go h-éag mé gan faoiseamh 'na diaidh.

The text in Ní Annagáin & De Chlanndiolún, *Londubh an chairn*, No. 19, differs considerably from ours and has a different air.Mac Coluim's note in *Cosa buidhe árda* 2, 35, says that the air of the song was similar to that of *Cá rabhais ar feadh an lae uaim?* (the Irish version of *Lord Randal*).

123

Roll on, silvery moon

Note Title only in one of Bess's song-lists. **Printed Sources** Fitzgerald, 'An account of the old street ballads of Cork', *Jnl of the Cork Hist. & Arch. Soc.* 1/4 (1892) 63–71 68 (1 v. + refrain); McClaskey, *200 favorite songs*, No. 2, 34; Williams, *Folk-songs of the Upper Thames*, 128; *Walton's treasury of Irish songs and ballads*, 162. **Notes** There is one verse and a refrain published in Fitzgerald, 'An account of the old street ballads of Cork', 68:

> As I strayed from my cot at the close of the day,
> About the beginning of June,
> 'Neath a jessamine shade I espied a fair maid,
> And she sadly complain'd to the moon.
>
> Roll on, bonny moon, guide the traveller's way,
> While the nightingale's song is in tune,
> For never again with my Edwin I'll stray,
> By the sweet silver light, bonny moon.

A near neighbour of Bess's, John O'Connell of Daingean na Saileach, had a very fine version of the song. The *Walton treasury of Irish songs and ballads*, 162, has the following second and third verses:

> A. 'As the hart on the mountain my lover is brave,
> And so handsome, so manly, and clean;
> So kind, so sincere, and he loved me so dear,
> Oh, Eamon, thy equal was never yet seen.
> But now he is dead and gone to his lone bed,
> Cut down like a flower in full bloom;
> He had fallen asleep, and poor Jane's left to weep
> By the bright silvery light of the moon.'
>
> B. 'For he died for his country, my sweetheart so true,
> For Ireland he gave his young life;
> He fell with our heroes, when mourners were few,
> Mid the rifle-fire, cannon, and strife.
> And his brothers-in-arms, 'neath that bright Easter sun,
> Fought and prayed that the dawn would come soon —
> 'Gainst the fierce, foreign, foe, till the Vict'ry was won
> By the sweet silvery light of the moon.'

Williams, *Folk-songs of the Upper Thames,* 128, has the following additional verse:

> C. 'His grave will I seek till morning appears,
> I'll weep for my lover so brave,
> I'll embrace the cold turf, and I'll wash with my tears
> The daisies that bloom on his grave;
> No, never again shall my bosom know joy,
> With my Edwin I trust to be soon,
> And lovers shall weep o'er the spot where we sleep,
> By thy sweet, silver light, bonny moon.'

McClaskey, *200 favorite songs*, 34, has the following final verse:

D.   Ah, me! ne'er again may my bosom rejoice,
For my lost love I fain would meet soon;
And fond lovers will weep o'er the grave where we sleep,
'Neath thy soft silver light, gentle moon.

McClaskey attributes the song to a J. W. Turner.

124

Scoil Bhárr d'Ínse

1.   Bhíomair oíche i Scoil Bhárr d'Ínse,
Bhíomair go léir 'nár dhá pháirtí ann.
Bhí púic ar gach éinne 'gus fonn chun bruighne,
Agus chífeá fuil ar chuid acu i ndeire na scríbe.

    Right-fol-the-dúril-éril-um,
    Dic ril-úril-éril um,
    Fol the-dúril-éril-úril,
    Um diddley-um.

2.   Conchubhar Ó Loingsigh, an máistir a bhí againn,
'S Máire Ní Churnáin, ceann de mhnáibh Chiarraí ann.
Ón Muileann a tháinig na Cruadhlaoigh ann,
Amhlaoibh agus Seán 's iad a' rá na n-eachtraí dhúinn.

    Curfá

3.   Bhí muintir Luasa ó Screathan na nGamhann ann,
Muintir Chróinín agus muintir Thuama,
Muintir Mhulláin agus muintir Ghruama,
Agus bhíodar na Pléimeannaigh ó iarthar an domhain ann.

4.   Bhí clann Mhuirtí ó Bhárr d'Ínse ann,
Bhí J.J. agus Seán Dhiarmín ann;
Clann Sheáin Fhada tháinig treasna an linn ann,
Is bhíodar clann Mhaidhc Thaidhg Uí Chuill ann.

5.   Tháinig na sluaite ón Ínse Mhór ann:
Muintir Scannaill agus muintir Ghruama,
Muintir Mhuirithe agus muintir Shíocháin,
Muintir Chéilleachair 's Con Amhlaoibh ann.

6.   Bhí Hyde a' tSleasa agus Dónal Ó Móráin ann,
An Pléarach Dheansail, 's é go fiain ann,
Bhí 'gainn muintir Chuill na Luachra,
Diarmuid Phaid, 's a chrúbaí móra.

7. Bhí clann Sheáin Pheaidí ós na Millíní,
    Clann Mhaidhc Óig ón mbóthar íochtar,
    Dhá líon-tí 'cu os na Doirí ann,
    'S a Dhia, nach flúirseach muintir Chuill ann!

8. Ó Dhoire 'n Chuilinn, bhí muintir Dhuinnín ann,
    Muintir Shúilleabháin, 's muintir Ríordáin,
    Muintir Laoire, agus bhíodar na Ceallaigh ann,
    Agus bhí againn an deidhrí, mac do' tuing ann.

9. Bhí muintir Raghallaigh os na Fuithirí ann,
    Muintir Bhuachalla agus muintir Dhuinnín ann,
    Ón Lománach, na Carrthaigh a bhí ann,
    'S clann Shiobháin aniar ón gcoill ann.

10. Bhí Eoin a' Droichid ó Shráid a' Mhuicín ann,
    Bhí, nuair a mhair sé, an spriúnlín bocht;
    Beannacht Dé len' anam, níor mhair sé críonna,
    Níor tharraing sé an pinsean ach an dá Dhé hAoine.

11. Tháinig na sluaite ó Chúil Aodha 'noir,
    Sclábhaithe, gabhainne agus siúinéirí,
    Muintir Shuibhne agus muintir Chearaí,
    Agus bhíodar na Scannallaig ó 'n-aice an tSéipéil ann.

12. Bhí clann Dhonncha Bán ón Kerry Yard ann,
    Agus bhíodar leis na Seitheachánaigh;
    Ní raibh againn bacaigh ná tíncéirí,
    'S a Dhia nach sinn-ne bhí go h-aerach!

13. Bhí Séamus Ó Dónaill ó Chathair Saidhbhín ann,
    'S é ag amhrán go h-ard le binn-ghuth;
    Ón gCarraig a tháinig Dochtúir Ó Loingsigh,
    Agus Seán Ó Cearúil, ón gCaiseal aníos ann.

14. Bhí Conchubhar Ó Luasa ag rínce at stáitse ann,
    Seán Ó Mulláin 's é ag déanamh geaitsí;
    Seán Mhuirtí 's a phláinín bán air,
    A's — h-anam an diabhal! — cár ghaibh an Carrthach?

15. Bhí *fire-crackers* á lasadh ag seó acu,
    Agus iad a' cnagarnaigh mar a bheadh tóirneach;
    Piobar dearg i gceart á dhó ann,
    Gach éinne a' casachtaigh, 's é dul 'n-a scórnaigh.

16. Siúd amach gach éinne, a' sraotharnaigh go seoidh ann,
    Do mhúchadar na soillse a's do ghlasadar na dóirse,
    Nuair a leagadar an geata tháinig fearg ar an Loingseach,
    'S nuair a h-ínseadh é don sagart cuireadh deireadh leis an rínce!

English Summary The song describes a gathering of local families for an evening's singing and dancing at the School of Barr d'Ínse. When the merriment was at its greatest, however, the local priest arrived and stopped the dancing!   **Text** I have the text of the last verse only and the refrain from Seamus Ennis's CBÉ transcription(Sept. 1946).   **Printed Sources** *Múscraí* 1 (1983) 5–7.   **Notes** Ennis has the following note preceding the song 'Fonn an *Claisceadail do Fhiadhach a' Mhada Ruaidh* — an píosa seo dhe ag Bean Uí Chróinín':

> [17.]   Do mhúchadar na soillse, do bhriseadar na dóirse,
>   'S do ghabhadar go léir amach fé'n mbóthar.
>   Do bhriseadar an geata 's tháinig fearg ar an Loínseach
>   An uair adúirt an sagart go raibh deireadh leis an rinnce.

Following this Ennis has the note '"Port Béil" was called "Puss-Music" in Baile Mhúirne and district — Mrs Cronin'. For the full text — which I have used here — see Gobnait Ní Shúilleabháin, 'Comhartha cuimhneacháin ar chomóradh céad blian Sgoil Bharr d'Inse, 1883–1983', *Múscraí* 1 (1983) 5–7. This article has a very full account of the authors (Dónal and Pádraig Ó Súilleabháin, Doire 'n Chuilinn) and the song, which they composed in 1922. Bess's father, Seán Máistir Ó hIarlaithe, was the first headmaster in Scoil Bharr d'Ínse.

125

'Sé Pead Buí atá thíos leis an ní seo go léir

1.   'Sé Pead Buí atá thíos leis an ní seo go léir
        Do cheannaigh trí slata beaifití 'gcóir gach aon lae.
        Nuair a bhí an mhaighdean á ghearradh do loit sí'n coiléar;
        Do bhí an *sweetheart* 'na h-aice agus do scaoil air a' faobhar.

Text From a notebook of DÓC's (dated 29 Aug. 1944).   **Notes** The notebook introduction provides a neat summary of the song 'Cheannaigh sé trí slata beaifití chun léine dhéanamh agus thug sé an beaifití do chailín éigin chun í dhéanamh. Do loit sí an léine air agus seo mar adúirt sé' [*'The poet bought three yards of course cotton (baft) and gave it to a young girl to make a shirt for him with, but she ruined the shirt and he composed this satirical verse about it'*].

126

Seán a' Bhríste Leathair

1.   Nuair a bhíos i dtúis mo shaoil ag éirí suas im' leanbh
        Do bhí orm greann gach éinne, mar ba mé peata 'n cheana.
        Nuair a bhíos ag éirí, 'sé idir a naoi 's a ceathair,
        Bhí mo thóin dá thé ag sceilp 'e bhríste leathair.

        Téir-a-léir a leá, téir-a-léir a leaidí
        Téir-a-léir a leá, Seán a' Bhríste Leathair.

2.   Nuair a bhíos ag dul isna déagaibh théinn imeasc na bhfear ann;
        Níor mhór dhom fhéin 'na dhéidh sin iompáil amach im' ghaige.
        Do bhíos ag suirí le *lady* go raibh uirthi *veil* is *bonnet*;
        Shaoileas go bhfaghainn gach aon bhean, ó bhí orm bríste leathair.

Téir-a-léir a leá, téir-a-léir a leaidí
Téir-a-léir a leá, Seán a' Bhríste Leathair

3. Nuair a bhíos-sa bliain is fiche d'aos, sin é an uair a ndéanfainn gaisge;
   Ní iarfainn ach naoi gcoiscéim chun dul le léim thar geata;
   Thógfainn sé leath-chéad le neart mo ghéag ón dtalamh,
   'S b'é rá gach spéirbhean óg, 'Dia led' bhríste leathair!'

   Téir-a-léir a leá, téir-a-léir a leaidí
   Téir-a-léir a leá, Seán a' Bhríste Leathair

4. Do bhí orm c'laith dheas éadaigh in iúil do righ mo Mharcus,
   Casóigín deas bhréide agus bheistín gléigeal phláinín;
   Stoicín dubh-ghlas caorach agus bróigín Gaelach smeartha,
   Agus haitín íseal *Quaker* agus smeig don bhríste leathair.

   Téir-a-léir a leá, téir-a-léir a leaidí
   Téir-a-léir a leá, Seán a' Bhríste Leathair

5. Chuas-sa lá go dtí'n t-aonach suas ar fad go *standing*;
   Cé chífinn ach an chúilfhionn agus í 'ceannach úll a's *crackers*;
   Chonnaic sí 'druidiúint léi mé agus thóg sí an *veil* dá *bonnet*,
   Agus is cruinn do thug fé ndeara *shape* mo bhríste leathair.

   Téir-a-léir a leá, téir-a-léir a leaidí
   Téir-a-léir a leá, Seán a' Bhríste Leathair

6. Nuair a bhí an tráthnóinín ann go déanach agus sinn chun teacht abhaile
   Cé chífinn ach an chúilfhionn agus í ag iompáil orm 's ag bagairt;
   Do dhruid sí liom go dlúth, do labhair sí liom go cneasta,
   Agus chuir sí nimh a súl i dtóin mo bhríste leathair.

   Téir-a-léir a leá, téir-a-léir a leaidí
   Téir-a-léir a leá, Seán a' Bhríste Leathair

7. Do ghluais a hathair 's a máthair dhá lorg ar fuaid na mbailte,
   Fuaradh mise is Máire i dtí'n tabhairne, geallaim;
   Nuair a fhágamair an áit sin chuamair go tigh an tsagairt,
   Agus fuaireas baile 'stát de bhárr mo bhríste leathair!

   Téir-a-léir a leá, téir-a-léir a leaidí
   Téir-a-léir a leá, Seán a' Bhríste Leathair

8. Nuair a bhí na focail ráite agus sinn ag teacht abhaile,
   Do riug a hathair ar láimh orm am' fhásgadh le neart ceana;
   Dúirt sé féin 's a máthair, dá mba leó 'stát an Mharcuis,
   Ná faghadh aon fhear go brách í ach Seán a' Bhríste Leathair.

   Téir-a-léir a leá, téir-a-léir a leaidí
   Téir-a-léir a leá, Seán a' Bhríste Leathair.

English Summary A comic song in which the poet recounts his amorous successes from early youth, all supposedly due to his attractive leather britches! He finally wins the heart of a wealthy young heiress and weds her.   **Text** From DÓC papers. **Printed Sources** Mac Coluim, 'Racaireacht na tuaithe', *An Lóchrann* (Bealtaine 1925) 165–68 (11 vv.).   **Notes** The text in *Racaireacht na tuaithe*, 165–68, has eleven verses in the order 1/2, 4, 2/5/6, 7, 8 (where some verses are composite, with lines from different verses of our text); the *Racaireacht* text follows our v. 8 with six more:

A.   Nuair a dh'itheamair ár ndóthain,
       Agus d'ólamair ár n-acfuinn,
       Chuas is Máire ag rinnce,
       'S is ró-bhreágh bhuail an talamh,
       D'fhiafraigh na daoine go léir díom,
       Cad é an sórt mo bhríste leathair,
       Dubhart-sa leó go béasach,
       Gur smut de chroicean reith' í.

B.   The Piper, to help the sport,
       He played some tunes so merry,
       Faith he played some charming notes,
       To banish melancholy,
       When he put on the pipes,
       He played 'Sweet Highland Mary,'
       You'd laugh until you'd cry O
       To hear poor 'Paddey Carey.'

C.   'Nora Criona' he did play,
       With the greatest variations,
       'The Rambler from Tralee.'
       And 'The Diggle among the Tailors,'
       'The Job of Journeywork' and
       'The Girl I left behind Me,'
       The song of 'Paddy Whack' and
       'Tally heigh ho the Grinder!'

D.   He played the tune of 'Cailín Donn',
       'The Hare was in the Corn,'
       He played 'The Peeler's Cap'
       And 'The Irish Washerwoman,'
       'The Clonmel Rakes' in style,
       Likewise 'The Banks of Claudy,'
       'Saddle the Pony,' too,
       And 'The Wind that Shook the Barley.'

E.   He played 'The High Caul Cap,'
       The tune of 'Kitty's Rambles,'
       'The Charms of the Bottle of Punch,'
       And 'The Bonnie Highland Laddie'
       'The Maids of Sweet Tralee,'
       The lively 'Drops of Brandy,'
       The roving sporting reel —
       'My love he is a Dandy.'

F.   He played 'Aughrim Overthrown,'
       With 'Judy Joyce the Joker,'
       He played 'The Jig Polthogue,'
       That was made for Captain Croker,
       The famous 'Geese in the Bog,'
       The song of 'Bean a Leanna,'
       'Planncum,' 'Moll in the Wad,'
       And 'Seán Ó Duibhir a' Ghleanna.'

127

Sean O'Farrell

1. Young lovers pay attention to my feelings
    And the truth unto you I'll reveal:
    I once courted a brave Irish hero,
    Sean O'Farrell they call him by name.
    But now that he's gone and has left me —
    He's gone across the salt sea —
    I'll follow my brave Sean O'Farrell,
    For I know he loves Ireland and me.

2. The day that my love sailed o'er the waters —
    It was a grand sight to be seen —
    With twelve hundred together,
    And they cheering for Erin the Green.
    The pipers played up in a moment
    Garryowen and *St Patrick's Day*,
    And the toast that he drank towards the yankees —
    That the shamrock may never decay!

3. Do you remember the wedding of Molly?
    It was a grand sight to be seen!
    Twelve hundred together,
    and they cheering for Erin the Green.
    Those men, they were brave, I can tell you,
    And their hearts were as true as could be.
    And I'll follow my darling tomorrow,
    For I know he loves Ireland and me.

Text From CBÉ 283, 182–83. **Notes** The title occurs in one of Bess's song-lists as *You (sic) lovers pay attention to my feelings*. For a more recent (1987) recording of the song, see Tom Munnelly, *Mount Callan garland*, 133–34 (5 vv., with the title *Miss Green*), from the singing of Tom Lenihan, Knockbrock, Co. Clare.

128

Seoithín-seó [1/15]

1. A bhean úd thíos ar bruach an tsrutháin
    Seoithín seó, úileó leó,
    A' dtuigeann túsa fáth mo ghearáin?
    Seoithín seó, úileó leó.
    Seoithín, seoithín, seoithín, seoithín,
    Seoithín seó, úileó leó,
    Seoithín, seoithín, seoithín, seoithín,
    Seoithín seó, úileó leó.

2.   Abair lem' chéile teacht amáireach
     Seoithín seó, úileó leó,
     Agus scian coise duibhe a thabhairt 'na láimh leis,
     Seoithín seó, úileó leó.
     Nó mara dtige sé san tráth so,
     Seoithín seó, úileó leó,
     Beadsa im banríon ar na mnáibh seo,
     Seoithín seó, úileó leó.
     Seoithín, seoithín, seoithín, seoithín,
     Seoithín seó, úileó leó,
     Seoithín, seoithín, seoithín, seoithín,
     Seoithín seó, úileó leó.

English Summary A woman taken by the fairies and held in their *sídh* (fairy-fort) implores another woman (who is washing clothes in the river) to take word to her husband, with instructions on how to release her.   **Recordings** BBC 11988 (1947) = Kennedy, *Folktracks* F–60–160 (1981) A8 — JR-GP (Nov. 1952).   **Text** From the BBC recording.   **Printed Sources** Petrie, *The Petrie collection of the ancient music of Ireland,* 72–73 [a fuller version, with music (and with very interesting note by Eugene O'Curry on the theme of the song)]; cf. Petrie & Stanford, *The complete collection of Irish music,* 384, No. 1532 (music only); O'Daly, *Irish language miscellany,* 109–111; Sigerson, *Bards of the Gael and Gall,* 353–54 [English only]; see also Ní Chróinín, *An Lóchrann* 1 (Abrán 1916) 5; Breathnach, *Ár gceól féinig,* 196–98 (5 vv.); Ní Ógáin, *Duanaire Gaedhilge,* 12; Mac Coluim, *Cosa buidhe árda* 2, 24–26 (5 vv.); Maguidhir, *Pilib an cheóil,* 14–15; Goodman, *The Irish minstrel a collection of songs for use in Irish schools,* No.1, 37–38, No. 29 (5 vv.); Ua Braoin, *An cuaichín ceoil,* 54–55, 110–12.   **Notes** This version from Petrie, *Ancient music of Ireland* (Dublin 1855) 74 (who also adds a translation):

1.   A bhean úd thíos ar bhruach an tsrutháin,
     Seó hú leó, seó hú leó,
     An d-tuigeann tusa fáth mo ghearáin,
     Seó hú leó, seó hú leó,
     'Sgur bliadhain 'sa lá 'niu 'fuadaigh mé dhom 'ghearrán,
     Seó hú leó, seó hú eó,
     'Sda rugadh asteach mé a Lios an Chnocáin,
     Seó hú leó, seó hú leó.
     Seó hín, seó hín, seó hín, seó hín,
     Seó hú leó, seó hú leó,
     Seó hín, seó hín, seó hín, seó hín,
     Seó hú leó, seó hú leó.

2.   'Seo é annso mo theagh mór maiseach,
     Seó hú leó, seó hú leó,
     As iomdha leann úr agus leann sean ann,
     Seó hú leó, seó hú leó,
     As iomdha mil bhuidhe agus céir bheach ann,
     Seó hú leó, seó hú leó,
     As iomdha sean duine ar a nasg ann,
     Seó hú leó, seó hú leó,
     Seó hín, seó hín, seó hín, seó hín,
     Seó hú leó, seó hú leó,
     Seó hín, seó hín, seó hín, seó hín,
     Seó hú leó, seó hú leó.

3.   As iomdha buachaill cúl-donn cas ann,
     Seó hú leó, seó hú leó,
     As iomdha cailín cúl-bhuidhe deas ann,
     Seó hú leó, seó hú leó,
     'Tá dhá bhean déag ag iomchar mac ann,
     Seó hú leó, seó hú leó,
     'Tá an oiread eile re na n-ais ann,
     Seó hú leó, seó hú leó,
     Seó hín, seó hín, seó hín, seó hín,
     Seó hú leó, seó hú leó,
     Seó hín, seó hín, seó hín, seó hín,
     Seó hú leó, seó hú leó.

4. Abair lem' chéile teacht a márach,
    Seó hú leó, seó hú leó,
    'San choinneall chiarach a g-croidhe a dheárnann,
    Seó hú leó, seó hú leó,
    Scian choise duibhe 'thabhairt na láimh leis,
    Seó hú leó, seó hú leó,
    'San capall tosaigh do bhualadh 'san m-bearnainn,
    Seó hú leó, seó hú leó,
    Seó hín, seó hín, seó hín, seó hín,
    Seó hú leó, seó hú leó,
    Seó hín, seó hín, seó hín, seó hín,
    Seó hú leó, seó hú leó.

5. An luibh a bhuain 'tá a n-dorus an leasa,
    Seó hú leó, seó hú leó,
    Mar shúil re Dia go raghainn leis a bhaile,
    Seó hú leó, seó hú leó,
    Nó mar a dtigi sé fá'n tráth sin,
    Seó hú leó, seó hú leó,
    'Go m-biadsa am bainríoghain ar na mná so,
    Seó hú leó, seó hú leó,

Seó hín, seó hín, seó hín, seó hín,
Seó hú leó, seó hú leó,
Seó hín, seó hín, seó hín, seó hín,
Seó hú leó, seó hú leó.

Verses 2 and 3 above are clearly extraneous. Breathnach, *Ár gceól féinig*, 196–98, reproduces Petrie's text in its entirety; Maguidhir, *Pilib an cheóil*, 14–15, reproduces vv. 1–3 of Petrie's version. Fionán Mac Coluim's text is composite, with the first verse of the lullaby *Seoithín-Seó* [No. **129**] as v. 1, followed by variants of vv. 2, 3 and 4 above. The story in *An Lóchrann*, incorporating verses of the song, was collected from Siobhán Ní Chróinín ('Siobhán an tSagairt') of Ballingeary, who was an acquaintance of Bess Cronin's and whose songs she occasionally referred to. There is a recording of the lullaby, from the singing of Maire O'Sullivan, of Ballylicky, Co. Cork, in Alan Lomax's *Columbia World Library of Folk and Primitive Music* (New York 1955) SL–204. The lullaby given by Joyce, *Ancient Irish music*, 90, No. 88, could be a version of this tune, I think.

129

Seoithín-seó

1. *Seo mar a chuirfinn-se mo leanbh a chodladh,*
   Seoithín seó, úileó leó
   I gcliabhán óir 'san ghaoth á bhogadh,
   Seoithín seó, úileó leó

2. *Seo mar a chuirfinn-se mo leanbh a chodladh,*
   Seoithín seó, úileó leó
   I mbairlín lín ar úrlár shocair,
   Seoithín seó, úileó leó

3. *Seo mar a chuirfinn-se mo leanbh a chodladh,*
   Seoithín seó, úileó leó
   Lá breá gréine 'dir dhá Nollaig,
   Seoithín seó, úileó leó

4. Baby sleep, and o'er thy slumbers,
   Seoithín seó, úileó leó
   Angels bright shall chant their numbers,
   Seoithín seó, úileó leó

5. Sleep my baby free from sorrow,
   Seoithín seó, úileó leó
   Bright thou'll open thine eyes tomorrow,
   Seoithín seó, úileó leó

6. Through the branchy trees the breeze is sweeping,
   Seoithín seó, úileó leó
   And my baby dear is sweetly sleeping,
   Seoithín seó, úileó leó.

English Summary The Irish verses describe how the mother put her baby to sleep (1) in a gold crib, rocking in the breeze; (2) in a linen sheet on the floor; and (3) on a fine sunny day between Christmas and Little Christmas. **Text** From a DÓC notebook (dated 3 Jan. 1948). **Printed Sources** Petrie, *The Petrie collection of the ancient music of Ireland*, 144–46, a composite text, from different informants, including Eugene O'Curry, whose recollection of the first two verses was different from Petrie's printed version; Moffatt, *The minstrelsy of Ireland*, 228–29. See also Borthwick, *Ceól-sídhe* 1, 94 (= Petrie's vv. 1, 2, 4); Mac Coluim, *Cosa buidhe árda* 2, 24–26 (which combines verses from this and the previous song); cf. also Breathnach, *Sídh-cheól* 1, 66–67, No. 66 (to the air of *Síle Ní Ghadhra*); idem, *Ár gceól féinig*, 192–93 (4 vv.); Goodman, *The Irish minstrel*, No. 1, 25–26, No. 21 [English verses only]; Graves, *The Irish song book*, 168, No. 109 (English only); Walton's *treasury of Irish songs and ballads*, 25. **Notes** Petrie prints the following version in his *Ancient music of Ireland*, 146:

1.   Do chuirfinn-si féin mo leanabh a chodhladh,
     'Sní mar do chuirfeadh mná na m-bodach,
     Fá shúisín bhuidhe ná a m-bratlín bhorraigh,
     Acht a g-cliabhán óir is an ghaoth dhá bhoghadh.
     Seó h-ín seó, h-uil leó leó,
     Seó h-ín seó, as tú mo leanabh;
     Seó h-ín seó, h-uil leó leó,
     Seó h-ín seó, 'sas tú mo leanabh.

2.   Do chuirfinn-si féin mo leanabh a chodhladh,
     Lá breágh gréine idir dhá nodhluig,
     A g-cliabhán óir ar úrlár shocair,
     Faoi bharra na g-craobh is an ghaoth dhá bhoghadh.
     Seó h-ín seó, h-uil leó leó, &c.

3.   Codail a leinibh 'sgus ba codhladh slán dhuit,
     Is as do chodladh go d-tugair do shláinte.
     Nár bhuailidh treighid ná greim an bháis tú,
     Galar na leanabh ná'n bholgach ghránna.
     Seó h-ín seó, h-uil leó leó, &c.

4.   Codail a leinibh 'sgus ba codladh slán dhuit
     Is as do chodladh go d-tugair do shláinte;
     As do smaointe do chroidhe nár chráidhtear
     Is nár ba bean gan mac do mháthair
     Seó h-ín seó, h-uil leó leó, &c.

Petrie's English translation of these verses is not identical with Bess's English verses, for which see further below, but it is very similar to George Sigerson's English version, *Bards of the Gael and Gall* (1897), 351–52, which is reproduced in turn by Halliday Sparling, *Irish minstrelsy*, 247–48. Breathnach's two texts, *Sídh-cheól* 1, 66–67, and *Ár gceól féinig*, 192–93, are taken from Petrie's edition. Fionán Mac Coluim's version in *Cosa buidhe árda* 2, 24–26, has these three verses, which belong to the previous song (cf. Petrie):

A.   Siúd é thall mo thig mór geal-sa,
     Seothúleó! Seothúleó
     Is mó bealach isteach 's amach ann,
     Seothúleó! Seothúleó
     Is mó leann úr agus leann sean ann,
     Seothúleó! Seothúleó!
     Is mó mil agus céir bhuidhe beach ann,
     Seothúleó! Seothúleó!
     Seoithín! Seóithín! 7rl.

B.   Is mó cailín cúl-bhuidhe cas ann,
     Seothuleó! Seothúleó!
     Is mó buachaill fuadrach deas ann,
     Seothúleó! Seothúleó!
     Is mó crann-laoch do chaill a neart ann,
     Seothúleó! Seothúleó!
     Is mó bean óg i bhfeidhil clann mac ann,
     Seothúleó! Seothúleó!
     Seóithín, Seóithín, 7rl.

C.   A bhean úd thall ar lic an nigheacháin,
     Seothúleó! Seothúleó!
     Abair lem' dhian-ghrádh teacht am láthair,
     Seothúleó! Seothúleó!
     Sgian coise duibhe a thabhairt n-a láimh leis.
     Seothúleó! Seothúleó!

Nó beidh an téarma dúbalth' orm amáireach.
Seothúleó! Seothúleó!
Seóithín, Seóithín, 7rl.

For the English words in Bess's version see Alfred Moffatt, *The minstrelsy of Ireland*, 229 [from Edward Walsh, *Irish popular songs* (Dublin 1847)], reproduced in P. Goodman, *The Irish minstrel*, 26–27, No. 21, which might be a more likely immediate source for Bess's text. Moffatt, *Minstrelsy*, 228, has references to Horncastle's *Music of Ireland* 3 (1844) and McCarthy's *Irish ballads* (1846), which I've not seen.

1.   Sweet babe, a golden cradle holds thee,
     Shoheen sho lo, lu lu, lo lo;
     Soft a snow-white fleece enfolds thee,
     Shoheen sho lo, lu lu, lo lo; etc.

Compare A. P. Graves, *The Irish song book*, 168, No. 109, v. 2:

2.   Oh sleep, my baby, free from sorrow,
     Bright thou'lt ope thine eyes to-morrow;
     Sleep, while o'er thy smiling slumbers
     Angels chant their numbers.

For a different lullaby incorporating the same kind of refrain, see Joyce, *Ancient Irish music*, 74, No. 73.

     Shoheen sho, lu lo lo;
     Thro' branchy trees the breeze is sweeping,
     Shoheen sho, lu lo lo;
     And my baby dear is now sweetly sleeping,
     Shoheen sho, lu lo lo.

Sam Henry published a song (28 Dec. 1935) with the title *Irish lullaby for the Christ-Child*, to the air of *The Old Man Rocking the Cradle*, in which the first words are 'Shoheen, shoho'. See Huntington & Hermann, *Sam Henry's Songs of the People*, 7. For a different song, set to the same tune, see Breathnach, *Songs of the Gael, 68*. See also Hugh Shields, Douglas Sealy, & Cathal Goan (eds), *Scéalamhráin Cheilteacha* (Dublin 1985) 15–17 *(A Bhean údaí thall a shíogó)*.

130

Seoladh na ngamhan faoi'n bhfásaig

1.   A' lorg na ngamhan 'sea chuireas-sa mo leanbh,
     'S níor fhill sí in am ná i dtráth chugham.
     Bhí Cormac roímpi i lúibín na coille
     Agus Peadair Ó Laéire láimh leis …

     Má tá dlí le fáil in aon tír 'nár n-aice
     Ní foláir nú geoimíd sásamh […].

English Summary The poet recounts how he sent his daughter to fetch the calves, but she fell into bad company. The song seems to imply that some local braves had their way with her, and the father is now seeking redress. **Text** From a DÓC notebook (fragment only). **Printed Sources** Ó Laoghaire, *Irisleabhar na Gaedhilge* 12, Uimh.140 (Bealtaine 1902) 77–78 (6 vv.). **Notes** A note after the song in DÓC's notebook says 'Is féidir an *Spailín Fánach* a chur leis a' bhfonn so leis' *[The* Spailín Fánach *can be set to this tune also']*. Not to be confused with *Seoladh na nGamhnadh*, e. g. in Edward Walsh, *Irish popular songs* (2nd ed., Dublin 1883) 51–52. The text in *Irisleabhar na Gaedhilge* 12, 77–78, is as follows:

A.   Ar lorg na ngamhan 'seadh chuireas mo leanbh:
        Ceann ní bhfuair go lá 'ca;
        Do bhí Cormac roímpi ag pointe an gleanna
        Agus Peadar na Péice láimh léi, —
        Dís atá riamh i ndiaidh na mbruinneall
        As srian níl chur go brách leó,
        Acht má [tá] dlighe le fághail ann san áit-seo 'bhfuilim
        Gheóbhad-sa díol as Cáitín.

B.   Tá oileáinín cubhartha i lúib na coille,
        ('Gus ragham araon go lá ann)
        Mar a mbíonn ceól na n-éan ag síor-dhul a chodladh
        Is gheóbham na gamhna i mbárach.
        Gheóbham cead saor ó mhaor na coille
        Féar a thabhairt go lá dhóibh,
        Is le fáinne an lae beam araon 'nár seasamh
        Ag seóladh na ngamhan faoi'n bhfásach.

C.   'Mo mhallacht-sa go léir do mhaor na coille
        'S gach stiobhart chuir chum fáin mé,
        D'fhág m'athair bocht féin gan chéill 'gan mbaile
        Is cionnus a raghad d'á láthair?'
        'A chogair dhil mo chléibh, ná bíodh ort mairg
        Is deas é dhein do mháithrín;
        Is má's ag siubhal dúinn araon ó chéile ar maidin,
        Seo póg as barra mo lámh dhuit.'

D.   Táim-se teinn, mo leigheas ní bhfachtar,
        Fóraoir daingean cráidhte!
        Táid mo ghéaga go léir gan tapadh —
        Céad moladh le Muire gheal Mháthair.
        Dhá mbeidhinn-se ar na sléibhtibh nó taobh an ghleanna
        Mar a mbíonn sonn ag bádaibh,
        An liugh breágh séimh, an glaodh o'n marcach
        Is guth na ngadhar ar árdaibh.

E.   'Sa ngleann úd thall do chómhnuidheas sealad —
        Gleann fial fairsing fáilteach
        Mar a mbíonn an breac breágh lúthmhar, buigiún slaite,
        An fúnsa, is feac na rámhainne,
        Cailínidhe óga, gleoite, deasa,
        Ciuin, tais, banamhail, nárach,
        A sláinte dhá ól ar bórd ag fearaibh
        Is cé nách dtiubhradh grádh dhóibh?

F.   'Is buachaill óg me a nduaidh ó Mhalla,
        Figheadóir socair sásta
        Do chaithfeadh an spól go ceól ar anairt,
        D'fhighfeadh sac no mála;
        Do dhéanfainn rómhar mar gach fear
        Lá breágh earraigh Márta;
        Thiomáinfinn céacht i ndiaidh sé gcapall
        Threabhfadh cnuic is bánta.'

131

Seothó-leó, a thoil[2/20]

1.   A éigse an aitis ó Chaiseal go Bóinn,
        Is gach n-aon den aicme nárbh aithin mo threod,

Éistíg feasta lem' theagasc le meon,
Agus féach mar a caitheadh an ainnise im' threo!

Agus seóthó leó, a thoil, ná goil go fóill.
Seóthó, a thoil, ná goil aon deoir.
Seóthó, a linbh, a chumann 's a stór
Atá a' sileadh na súl agus do chúm gan lón.

2.   Agus b'fhearra liom cácaí fáiscithe à beoir,
Nó dá n-abrainn árthaí lán d'fhíon leo,
Banarthla bhláth-bhínn bhán-chíoch óg
Ná duanaireacht folamh le file dem' shórd.

Agus seóthó leó, a thoil, ná goil go fóill.
Seóthó, a thoil, ná goil aon deoir.
Seóthó leó, a linbh, a chumainn 's a stór,
Atá a' sileadh na súl agus do chúm gan lón.

3.   Dá chífinn do […   …] chugham san ród
[…   …   …] luisne 'na snódh
D'fhág sí mise faoi iomarca 'en brón
[…   …   …] a' sileadh na ndeor.

A's seóthó leó, a thoil, ná goil go fóill.
Seóthó, a linbh, ná goil aon deoir.
Seóthó, a linbh, a chumann 's a stór
Atá a' sileadh na súl agus do chúm gan lón.

English Summary The poet laments a lost love and the fact that his poetry is no longer respected. He would prefer food and drink than vain composing such as he attempts. **Recordings** BBC 11988 (7 Aug. 1947) — JR-GP (2 Nov. 1952). **Text** From the JR-GP recording.   **Notes** The BBC text is slightly different it also has three verses, but in the order 1, A, 2.

A.   Agus cad a dhéanfad feasta le daltha dod' shórd,
Gan braon im' ballaibh ná beatha bhog shóil?
Éist, a linbh, agus tearman gheobhair,
Mar tá gréithre maithe agam beartaithe id' chóir.

Not to be confused with a lullaby of the same title, attributed to Eoghan Rua Ó Súilleabháin, which goes as follows:

Gheobhair an capall agus gheobhair an tsrian,
Gheobhair an fhalaing agus gheobhair an diallait,

Seothó-leó, a thoil, seothó-leó, a thoil,
Seothó-leó, a thoil, ná goil go fóill!

Gheobhair gan dearmad taisce gach seoid
Do bhí ag do mhuíntir ríoga romhat,

Is seothó-leó, a thoil, is seothó-leó, a thoil,
Is seothó-leó, a thoil, ná goil go fóill!

(from a DÓC notebook); for the full text, see Ní Ógáin, *Duanaire Gaedhilge* 2, 20–22.

A éigse an ai-tis - ó ___ Chaiseal go Bóinn, ___

Is gach ___ n-aon den aic -me ___ nár- bh ait-hin mo threod,

Éis - - tig feas-ta ___ lem'___ thea-gasc le meon, ___ A-gus

féach mar a cait - headh an ___ ainni-se im' threo! ___

A- gus seó - thó leó, ___ a ___ thoil, ___ ná ___ goil go fóill.

(m) Seó-thó, a thoil ___ ná ___ goil ___ aon deoir.

(m) Seó-thó, a ___ linbh, ___ a ___ chu-mann's a stór ___

A - tá a' si - leadh 'súl ___ a - gus do chúm gan lón.

132

Shades of evening

Note Title only from one of Bess's song-lists.

133

She called me upstairs

Note Title only from one of Bess's song-lists.

134

She's a dear maid to me

1. My name is Hugh Reynolds, I come of honest parents,
   Near Cavan I was born, as plainly as you may see.
   By loving of a maid, one Catherine MacCabe,
   My life has been betrayed — she's a dear maid to me.

2. The country were bewailing my doleful situation,
   But still I'd expectation this maid would set me free.
   But oh! she was ungrateful, her parents proved deceitful,
   And though I loved her faithful — she's a dear maid to me.

3. Young men and tender maidens throughout this Irish nation
   Who hear my lamentation — I hope you'll pray for me!
   The truth I will unfold, that my precious blood be sold,
   In the grave I must lie cold — she's a dear maid to me.

4. For now my glass is run and the hour it is come,
   And I must die for love and the height of loyalty.
   I thought it was no harm to embrace her in my arms,
   Or take her from her parents — she's a dear maid to me.

5. Adieu, my loving father, and you my tender mother,
   Farewell my dearest brother, who has suffered sore for me!
   With irons I'm surrounded, in grief I lie surrounded,
   By perjury confounded — she's a dear maid to me.

6. Now I can say no more, to the Lawboard I must go,
   There to take the last farewell of my friends and country.
   May the angels shining bright receive this soul tonight,
   And convey me into heaven to the Blessed Trinity!

Text From CBÉ 283, 336–39.   **Printed Sources** Sparling, *Irish minstrelsy*, 277–78 (6 vv.); Joyce, *Old Irish folk-music and song*, 135; Colum, *Broad-sheet ballads, being a collection of Irish popular songs*, 24–25 (6 vv.); Ó Lochlainn, *Irish street ballads*, 132–33, No. 66; Mac Mathúna, *Traditional songs and singers*, 64–65 (vv. 1, 3, 5).   **Notes** In CBÉ 283 the song is preceded by the following brief explanation, by Bess Cronin, of the circumstances surrounding its composition:

> There was once a certain man away up the country and he was acquainted with a certain young woman in the neighbourhood, and he wished to marry her; but the girl's parents — who were of English stock — would not hear of it.
> One night the man decided that he would take away the girl from her house and so he arrived when it was dark. He succeeded in taking the girl, but it was soon discovered and they were closely followed. However, they succeeded in getting away, but the young man was later captured when he went into a certain town.
> He was tried for abduction and the penalty for the crime was death. The girl gave evidence and she swore that he took her away by force. He was convicted and was sentenced to be hanged, and the sentence was carried out.

A note in *Sparling's Irish minstrelsy*, 370, says that the hero of this ballad was hanged on 28 March 1826. The title there given is *The Lamentation of Hugh Reynolds*, the title by which it is, in fact, more popularly known. See the account in Joyce, *Old Irish folk-music and song*, 135; Joyce knew Catherine McCabe personally.

135

She's at the bar selling soap, soda and blue

1. She's at the bar, selling soap, soda and blue,
   And things too superfluous to mention to you!
   Rally-ra-fol-the-da,
   Rally-rights-fol-the-dee.

Text From a DÓC notebook.   **Notes** The notebook heading reads 'Fragment of song by Poet of Lisbee', for whom see the songs entitled *All Ye That's Pierced By Cupid's Darts* [No. **6**] and *An Bothán ín Íseal gan Fálthas* [No. **13**].

136

Shore, shore;
if I can't get this maid from the shore

Note Title only from one of Bess's song-lists.   **Printed Sources** Joyce, *Old Irish folk music and songs*, 152 (air + v. 6); Corcoran, 'Two songs', *Ceol* 3/3 (1969) 66–70 68–70; Laws, *American balladry from British broadsides*, 154 (K 27); cf. Lomax, *The folk songs of North America in the English language*, 142–43, No. 73; Palmer, *Everyman book of British ballads*, 62–63 No. 24.   **Notes** Bertrand H. Bronson, *The traditional tunes to the Child ballads*, 4 vols (Princeton 1959–72), by including this (vol. 1, 337) as a version of Child 43 *(The Brownfield Hill)*, was stretching the evidence somewhat. For a modern recorded version, see Ewan McColl & Peggy Seeger, *The Long Harvest* 3, Argo Records (London 1967). There is a version, recorded from Tom Curran of Tenure, Co. Louth, in *Ceol* 3/3, 68–69:

1. There was a sea-captain went ploughing the main,
   And he ploughed o'er the water so clear, clear,
   Saying 'What will I give you my merry sea-men
   If you bring me that maid from the shore, sea-shore,
   If you bring me that maid from the shore'.

2. So the sailors they hauled out their merry wee boat,
   And straight to this lady did oar, oar,
   Saying 'Our captain he has sent us to your fair ladies bower,
   For to buy of your costly fine ware, ware,
   For to buy of your costly fine ware'.

3. 'I have got no riches' this maiden replied,
   'Nor have I got costly fine ware, ware',
   'Our captain he is kindly he is generous in mind
   He will keep you until you can spare, spare,
   He will keep you until you can spare'.

4. The captain he welcomed her up on the ship
   And down in his cabin did hide her,
   Saying 'This very night by my side you will lie,
   And tomorrow I'll make you my bride, bride,
   And tomorrow I'll make you my bride'.

5. 'I'll sing you a song, O! my merry sea-men,
   I'll sing you a song I declare, declare,
   It's concerning the waves, it's concerning the wars',
   And the captain said 'Hand her a chair, a chair',
   And the captain said 'Hand her a chair'.

6. She sang it so graceful, she sang it so sweet,
    She sang it so nice I declare, I declare,
    That she sang the sea-captain and his men asleep,
    Saying 'Fly away sorrow and care, care,
    Saying 'Fly away sorrow and care'.

7. She took up the captain's bright sword in her hand,
    Saying 'This will do me for an oar, an oar,
    As the God upon land he is also on sea,
    He'll protect me till I get on shore, sea-shore,
    He'll protect me till I get on shore'.

8. 'O! It's were my men crazy or were my men mad,
    Or were my men all in despair, despair?
    For to let her away with my bright golden sword,
    And she's now the free maid on the shore, sea-shore,
    And she's now the free maid on the shore'.

A fragment recorded by Seamus Ennis for the BBC from Michael Cronin, 7 May 1954, is from our song:

She sang it so sweet, so mild and complete
It caused both the captain and crew for to sleep.

Seán Corcoran points out that this song is very rare in Britain, though quite common in North America. A fragment was published by Joyce, *Old Irish folk-music and song*, No. 327 (*The Mermaid*), but apparently only one (unpublished) version has turned up in the oral tradition of the British Isles; see Palmer, *Everyman book of British ballads*, 62–63 and 243. A fragment collected from Mrs Costello of Birmingham, and published in *JFDSS* 7/2 (1953) 99–100, is not part of this song, but is a version of *Short Jacket and White Trousers*.

137

Show me the lady that never would roam

1. Show me the lady that never would roam
    Far away from her fireside at night;
    And never go roaming out after the boys,
    But would sit by her fireside so bright.

2. My wife she is one of the different kind,
    Often causes me a lot of grief;
    She oft from her home [... ...]
    She leaves me alone to rick (?).

Text From a DÓC notebook. I have no printed version.   **Note** The text is very faint, and corrected in several places. It appears to be faulty in the second verse.

138

Siubá-ín baby

1. *Siubá-ín* baby, *siubá-ín* baby,
    Siubá-ín baby, cradle and all;
    When the wind blows the cradle do fall,
    Then down with the cradle, baby and all.

2. Siubá-ín baby, *siubá-ín* baby,
    Siubá-ín baby, cradle and all;
    When the wind blows the cradle do fall,
    Then down with the baby, cradle and all.

3. The birdeen is calling, screeching and bawling,
    The birdeen is calling abroad in the bush;
    Siubá-ín baby, *siubá-ín* baby,
    Siubá-ín baby, cradle and all;
    When the wind blows the cradle do fall,
    Then down with the baby, cradle and all.

Text From a DÓC notebook.   **Notes** Probably the best-known lullaby in the English language, see Opie & Opie, *Oxford dictionary of nursery rhymes*, 61–62. For a different song incorporating the same theme, see Joyce, *Ancient Irish music*, 67, No. 66.

139

Siúil, a rúin[1/22]

1. I would I were on yonder hill,
    It is there I'd sit and cry my fill,
    And every tear would turn a mill,
    A's go dté tú, mo mhúirnín, slán!

    Siúil, siúil, siúil, a riúin,
    Siúil go socair is siúil go ciúin,
    Siúil go doras agus éalaigh liúm,
    A's go dté tú, mo mhúirnín, slán.

2. I'll sell my rock, I'll sell my reel,
    I'll sell my only spinning-wheel,
    To buy my love a coat of steel,
    A's go dté tú, mo mhúirnín, slán!

    Siúil, siúil, siúil, a riúin,
    Siúil go socair agus siúil go ciúin,
    Siúil go doras agus éalaigh liúm,
    Is go dté tú, mo mhúirnín, slán.

3.   I'll dye my petticoats, I'll dye them red,
     And round the world I'll beg for bread,
     Until my parents shall wish me dead,
     Agus go dté tú, mo mhúirnín, slán!

     Siúil, siúil, siúil, a riúin,
     Siúil go socair agus siúil go ciúin,
     Siúil go doras agus éalaigh liúm,
     A's go dté tú, mo mhúirnín, slán!

Recordings BBC 21535 (Autumn 1951) = Kennedy, *Folktracks* F–60–160 (1981) A13 = Kennedy & Lomax, *Songs of courtship* [= *The folk songs of Britain* 10], Topic Records 12T157 (1961) A 10.   **Text** From the BBC recording.   **Printed Sources** *Elias Howe's songs of Ireland*, 73 'Shule agrah, or Johnny has gone for a soldier' (5 vv.); *Delaney's Irish song book*, No. 2, 5; Sparling, *Irish minstrelsy*, 232–33 (5 vv.); Moffatt, *The minstrelsy of Ireland*, 104–5 (4 vv.); Cambridge University Library Ballads, vol. 5, 646; Joyce, *Old Irish folk music and song*, 236–38, No. 425 (5 vv.) [close to our text]; Breathnach, *Songs of the Gael* 1, 214–15 (5 vv.). See also Graves, *The Irish song book*, 6–7 ('adapted by the Editor'); *The Sarsfield song and recitation book*, 17 (5 vv.). Modern editions in Colum, *Broad-sheet ballads*, 12–13; *Walton's treasury of Irish songs and ballads*, 8 (5 vv.); Vaughan Williams & Lloyd, *The Penguin book of English folk songs*, 53; also Lomax, *The folk songs of North America in the English language*, 47–48, No. 20 *Johnny has gone for a soldier*; Cole, *Folksongs of England, Ireland, Scotland and Wales*, 64–67 (2 versions, both 5 vv., second version from Patrick Galvin, to a tune resembling the last half of the Protestant hymn *Nearer, My God, to Thee*); no source is cited for version 1. See also McPheeley, *More than 1000 songs and dances of the Irish people*, 81 (5 vv.); no source cited; Dallas, *The cruel wars*, 11–12; Mac Mathúna, *Traditional songs and singers*, 26–27 (from a recording of Bess Cronin); Meek, *The land of libertie: songs of the Irish in America*, 28–29.   **Notes** Zimmermann, *Songs of Irish rebellion*, 32 n. 78, says that this song was very often reprinted in pedlars' garlands; modern reprints of it are legion. The version in Vaughan Williams & Lloyd, *Penguin book of English folk songs*, 53, is from Mrs Cecilia Costello. The text in Howe's *Songs of Ireland*, 73, is as follows:

A.   Oh, Johnny dear has gone away,
     He has gone across to Bombay;
     Oh, my heart is sad and weary today,
     Since Johnny has gone for a soldier,

     Shule, shule, shule, a-grah!
     Time can only ease my wo,
     Since the lad of my heart from me did go;
     Oh, Johnny has gone for a soldier.

B.   Some say my love has gone to France,
     There his fortune to advance,
     And if I find him, it's but a chance,
     Oh, Johnny has gone for a soldier.

     Shule, shule, &c.

C.   I'll sell my flax, I'll sell my wheel,
     I'll buy my love a sword of steel,
     So in the battle he may reel,
     Oh, Johnny has gone for a soldier.

     Shule, shule, &c.

D.   I wish I was on yonder hill,
     It's there I'd sit and cry my fill,
     So every tear may turn a mill, —
     Oh, Johnny has gone for a soldier.

     Shule, shule, &c.

E.   I'll dye my dress, I'll dye it red,
     And through the streets I'll beg my bread,
     Oh, how I wish that I was dead,
     Since Johnny has gone for a soldier.

     Shule, shule, &c.

In most versions verse B above comes at the end of the song. Moffatt points out that one verse appears to have been incorporated in the Scottish song called *Rantin' roarin' laddie*, preserved in David Herd's *Scottish songs* 2 (Edinburgh 1776):

> I'll sell my rock, my reel, my tow,
> My gude grey mare and hacket cow,
> To buy my love a tartan plaid,
> Because he is a roving blade.

The text in *Delaney's Irish song book* has the following final 2 verses:

> I wish, I wish, I wish in vain,
> I wish I had my heart again.
> And vainly think I'd not complain.
> Is go de tu mo murnin slan.

> But now my love has gone to France,
> To try his fortune to advance.
> If he e'er come back 'tis but a chance,
> Is go de tu mo murnin slan.

There is a version from CBÉ 629, 529 (Limerick 1938) published in Diarmuid Ó Muirithe, *An t-amhrán macarónach*, 40, and 196, No. 4. The refrain, *Siúil a rúin, siúil a ghrá*, etc., occurs in a song of that title (but with different words) published in Mac Coluim, *Bolg an tsoláthair*, 9. See likewise Ní Annagáin & De Chlanndiolúin, *Londubh an chairn*, No. 18; and J. P. Craig, *An ceoltóir* 1, X. There is a hilarious pastiche of the song in *Delaney's Irish song book*, No. 4 (New York, n. d. [c. 1900]) 20.

140

Sweet Boney, will I e'er see you more?[1/14]

1. Curiosity led a young native of Erin
    To view the gay banks of the Rhine,
    Where an empress he saw and the robe she was wearing
    All over with diamonds did shine.
    No goddess of splendour was ever yet seen
    That could equal this fair one so mild and serene.
    In soft murmurs she cried: 'My young linnet so green,
    Sweet Boney, will I e'er see you more?'

2. Neither Hannibal, Caesar, nor great Alexander,
    Or Hector, the Trojan so bold,
    Were ever more braver where'er you did wander —
    You cared not for heat nor for cold.
    It grieves me the hardships that you did undergo,
    And the mountains you travelled all covered with snow.
    In the valley sepulchre your courage lay low —
    Are you gone, will I e'er see you more?

3. The numbers of men that were eager to slay you!
    Their malice you viewed with a smile.
    Their gold through all England they sowed to betray you
    And they joined the Mamelukes on the Nile.
    Like ravens for blood, their wild passions did burn;
    The orphans they slew and caused widows to mourn.
    They say my linnet's gone and never will return —
    Are you gone, will I e'er see you more?

4. The crowned heads of Europe, when you were in splendour,
    They fain would have you submit;
    But the goddess of freedom soon made them surrender,
    And their standard was lowered by your wit.
    Old Frederick's colours into France you did bring;
    Yet his offspring found protection under your wing.
    That year in St Claud's you sweetly did sing —
    Sweet Boney, will I e'er see you more?

5. In famed Waterloo, where thousands lay sprawling
    All over the fields high and low,
    Fame through her trumpets on Frenchmen were calling,
    Fresh laurels to place on her brow.
    Usurpers did tremble to hear the loud call,
    And a third of old Babel's new buildings did fall.
    The Spaniards their fleet back to harbour did call —
    Are you gone, will I e'er see you more?

6.   I've roamed through the deserts of wild Abyssinia
But could find no relief for my pain.
Shall I go and enquire at the isle of St Helena —
Ah! no, I should whisper in vain!
Come, tell me you critics, now tell me in time
What nations shall I range my Green Linnet for to find?
Was he slain in Waterloo or on the banks of the Rhine,
Or did he die in St Helena's green shore?

Recordings BBC 11990 (7 Aug. 1947) — BBC 21996 (Aug. 1954). **Text** From the BBC 1954 recording. **Printed Sources** Fitzgerald, 'An account of the old street ballads of Cork', *Jnl Cork Hist. & Arch. Soc.* 1/4 (1892) 63–71: 66 (2 vv.); *Delaney's Irish song book*, No. 1, 11; Joyce, *Old Irish folk music and songs*, 175–76, No. 372 *The Green Linnet* (5 vv.); Breathnach, *Songs of the Gael* 1, 314–15 (5 vv.); Zimmermann, *Songs of Irish rebellion*, 184–86, No. 30 (7 vv.); Milner, *The bonnie bunch of roses*, 158–59 (6 vv., from a broadside by Disley). **Notes** There is another text in CBÉ 476, 114–16 (dated 28 March 1938). The song is best known under the title *The Green Linnet*. John Fitzgerald, 'An account of the old street ballads of Cork', 66, remarks that the song 'though a great favourite, was very rare'. He has our verse 1 and this version of v. 2:

A.   Oh; the cold frosty Alps you so freely passed over,
Which nature had placed in your way,
And Marengo, where Bellona around you did hover,
All Paris rejoiced the next day.
It grieves me the hardship that you did undergo,
And the mountains you travelled all covered with snow,
And the Balance of Power where your courage was laid low;
Are you gone — will I ne'er see you more?

Delaney's song book has the same verse as follows:

The cold, lofty Alps you freely went over,
Which nature had placed in your way.
That Marengo Saloney [*sic!*] around you did hover,
And Paris rejoiced the next day, etc.

Joyce, *Old Irish folk music and songs*, 175, remarks that he had the song 'printed on ballad-sheets by Haly of Cork sixty or seventy years ago', which would date it c. 1839/1849. He omits verses 2 and 5. The text in CBÉ 476 has omitted v. 6, inverted the order of our verses 3 and 4, and has the following variants in v. 2:

It grieved me the hardships that you did undergo,
And the cold frosty Alps all covered with snow.
But your courage was by bribery and treachery laid low,
Are you gone, etc.

Zimmermann's text (which he dates to c. 1830), is from a garland printed by W. Kelly at Waterford, and is very close to ours; it has the title *Maria Louisa's lamentation for the loss of her lover*. The tune is the same as that for *Faiche Bhreá Aerach an Cheoil* [No. **57**] and for *The Charming Sweet Girl that I Love* [No. **154**].

Cur - i - os - it - y led __ a young na-tive of E - rin __

To view the gay banks of the Rhine,

Where __ an Emp-ress he saw and __ the robe she was wea - ring __

All o - ver with dia - monds did shine.

No __ God - dess of __ splen - dor __ was ever yet __ seen

That __ could eq - ual this fair one so mild and se - rene.

In soft mur-murs she cried: __ 'My young lin - net so green, __

Sweet Bo - ney, will I e'er see you more?'

141

Sweet Kilydysart[2/15]

1. In sweet Kilydysart, as Phoebus was dawning,
    I went to the fair and my cattle I sold
    For to buy for my father a vest and a breeches,
    A pipe for my mother, tobacco and brogues.
    I sold the two cows and a sheep to a dealer;
    He paid me down cash both in silver and gold;
    But Biddy came bouncing and scolding like blazes
    And threw me the child till we both were exposed.

2. To flatter this damsel I did my endeavours;
   I rolled up the child in the skirt of my coat.
   We called to an inn where I had an acquaintance;
   We drank and caroused till the cocks they were crowing.
   We drank a good health to the friends and the neighbours
   To sweet Lizzy Easy and Peggy Malone.
   That beautiful creature — the pride of the nation —
   Though down from the mountain, she's rare to behold.

3. This beautiful damsel is nicely accomplished;
   She's very well able to knit and to sew.
   To spin with her wheel when the wool is in season,
   And making up linen as white as the snow.
   In milking her cows and in minding her dairy
   Her butter has taken the sway in the store.
   She sprang from the prince of the Irish Milesians
   Who banished the Danes from invading our shore.

4. She could draw with her needle a map of old Erin,
   The Garden of Eden and Temple of Rome;
   The ship in full sail and she crossing the ocean,
   The fox in full chase and the goose that he stole.
   But Biddy abused me and called me a schemer
   For not getting married before she came home.
   She ruined my character by throwing me the baby,
   And left me blind drunk on the side of the road.

5. So now I'm returned to dear Lizzy Easy,
   Both tired and fatigued without money or clothes.
   Once down is no battle — what matter about it! —
   The sense that's well bought is worth silver and gold.
   I'll marry young Peggy that's full of good nature;
   There is plenty potatoes and bacon at home.
   She'll suckle her infant without hesitation,
   And we'll live as contented as a king on his throne.

Recordings BBC 19025 (21 Sept. 1952) — JR-GP (2 Nov. 1952). **Text** From the JR-GP recording. There is a copy in Bess's hand-written collection of songs, and another (identical) text in a DÓC notebook. **Printed Sources** Royal Irish Academy, RR 66 H 17 (Lord Moyne Coll.) 37. There are three other copies in Cambridge University Library Ballads, vol. 3, 152, vol. 4, 191 and 367 with the title *Favorite New Song, the Mountain Phoenix*; Healy, *The Mercier Book of Old Irish Street Ballads* 1, 279–80 *(The Mountain Phoenix)*. **Notes** The Royal Irish Academy broadside text is almost identical to ours. 'Lizzy Easy' in vv. 2f and 5a is Lissycasey, Co. Clare (and is correctly spelt in the ballad sheet). The song has the same air as *Nice Little Jenny from Ballinasloe* [No. **103**]. There are other recorded versions in CBÉ 77, 312 (Galway 1934); CBÉ 193, 619–22 (Clare 1936); CBÉ 275, 318–21 (Waterford 1936); CBÉ 275, 469–72 (Waterford 1936); CBÉ 317, 370–73 (Waterford 1937); CBÉ 318, 96–100 (Waterford 1937); CBÉ 1591, 180–82 (Cork 1960).

In sweet Kily - dy - sart, as Phoe - bus was daw - ning,

I went to the fair and my catt - le I sold

For to buy for my fath - er a vest and a bree - ches

A pipe for my mo - ther, tob - acc - o and brogues

I sold the two cows and a sheep to a deal - er;

He paid me down cash both in sil - ver and gold;

But Bid - dy came boun - cing and scol - ding like blaz - es

And threw me the child till we both were ex - posed.

142

Sweet Lisbweemore[1/27]

1. One morning in the month of June,
    as Sol's bright beams the air illum'ed,
    My cattle from the bawn I drove,
    and then stretched at my ease.
    The skylark sang melodiously,
    a lovely lass appeared to me,
    Down by the turbary
    in sweet Lisbweemore.

2. When I saw this maid approaching me
my heart rose to a height of glee,
I stood with great alacrity
to accost this comely maid.
She says: 'Kind sir, I'm going astray;
please, now, would you show me the way
That leads to the weaver's house
in sweet Lisbweemore?'

3. When I beheld this charming maid,
my heart began to palpitate,
My eyes began to dazzle
and her figure I could not state.
She was loaded with some balls of thread,
the same she had upon her head,
Passing by the turbary
in sweet Lisbweemore.

4. 'Come along, my pretty maid,
don't be of me the least afraid;
I'll lead you through this rugged place
you never went before.
Your guardian I will surely be,
until that young man's face you'll see,
Down by the turbary
in sweet Lisbweemore.

5. There is no other human being
in showing the way can surpass me;
I know it from my infancy,
so come along, *a stóir*.
Or if you will abide with me,
I'll always style you '*grá mo chroí*',
Here by the turbary
in sweet Lisbweemore'.

6. She soon replied: 'Indeed, I won't;
you are a scheming, naughty rogue!
So please desist from flattery
with a simple, honest maid.
But if you're inclined to show the way,
then come along, don't me delay,
Down by the turbary
in sweet Lisbweemore'.

7. What she said I did excuse,
her request I could not refuse,
As we walked along together
she this to me did say:
'Where lives the man they call "D.D."?
his residence I'd like to see,

Down by the turbary
in sweet Lisbweemore'.

8.   'The truth to you I will relate:
I do not wish to see his face;
The reason, too, I'll tell to you:
'tis early in the day.
For if he'd see us two alone,
a song for us he would compose,
Down by the turbary
in sweet Lisbweemore'.

9.   'To do his best, what can he say —
are we not honest going the way?
Besides, he has the [? tendency]
never to dispraise.
But if another man were in my shoes
he'd spoil your thread, both warp and woof,
Down by the turbary
in sweet Lisbweemore'.

10.   When this I said, without delay,
upon my word! she ran away!
In vain I tried to follow her
through flat and steeplechase.
No roe-buck in the park so quick could lep
beyond each *ceap* and ditch
As she did through the turbary
in sweet Lisbweemore!

11.   And as she was too smart for me,
though I ran with great rapidity,
I was troubled with the dint of speed
and topsy-turvy thrown.
Ere again on ground my foot I lay
At least, from the turbary
in sweet Lisbweemore.

Recordings: CBÉ 393a (1947) — BBC 11989 (7 Aug. 1947) — Seamus Ennis (May 1947) — BBC 19021 (8 Sept. 1952) = Kennedy, *Folktracks* F–60–160 (1981) B1.   **Text:** From the BBC 11989 recording.   **Notes:** The BBC 1947 version is basically the same text as BBC 1952, but better (and with no crackle). The BBC version has 10 verses; CBÉ 393a has only vv. 1–4 (the BBC versions have v. 4 as v. 6). Seamus Ennis's BBC note reads: 'Song is fairly old as the girl was going to the weaver's house carrying balls of thread on her head, as was the women's custom in older times, when the bard met her. It is probably a product of the bardic schools of the early 19th century'. The 'D. D.' mentioned in verse 7e is possibly to be identified with Dinny Denis (*alias* Parthalán Ó Conaill), of Cnocán an Bhóthair, between Lios Buí Mór and Lios Buí Beag (for whom see *An Botháinín Íseal Gan Fálthas* [No. **13**]).

One___ mor-ning in _ the month of June, as _ Sol's bright beams the air il - lum'ed

My_ catt-le from. the yard I drove, and then stretched at _ my_ ease.

The sky-lark sang me-lo-dious-ly, a _ love-ly lass a-ppeared to me,

Down__ by _ the tur - bar - y in sweet ___ Lis - bwee-more.

143

Sweet Liscarrol Town

1. You roving boys of pleasure, give ear unto my song!
   I'll sing for you a verse or two that won't detain you long.
   I'm pressed in grief and no relief, in slavery I'm bound.
   I am far from those who wished me well in sweet Liscarrol Town.

2. 'Tis there you'd see the pretty girls dressed up in silk so fine;
   They far exceed bright Venus or fair Helen in her prime.
   Their hair hangs o'er their shoulders, so neatly hanging down.
   There's no beauty there I could compare to you, Liscarrol Town.

3. 'Tis there you'd see fine horses, fine carriages and carts.
   Noble men of honour there come from foreign parts.
   There's a convent situated on an elevated tower,
   And valleys to submit them all in sweet Liscarrol Town.

4. If I were in Liscarrol Town I'd count myself at home.
   I think I'd be as happy as a king upon his throne.
   But now, when I am far away and strangers on me frown,
   How can I help to shed a tear for you, Liscarrol Town?

5. So fare thee well, Liscarrol Town, to tell the candid truth,
   I hope you will excuse me for being a foolish youth.
   With a cheerful voice I do rejoice, the pride of all renown.
   I curse the day I chanced to stray from you, Liscarrol Town.

Text From Bess's handwritten collection of songs. I have no printed version.

144

Táim cortha ó bheith im' aonar im' luí[1/28]

1. *Tráthnóinín déanach is mé a' dul a' bhálcaeracht*
   'sea do dhearcas spéirbhean a' caoi.
   D'fhiosraíos féin di — do labhair sí go séimh liom:
   'Táim cortha ó bheith am' aonar am' luí, am luí,
   Táim cortha ó bheith am' aonar am' luí'.

2. One evening of late as I carelessly strayed
   I espied a fair maid in great moan.
   I asked her the matter, she quickly made answer:
   'I'm weary from lying alone, alone,
   I'm weary from lying alone'.

3. *A's a mhúirnín donn dílis, suidh anso taobh liom,*
   Agus aithris scéal dom ar t'aois.
   'A cúig agus a sé agus a' sárú dhá naoi,
   A's táim cortha ó bheith am' aonar am' luí, am' luí,
   Táim cortha ó bheith am' aonar am' luí'.

4. My comely young damsel, sit down here alongside me,
   And tell me the years that have flown.
   'Oh! there's seven and one and eleven years long,
   And I'm weary from lying alone, alone,
   I'm weary from lying alone'.

5. *Agus dá bhfaighinn ógánach éigin do thógfadh gan spré mé,*
   A's go mbeinn aige féinig mar mhnaoi,
   Ní cheilfinn ar éinne é 's do neosfainn don tsaol é,
   Go bhfuilim cortha ó bheith am' aonar am' luí, am' luí,
   Táim cortha ó bheith am' aonar am' luí'.

6. If I got some comely young man that would take me without fortune
   And would make me a wife of his own!
   But the truth I'll explain — that I'll die in despair —
   If I lie any longer alone, alone,
   If I lie any longer alone'.

7. *Is tá róisín breá néata sa gháirdín seo taobh linn,*
   Á, baineam is déanam é fhí,
   Mar is ró-ghearr 'na dhéidh sin go mbeidh sé chomh traochta
   Leis a' mnaoi a bhíodh 'na haonar 'na luí, 'na luí,
   Leis an mnaoi a bhíodh 'na haonar 'na luí.

8. There's a neat sweetly flower in this garden 'longside us:
   Take it and make it your own.
   For the flower it will fade, so also the maid,
   That is weary from lying alone, alone,
   That is weary from lying alone.

Recording CBÉ 389 (1947). **Text** From the CBÉ recording. **Printed Sources** Shepard, *The broadside ballad: a study in origins and meaning*, 142 [facsimile]; cf. McCarthy, *Bawdy British folk songs*, 124–25. **Notes** The broadside published in facsimile by Leslie Shepard, *The broadside ballad*, is called *A New Song, called, Weary of tumbling Alone* and reads as follows:

1. One morning of la[t]e as I walk'd in great state,
   I heard a maiden making sad moan;
   I ask'd her the matter, she said, sir, I won't flat[t]er,
   I am weary of tumbling alone.

2. O that is [a] pity, that a maiden so pretty,
   And the young men so idle are grown,
   But a curse light upon it, and worse may come on it,
   If I leave you a tumbling alone.

3. O then, says the sailor, can you fancy me,
   I have got gold, and got silver in store,
   I have brought from the sea, such a fine remedy,
   That will ease you of tumbling alone.

4. O then, says the fair maid, if you can fancy me,
   I have got plenty of money in store,
   No more cross the main[,] to fight France nor Spain,
   Nor go where the cannons loud roar.

5. O then, says the sailor, I can fancy you,
   As long as your money doth last,
   She grows thick in the waist, and thin in the face,
   But the sailor he steers off at last.

6. As down in the garden there grows a red rose,
   I'll pluck it, and call it my own,
   In an hour it will fade, and so will a maid,
   That's weary of tumbling alone.

McCarthy, *Bawdy British folk songs*, 124–25 has this text. The song was doubtless originally an English broadside ballad, which was translated into Irish and fashioned into this macaronic version. There are slight discrepancies between the Irish and English verses occasionally, e.g. verses 3 and 4 give different ages for the young woman. That the song may have been older still is suggested by

Tráth-nói - nín déan - ach is mé a' dul a' bhál - cae - racht

'sea do dhear - cas _____ spéir - bhean a' caoi.

D'fhios-raí - os féin _____ di do labh - air sí _____ go séimh liom:

Táim __ cor - tha ó bheith am' ao - nar am'_ luí, am __ luí,

Táim _____ cor - tha ó bheith am' ao - nar am'_ luí.

the fact that in one of the Pepys ballads (dated probably 1615) there is reference to another ballad called A Maiden's Lamentation for a Bedfellow. Or, I can, nor will no longer lye alone, 'as it hath been often sung at the Court'; see Rollins, *A Pepysian garland*, 78. Joyce, *Old Irish folk music and songs*, 315, No. 611, has an air called 'I'm weary of walking alone', but it differs from the air of our song here. For the term *bhálcaeracht*, in v. 1, cf. the song called *Casam Araon na Géanna Romhainn* [No. **37**] v. 4 (g), and another entitled *Rachadsa 's mo Chití ag bhálcaeracht* in Breathnach, *Sídh-cheól* 2, 34–36 (from the *JIFSS*), written down in Kilmalchedar, Co. Kerry, in 1901 (ibid. 198). For a recent recording, see Sarah McQuaid, *When two lovers meet*, Mongrel Music (Dublin 1997), MMCD001 (8) (learned from the singing of Iarla Ó Lionaird, a grand-nephew of Bess's).

145

The banks of Sullane[1/24]

1.   How pleasant, on a fine summer's morning,
        To stroll by the banks of Sullane,
        And to gaze on the beauties of nature
        That embellished the woods and the lawns.
        The prospect is surely enchanting,
        With gay lasses in juvenile bloom
        Perambulating by the banks of that river,
        As it flows through the town of Macroom.

2.   I being airy and fond of enjoyment
        By this river I chanced for to rove,
        Until wearied of my rambles and walkings
        I laid myself down by a grove.
        In contentment I sat meditating
        Until Sol had his rays all withdrawn,
        When a damsel of queenly appearance
        Came down by the banks of Sullane.

3.   Then I stood with great joy and emotion
        On perceiving that angelic fair
        Whose apparel in the greatest profusion
        Was bespangled with jewels so rare.
        Her fine and her majestic figure —
        To describe it I will not presume —
        For like Venus she appeared by that river
        As it flows through the town of Macroom.

4.   However, we walked on together,
        Inhaling the pleasant fine air,
        Until at length with a voice much dejected
        She says: 'See, my father comes there!'
        His appearance to me was appalling;
        His cross angry look and his frown;
        For it pierced through my heart like an arrow,
        On my way down through sweet Massey-town.

5.   I quickly retreated from my storeen
        With a heart full of sorrow and grief;

For no joy here on earth can console me,
Or bring me the slightest relief.
Sure, I'll wander o'er the African deserts
Until death shall bring me to the tomb;
For my lovely and charming young Helen
That I met near the town of Macroom.

Recordings CBÉ 911 (1947) — BBC 11991 (7 Aug. 1947). **Text** BBC 11911. Another in Bess's handwritten collection of songs; a third in CBÉ 737, 70–72. **Printed Sources** Cf. Ó Canainn, *Songs of Cork*, 70–71 (a modern version). **Notes** Seán Ó Cróinín has a note in CBÉ 737 which reads 'Poet Ahern ó Chluain Droichid a chúm é seo, is dóigh liom', *['The Poet Ahern from Clondruhid composed this, I think']* For another manuscript version, see CBÉ 1591, 554–55 (Cork 1960); for fragments of two other songs on the same subject (both composed by Peter Goulden), see CBÉ 1591, 404 and CBÉ 1592, 69–70 (Cork 1960).

146

The banks of the Lee

1.   On the banks of the Lee the angler finds pleasure
     While casting his flies by his judgement and skill;
     Each purling fine stream he can fish at his leisure,
     The salmon and trout he is sure for to kill.

Recording BBC 21996 (Aug. 1954).   **Text** From the BBC recording.   **Notes** This much only of the song is in the BBC recording. Ennis, in his BBC notes, describes it as a 'portion of a song in praise of the River Lee in Co. Cork', and adds that the tune 'is that commonly known as *Haste to the wedding*'. [Note that our song is not the same as Joe Heaney's *Banks of the Lee* ('When true lovers meet down beneath the green bowers …').]

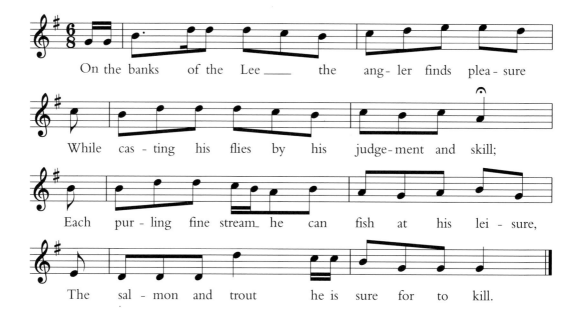

147

The bells of Heaven[2/29]

1.   The bells of heaven began to ring, began to ring, began to ring,
       The bells of heaven began to ring on a Christmas Day in the morning.

2.   The bell's of hell began to blow, began to blow, began to blow,
       The bell's of hell began to blow on a cold and frosty morning.

3.   The gates of heaven were dressed in white, were dressed in white, were dressed in white,
       The gates of heaven were dressed in white on a Christmas Day in the morning.

4.   The gates of hell were dressed in black, were dressed in black, were dressed in black,
       The gates of hell were dressed in black on a cold and frosty morning.

5.   I'll buy for you a red little book, a red little book, a red little book,
I'll buy for you a red little book on a Christmas Day in the morning.

6.   And I'll send you up to school to heaven, to school to heaven, to school to heaven,
I'll send you up to school to heaven on Christmas Day in the morning.

Recording JR-GP (24 Nov. 1952).   **Text** From the JR-GP recording.   **Note** This is a version of the carol *I Saw Three Ships*.

The bells of heaven be-gan to ring, be-gan to ring, be-gan to ring,
The bells of heaven be-gan to ring on a Christ-mas Day in the mor-ning.

148

The bonny blue-eyed lassie^{2/9}

1.   How can I live on the top of a mountain,
Without gold in my pocket or money for to count it?
I'll leave the money go, all for to please her fancy;
For I'll marry none but the bonny blue-eyed lassie.

2.   The bonny blue-eyed lassie, with her fair hair so tender;
Her red rosy cheeks and her waist neat and slender.
I'd roll her in my arms and fondly I'd embrace her,
But how can I love her, ah!, when my people hate her?

3.   Some people say she is very low in station,
While more of them say she is the cause of my ruination.
But let them all say what they will, to her I will prove constant still.
Until the day that I'll die she's my charming girl, believe me.

4.   Brightly swims the swan in the broad streams of Youghal,
And loudly sings the nightingale, all for to behold her.
In the cold frost and snow the moon shines deeply,
But deeper by far between me and my true love.

Recordings CBÉ 394a (1947) — BBC 19021 (8 Sept. 1952) — Diane Hamilton (1955).   **Text** From the Diane Hamilton recording.   **Printed Sources** Lyle, *Andrew Crawfurd's collection of ballads and songs*, vol. 1, 82, No. 33; Moulden, 'Ag déanamh ceoil', *Treoir* 16/1 (1984) [18] (from the BBC recording) [see corrections in *Treoir* 16/2 (1984) 4 and 25].   **Notes** The BBC version is taken in a lower key, though the same style. The words are clearer in the BBC version than in the CBÉ one (the latter recording being rather high-pitched). Seamus Ennis says, in his note to the BBC recording 'An old song origin unknown'. For another version, see CBÉ 219, 533–34 (Cork 1936). The version in Emily Lyle's *Crawfurd collection of ballads and songs* 1, 82, No. 33, is as follows:

1.   O gin I were at the tap of yon mountain
     Gold in my pocket and money for the counting
     I wad gar the guinea gang I wad hae my fancy
     I wad marry nane but the bonnie blue eyit Lassie

2.   She has tway bonnie blue een her looks are sae tender
     Her rosy cheeks and her body lang and sklender
     And I wad take her in my arms sae fond I wad embrace her
     For how I can love her when all the world hates her

3.   For sum folk say she is o a bad station
     And ither folks say she is o a bad nation
     But let them aw say as they will it never will grieve me
     For to the day I die she is my deir girl

4.   Though my fause friends they'd revile thee
     Here is the hand that never will beguile thee
     Here is the hand although in the dark love
     The next place ye'll find it will be in the kirk love

5.   Sweet sweet swims the swans on yon high streams o Yarrow
     Sweey sing the nightingales theire voice is like to an arrow
     It's cauld frost and snaw the mune shining clearly
     Deep runs the river between me and my dearie

How_____ can I live __ on __ the top of that moun - tain,
With- out gold in my __ poc-ket or __ mo-ney for_ to_ count_ it?
I'll _ leave the mo-ney_____ go, __ all for to please_ her fan - cy;
For _ I'll _ ma -rry_ none_ but_____ the bo- nny. blue - eyed _ la - ssie.

149

The Boston burglar

1.   I belong to Boston City, that place you all know well;
     Brought up by honest parents, the truth to you I'll tell;
     Brought up by honest parents and reared most tenderly,
     Until I became a roving chap at the age of twenty-three.

2.   My character was broken and I was sent to jail,
The neighbours tried to bail me out, but all of no avail;
The jury heard my charges, the clerk he took them down,
The magistrates found me guilty, and I was sent to Charlestown.

3.   As I passed on the eastern train on a cold December day,
At every station I stepped out you could hear the people say:
'Here comes the Boston Burglar, in strong irons he is bound,
For the robbing of the Provincial Bank he is sent to Charlestown'.

4.   As I was standing at the bar, who do you think I espied! —
I espied my aged father with the salt tear in his eye;
I espied my aged mother and the tears were travelling down,
Saying: 'Son, dear son, what have you done, that you're sent to Charlestown?'

5.   I have friends in Boston City, that place you all know well,
And if ever I get my liberty it is there I mean to dwell;
If ever I get my liberty, bad company I'll shun,
And never break the laws of man by the drinking of strong rum.

6.   Young men who have your liberty, pray, keep it while you can!
Don't ever roam the streets at night, or break the laws of man!
Or if you do, you'll surely rue, and become a man like me,
And be serving out your twenty-one years in a penitentiary.

Laws L 16 B.   **Text** From CBÉ 283, 165–67.   **Printed Sources** Sam Henry, 'Songs of the People', *Northern Constitution* (24 Sept. 1927), No. 202 (*The Boston Burglar*, 6 vv.) = Huntington & Hermann, *Sam Henry's Songs of the People*, 119–20; Ó Lochlainn, *Irish street ballads*, 88–89, No. 44 (*Boston City*); Laws, *American balladry from British broadsides*, 175; Loesberg, *Favourite Irish ballads* 5, 49–50.   **Notes** 6c 'you'll surely ruin' CBÉ MS. Sam Henry's text is similar to ours, but by no means identical. Our song occurs in one of Bess's handwritten lists under the title *I belong to Boston city* (the title it has, e.g., in Loesberg's edition); I have given it its better-known title here, for ease of reference.

150

The boy in love that feels no cold

1.   The boy in love that feels no cold, like me some time ago,
Like a hero brave through frost and snow to meet my girl did go.
The moon a-gently shone me light upon my dreary way
Until I came to my true love's gate, where all my fancy lay.

2.   And when I came to my true love's gate it's there I rapped quite slow.
She arose and left me in, most lively(?) she did go.
Her hands were soft and her breath was sweet and her [tongue did?] gently play;
And from her sweet lips I stole a kiss where all my fancy lay.

3.   'Oh, take me to your chamber, love, or take me to your room,
Or take me to some silent place and we'll wed in the afternoon'.
'To take you to my chamber, love, to that I'll not agree,
But I'll seat you down by my own fireside until daylight dawns on thee'.

4.   'Many a dark and dreary night, my love, I courted thee,
     Tossed about in the winter wind and out in the summer dew.
     For seven long years I courted you against my parents' will;
     I always intended to make you my bride, but now, sweet girl, farewell!'

5.   'Our ship lies on the ocean, just ready for to sail;
     I wish her safely landed in a sweet and pleasant gale.
     But if the wind blew from the west, bound for East Columbia's shore,
     You may then look out for another sweetheart — you'll not see me anymore'.

Laws O 20.   **Recordings** BBC 19026 (21 Sept. 1952) = Kennedy, *Folktracks* F–60–160 (1981) B13.   **Text** From the BBC recording.   **Printed Sources** McWilliams, *Poems and songs on various subjects 2*, 116; Moulden, *Songs of Hugh McWilliams, schoolmaster, 1831, 2*, 20; Dean, *The flying cloud,* 110; Sam Henry, 'Songs of the People', *Northern Constitution* (26 Nov. 1927), No. 211 (*When a man's in love*, 6 vv) = Huntington & Hermann, *Sam Henry's Songs of the People*, 479; Lomax, *The folk songs of North America in the English language*, 146–47, No. 76; Tunney, *The stone fiddle: my way to traditional song*, 96–97; Shields, *Shamrock, rose and thistle: folk singing in north Derry*, 158. See also Karpeles, *Folk songs from Newfoundland*, x, No. 59; Kennedy, *Folksongs of Britain and Ireland*, 320, No. 143 (and notes, 335); Laws, *American balladry from British broadside ballads*, 235.   **Notes** A note by DÓC in his 1947 diary (flyleaf) says that this song was composed by Seán Máistir Ó hIarlaithe, i.e. Bess's father. Presumably this is intended to mean that Bess learned it from her father. Hugh Shields, *Shamrock, rose and thistle*, 158, wrote 'The song is hardly older anyway than mid-nineteenth century, and may be less old. I have seen no popular edition of it, though it must have been circulating among the Irish in America by the early 1900s [ref. to O'Neill, *Music of Ireland* (New York 1903) 29 (air only)]. Undoubtedly Irish, it has been found chiefly in the northern half of Ireland and in parts of Canada colonized from there'. Lomax, *Folk songs of North America*, 146, says 'Probably composed by Irish bard in the 18th century, S. W. Ireland'. Kennedy, *Folksongs of Britain and Ireland,* 335, has no comment on the song's origins. However, John Moulden has given strong grounds for believing that the song was composed by Hugh McWilliams c. 1831; see his booklet, *Songs of Hugh McWilliams, 2,* 20. The air is similar to the well-known *Will you go, lassie, go?*

The boy in love that feels no cold, like me some time a-go,

Like a he-ro brave through frost and snow to meet my girl did go.

The moon a-gent-ly shone me light u-pon my drear-y way

Un-til I came to my truelove's gate where all my fan-cy lay.

151

The braes of Balquidder [1/16]

1.   Let us go, lassie, go, to the braes of Balquidder,
     Where the blawberries grow on the bonny highland heather;
     Where the deer and the doe lightly bounding together
     Sport the long summer's day on the braes of Balquidder.

2. I will twine thee a bower by the clear crystal fountain,
    And I'll cover it o'er with the flowers of the mountain.
    I will range through the wild and the steep glens so dreary,
    And return with the spoil to the bowers of my dearie.

3. Now the rude wintry winds lightly raise round our dwelling,
    And the roar of the lind on the night breezes swelling.
    How merrily we will sing when the storm rattles o'er us,
    And the dear shieling rings and the light lilting chorus!

4. Now the summer is in prime and the flowers richly blooming.
    The wild mountain thyme and the moorlands perfuming.
    To the dear native scene we will journey together,
    Where bright innocence reigns in the braes of Balquidder.

Recordings BBC 18758 (29 Aug. 1952) = Kennedy, *Folktracks* F–60–160 (1981) B6. **Text** From the BBC recording. **Printed Sources** McClaskey, *200 favorite songs*, 94; *Harding's Dublin songster*, new series, Vol. 2, No. 13, 302; *Delaney's Irish song book*, No. 1, 15; Buchan, *101 Scottish songs*, 129 (3 vv.). **Notes** The song was composed by the Scottish poet Robert Tannahill and set to music by R. A. Smith. Seamus Ennis notes that the same air was set to a song called *The Bogs of Shanaheever*, sung by Seán Mac Donnchadha of Carna, Co. Galway.

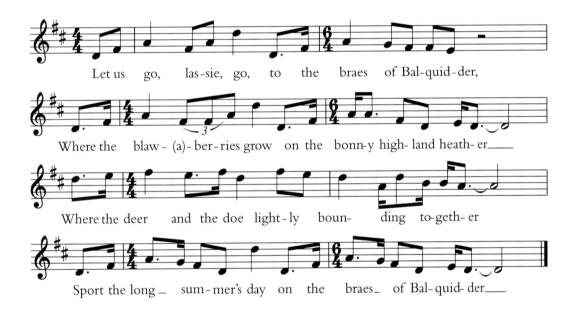

152

The Buachaill Rua[1/18]

1. Come all you pretty fair maids, give ear now and join with me,
    All for a conversation bewailing my sad destiny;
    For the lad I love so dearly from my arms from first he flew,
    And he left me here bewailing the loss of my Buachaill Rua.

2.   My love is tall and handsome, his age it is twenty-three.
      If you travelled all the nations his equals you would not see;
      With his two black eyes and ruby lips, his skin as white as any snow,
      He is a credit to Old Ireland, he's my charming sweet Buachaill Rua.

3.   My love he is undaunted, of honour and of noble blood,
      And against the foes of England in battlefield he often stood.
      He never yet retreated, although his wounds they were deep and sore.
      And I'll crown my love with laurels on the banks of Lough Erne's shore.

4.   Lough Erne is crowded, surrounded by a mist of rain;
      And so is Enniskillen, where my love he did once remain.
      Where the gentle thrush forsakes the bush and the blackbird will sing no more;
      And I'll crown my love with laurels on the banks of Lough Erne's shore.

5.   If I had the wealth of Homer and the Muses to be my friend
      I would write a letter and to England I would it send,
      In hopes that the Queen might pardon him, for he's always my grief and woe,
      And I'll crown my love with laurels on the banks of Lough Erne's shore.

6.   So now to conclude and finish with my sad destiny:
      She has granted me my darling from bondage and set him free.
      She has granted me my darling, he's the lad that I do adore,
      And I'll crown my love with laurels on the banks of Lough Erne's shore.

Recordings CBÉ 1061a (1947) — BBC 19023 (20 Sept. 1952). **Printed Sources** Royal Irish Academy, RR 66 H 17 (Lord Moyne Coll.) 131. Same broadside in NLI General Collection, and apparently also in Cambridge University Library Ballads, vol. 6, 245; Tunney, *Where songs do thunder*, 147–48. **Text** From the BBC recording; another in Bess's handwritten collection of songs. **Notes** The Royal Irish Academy and NLI broadside texts are similar to ours, but not identical. Their texts are as follows:

Come all you pre-tty_ fair _____ maids_ give ear_ now_ and join with me

All   for a con-ver-sat-ion be-wail-ing my sad des-tin-y;

For the lad I love so dear-ly from my ar - ms from first_ he flew

And he left me here_ be - wail - ing the loss of _ my Buach-aill Rua.

The Bouchael Rua

Come all you pretty fair maids give ear now & join with me
All for a conversation bewailing my sad destiny
For the lad of love so dearly from my arms from first he flew
And he left me here bewailing the loss of my Bouchaiel Rua

My love is tall & handsome his age it is twenty three
If you travelled all the nations his equals you would not see
With his two black eyes & ruby lips his skin as white as any snow.
He is a credit to Old Ireland his my charming sweet B.R

My love he is undaunted, of honour & of noble blood.
And against the foes of England, in battlefield he often stood,
He never yet retreated altho' his wounds they were deep & sore,
And I'll crown my love with laurels, on the banks of Lough Ernes Shore.

Lough Erne is crowded, surrounded by a mist of rain,
And so is Enniskillen where my love he did once remain,
Where the gentle thrush forsakes the bush & the black bird will sing no more,
And I'll crown my love with laurels on the banks of L. E shore.

If I had the wealth of Homer & the Muses to be my friend
I would write a letter & to England I would it send

'The Buachaill Rua' written by Bess herself (private collection).

A.   Come all you pretty fair maids, give ear now and join with me,
        All in a conversation concerning my love's destiny,
        A lad whom I loved dearly from my arms he was forced to go,
        I never can forget him, he is my charming young Bochal Row.

B.   He was a youth undaunted, his age was twenty three,
        Search this Irish nation, my love's equal you could not see,
        With his two black eyes and rosy cheeks, his skin as white as snow,
        I own I love him dearly, he is my charming young Bochal Row.

C.   If I had the skill of Homer, or the minister to be my friend,
        I'd sit and write a letter, to old England I would it send,
        In hopes the Queen would pardon him, to heal all my grief and woe,
        And restore him to my arms, he is my charming young Bochal Row.

D.   He was a youth undaunted, of courage and of noble blood,
        Against the foes of Erin in battle he has often stood
        He never yet retreated, though his wounds were deep and sore,
        He is a credit to old Erin, he is my charming young Bochal Row.

E.   Lough Erne is overclouded, and surrounded with mist and rain,
        And so is Enniskillen, where my darling he did once remain,
        The gentle thrush forsook the groves, the black birds will sing no more,
        With a voice of consolation bewailing my Bochal Row.

F.   Could I set forth great praises with honour to her Majesty,
        She granted me my darling, and from bondage set him free,
        So now I'll build a castle on the banks of Lough Erne shore,
        And plant the walk with laurel for my charming young Bochal Row.

See the air of this title published by Edith Wheeler, *JIFSS* 3/3–4 (1905–06) 28. Paddy Tunney, *Where songs do thunder*, has described this as 'one of Fermanagh's loveliest songs' (he gives 4 vv.); see also his record, *A wild bee's nest*, Topic 12T139 (London 1965).

153

The Cappabwee murder[1/20]

1.   One and all, on you I call, your attention now I'll crave.
        I'll sing for you a verse or two of a sad and mournful tale.
        Doubtlessly you must have heard of that life I took away
        At Cappabwee, near Keimaneigh, on that September's day.

2.   The details of this mournful crime to you I will unfold,
        Though oftentimes round your fireside the story has been told.
        Whilst here in irons cold I lie, and now it grieves me sore,
        To be thinking on that awful hour when I shall be no more.

3.   Before my name I'll mention I have one word to say:
        It was my inclination to take his life away;
        And then to plead my innocence, as any man would do,
        But the light of powerful will has brought this story true.

4.   My name it is John Sullivan, in shame I tell to ye,
        I spent my youthful happy days in mirth and jollity.
        For the wilful murder of Jim Ring I am in captivity,
        Far from the land where I was born and reared from infancy.

5. Returning from a funeral before the break of day
    And knowing that he would pass the way whilst I in ambush lay;
    Instantly across his throat a knife with force I drew
    And I dragged him to a stable floor to hide him there from view.

6. There he lay from early morning until the dark of night,
    Without a consoling friend to quench his thirst, or to offer him a bite.
    I own to God I do not know how he managed to get home
    Along that rough and rugged path and the river stepping-stones.

7. Next day I was arrested and placed in custody
    And taken to his dying bedside that he might swear on me.
    Positively, so he did, identify me plain,
    And told the story as it was both to my grief and shame.

8. So now my song is ended and my trial is coming on.
    By the forces of the Crown bound with an iron band.
    By a jury of my countrymen there is no chance for me
    But transportation all my life, or step the gallows tree.

Recordings BBC 19022 (11 Sept. 1952) = Kennedy, *Folktracks* F–60–160 (1981) B10.   **Text** From the BBC recording.   **Notes** This ballad is the confession of John Sullivan, who murdered Denis Ring and was condemned to death. The murder was committed at Cappabwee, near the Pass of Keimaneigh, west of Ballingeary, Co. Cork. The following conversation between Bess and the collector occurs at the end of the recording (BC) 'There is another verse in it, but I'd say that I couldn't manage it because it is "So farewell to his friends —", or something like that. Is that much all right mister?' 'That's fine'. 'Is it?'

154

The charming sweet girl that I love[2/21]

1. In heartrending anguish by love I am wounded
    most sadly those five or six years,
    For in secret I sigh, I lament and I mourn,
    most compassionately wasting my tears.
    'Tis all for the sake of a charming young dame
    who in my bosom have kindled a flame.
    I could not make her known to you by any other name
    but the charming sweet girl that I love.

2. Last May I saw my darling in the morning very early
    in the sweet little town of Macroom;
    She took me by the hand and treated me most kindly,
    and remained in my company till noon.
    Sharing the caresses of my approaching doom,
    She would pay me a visit, which was forgotten very soon,
    by the charming sweet girl that I love.

3. And why should not I have loved her, because she is charming
    and perfect in every degree?

And why should not I love her, because she is charming
and always proved pleasing to me.
I love her in my heart and I love her in my soul;
There's no human being on earth that could my love for her control.
I could not find to please my mind, I mean from pole to pole,
But the charming sweet girl that I love.

4.   With her I often walked through the borders of green hedges,
       when the dewdrops were sprinkled on the lawn,
       Not far from the demesne of the late-lamented Hedges,
       near the lovely sweet banks of Sullane.
       With her I often ventured in the stillness of the night
       Through the thicket of each grove where the moon could show no light,
       And where I often said: 'You are my joy and heart's delight,
       You are the charming sweet girl that I love!'

5.   If my song it were sung near Macroom where I was born,
       and now very shortly shall die;
       For it's now I am rejected, forsaken and forlorn,
       for the sake of that fair one I am dying.
       It's now I am repenting in sorrow and in grief.
       My health is fast declining, I'm despairing of relief.
       This fair one stole away my heart, although being not a thief,
       But the charming sweet girl that I love.

6.   If my song it were sung by that worthy good man Haly,
       it would soon find its way to Macroom;
       And it's there 'twould be purchased at fairs and at markets,
       where young men and fair maids are in bloom.
       Where songsters they would sing it with voices long and loud,
       And who knows but my dear darling might chance to be in the crowd!
       Oh! it's then that I would sigh and I'd say in a shout:
       'How I long for the girl that I love!'

Recordings CBÉ 396a (1947) — BBC 18759 (29 Aug. 1952) = Kennedy, *Folktracks* FSP 60–160 (1981) — JR–GP (2 Nov. 1952)
A12 (under the title *The Darling Sweet Girl of Macroom*).   **Text** From the JR–GP recording.   **Notes** The BBC 1952 recording has
only vv. 4, 5, and 6. There is a note in a DÓC notebook, taken down 30 July 1947 from Máire Bean Í Chonaill (= 'Máire Bhill'?),
which appears to attribute the song to 'The Poet of Mushera', perhaps to be identified with Tadhg Ó Síocháin, mentioned in
manuscripts of the Tórna collection in the National University of Ireland, Cork (according to a note from Seán Ua Súilleabháin).
He composed a song entitled *Muisire an Mháma* (cf. Pádraig de Brún, *Clár láimhscríbhinní Gaeilge in Ollscoil Chorcaí*, Lss Thórna, 1,
266); see also Seán Ó Cróinín & Donncha Ó Cróinín, *Seanachas Phádraig Í Chrualaoi*, 57 and 232–33. Alternatively, our poet may
be Diarmaid Ó Longaig, from the same area as Ó Síocháin, several of whose compositions have survived in manuscripts (see
Seanachas Phádraig Í Chrualaoi, 56 and 231). However, neither of these two local bards is known to have composed songs in English.
Seamus Ennis's BBC note states that it was composed 'by a bard of the Macroom area'. The DÓC notebook also has the title *The
Darling Sweet Girl that I Love*. The song has the same air as *Sweet Boney will I e'er see you more?* [No. **140**] and *Faiche bhreá aerach an
cheoil* [No. **57**].

In _____ heart-ren-dring__ an - guish__ by love ____ I am woun-ded__

most sad- ly those five or six years,

For in sec - ret I sigh, _____ I la - ment and__ I mourn._____

most com- pas-sio- ate- ly was - ting my tears.

'Tis all __ for the __ sake . of _____ a char-ming_____ young dame

who ___ in my bo-som_____have kin- dled a flame.

I _____ could not make her known to you _ by an-y o - ther name

but _____ the char- ming sweet girl that I love.

155

The Croppy boy

1. It was early, early in the spring,
    The small birds whistled and sweetly did sing;
    Changing their notes from tree to tree
    And the song they sang was *Old Ireland Free*!

2. It was early, early, last Sunday night,
    The yeomen cavalry gave me a fright.
    The yeomen cavalry was my downfall,
    When taken I was by Lord Cornwall.

3.   'Twas in his guard-house where I was laid,
      And in his parlour where I was tried;
      My sentence passed and my spirits low,
      And to New Geneva I was forced to go.

4.   As I was passing my father's door
      My brother Willie stood on the floor.
      My poor aged father in grief full sore,
      And my tender mother her hair she tore.

5.   When my sister Mary heard the express
      She ran downstairs in her morning dress,
      Saying 'Five hundred pounds I would lay down
      To see you walking through Wexford Town'.

6.   When I was walking through Wexford Town —
      Now who would blame me to cry or frown?
      I looked behind and I looked before,
      But my tender mother I ne'er saw more.

7.   I chose the dark and I chose the blue;
      I chose the pink and the orange too.
      I forsook them all and did them deny
      And the name I got was 'The Croppy Boy'.

8.   'Twas in old Ireland this young man died;
      And in old Ireland his body's laid.
      Now all good people who do pass by
      Say 'The Lord have mercy on The Croppy Boy'.

Laws J 14. Text From Seamus Ennis's CBÉ copybooks (Sept. 1946); another in a DÓC notebook (handwritten by Bess).
Printed Sources Royal Irish Academy, RR 66 H 17 (Lord Moyne Coll.) 30; several broadside copies in the National Library of Ireland, General Collection, and in Cambridge University Library Ballads, vol. 3, 214; vol. 4, 346; vol. 5, 262; vol. 6, 14; Sparling, *Irish minstrelsy*, 73–74 (9 vv., 'taken from a London ballad-slip of 1830'); Joyce, *Old Irish folk music and songs*, 192–93, No. 385; cf. idem, *Ancient Irish music*, 62 (music, with words of v. 2 only); *Delaney's Irish song book*, No. 1, 12 (12 vv.); Colum, *Broad-sheet ballads*, 52–53 (10 vv.); Ó Lochlainn, *More Irish street ballads*, 80–81 (8 vv.); Zimmermann, *Songs of Irish rebellion*, 161–65, No.19 two broadsides, one printed by Haly in Cork (10 vv.), another anonymously in Dublin (7 vv.); a third text is given from R. R. Madden's *Literary remains of the United Irishmen* (6 vv.). See Karpeles, *Cecil Sharp's collection of English folk songs*, 2, No. 309 (6 vv. + 2 ll.) [text corrupted].   **Notes** There is a good discussion of this song in Zimmermann, *Songs of Irish rebellion*, 96–97, who also gives texts from various broadsides, 161–65. He lists the different airs to which the song is sung, and points out that it also appears in North American ballad collections, with reference to Laws, *Amerian balladry from British broadsides* (Philadelphia 1957) 135, and Helena Creighton, *Gaelic songs and ballads from Nova Scotia* (1964) No. 85. The version in Sparling's *Irish minstrelsy*, 73–74, is set in Dungannon, and the hero dies there rather than in New Geneva. Two of the NLI broadsides have this detail. Bess's version is perhaps closest to the NLI broadside printed by Haly of Cork, with 10 vv. The Royal Irish Academy broadside (and the version in *Delaney's Irish song book*) has, after our v. 3, the following lines:

A.   When I was marching through the streets,
      The drums and fifes did play so sweet,
      The drums and fifes did so sweetly play
      When to New Geneva I was forced away.
      [As we were marching so far away, *Delaney's Song Book*]

The two texts are otherwise almost identical. The text in Sparling's *Irish minstrelsy*, 73–74, has 9 verses in the order: 1, 2, 3, 4, a, 5, 6, b, 8, but lacks our v. 7; the additional verses a, b are as follows:

a.   As I was walking up Wexford Street
      My own first cousin I chanced to meet;

1st   The Croppy Boy.

It was early early in the Spring
~~The small birds whistled & sweetly did sing~~
~~My love sailed out for to serve the King~~
~~# Changing their notes from tree to tree~~
~~The raging seas & the winds blew high~~
~~And the Song they sang was Old Ireland free.~~
~~Which parted me from my Sailor boy.~~

2nd

It was early last Sunday night
The Yeomen Cavlary gave me a fright
The Yeomen Cavlary was my downfall
When taken I was by Lord Cornwall

3rd

I was in his guard-house where I was laid
And in his parlour where I was tried
My sentence passed & my spirits low
And to New Geneva I was forced to Go.

~~4th~~

As I was passing my fathers door
My brother Willie stood on the floor
My poor aged father in grief full sore.
And my tender Mother her hair she tore,

'The Croppy boy' written out by Bess Cronin (with corrections) (private collection).

My own first cousin did me betray,
And for one bare guinea swore my life away.

b.   As I was mounted on the platform high,
My aged father was standing by;
My aged father did me deny,
And the name he gave me was the Croppy Boy.

Verse (b) is the penultimate verse in *Delaney's song book*. Delaney has the following version of v. (a) and a closing verse:

As I was marching through Wexford Street,
My sister Mary, I chanced to meet;
That false young woman did me betray,
And for one guinea she swore my life away.

And when I am dead and taken to my grave,
A descent (*sic*) funeral, pray, let me have!
And over my head plant a laurel tree,
In sweet remembrance, remembrance of me.

The Haly broadside in the NLI also has verse (a) above, and this second additional verse:

c.   Farewell father, and mother, too,
And sister mary, I have but you;
As for my brother, he's all alone,
He's pointing pikes on a grinding stone.

Padraic Colum's version in *Broad-sheet ballads* appears to be based on this Haly text. The first verse in Bess's handwritten text is written over the following:

It was early early in the Spring
My love sailed out for to serve the King
The raging seas and the winds blew high
Which parted me from my sailor boy.

Cf. song No. **75**. The song called *The Small Birds Whistled* in one of Bess's song-lists is probably identical with this song here.

156

The Dingle puck goat

1.   I am a young jobber, both foolish and airy,
The green hills of Kerry I came for to see.
I went back to Dingle to buy up some cattle,
I hope you will listen to what happened me.
I entered the fair on a Saturday morning,
The first thing I saw was a long-legged goat.
'Bedad then!', said I, for to commence the dealing,
'I think, my bold hero, you're worth a pound note!'

2.   This darling old fellow, I stood and I stared him,
While I knew that I feared the old monster to see.
He wore a long *meigeal* as grey as a badger
That would reach from Dingle as far as Tralee.
He had a pair of long horns, like any two bayonets,
And just like a needle were pointed in top.

And you may be sure you would give a week laughing,
If he only happened to give you a rap.

3. I made myself known to the owner who held him
And a bargain we struck on without much delay.
He said 'As you paid me my twenty-two shillings,
Advice I will give you before going away:
This daring old fellow was reared on the mountain.
In the year '64 he learned some drill;
And some of his comrades, I'm told, were transported,
Since they were determined some blood for to spill'.

4. The owner departed and I was for starting,
Though the news that he gave left me deep in despair.
Then a tug at my arm — the battle had started —
I jumped on his back and took hold of his hair.
Says I, 'My old ranger, up here I am landed,
Unless that I fall, you may go where you will!'
Then he ran through the streets like something demented,
And soon we were making on up Connor Hill.

5. When we came to Brandon I thought it was London,
Regretting the journey when I saw the sea.
He jumped in the water and swam right across it,
And towards Castlegregory he made a near way.
The waves of the ocean were in a commotion,
The fishes they eat all the nails off my toes.
A mighty big mackerel, he snapped at my nostril,
And thought to do away with a part of my nose.

6. When we came to the strand he stood and he scanned it,
Then away o'er the hills like mad we did tear,
Through Milltown, Killorglin, and likewise Killarney,
We never cracked whip till we came to Kenmare.
'Twas then he first spoke, saying 'We've passed over headquarters,
Where my ancestors bold they always have been.
We'll go back to there now, and take up our quarters,
With *Cailichín na Gabhar*, where there's plenty of poteen'.

7. When I heard him speaking, my heart began beating;
Says I, 'It's a spirit called Petticoat Loose,
Or something contrary that came into Kerry,
Or if it's not that, I'm surely a goose!'
Just then we got back there and stopped until morning,
But during the night I remained on his back.
When the day it was dawning, he jumped from the corner,
And towards Castleisland he went in a crack.

8. To the town of Tralee he next took his rambles —
He surely was anxious to see plenty folk! —
'Twas outside of the town that we met a Highlander,

He ups with his horns and he tears at his cloak.
The Highlander he roared and he bawled 'Meela Murder!',
While peelers galore came to take him to jail.
The whole British Army was coming behind them,
So my hero he turns and shows them his tail.

9.   He jumped o'er the Basin and left me behind him,
      Away went my goat and I saw him no more.
      Perhaps he is gone to where he belongs to,
      Or maybe he'll steer to a far distant shore.
      If he's in Ireland, he's in Camp or in Brandon,
      Away in the mountains in some place remote.
      But as long as I'll live, I'll always remember,
      The time that I spent with the Dingle Puck Goat.

Text From Bess's handwritten songs.   **Printed Sources** Hughes, *Irish country songs* 4, 101–6.   **Notes** 6h *Cailichín na Gabhar* = 'The little hag of the goat(s)'. I do not know what — if anything — is being alluded to here; 7b 'Petticoat Loose' — I do not know what is being alluded to here, either.

157

The factory girl

1.   As I went out walking on a bright summer's morning
      The birds on the bushes did warble and sing;
      Gay laddies and lassies and couples were sporting,
      Going down to the factory, their work to begin.

2.   I spied one young damsel was fairer than any:
      Her cheeks like the red rose that none could excel;
      Her skin like the lilly that grows in yon valley,
      And she but a hard-working factory-girl.

3.   I stepped up beside her, the better to woo her,
      But on me she cast such a look of disdain,
      Saying: 'Young man, have manners, and do not come near me,
      Ah, because I'm a hard-working factory-maid'.

4.   'Oh, it is not to slight you — fair maid, I adore you! —
      But grant me one favour: say, where do you dwell?'
      'And kind sir, have patience and do not come near me,
      For yonder's the sound of my factory-bell'.

5.   'I have lands, I have houses adorned with ivy;
      I have gold in my pocket and money in my purse;
      And if you'll come with me, a lady I'll make you,
      And never more need you heed your sweet factory-bell'.

6. 'Love and sensation rules many a nation —
   Go marry a lady, and may you do well!
   But I am an orphan with ne'er a relation,
   Whereby I'm a hard-working factory-girl'.

7. With these words she turned and with less she had left me,
   And it's for her dear sake I'll go wander away;
   And in some deep valley, where no one shall know me,
   I'll mourn for the sake of my factory-maid.

Recordings JR-GP (2 Nov. 1952) — Diane Hamilton (1955). **Text** From the JR-GP recording. **Printed Sources** Sam Henry, 'Songs of the People', *Northern Constitution* (17 Apr. 1926), No. 127 = Huntington & Hermann, *Sam Henry's Songs of the People*, 368; Shields, 'A latter-day "pastourelle" The Factory Girl', *Ceol* 1/3 (1963) 5–10; Purslow, *The constant lovers: more English folk songs from the Hammond and Gardiner Mss.*, 29 and 123; Kennedy, *Folksongs of Britain and Ireland*, 501, No. 221 (and notes, 529) 9 vv.; Mac Mathúna, *Traditional songs and singers*, 37–38. **Notes** Hugh Shields, 'A latter-day "pastourelle"', 7, reports a text printed in Waterford by Walter Kelly c. 1843, in a booklet together with a lamentation on the catastrophic loss of 37 lives at a Christmas Day mass in Galway; this version makes the subject of the song a 'Country Girl'. Shields knows of no surviving broadside version. Purslow, *The constant lovers*, 123, states it as his belief that the song is of Northern Irish origin, but without giving reasons. His text is quite different in some verses, and has a 'happy ending', in which the wooer and factory-girl are wed. This is the case also in Sam Henry's text; his and Kennedy's version, *Folksongs of Britain and Ireland*, 501, have a 'happy ending', concluding with the following two verses:

A. Now this maid's she got married and become a great lady
   Become a great lady of fame and renown
   She may bless the day and the bright summer's morning
   She met with the squire and upon him did frown

B. Well now to conclude, and to finish these verses
   This couple got married, and both are doing well
   So, lads, fill your glasses, and drink to the lasses
   Till we hear the sweet sound of the factory bell.

Hugh Shields has (rightly, I think) dismissed this 'happy ending' as intrusive. Kennedy reports Margaret Barry as stating that she had learnt the song in Cork and believed it to refer to a factory in Blackpool, Cork. There is another very fine recording of the song by John O'Connell, Danganasillagh, Macroom, recorded by Diane Hamilton; John was a friend and neighbour of Bess's and often sang at the Plantation.

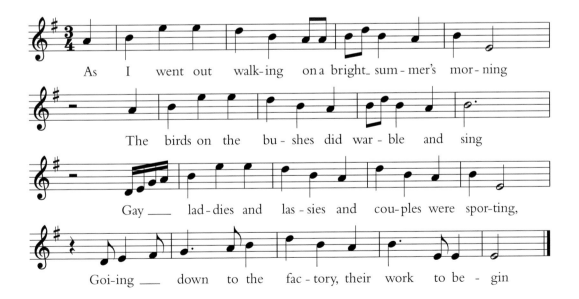

As I went out walk-ing on a bright summer's mor-ning

The birds on the bu-shes did war-ble and sing

Gay ___ lad-dies and las-sies and cou-ples were spor-ting,

Goi-ing ___ down to the fac-tory, their work to be-gin

158

The fair of Ballyally-o[x/y]

1. As I was coming home from the fair of Ballyally-O
    I spied a comely maid, she was fairer than Diana-O!
    I asked her for to [...   .]
    [...   .]

2. [...   ...   .   among the heather-O!
    [...   .]
    [...   .]
    [...   .]

3. [...   .]
    Young man, do you think that I am   [...   ...]
    I am happy here at home with my father and my mother-O!
    [...   ...   ... for to see the charming [... ...]
    [...   .]

Recording CBÉ 1064b (1947).   **Text** From the CBÉ recording.   **Printed Sources** Greig, *Folk-song of the North-East*, No. xliv *(The Fair of Ballinaminna); The Greig-Duncan folk song collection*, vol. 4, 385–387, No. 873 A, B (*The Fair o' Balquhither* and *The Fair o' Balnaminnna*).   **Notes** One of Bess's song-lists has both *The Lass Among the Heather-O* and *The Fair of Ballyally-O*, but the two are possibly identical. Gavin Greig, *Folk-song of the North-East*, No. xliv, remarked that the tune for his version was very similar to that for *The Braes of Balquidder*, and the Greig-Duncan Collection gives *The Fair o' Balquhither* and *The Fair 'o Balnaminna* with more-or-less identical words and variant versions of the one tune. The quality of this recording is, unfortunately, very poor, hence the lacunae in the text here.

159

The flower of Kilkenny

1. I once loved a flower in Kilkenny,
    and a beautiful creature was she.
    I loved her far better than many,
    and I know that young darling loves me.
    She's the beautiful Flower of Kilkenny —
    shall I gaze on her fair face no more?
    I have roamed over lands and seen many,
    but none like my Eileen, *a stór*.

2. As she left me she gave me a token,
    and that was an outburst of tears;
    And the words that were generally spoken,
    they've reigned in my memory for years.
    She's the beautiful Flower of Kilkenny —
    shall I gaze on her fair face no more?
    I have roamed over lands and seen many,
    but none like my Eileen, *a stór*.

3. For this was the last and fond token,
    to be given with a fond loving will;
    And the words that were generally spoken,
    they've reigned in my memory still.
    She's the beautiful Flower of Kilkenny —
    shall I gaze on her fair face no more?
    I have roamed over lands and seen many,
    but none like my Eileen, *a stór*.

Recording BBC 19023 (20 Sept. 1952).   **Text** From the BBC recording.   **Note** Seamus Ennis, in his BBC note, says that the 'tune is a nice little snatch reminiscent of others at various points'.

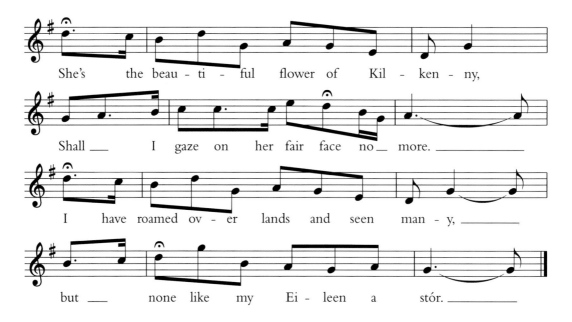

She's the beau - ti - ful flower of Kil - ken - ny,

Shall ___ I gaze on her fair face no ___ more. ___

I have roamed ov - er lands and seen man - y, ___

but ___ none like my Ei - leen a stór. ___

160

The fox went out

1.   The fox went out in a hungry plight,
       And he begged of the moon to give him light,
       For he had a long way to travel that night
       Before he reached his den-o, his den-o,
       Before he reached his den-o.

2.   Mrs Slipper Slapper jumped out of her bed,
       And out of the window she stuck her head,
       Saying: 'John, John, John, the grey goose is gone
       And the fox he is off to his den-o, his den-o,
       And the fox he is off to his den-o!'

3.   The fox took it home to his hungry wife,
       They ate it up without fork or knife,
       They never ate a better duck in all their life
       And the little ones picked the bones-o, the bones-o,
       And the little ones ate the bones-o.

Recordings BBC 21997 (Sept. 1954) = Kennedy, *Folktracks* F–60–160 (1981) A7.   **Text** From the BBC recording; another in a DÓC notebook.   **Printed Sources** Baring-Gould, Sheppard & Bussell, *Songs of the West folk: songs of Devon and Cornwall*, 112–13, No. 55 *The Fox* (7 vv.) [text very similar to ours]; Sam Henry, 'Songs of the People', *Northern Consitution* (2 Aug. 1924), No. 38 = Huntington & Hermann, *Sam Henry's Songs of the People*, 29. See Opie & Opie, *The Oxford dictionary of nursery rhymes*, 173, No. 171. See also Purslow, *The wanton seed*, 89 (4 vv.); Karpeles, *Cecil Sharp's collection of English folk songs*, vol. 2, No. 333 (2 versions); Kennedy, *Folksongs of Britain and Ireland*, 656–57, and 678, No. 301 (8 vv.). See also Petrie & Stanford, *The complete collection of Irish music*, 162, Nos 645, 646 (music only).   **Notes** Bess, in the recording, says there was a fourth verse, in which the husband jumps up and follows the fox, but returns empty-handed, etc.; see Kennedy, *Folksongs of Britain and Ireland*, 657, v. 6:

6.   Now John rushed up to the top of the hill
     And blowed his horn both loud and shrill
     Blow on, said the fox, your pretty music still
     Whilst I trot back to my home-o

Baring-Gould et al. say (p. 16): 'In the early part of the last century this song was sung at all harvest suppers in the West of England'. They have interesting notes on 19th-c. editions, and a ref. (p. 17) to a broadside ballad in the British Library by Harkness of Birmingham (n. d.). The Opies, *Oxford dictionary of nursery rhymes*, 173, No. 171, note early editions and have the following text:

A fox jumped up one winter's night,
And he begged the moon to give him light,
For he'd many miles to trot that night
Before he reached his den O!
Den O! Den O!
For he'd many miles to trot that night
Before he reached his den O!

The first place he came to was a farmer's yard,
Where the ducks and the geese declared it hard
That their nerves should be shaken and their rest so marred
By a visit from Mr. Fox O!
Fox O! Fox O!
That their nerves should be shaken and their rest so marred
By a visit from Mr. Fox O!

He took the grey goose by the neck,
And swung him right across his back;
The grey goose cried out, Quack, quack, quack,
With his legs hanging dangling down O!
Down O! Down O!
The grey goose cried out, Quack, quack, quack,
With his legs hanging dangling down O!

Old Mother Slipper Slopper jumped out of bed,
And out of the window she popped her head:
Oh! John, John, John, the grey goose is gone,
And the fox is off to his den O!
Den O! Den O!
And the fox is off to his den O!

John ran up to the top of the hill,
And blew his whistle loud and shrill;
Said the fox, That is very pretty music; still,
I'd rather be in my den O!
Den O! Den O!
Said the fox, That is very pretty music; still,
I'd rather be in my den O!

The fox went back to his hungry den,
And his dear little foxes, eight, nine, ten;
Quoth they, Good daddy, you must go there again,
If you bring such good cheer from the farm O!
Farm O! Farm O!
Quoth they, Good daddy, you must go there again,
If you bring such good cheer from the farm O!

The fox and his wife, without any strife,
Said they never ate a better goose in all their life:
They did very well without fork or knife,
And the little ones picked the bones O!
Bones O! Bones O!
They did very well without fork or knife,
And the little ones picked the bones O!

The text in Kennedy, *Folksongs of Britain and Ireland*, 656–57, is more or less identical. Sam Henry's text is in the *Reynard the Fox* tradition.

The fox went out in a hun - gry __ plight,

And he begged of the moon to __ give him __ light,

For he had a long way to (a) tra - vel that __ night

Be - fore he __ reached his den - o, his __ den - o,

Be - fore he __ reached his den - - o.

161

The geall sidhe

Note Title only from one of Bess's song-lists.   **Printed Source** Cf. *An Lóchrann* (Meadhon Fómhair 1920) 5.   **Notes** If this is an anglicisation of an English title, it might possibly be a song called *Do Gheall Sí* ('She Promised'); cf. *An Lóchrann* (1920) 5, which has the following, collected by Fionán Mac Coluim:

> Do gheall sé's do gheall sé's
> Do gheall sé go dtiocfadh sé
> Do gheall sé's do gheall sé's
> Ní fheadar cad do choingibh é.
> Do gheall sé's, 7rl.
> Poll a bhí 'na bhróig
> Is dócha gurb é do choingibh é.
>
> Do gheall sé's, 7rl.
> Ní fheadar cad do choingibh é.
> Do gheall sé's, 7rl.
> Tuilre a bhí 'san abhainn
> Is docha gurb é do choingibh é.
>
> Do gheall sé's, 7rl.
> A mháthair do bhí breoite
> 'S is dócha gurb é do choingibh é.
>
> Do gheall sé, 7rl.
> Crochán de faoit an stócach
> Is dócha gurb é do choingibh é.

The words are accompanied by music in tonic sol-fa notation.

162

The grand conversation on Napoleon

1.   'Ah England!', he cried, 'you did persecute that hero bold,
Much better had you slain him on the plains of Waterloo;
Napoleon he was a friend to heros all, both young and old,
He caused the money for to fly wherever he did go'.

2.   When plans were ranging night and day, the bold commander to betray,
He cried, I'll go to Moscow, and then 'twill ease my woes,
If fortune shines without delay, then all the world shall me obey;
This grand conversation on Napoleon arose.

3.   Thousands of men then did arise, to conquer Moscow by surprise,
He led his men across the Alps, oppressed by frost and snow,
But being near the Russian land, he then began to open his eyes,
For Moscow was a burning and the men drove to and fro.

6.   Napoleon dauntless viewed the flame, and wept in anguish for the same,
He cried, retreat my gallant men, for time so swiftly goes;
What thousands died on that retreat, some forced their horses for to eat;
This grand conversation on Napoleon arose.

Recording BBC 21996 (Aug. 1954).   **Text** From the BBC recording.   **Printed Sources** Holloway & Black, *Later English broadside ballads* 2, 206–8 (with a facsimile of a broadside signed 'George Brown'); Milner, *The bonnie bunch of roses*, 161–62 (10 vv. from a broadside by Disley); cf. Cambridge University Library Ballads, vol. 5, 717; vol. 3, 235 and 4, 378.   **Notes** I give here the full text (from a broadside by Disley) printed in Milner's *The bonnie bunch of roses*, 161–62:

1.   It was over that wild beaten track, a friend of bold Bonaparte,
Did pace the sands and lofty rocks of St. Helena's shore.
The wind it blew a hurricane, the lightning's flash around did dart,
The sea-gulls were shreiking, and the waves around did roar.

2.   Ah! hush, rude winds the stranger cried awhile I range the dreary spot,
Where last a gallant hero his envied eyes did close.
But while his valued limbs do rot, his name will never be forgot,
This grand conversation on Napoleon arose.

3.   Ah England! he cried, you did persecute that hero bold,
Much better had you slain him on the plains of Waterloo;
Napoleon he was a friend to heros all, both young and old,
He caused the money for to fly wherever he did go.

4.   When plans were ranging night and day, the bold commander to betray,
He cried, I'll go to Moscow, and then 'twill ease my woes,
If fortune shines without delay, then all the world shall me obey;
This grand conversation on Napoleon arose.

5.   Thousands of men then did arise, to conquer Moscow by surprise,
He led his men across the Alps, oppressed by frost and snow,
But being near the Russian land, he then began to open his eyes,
For Moscow was a burning and the men drove to and fro.

6.   Napoleon dauntless viewed the flame, and wept in anguish for the same,
He cried, retreat my gallant men, for time so swiftly goes;
What thousands died on that retreat, some forced their horses for to eat;
This grand conversation on Napoleon arose.

Ah Eng - land! he cried, did-n't you per - se -cute that he - ro bold,

Much __ bet-ter had you slain him in the plains of Wa - ter - loo;

Na - pol - eon he was a friend to her - os, both young and old,

He caused the mo - ney for to fly wher- ev - er he did go.

When plans were rang- ing night and day, this bold com-man- der to be - tray,

He cried, I'll go to Mos - cow and that will ease my woes,

But being near the Rus - sian land, he then be - gan to op- en his eyes,

For Mos - cow was bur - ning and the men drove to and fro.

Na - pol- eon daunt-less viewed the flames and in an - guish forth a - gain,

He cried re-treat my gal-lant men for time im - por - tant goes;

What thous - ands died on that re- treat some forced to take their horse to eat;

This grand con - ver - sa - tion on Na- pol - eon a - rose.

7.   At Waterloo his men they fought, commanded by great Bonaparte,
        Attended by field-marshal Ney, and he was bribed with gold;
        When Blucher led the Prussians in, it nearly broke Napoleon's heart,
        He cried, my thirty thousand men were killed, and I am sold.

8.   He viewed the plain, and cried it's lost, he then his favorite charger crossed,
        The plain was in confusion with blood and dying woes.
        The bunch of roses did advance, and boldly entered into France —
        This grand conversation on Napoleon arose.

9.   But Bonaparte was planned to be a prisoner across the sea
        The rocks of St. Helena, it was the fatal spot,
        And as a prisoner there to to be, till death did end his misery,
        His son soon followed to the tomb, it was an awful plot.

10.   And long enough they have been dead, the blast of war is round us spread,
        And may our shipping float again, to face the daring foe;
        And now my boys when honour calls, we'll boldly mount the wooden walls;
        This grand conversation on Napoleon did close.

Seamus Ennis, in his BBC notes, described it as 'a discussion pro and versus Napoleon among folk-bards'. The tune is that of *O'Donnell Abu*! For another version, with music, see *JFSS* 2/8 (1906) 188–89).

163

The green fields of America

1.   Más maith leat me bheith láidir, cuir 'rán dom ar anairthe,
        Cuir 'rán dom, cuir 'rán dom, cuir 'rán dom ar anairthe;
        Más maith leat me bheith láidir, cuir 'rán dom ar anairthe,
        Agus bíodh mo chuid go sásta sa tsáspan am' chóir!

Engish Summary The poet asks for bread and soup, and lots of it.   **Text** From a DÓC notebook.   **Notes** Petrie & Stanford, *Complete collection*, 375 No. 1499, has an air entitled 'Má is maith leat', but the facsimile at the beginning of the vol. shows the full title is 'Mas maith leat me bheith laidir déin eanbhruith maith coilig dham' and is there given the alternative title *An Seanduine*. A heading (misplaced?) in the DÓC notebook reads 'Words for *The Green Fields of America*'. Another note after the verse reads 'No more in it'. Our text has the look of a chorus, and may be no more than a mnemonic for the well-known reel called *The Green Fields of America*; cf. Francis O'Neill's *1001 gems the dance music of Ireland* (Chicago 1907) 97, No. 513, though it does not appear to fit very snugly. The usual words (e.g., in *Delaney's Irish song book*, No. 2 (New York, n. d. [c. 1900]) 15), bear no relation to our text above.

164

The green mossy banks of the Lee

Laws O 15.   **Note** Title only from one of Bess's song-lists.   **Printed Sources** *Delaney's Irish song book*, No. 5, 24; *Weyman's Irish song book*, 1, 9 (M); Ó Lochlainn, *More Irish street ballads*, 194–95, No. 98 [from a broadside?]; Laws, *American balladry from British broadsides*, 87, 233; Palmer, *Songs of the Midlands*, 38.   **Notes** The text in Ó Lochlainn's *More Irish street ballads*, 194–95, is as follows:

1.   When first in this country a stranger,
        Curiosity forced me to roam.
        To Europe I came as a ranger,
        When I left Philadelphia my home.
        We swiftly sailed over to Ireland,

Where forms of great beauty do shine,
Till at length I beheld a fair damsel,
And I wished in my heart she was mine.

2.   One morning I careless did ramble,
Where the winds and sweet breezes did blow,
It was down by a clear crystal river,
Where the sweet purling waters did flow:
'Twas there I espied a fair creature,
Some goddess appearing to be,
As she rose from the reeds by the water,
On the green mossy banks of the Lee.

3.   I stept up and wished her good morning,
Her fair cheeks did blush like a rose,
Said I, 'The green meadows are charming,
Your guardian I'll be if you choose.'
She said 'Sir, I ne'er want a guardian,
Young man you're a stranger to me,
And yonder my father is coming,
O'er the green mossy banks of the Lee.'

4.   I waited till up came her father,
And plucked up my spirits once more,
Saying 'Sir, if this is your fair daughter,
That beautiful girl I adore.
Ten thousand a year is my fortune,
And a lady your daughter shall be,
She may ride with her carriage and horses,
O'er the green mossy banks of the Lee.'

5.   Then they welcomed me home to their cottage,
Soon after in wedlock to join,
And there I did build a fair mansion,
In grandeur and splendour to shine.
And now the American stranger,
All pleasure and pastime can see,
With adorable gentle Matilda
On the green mossy banks of the Lee.

6.   Now all pretty maidens attention,
No matter how poor you may be,
There is many a poor girl as handsome
As those with a large property.
By flattery let no one deceive you,
Who knows but your fortune may be,
Like that sweet and lovely Matilda
On the green mossy banks of the Lee.

Palmer's text in *Songs of the Midlands*, 38, collected from an Irish traveller, P. Murphy, at Brownhills, Staffordshire in 1967, is as follows:

A.   Well, for once I was carelessly strolling,
Curiosity caused me to roam;
Aye, 'twas down by the banks of the river,
Where the pure crystal waters do flow.

B.   Over yonder I spies a young maiden,
And her equal I ne'er saw before;
I sat down for to bid her good evening,
O'er the green mossy banks of the Lea.

C.   For she says, 'Sir, I don't want your escort,
Young man you're a stranger to me,
Over yonder my father is coming,
O'er the green mossy banks of the Lea.'

D. So I waited and down comes her father,
And for courage I just picked up once more,
I says, 'Sir, if this be your daughter,
She's the girl that I really adore.

E. 'Ten thousand a year is my income,
And a lady your daughter may be,
She can ride in her horses and waggons
O'er the green mossy banks of the Lea.'

F. O, they advited me home to their mansion,
And for courage I'd welcome galore,
Musha, God bless the hour of our meeting,
That's the green mossy banks of the Lea.

165

The hat my father wore

1. I'm Paddy Myles, an Irishman, that comes from sweet Fermoy.
For singing and for dancing with merriment and joy
I can dance and sing with any man, as I did in days of yore;
But on St Patrick's Day I love to wear the hat my father wore.

2. 'Tis old but it is beautiful, the best you've ever seen;
'Twas worn more than ninety years, and 'tis all trimmed with green.
It descended from my ancient sires with harmony galore;
'Tis the relics of ould decency — the hat my father wore.

3. For the wearing of this ancient hat they sent me far away,
They sent me off an exile across the stormy sea;
In the joining of the Brotherhood in the year of '64,
They transported Irish Paddy with the hat my father wore.

4. When I landed safely in New York, the girls did dance with joy,
And they welcomed Paddy Myles from the town of sweet Fermoy.
They asked me to play 'St Patrick's', or 'Dance the Reel of Four',
Or would I e'er return again to the hat my father wore?

5. 'Twas from Queenstown Harbour our gallant ship set sail,
With thousands of young Irishmen, true sons of Granuaile.
When we landed safely in New York the green was spangled o'er,
With a *Céad Míle Fáilte* for the hat my father wore.

Text From CBÉ 283, 183–85.   **Printed Sources** *Delaney's Irish song book*, No. 1, 28; *Harding's Dublin songster*, new series, Vol. 2, No. 18, 419, and Vol. 2, No. 22, 509; Greig, *Folk-song of the North-East*, No. clxviii; cf. *Songs the Irish people love*, No. 38.   **Notes** The version in *Songs the Irish people love* is stated to have been written and composed by Edwin Ferguson. *Delaney's song book* has our v. 1 and the chorus, and the following 2 vv.

I bid you all good evening, good luck to you, I say;
And when I cross the ocean, I hope for me you'll pray.
I'm going to my happy land, in a place called Ballymore;
To be welcomed back to Paddy's land with the hat me father wore.

And when I do return again, the boys and girls to see,
I hope that with old Erin's style you'll kindly welcome me.
With the songs of dear old Ireland, to cheer me more and more,
And make my Irish heart full glad with the hat me father wore.

This ditty is, of course, a parody of the well-known Ulster song, *The Sash My Father Wore*.

166

The Irish Jubilee

A short time ago, boys, an Irishman named Doherty
Was elected to the Senate by a very large majority.
He felt so elated he said to Mr Cassidy,
Who owned a bar-room of very large capacity,
He said to Cassidy to go over to the brewer
For a thousand kegs of lager beer and give it to the poor
And go over to the butcher's shop and order up a ton of meat —
'Be sure to see the boys and girls have all they want to drink and eat!
Send out invitations in twenty different languages,
And don't forget to tell them to bring their own sandwiches!
They have made me their Senator, and then to show my gratitude,
They'll have the finest supper ever given in this latitude!
Tell them the music will be furnished by O'Rafferty,
Assisted on the bagpipes by Felix McCafferty.
Whatever the expenses are, remember that I'll put up the tin!
Anyone that doesn't come, be sure and do not let him in!'
Cassidy at once sent out an invitation,
And everyone that came was a credit to his nation.
Some came on bicycles because they had no fare to pay,
And those that didn't come at all made up their minds to stay away.
Two by three they marched into the dining-room:
Young men, old men, girls who were not men at all;
Blind men, deaf men, men who had their teeth in pawn;
Single men, double men, and men who had their glasses on.
Before many minutes every chair was taken
Til the front rooms and mushrooms were packed to suffocation.
When everyone was seated they started to lay out the feast;
Cassidy said: 'Rise up and give us each a cake of yeast!'
He then said, as manager, he would try and fill the chair.
We all sat down and we looked at the bill-of-fare:
There were pigs' heads and goldfish, mocking-birds and ostriches,
Ice cream, cold cream, vaseline and sandwiches;
We ate everything that was down on the bill-of-fare,
Then looked at the back to see if anymore was there.
We had dressed beef, naked beef, beef with all its dresses on;
Soda-crackers, fire-crackers, lumberger cheese with tresses on;
Beef-steaks and mistakes were down on the bill-of-fare,
Roast ribs, spare ribs, and ribs that we couldn't spare;

Hob corn, cold corn, corn-salve and honeycomb;
Red birds, red books, sea-base and sea foam.
Fried liver, baked liver, Carters' little liver pills;
And everyone was wondering who was going to pay the bills.
We had red herrings, smoked herrings, herrings from Old Erin's Isle;
Bull eyes, fruit cakes and sausages a half-a-mile.
We had red-deer, reindeer, dear me, and antelope.
And the women ate so much melon that the men said 'They can't elope'.
For dessert we had tooth-pick, ice-pick and skipping rope.
And we washed them all down with a fine piece of shaving soap.
The band played hornpipes, gas-pipes, and Irish reels.
And we danced to the music of the wind that shakes the barley field.
They welted the doors 'til they could be heard for miles around —
When Cassidy was in the air his feet were never on the ground.
Such a fine set of dancers you never set your eyes upon,
And those that didn't dance at all, they were dancing with their slippers on.
When the fun was over, Cassidy then told us
To join our hands together and to sing this grand old chorus:
'Should auld acquaintance be forgot,
Wherever we may be,
Think of the grand old time we had
At the Irish Jubilee'.

Text From a DÓC notebook (handwritten by Bess).   **Printed Sources** *Echoes from Erin: an album of ballads, novelties, comics (old and new), compiled expressly for and dedicated to those who love IRISH SONG*, 12–15 ('words by James Thornton, Music by Chas. Lawler'. Copyright is dated '1890'); McPheeley, *More than 1000 songs and dances of the Irish people*, 58–61 (identical with Witmark ed.).   **Note** For a modern version of this song, with music, see Robbie Morton, *Folksongs sung in Ulster* (Cork 1970) 88–90, which reproduces the text of a version recorded from Michael Higginbotham (84 at time of recording) by Robbie Morton and heard on Cathal McConnell & Robin Morton, *The Irish Jubilee. Traditional Irish Songs and Music*, Topic Records 12T290 (London 1976) [first issued by Mercier Press (Cork 1970)] B 7.

167

The Kerry cow[2/22]

1.   *Is trua gan gáirdín úll agam,*
     Is trua gan gáirdín úll agam,
     Is trua gan gáirdín úll agam,
     Is cúpla tor cabáiste

     Ó míle gile tu, grá mo chroí 'gus míle tu
     Ó míle gile tu, 's tú peata geal do mháthar

2.   *Is trua gan maoilín bán agam,*
     Is trua gan maoilín bán agam,
     Is trua gan maoilín bán agam,
     Is na gamhna beaga bána

     Ó míle gile tu, grá mo chroí 'gus míle tu
     Ó míle gile tu, 's tú peata geal do mháthar

3.   I wish I had a Kerry cow,
      A Kerry cow, a Kerry cow,
      I wish I had a Kerry cow
      And Mary from her father!

      Ó míle gile tu, grá mo chroí 'gus míle tu
      Ó míle gile tu, 's ní a' magadh leat atáim-se

Recording JR-GP (24 Nov. 1952).   **Text** From the JR-GP recording.   **Printed Sources** Petrie, *The Petrie collection of the ancient music of Ireland*, 42–43 (2 vv.); cf. Petrie & Stanford, *The complete collection of Irish music*, 375, No. 1501 (air only) [cf. 291, No. 1151]; O'Daly, *Irish language miscellany*, 70; *Fáinne an Lae* (12 Márta 1898) 3; Mac Coluim, *Duanaireacht do leanbhaíbh*, 24–25; idem, *Cosa buidhe árda* 1, 15–16 (5 vv.); Borthwick, *Ceól-sídhe* 1, 24; Breathnach, *Cnuasachd bheag amhrán* 1, 3 [3 vv. 'Is truagh gan peata 'n mhaoir agam']; idem, *Ceól ár sínsear*, 3 [same as previous text]; cf. Maguidhir, *Mo stóirín cheóil*, 4–5; Ua Braoin, *An cuaichín ceoil*, 23; Ní Ógáin, *Duanaire Gaedhilge*, 25.   **Notes** This song is better known as *Peata an Mhaoir* ('Is trua gan peata an mhaoir agam'), and was written down from Bess by Seamus Ennis under the title *Dá mbeadh mac an mhaoir agam*. There is an English translation in Eleanor Hull, *The poem-book of the Gael* (London 1913) 341, and in Joyce, *Old Irish folk music and songs*, 238, No. 426. Joyce's text is as follows:

I wish I had the sheperd's lamb,
The sheperd's lamb, the sheperd's lamb,
I wish I had the sheperd's lamb,
And Katie coming after,

Iss o gurim gurim hoo, etc.

I wish I had the yellow cow,
The yellow cow, the yellow cow,
I wish I had the yellow cow
And welcome from my darling.

> I wish I had a herd of kine,
> A herd of kine, a herd of kine,
> I wish I had a herd of kine,
> And Katie from her father!

Compare the song *Dá bhfaghainn mo rogha dhe thriúr acu* [No. **44**], which is sung to the same air.

168

The lakes of Coolfin

1. 'Twas early one morning young Willy arose,
    And up to his comrade's bed-chamber he goes:
    'Arise, my dear comrade, and let no one know,
    'Tis a fine sunny morning and a-bathing we'll go'.

2. To the Lake of Coolfin the companions soon came,
    And the first man they met was the keeper of game: —
    'Turn back, Willy Leonard, return back again;
    There is deep and false water in the Lake of Coolfin!'

3. Young Willy plunged in, and he swam the lake round;
    He swam to an island — 'twas soft marshy ground:
    'O, comrade, dear comrade, do not venture in;
    There is deep and false water in the Lake of Coolfin!'

4. 'Twas early that morning his sister arose;
    And up to her mother's bed-chamber she goes: —
    'O, I dreamed a sad dream about Willy last night;
    He was dressed in a shroud — in a shroud of snow-white!'

5. 'Twas early that morning his mother came there;
    She was wringing her hands — she was tearing her hair.
    'O, woeful the hour your dear Willy plunged in: —
    There is deep and false water in the Lake of Coolfin!

6. And I saw a fair maid, standing fast by the shore;
    Her face it was pale — she was weeping full sore;
    In deep anguish she gazed where young Willy plunged in:
    Ah! there's deep and false water in the Lake of Coolfin!'

Laws Q 33.   **Recording** CBÉ 1061b (1947).   **Text** From the CBÉ recording.   **Printed Sources** Royal Irish Academy, RR 66 H 17 (Lord Moyne Coll.) 94; Cambridge University Library Ballads, vol. 3, 242 *(Willy Leonard)*; Joyce, *Ancient Irish music*, 103–4, No. 100; *Delaney's Irish song book* No. 5, 3; *JIFSS* 9 (Jan.-June 1911) 15–16; Graves, *The Irish song book*, 34–35, No. 24; Joyce, *Old Irish folk music and song*, 227; Sam Henry, 'Songs of the People', *Northern Constitution* (26 March 1927), No. 176 *(Willie Lennox, 7 vv.)* = Hermann & Huntington, *Sam Henry's Songs of the People*, 146, No. H176; Laws, *American balladry from British broadsides*, 289. **Notes** The broadside version in the Royal Irish Academy, Lord Moyne Collection, lacks our verses 2, 3, and 6, but has an additional verse at the end about Willy Leonard's funeral. Verse 2 of the *Delaney Song Book* text reads 'So they walked right along till they came to Long Lane', which is possibly a corruption of Lough Lein (in Killarney), and perhaps an indication of the area where the song originated. This song is found also in England and Scotland, where the name of the lake takes on correspondingly different forms. On English broadsides the setting is the Lakes of Cold Finn, and in Scotland the Lakes of Shallin (or Shillin).

Though undoubtedly Irish in origin, the exact location of the events in the song has not been established. Sam Henry's version, *Willie Lennox*, recorded in Derry, is set apparently at Inisholeen, Co. Derry. There is a broadside version of this song in the NLI General Collection. Joyce, *Ancient Irish music*, 103, remarks that 'the ballad, as I received it, … is a singular mixture of vigour and imbecility; in some parts vivid and true to nature; in others, vulgar, feeble and prosy'. In consequence he 'curtailed the tedious matter of fact narrative at the end, and retrenched other parts also; added something of my own; changed many of the lines; and restored the rhythm where it was necessary. But I have retained as much of the old ballad as possible'. It is difficult to know how much of the original ballad survived this editorial treatment. The Royal Irish Academy, Lord Moyne Collection, 94, has the following additional verse at the end:

> The day of his funeral it was a grand sight,
> There was four and twenty young men and all dressed in white,
> They carried him along and laid him in the clay,
> Saying adieu Willy Leonard and they all marched away.

The final verse in *Delaney's Irish song book*, on the other hand, is as follows:

> So it was early one morning when his uncle went there,
> He rode round the island like one in despair;
> Saying: Where was he drowned, or did he face in?
> For there's depth in false water in the lakes of Cold Finn!

For a modern version, with tune, see Tom Munnelly, *Mount Callan garland*, 103–6 (with interesting remarks on the song's origins).

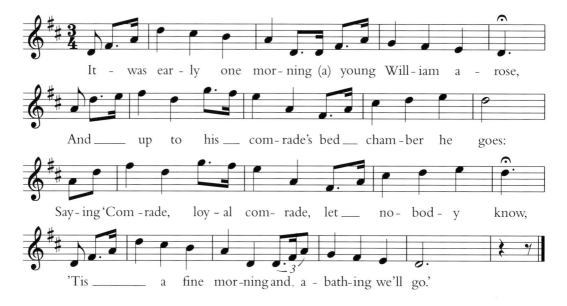

It - was ear-ly one mor-ning (a) young Will-iam a - rose,

And ___ up to his __ com-rade's bed __ cham-ber he goes:

Say-ing 'Com-rade, loy-al com-rade, let __ no-bod-y know,

'Tis ___ a fine mor-ning and a - bath-ing we'll go.'

169

The lass among the heather-o

Notes Title only from one of Bess's song-lists. It is perhaps identical with *The fair of Ballyally-O*. Mairéad Bean Uí Lionaird, a niece of Bess's, remembers her singing this song. **Printed Sources** McWilliams, *Poems and songs on various subjects*, 106; cf. Greig, *Folk-song of the North-East*, No. xliv *(The Fair of Ballinaminna)*. **Notes** John Moulden supplied the following text from a ballad-sheet entitled *The lass among the heather*, which goes as follows:

> A. One night as I came home,
>   Frae the town o' Ballymena,
>   A lass I overtaen,
>   That was fairer than Diana,
>   I as't her whar she lived,
>   As we jogged on together
>   On the friendly mountain side,
>   She reply'd amang the heather.

B.   Sweet lassie I'm in love,
Ye hae so many charms,
Then dinna let me grive,
For my breast to you warms,
The glances o' your eye,
And your form that's so clever,
I could freely wed with thee,
Dearest lassie o' the heather.

C.   Do you think I'm sic a fool,
As to believe what you've spoken,
Na, laddie, let me tell,
You are sairly mistaken,
I'm happy, and I'm weel,
With my father and my mother,
He would be a cany chiel,
That would coax me frae the heather.

D.   Dear lassie condescend now,
And dinna be so cruel,
I hope I'll no offend now,
My dearest, my jewel,
My heart frae love was free,
And as light as any feather,
Till this night I met with thee,
Bonny lassie o' the heather.

E.   On the friendly mountain side,
Where the heather is blooming,
Where flocks are feeding wide,
And the streams gently running,
'Tis pleasant there to stray,
In the warm summer weather,
So you need na' bid me gae,
From my dear, my native heather.

F.   Ah! cruel, cruel, lass now,
My heart's nearly broken,
Will you gi'e to me a kiss,
As a last parting token,
If I would gi'd you ane,
You would may be seek anither,
But I kissed and kissed again,
The bonny lassie o' the heather.

G.   Now I will visit you,
So you must not deny it,
Na, that you minna do,
With a smile she replied,
But if you're late in town,
In the stormy wintry weather,
A lodging you will find,
In the cot among the heather.

H.   O how my heart did glow,
At the knd invitation,
My breast was in a low,
O' the warmest sensation,
Since my suit she now approves,
I will shortly ask her father,
And if he does refuse,
I will steal her frae the heather.

170

The letter that he longed for
never came

1.   'Any letter here today?' was the question that he asked
     of the mailman at the closing of the day.
     He turned sadly with a sigh and the tears stood in his eye,
     he bowed his head and slowly walked away.
     Was it for a grey-haired mother, or a sister or a brother,
     that he waited all those weary years in vain, all in vain?
     And from the early moning light he would watch from dawn till night,
     still the letter that he longed for never came.

2.   As he waited many years, joy had mingled with his tears,
     the postmaster would meet him with a smile;
     His features they would brighten and his poor heart seeemed to lighten,
     for his vain hopes only lasted for a while.
     But as the postmaster would say: 'There's no letter here today'
     he bemoaned his fate, yet no one could he blame;
     Still he murmured 'Can it be? Will she ever think of me?'
     And the letter that he longed for never came.

     Was it for a grey-haired mother, or a sister or a brother
     that he waited all those weary years in vain, all in vain?
     And from the early morning light he would watch from dawn till night,
     Still the letter that he longed for never came.

3.   One morn' upon the shore he was found, but life was o'er,
     his poor soul it had gone out with the tide.
     In his hand was found a note — the last words that he wrote:
     'If a letter comes, please place it by my side'.
     Sweetest flowers entwine around o'er the tombstone on his mound
     on which were engraved his age, also his name;
     Many years have gone, they say, since his shadow passed away,
     Still, the letter that he longed for never came.

     Was it for a grey-haired mother, or a sister or a brother,
     that he waited all those weary years in vain, all in vain?
     And from the early morning light he would watch from dawn till night,
     Still, the letter that he longed for never came.

Recordings BBC 11989 (7 Aug. 1947) = Kennedy, *Folktracks* F–60–160 (1981) B2 — CBÉ 915 (1947) — JR–GP (24 Nov. 1952)
Text From the BBC recording.   **Notes** Ennis, in his BBC note, describes this as 'an English popular song, learned probably from a broadsheet'.

'An - y let-ter here to-day?' was ___ the ques-tion that he asked

of the mail-man at the clos-ing of the day. ___

He turned sad-ly with a sigh and the tears stood in his eye,

he bowed his head and slow-ly walked a - way.

Was ___ it for a grey-haired mo-ther, or a sis-ter or a bro-ther, ___

that he wai-ted all these wear-y years in vain, all in vain?

And from the ear-ly mor-ning light he would watch from dawn till night,

Still the let - ter that he longed for nev-er came.

171

The little pack of tailors[2/8]

1.   O-ro, we rattled them, and o-ro, we chased them,
    And o-ro, we rattled them, the little pack of tailors;
    O-ro, we rattled them and o-ro we chased them,
    O-ro, we rattled them, the little pack of tailors.

2.   I went to Dublin and met a little tailor,
    I stuck him in my pocket, for fear the ducks would eat him.
    The dogs began to bark at him and I began to beat him,
    And I threw him in the water for fear the ducks would eat him.

O-ro, we rattled them, o-ro, we chased them,
And o-ro, we rattled them, the little pack of tailors;
O-ro, we rattled them, o-ro, we chased them,
O-ro, we rattled them, the little pack of tailors.

Tie-aye the-dye-aye, the dye-eye the day-dee
Tie-aye the-dye-aye, the dye-the-diddle day-dee
Tie-um the die-um, the dye-um the-day-dee
the dye the-diddle day-dee

Recordings JR-GP (24 Nov. 1952)= Kennedy, *Folkways* FW 8872.   **Text** From the JR-GP recording; another in Bess's handwritten collection of songs.   **Notes** The text in Bess's own handwritten collection goes like this:

A.   As I went down to Dublin, I met a little tailor,
          I stuck him in my pocket, for fear the ducks would ate him.
          The dogs began to bark at him, and I began to bate him,
          And I threw him in the water, for fear the ducks would ate him.

        And O Ro we rattled em and O Ro we chased em
        And O Ro we rattled em, the little pack of tailors.

B.   I went into [a] tailor's shop, I picked up a needle,
        I stuck it in the tailor's pocket — pop goes the weasel!
        A halfpenny for a cotton ball, a penny for a needle,
        That's the way my money goes — pop goes the weasel!

C.   Johnny will you marry me, Johnny will you take me?
        Johnny will you marry me — or what the devil ails you?

        Towdy dowdy diddley dom towdy dowdy deed e
        Towdy dowdy diddley dom — pop goes the weasel!

In another DÓC notebook, our text is followed by these verses (to the same air?) :

1.   Get up ould woman and shake yourself!
        Get up ould woman and shake yourself!
        Get up ould woman and shake yourself!
        Don't be sitting all day in the corner!

2.   When old women are drunk it is tay they want,
        When old women are drunk it is tay they want,
        When old women are drunk it is tay they want
        At eight o'clock in the morning.

John Moulden refers me to Len Graham, *Wind and water*, Topic 12TS334 (London 1977); Paddy Tunney, *The lark in the morning*, Tradition TLP 1004 (N.Y. 1955); Jeannie Robertson, *Bonnie lass come over the burn*, Transatlantic XTRA 5041 (London 1967), and *Love will you marry me?*, sung by Johnny Moynihan on *Dé Danann: selected jigs, reels and airs*, Decca SKCR 5287 (London 1977). The song is also known as *Some say the devil's dead*.

172

The lover and darling[1/2]

1.   One evening as Sol reclined in his ways
      I commenced my usual excursions.
      The birds that sang sweetly were just going away
      And most enchanting lay nature's exertions.
      When at length in the dusk I espied a young pair —
      I seldom beheld a beauty so rare! —
      My heart felt astonished when I heard him exclaim:
      'Fair maid, won't you call me your darling?'

2.   I waited a moment to hear the reply,
      Disliking, of course, to disturb them.
      In the meantime I wished I had been far away,
      Though I apparently couldn't prevent it.
      Her blushes and kisses seemed his heart to beguile,
      And he holding his hand round her neck all the while.
      'How soon you expected', she said with a smile,
      'Young man, that I'd call you my darling!'

3.   'An abundance of money I'll give you', said he,
     'And in robes I will dress you most splendid;
     A farm of land and to hold it rent-free,
     And servants in plenty attending.
     I'll give you a carriage and horses to drive,
     And a supply of spirits that might serve to deprive,
     Or to drown discontention in your heart that might thrive,
     And fair maid, won't you call me your darling?'

4.   'If you were to give me all ships on the main,
     Britannia's powerful dominions,
     With Persia and Turkey and fertile Lorraine,
     And also the East and West Indies.
     If you were to give me Hibernia of old,
     Or were you to give me large trunks full of gold,
     Such comical things can't my senses blindfold,
     And for such I'll not call you my darling.'

5.   'I'll give you, my love, contentment and ease,
     Though exalted or low be your station;
     And with much satisfaction I'll try for to please
     And to serve you with much consolation.
     I'll promise to chase from your heart all its woes
     And in bed you can lie undisturbed till you chose;
     In the morning at parting I'll settle the clothes,
     And fair maid, won't you call me your darling?'

6.   Most lovely and noble and charming to view,
     Her countenance changed in a moment.
     Her cheeks that were tinged with a little of blue
     Grew red like the tincture of roses.
     When this damsel at last by those means he did gain,
     With extended arms he embraced her again,
     And from laughing I thought I could never refrain
     When I heard her exclaim: 'You're my darling!'

7.   Confounded I felt and my heart got amazed,
     Sunk deep in a retrograde motion.
     I stepped through the bushes, not knowing where to range,
     Like a ship in the midst of the ocean.
     Ever since, when I would cast a glance at the same,
     My heart, when transported, uprises again;
     And soon it disperses all trouble and pain,
     When I think of the Lover and Darling.

Recording BBC 19023 (14 Sept. 1952).   **Text** From the BBC recording. There is another copy in Bess's handwritten collection of songs; there is a third text, basically identical, in CBÉ 283, 170–72.   **Notes** In CBÉ 283 (175) a note added by Seán Ó Cróinín states that the song was composed by Bess's father, Seán Máistir Ó hIarlaithe. Ennis's BBC note reads 'Tune is old Munster narrative-type song-tune. Compare with [BBC] 19027 Back, Bd. 1, 'The little low hut' and also 'The wife of the bold tenant farmer' recorded from Michael Cronin. It is a variant of 'The Limerick Rake' tune (Ó Lochlainn, *Irish street ballads*)'. The air is the same as that for *The Trip o'er the Mountain*.

One eve - ning as Sol __ re - clined in his ways __

I com - menced my us - ual ex - cur - sions.

The birds that sing swee - tly were just going a - way

Most en - chan - ting lay na - ture's ex - er - tions. ___

At length in the dusk I es - pied a young pair ___

I sel - dom be - held a ___ beau - ty so rare!

I ___ then felt as - ton - ished when I heard him ex - claim:

'Fair_ maid, will you call me your dar - ling?'

173

The maid of the sweet brown Knowe

Laws P 7.   **Note** Title only from one of Bess's song-lists.   **Printed Sources** See Laws, *American balladry from British broadsides*, 251 (The Foot of the Mountain Brow). Ó Lochlainn, *Irish street ballads*, 38–39, No. 19) has a text in 6 verses.

174

The man that came home from Pretoria

1.   'Although I have travelled far over the seas,
     My rags, they are ravelled and flowing in the breeze;
     They'll get me entangled in brambles and trees
     On my way coming home from Pretoria.
     I thought in my heart when I was going away
     I'd make a good start and have wonderful pay.
     But I found it was harder to act than to say',
     Said the man that came home from Pretoria.

2.   'Believe me, De Wett gave them something to do;
     I remember him yet, and I think so would you.
     Three of those chaps were a match for three score
     Of the English force in Pretoria.
     I worked liked a bugger to come back again
     On board of the lugger 'mid torrents of rain.
     The roar of the surges 'nigh drove me insane',
     Said the man that came home from Pretoria.

3.   'After fourteen days' sailing we came to Dundalk.
     My limbs they were failing, I scarcely could walk.
     The peelers they gazed with the eye of a hawk
     At the man coming home from Pretoria.
     There was one with a squint that insisted to know
     My name and my way of existing also:
     "You have not got the build and identical go
     Of the man that came home from Pretoria"'.

4.   'He says: "You have got no means of support.
     Your movements are strange since you came into port.
     You will be detained to explain it in court,
     Why you're tramping it home from Pretoria".
     'I'll tell you where then they lodged me that night:
     In a dreary stone closet shut off from the light,
     Where the fleas in battalions were having a fight
     For the man that came home from Pretoria'.

5.   'It was early next morning a raw-boned J.P.
     Subjected the law to a close scrutiny.
     "The devil a harm at all can I see
     In the man coming home from Pretoria".
     I craved and protested with tears in my eyes,
     For all that had left him and fled to the skies
     Not to have me arrested and let me pass by
     On my way coming home from Pretoria'.

6. When I'm back in Struicín, as you see in the fall,
    'Tis the fairest I see from the Lee to Dundalk;
    [Of the fair spots I've seen from Beleek to Bengal,]
    And I'll stop there till my whiskers are hoary.

Text From Bess's collection of handwritten songs; I have another text, transcribed by SÓC (vv. 1, 2 only). See also *An Múscraíoch*
11 (Iúil 1992) 8.   **Notes** This song was composed by George Curtin (= Mícheál Ó Tuama), who was the author also of the song
I'll Tell You a Comical Story [No. **71**]. Dr Seán Ua Súilleabháin has kindly supplied me with the background story: George inherited
some money from an aunt in Cardiff, and travelled over to collect it. However, he spent the money on drink, and found himself
with nothing left to pay for his ticket home. He worked a passage on a ship coming back to Dundalk, where the ship's captain sent
him to buy bread. George then made his way as far as Drogheda, where he earned £6 by singing *The Youth Who Belonged to
Milltown* and passing round a hat! From Drogheda George then made his way to Dublin and Wicklow, and on southwards, till he
returned home around Christmas 1900, when he composed the song about his supposed adventures. He pretended that he had
been in Pretoria, in South Africa! The words missing in verse 6c above were supplied from Seán Ua Súilleabháin's text. Bess's
version has accidentally dropped the following four lines from v. 2:

> The long hours in ambush whilst dodging the Boers,
> In anguish we languished while patching our sores,
> For three of those chaps were a match for three score
> Of the lads that came home from Pretoria.

There is a later version in CBÉ 1591, 224–29 (Cork 1960). The text in *An Múscraíoch* is from the singing of John Connell, of
Danganasillagh.

175

The prayerbook[1/12]

1. Once I had a prayerbook inlaid well with gold.
    I thought myself a happy man when first I got the hold.
    To Mass or Service, when I'd go, fair maids would at me stare
    In hopes to gain myself and same, we were so nice a pair.

2. My sweetheart came to me one day and begged it for a time;
    Willingly I gave it to her, for I thought she would be mine.
    She took this pretty keepsake and kept it for a week;
    And ever since that time to me she did not speak.

3. My love she is a sprightly lass, she has skin as white as snow.
    Her golden hair in ringlets along her back do flow.
    Her cherry cheeks and ruby lips in vying with the rose;
    She's kind of heart, both tall and smart, wherever that she goes.

4. It was your cruel father first parted you and I,
    And caused our separation now and in aftertime.
    But now as I have nothing left, but pine away and moan,
    Until some kind one takes me in hand and cures the heart that's sore.

5. Fair maids remark in time to pass, mind what the poet says:
    You will repent in aftertime, but then 'twill be too late.
    You'll wed unto another man — a stick he'll give your side,
    And, mind you, the day's long passed away when I'd make you my bride.

6.   I never wrote a verse before, nor never would, I'm sure,
     But in order to remind you of what may be your doom.
     Some other lass will have the chance of wedding me one day,
     So fare thee well, my former love, my heart lies far away!

Recording BBC 19022 (14 Sept. 1952).   **Text** From the BBC recording.   **Notes** A second text, in CBÉ 283, 173–74, lacks our v. 4. A third text in CBÉ 476, 287–88, lacks v. 6. There is an interesting account, in CBÉ 476, 288–89, of Seán Ó Tuama, a Kerryman who had relations next-door to Bess's place and who visited frequently. He had a great collection of songs, and neighbours all crowded in whenever he arrived. He composed *Cois a chatharaig is breátha in Éirinn*, amongst others (1st v. ibid, 289). Seamus Ennis, in his BBC note, remarks that *The Prayerbook* was 'learned in childhood from the old singers in the neighbourhood in the same way as the rest of her songs. She can't recall learning any individual song from an individual singer'.

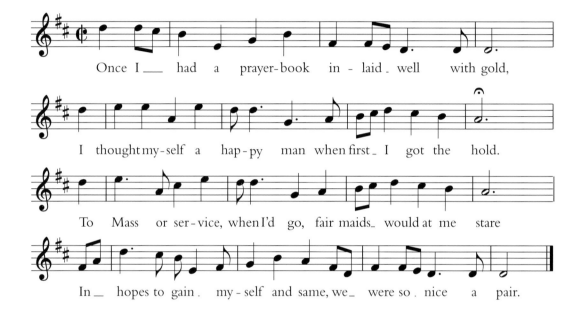

176

The sun is gone down in the west, love[2/5]

1.   The sun is gone down in the west, love,
     The evening falls with the dew.
     No more shall the shamrock be green, dear,
     Since I lost my remembrance of you.

     Since I lost my remembrance of you, dear,
     Since I lost my remembrance of you,
     No more shall the shamrock be green, dear,
     Since I lost my remembrance of you.

2.   Last night you were in with another,
     As you sat 'neath the old oaken tree.
     I hope you won't leave her in sorrow
     Alone, as you've gone and left me.

The Sun is gone down in the West love.
The evening falls with the dew.
No more shall the shamrock be green. dear.
Since I lost my remembrance of you
Since I lost my remembrance of you dear
Since I lost my remembrance of you
No more shall the Shamrock be green dear.
Since I lost my remembrance of You.
            2 nd Verse.
Last night you were in with another
As you sat neath the old oaken tree
I hope you wont leave her in sorrow.
Alone as youre gone & left me.
Alone as youre gone & left me dear.
Alone as Youre gone & left me
I hope you wont leave her in sorrow.
Alone as youre gone & left me.
            3 rd Verse.
I have but the one heart to give thee
Tis hard to divide it in two
So darling you may have it all
For I never loved any but you

'The sun is gone down in the west, love' written out by Bess Cronin (private collection).

Alone, as you've gone and left me, dear,
Alone, as you've gone and left me;
I hope you won't leave her in sorrow,
Alone, as you've gone and left me.

3. I have but the one heart to give thee.
    'Tis hard to divide it in two.
    So, darling, you may have it all,
    For I never loved any but you.

    I never loved any but you, dear.
    I never loved any but you.
    So, darling, you may have it all,
    For I never loved any but you.

4. Death in this world shall divide us;
    It's then I shall bid thee adieu.
    I have nothing to leave thee behind, dear,
    But numberless blessings on you.

    But numberless blessings on you, dear,
    But numberless blessings on you.
    I have nothing to leave thee behind, dear,
    But numberless blessings on you.

5. And when I am laid in my coffin,
    And my bones are all gone to decay,
    I'll think on the promise you made me,
    Alone on that bright summer's day.

    Alone on that bright summer's day, dear,
    Alone on that bright summer's day.
    I'll think on the promise you made me,
    Alone on that bright summer's day.

Recordings CBÉ 430b (1947) — JR‑GP (2 Oct. 1952) — Diane Hamilton (1955).   **Text** From the JR‑GP recording. There is a copy also in Bess's handwritten collection of songs, and another in a DÓC notebook; the two texts are identical.   **Printed Sources** *JIFSS* (Dec. 1921) 32, No. 17 (5 vv).   **Notes** This song is also known under the title *Since I Lost My Remembrance of You*.

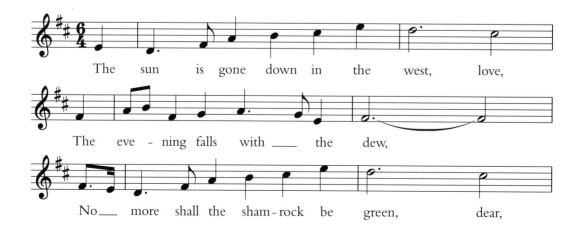

The sun is gone down in the west, love,

The eve - ning falls with ____ the dew,

No ____ more shall the sham - rock be green, dear,

Since I lost my re-mem-brance of you,

Since I lost my re-mem-brance of you, _____ dear,

Since I lost my re-mem-brance of you, _____

No ___ more shall the sham-rock be green, dear,

Since _ I lost my re-mem-brance of you

177

The Tailor Bawn

1. A dozen long years I am shaping, singing and making rhymes;
    Very often contrary and putting out airy times;
    Sleeping in very cool places and often out late till dawn,
    And it's now I do hear them comparing myself and the Tailor Bawn.

2. A pair of rollicking sporters nearly both one size;
    Very fond of this porter — 'tis bulging out both our eyes.
    The people know well we are topers and coming in home at dawn.
    The dogs will be barking before us and welcoming home Dan Bawn.

3. 'Tis often I drank with the Tailor at market and fair each time.
    On Sundays there was not a failure, we thought that our game was fine.
    He used to be acting old capers and singing up queer *rócáns*;
    The landlady looking for payment and cursing the Tailor Bawn.

4. There was not a tramp in the nation, ugly, fair or fine,
    And people of very low station were pulling out airy times.
    We drank with journeymen bakers and every queer *spréachán*.
    You'd think, when you'd look at their features, they were cousins of Tailor Bawn!

5. I struck on a comical bargain, myself and Dan Bawn, last June;
    To meet him at old Kilafada, and it's there we'll be marching soon.
    Then we'll be setting the garden and turning out sods of bawn;
    And we'll take an odd trip to Kilgarvan, myself and the Tailor Bawn.

6. Myself will go in for Moll Foley, for everyone knows she's fine.
    Her parents, they often had told me her money, of course, was mine.
    The Tailor and Jackeen are poaching and coming in late at dawn.
    The meat and the fish they'll be roasting for myself and the Tailor Bawn.

7. 'Tis then I'll have a fine farm, myself and my charming wife.
    I need not be afraid of the storm that's crushing me all my life.
    And if there's a son or a daughter and fortune may favour Seán,
    'Tis easily known who's the father, myself or the Tailor Bawn.

8. 'Tis often I sat with this Tailor, expecting to make things fine;
    In a kind of a happy-go-easy from drinking strong ale and wine.
    We'll turn out riggedy-rero, for he is a queer *creachán*,
    And we will have women — by japers! — myself and the Tailor Bawn.

9. By herrings! — he was a good Tailor for cutting and making frieze.
    'Tis very often he teased us, splitting and shaping lies.
    He turned out drinking completely, an ugly queer *clampán*,
    And I have nothing to add to his failures, but bad luck to the Tailor Bawn!

Text From Bess's handwritten collection of songs (2 copies); a third handwritten copy in an SÓC notebook. Another text in CBÉ 912, 539–43 (dated 17 June 1943). **Printed Sources** Tomás Ó Canainn, *Songs of Cork*, 76–77, 123 (a modern text). **Notes** In CBÉ 912, 543, Seán Ó Cróinín adds the following note 'Johnny Nóra Aodha (Seán Ó Tuama) a dhein an t-amhrán san — 'The Tailor Bawn'. Thiar tímpeall Chíll Gharbháin a bhíodh an táilliúr sin — agus is dóigh liom gur do mhuíntir Dhonnchúdha é — Dómhnall Ó Donnchúdha. Fear aerach ab eadh é go háirighthe. Fear aerach go maith ab eadh Johnny Nóra Aodha, leis. Tá sé marbh le fada. Ansan thiar a chaith sé a shaoghal (i bparr. Chíll Gharbháin), ach ó Bhaile Mhúirne ab eadh a mhuíntir. Do mhuíntir Thuama na Seana-Chluan anso (baile f. i mB. Mhúirne) ab eadh a mháthair, driofúr do Phead Aodha. Dhein Seán seó amhrán, agus bhíodar go léir i mBéarla. Ach do bhí an Ghaoluinn aige chómh maith leis an mBéarla. Bhíodh an "Tailor Bawn" ag ga héinne roinnt bhlianta ó shoin; aon áit go mbeadh rínnce, nú pósadh, bheadh an "Tailor Bawn" ar siúbhal ann agus daoine ag gáirí go seóig, mar do bhí spórt ann. (E Ní Ch)' *[Johnny Nóra Aodha (Seán Ó Tuama) composed this song … He used to be around Kilgarvan, and I think he was one of the Donoghues — Donal O'Donoghue. He was an odd sort, and Johnny N.A. was odd too. He's long dead. He spent his life in the parish of Kilgarvan, but his people were from Ballyvourney. His mother belonged to the Twomey's of Seana-Chluan here in the parish of Ballyvourney; she was a sister of Pead Aodha's. He composed a lot of songs, and they were all in English; but he had Irish as well as English. Everybody knew The Tailor Bawn many years ago, and any place there was a dance or a wedding, The Tailor Bawn would always be sung, and people laughing heartily at it, because there's fun in it (Bess Cronin)'.]*

CBÉ 912, 539, has this opening verse

> You neighbours, come listen a moment, I'll sing you a sporting song.
> I'm not very good at composing, but I'd better not wait too long.
> The best of my strings they are broken, and more of them going quite wrong,
> But as far as I hear it outspoken that some of my notes are strong.

and our v. 8 precedes v. 6. The following Irish words occur: 4c *spréachán*: a lively sort of person; 8c *creachán*: lit. a small potato; 9c *clampán*: perhaps the same as *clamprán*, an antagonistic individual. See also the note to *Muirisheen went to Bonane* [No. **95**].

178

The town of Dunmanway

1. In the neat little town of Dunmanway
    an apprentice by trade I was bound,
    And many is the hour of happiness
    I spent in that neat little town.

Until ruin and misfortune came o'er me,
which caused me to leave my own land,
Far away from my friends and relations,
to be led by a black velvet band.

2. When I first took a walk down the broadway,
thinking not to stay very long,
I fixed my eyes on a pretty fair maid
as she tripped o'er the broadway along.
Her cheeks were as red as the roses,
and her skin was as white as the swan,
And the hair that fell down from her shoulders,
tied up by a black velvet band.

3. When I first took a walk with this pretty fair maid,
a gentleman just passed us by,
I knew he was on to something,
for the look in his roguish black eye.
But the watch he took out of his pocket
and slipped it right into my hand,
That was the first time I was taken —
bad luck to the black velvet band!

4. Next day before the grand jury —
in court I had to appear —
The gentleman swore to his jewellery —
the case against me was brought clear.
The gentleman swore to his jewellery —
the gold watch he held in his hand —
And for seven years I was transported,
a convict to Van Diemen's Land.

5. So all young men take warning,
to shun bad company,
For if you don't take this warning,
'twill happen you as it happened to me.
They'll treat you with strong ale and porter,
until you won't be able to stand,
And then before they will leave you,
they'll send you to Van Diemen's Land.

Recording CBÉ 1063b (1947).   **Text** From the CBÉ recording; a second copy in CBÉ 283, 180–82.   **Printed Sources** National Library of Ireland, General Coll. (8 vv.); Hughes, *Irish country songs* 4, 52–56 *(The black ribbon-band)*; Kennedy, *Folksongs of Britain and Ireland*, 695 and 725, No. 313 (4 vv.).   **Notes** This song is better known under the title of *The Black Velvet Band*, one of the most popular of Anglo-Irish broadside ballads, which is recorded also from England and Australia. It is usually sung with a refrain:

> Her eyes, they shone like diamonds,
> I thought her the pride of the land;
> Her hair it hung down o'er her shoulders,
> Tied up in a black velvet band.

The NLI broadside was published by [? name omitted] & Co., Printers, 2 & 3, Monmouth Court, Seven Dials, with the title *The Black Velvet Band*, to the air of *Tars of the Blanch*. The text is as follows:

A.   To go in a smack down at Barking, where a boy as apprentice was bound,
     Where I spent many hours in comfort and pleasure in that little town;
     At length future prospects were blighted, as soon you may all understand;
     So by my downfall take a warning — beware of a black velvet band.

B.   One day being out on the ramble, alone by myself I did stray,
     I met with a young gay deceiver, while cruising in Ratcliffe Highway,
     Her eyes were as black as a raven: I thought her the pride of the land;
     Her hair, that would hang o'er her shoulders, was tied with a black velvet band.

C.   She towed me in port, and we anchored, from virtue she did me decoy,
     When it was proposed and agreed to, that I should become a flash boy,
     And drinking and gaming to plunder to keep up the game was soon planned;
     But since, I've had cause to remember the girl with a black velvet band.

D.   Flash girl, if you wish to turn modest, and strive a connexion to gain,
     Do not wear a band o'er the forehead, as if to tie in your brain;
     Some do prefer Victoria fashion, and some their hair braided so grand
     Myself I do think it much better than a girl with a black velvet band

E.   Young men, by my fate take a warning, from all those gay ladie[s] refrain,
     And seek for a neat little woman that wears her hair parted quite plain,
     The subject that I now do mention, tho' innocent, soon me trapanned;
     In sorrow my days will be ended, far from the black velvet band;

F.   For she towed in a bold man-of war's man her ogle she winked on the sly,
     But little did I know her meaning, when I twigged her a faking his cly,
     He said, I'm bound for the ocean, and shortly the ship will be made,
     [B]ut still I've a strong inclination for the girl with a black velvet band.

G.   A snare was invented to slight and banish me out of her sight,
     A fogle she brought of no value, saying, more I will bring this night
     She slipped it sly into my pocket, false girl! and took me by the hand;
     They gave me in charge for the sneezer — bad luck to the black velvet band!

H.   [I?] Forkly was [j]ailed and committed, and cast in the jug for a lag,
     [ ] a wipe that she pinched and bunged to me, and valued no more than a flag,
     The judge said to me, you are s[e]ntenced to a free passage to V[an] Diemen's Land
     [last line missing: My curse to the black velvet band?].

Peter Kennedy's version is set in Belfast and he believed that the song originated there; see *Folksongs of Britain and Ireland*, 725. It must be said, however, that our version is more coherent than the version printed by him, and there is nothing in the content which would indicate a Belfast origin.

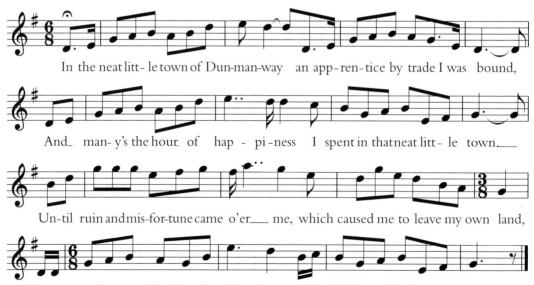

In the neat litt- le town of Dun-man-way   an app-ren-tice by trade I was   bound,

And_ man- y's the hour_ of   hap - pi-ness   I spent in that neat litt- le   town.___

Un-til ruin and mis-for-tune came o'er___ me, which caused me to leave my own land,

Far a-way from my friends and re- la - tions, to be led by a black vel-vet band.

179

The whistling thief

1. When Pat came over the hill, his colleen for to see
His whistle, low but shrill, the signal was to be.
'Oh, Mary!', the mother cried, 'there's somebody whistling sure' —
'Oh, Mother, it is the wind that's whistling through the door'.

> To me fol-the-dol-ah rull-ah
> To me fol-the-dol-ah rull-ee
> To me fol-the dol-ah rull-ah
> Rights fol-the-dol al-the-lol-ee

2. 'I have lived a long time, Mary, in this wide world, my dear,
But the door to whistle like that I never yet did hear!'
'But, Mother, you know the fiddle hangs close beside the chink,
And the wind upon the strings is blowing the tune, I think!'

> To me fol-the-dol-ah rull-ah
> To me fol-the-dol-ah rull-ee
> To me fol-the-dol-ah rull-ah
> Rights fol-the-dol al-the-lol-ee

3. 'The dog it is barking now, you know; the fiddle can't play the tune';
'But, Mother, you know they say dogs bark when they see the moon!'
'But how can he bark at the moon when he is old and blind? —
Blind dogs can't bark at the moon, you know, nor fiddles can't play with the wind!'

> To me fol-the-dol-ah rull-ah
> To me fol-the-dol-ah rull-ee
> To me fol-the-dol-ah rull-ah
> Rights fol-the-dol al-the-dol-ee

4. 'Mary, I hear the pig uneasy in his mind' —
'But, Mother, you know they say that pigs can see the wind!'
'That's true enough by day, but I think you may remark,
That pigs no more than we can see anything in the dark!'

> To me fol-the-dol-ah rull-ah
> To me fol-the-dol-ah rull-ee
> To me fol-the-dol-ah rull-ah
> Rights fol-the-dol al-the-lol-ee

5. 'I'm not such a fool as you think: I know very well it is Pat —
Go home you whistling thief and do get away out of that!
You go into bed and don't play upon me your jeers,
For although I have lost my sight, I haven't lost my ears!'

> To me fol-the-dol-ah rull-ah
> To me fol-the-dol-ah rull-ee
> To me fol-the-dol-ah rull-ah
> Rights fol-the-dol- al-the-lol-ee

6.   'You chaps when courting go and for your sweethearts wait,
      Take care not to whistle too loud, for fear the old woman might wake!
      For in the days when I was young — forget I never can —
      I knew the difference between a fiddle, a dog and a man!'

Recording BBC 11990 (7 Aug. 1947) CBÉ 380 (1947).   **Text** From the BBC recording; another in Seamus Ennis's CBÉ transcript of Sept. 1946; a third copy in a DÓC notebook (handwritten by Bess).   **Printed Sources** National Library of Ireland, General Coll., No. 152 (broadside); Sparling, *Irish minstrelsy*, 359–60; *Delaney's Irish song book* No. 1, 19; Henry, 'Songs of the People', *Northern Constitution* (3 July 1937), No. 710 = Huntington & Hermann, *Sam Henry's Songs of the People*, 264–65; *Walton's treasury of Irish songs and ballads*, 79–80.   **Notes** See also Paul Clayton, *British broadside ballads in popular tradition*. Folkways Records, Album No. FW 8708 (New York 1957) 4, a song learned from a Seamus Ennis recording of 1947 for the BBC (and by him presumably from Bess Cronin). Clayton refers also to Manus O'Conor, *Irish come-all ye's* (New York 1901), which I've not seen.

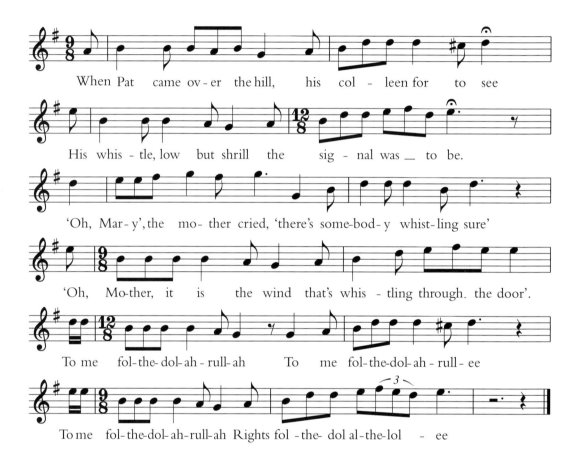

When Pat came over the hill, his col-leen for to see
His whis-tle, low but shrill the sig-nal was — to be.
'Oh, Mar-y', the mo-ther cried, 'there's some-bod-y whist-ling sure'
'Oh, Mo-ther, it is the wind that's whis-tling through the door'.
To me fol-the-dol-ah-rull-ah To me fol-the-dol-ah-rull-ee
To me fol-the-dol-ah-rull-ah Rights fol-the-dol al-the-lol — ee

180

The Yorkshire farmer [2/18]

1.   Come, listen to me, and a story I will tell,
      Concerning a farmer in Yorkshire did dwell!
      He had a youthful boy, he hired him as a man,
      All for to do his business, his name it was John.

      To me fol-the-day rul-aye-ro, fol-the-day rul-ee

2.   Early one morning he called to his man;
John to his master immediately ran.
'John', said the master, 'take this cow to the fair,
For she's in good order and I her can spare'.

To me fol-the-day rul-aye-ro, fol-the-day rul-ee

3.   John drove the cow out of the barn
And off to the fair he immediately ran;
He was not long there when he met with three men,
And he sold them the cow for five-pound and ten.

To me fol-the-day rul-aye-ro, fol-the-day rul-ee

4.   He went into an ale-house all for to drink,
The three men they came and down went the chink;
'What shall I do with the money?' he did say,
'Or where shall I put it, landlady, pray?'

To me fol-the-day rul-aye-ro, fol-the-day rul-ee

5.   'To the lining of your coat I will sew it', said she,
For fear of marauders robbed you might be.
A robber in the room was drinking up his wine
And says he to himself: 'Sure, this money shall be mine'.

To me fol-the-day rul-aye-ro, fol-the-day rul-ee

6.   John took his leave and he started for home;
The robber, he followed him straight out of the room.
He soon overtook him along the high-way:
'I'm glad of your company, young man', he did say.

To me fol-the-day rul-aye-ro, fol-the day rul-ee

7.   'Now', said the robber, 'you'd better for to ride:
'How far have you to go, then?', poor John, he replied:
'Three or four miles, far as I know';
He jumped up behind him and off they did go.

To me fol-the-day rul-aye-ro, fol-the-day rul-ee

8.   They rode all along till they came to a lane,
'Now', said the robber, 'I'll tell you quite plain:
To deliver up your money without any strife,
Or in this very moment I'll take away your life'.

To me fol-the-day rul-aye-ro, fol-the-day rul-ee

9.   'Now', says John, 'there's no time to dispute';
He jumped off his horse without neither fear or doubt.
From the lining of his coat he pulled the money out,
And among the green grass he threw it all out.

To me-fol-the-day rul-aye-ro, fol-the-day rul-ee

10.   The robber he alighted down off his horse —
       Sure, 'twas little he thought it was to his loss!
       When gathering up the money that was thrown along the grass
       John jumped in the saddle and he rode away his horse.

       To me fol-the-day rul-aye-ro, fol-the-day rul-ee

11.   One of the servants saw John coming home
       And it's in to her master she immediately ran;
       'John', said the master, 'did you make a swap,
       Or how did my cow turn out to be a horse?'

       To me fol-the-day rul-aye-ro, fol-the-day rul-ee

12.   'Indeed, and my dear master, the truth I will unfold:
       I was [stopped on the way] by a robber so bold;
       While gathering up the money that I threw among the grass
       For to make you some amends I brought you home his horse.

       To me fol-the-day rul-aye-ro, fol-the-day rul-ee

13.   The saddle-bag was opened and in it was found
       One-hundred bright guineas in silver and gold;
       A fine case of pistols, the farmer did avow,
       Saying: 'John, my dear fellow, you have well sold the cow!'

       To me fol-the-day rul-aye-ro, fol-the-day rul-ee

Laws L 1.   **Recording** JR-GP (24 Nov. 1952).   **Text** From the JR-GP recording; another text in an SÓC notebook. There are broadside versions in Royal Irish Academy RR 66 H 17, 52, and SR 3 C 39, 23, and in the NLI General Collection, almost identical to ours; they have the title *The Robber Outwitted*, and the text is identical in all four. Another broadside in the NLI, printed by John White, Rose Place, Liverpool, is titled *Crafty Ploughboy* and is in the *Yorkshire Bite* tradition. This is the version printed by Sam Henry.   **Printed Sources** Royal Irish Academy, RR 66 H 17 (Lord Moyne Coll.) 52; Royal Irish Academy, SR 3 C 39, 23; NLI General Coll., 2 copies; cf. also Cambridge University Library Ballads, vol. 3, 314; vol. 4, 104; vol. 6, 207, 431 (*The Robber Outwitted*); Child, *The English and Scottish popular ballads*, 5, 128–29, No. 283; Greig, *Folk-song of the North-East*, No. xxxv; Henry, 'Songs of the People', *Northern Constitution* (1 Nov. 1924), No. 51 (16 vv.) = Huntington & Hermann, *Sam Henry's Songs of the People*, 129–30; Purslow, *The wanton seed: more English folk songs from the Hammond and Gardiner Mss.*, 19 and 123; Laws, *American balladry from British broadsides*, 12–13, 72, 75–77, 165.   **Notes** This song is No. 283 in the famous Child collection, *The English and Scottish popular ballads*, 5, 128–29, *The Crafty Farmer*, who said of it 'This very ordinary ballad has enjoyed great popularity, and is given for that reason and as a specimen of its class' (128). There is a good discussion in George Malcolm Laws, *American balladry from British broadsides: a guide for students and collectors of traditional song*. Publications of the American Folklore Society, Bibliographical & Special Series Vol. viii (Philadelphia 1957) 72–77, where he compares *The Yorkshire Farmer (The Crafty Farmer)*, *The Lincolnshire Farmer's Daughter (The Highwayman Outwitted)*, and *The Crafty Ploughboy, or Highwayman Outwitted (The Yorkshire Bite)* — all believed to be different versions of the same original ballad. Purslow points out that the song may have a basis in fact: in the *JFSS* 1904 it is said that the incident described in the song was reported in *The Universal Museum* for February 1766, and first appeared in print c. 1782. This song is equally well-known in a version in which the farmer's daughter is the one who outwits the highwayman; see Maud Karpeles (ed), *Cecil Sharp's collection of English folk songs*, vol. 2, 45–48, No. 208 (two versions); Purslow, *The constant lovers*, 40–41, and 126. There is a Scottish version in Ewan McColl, *Folk songs and ballads of Scotland*. Oak Publications (New York 1965) 24–25.

Come, lis - ten un - to me, and a sto - ry I will tell,

Con - cern - ing a far - mer in York - shire did dwell!

He had a youth- ful boy, he hired him as a man.

All ___ for to do his busi - ness, his name it was John.

To me fol - the-day rul - aye - ro, fol - the-day rul - ee

181

The youth that belonged to Milltown

1. It's of a youth who came here to our country
   Among thousands who sailed far away;
   In hopes for to meet with employment,
   As thousands before him did stray.
   He resolved for to travel through England,
   For labour to seek up and down;
   But he never denied where he came from,
   From Kerry, a place called Milltown.

2. One day as he walked out through London,
   He met with John Bull on his way;
   And just as he passed by a corner
   We stopped and these words he did say:
   'Good evening, Pat, where are you bound for,
   Or when did you land on the shore?
   Or do you belong to those Fenians
   We had in the year '64?'

3. Says Pat: 'Now don't speak about Fenians,'
   As he looked at John Bull in surprise.
   'But remember the last words of Emmet,
   For they were the cause of great noise.
   But if it's because I'm from Ireland
   By your looking you do on me frown,

Remember you've met the wrong hero',
Said the youth that belonged to Milltown.

4. Says John Bull:'Though, stranger, you're saucy,
No doubt, your expressions are great!
But see how we did beat the Russians,
And the Zulus, we did them defeat.
We conquered all earth came before us —
Like thunder our cannons did roar —
We made proud Napoleon surrender,
When exiled to a far distant shore'.

5. Said the youth:'You may boast of your country,
Your soldiers and brave English men;
But tell me who is the right owner
Of the land where the shamrock do grow?
As long as the green flag is waving
An Irishman can't be put down;
While William O'Brien is our leader',
Said the youth who belonged to Milltown.

6. Said John Bull:'You have strayed from your country,
Like wild geese you do go away;
To America, New York and New Zealand,
You're never tired crossing the sea.
Why don't you some time be contented
A living to make of your own,
Like those that are here all around me
They don't go one mile from their home'.

Text CBÉ 476, 116–19.   **Printed Sources** National Library of Ireland, General Coll. (broadside).   **Notes** The NLI text (8 vv.), is stated to be 'by P. Connell'. There is a ballad in the Cambridge University Library collection, vol. 5, 281, entitled *Dialogue between John Bull and Irish Pat*, which may be identical with our song. The broadside in the NLI has the following text of vv. 5 and 6, plus two additional verses:

A. Says the youth, you may boast of your soldiers,
and many are brave Irishmen,
If it was not for them only,
a battle you never would win;
Will you show me one deed in your country
that the sword and the pistol cut down,
You are fond of spies and informers
says the youth that belongs to Milltown.

B. Says John Bull, why not stop in your own country
sometime and make home of your own,
Like those that you see here around us,
that never went a mile from their home;
Why not be sometime contented,
like wild geese you fly away,
To America, Queensland, and New Zealand,
you are never tired of crossing the sea.

C. Tis hard, if I could stop in my own country,
for England rules over us all,
Will you tell me who is the right owner
of the land where the great shamrock grows;

Whether the right or the wrong was the question,
he struggled to jink out the game,
I had a man here from your country,
it had been in the year 29.

D.   If you had a man here from my country,
his equals you never had seen,
And Daniel O'Connell they call him,
and remember from Kerry he came
Says the youth he was born in Caran,
its old ruins to day can be seen,
Close by the brink of the water
within a mile of Cahirciveen.
He was long the brave king of our country,
the harp and the shamrock crowned,
May God rest his soul he's in heaven,
ays the youth that belongs to Milltown.

Tom Munnelly informs me that this song is still common in the oral tradition; see his 'The long song singer', *Dál gCais* 8 (1966) 82–83. There are other texts in CBÉ 193, 631–37 (Clare 1936); and CBÉ 481, 318–21 (Wexford 1938).

182

There is no luck

Note Title only from one of Bess's song-lists.   **Printed Sources** *Delaney's Scotch song book* No. 1, 8 (6 vv.).   **Notes** Presumably intended is the Scottish song *There is nae luck about the house*, composed by William Julius Mickle. It was first published in Herd's Collection (1776) and was republished in James Johnson & Robert Burns, *The Scots musical museum 1787–1803* (repr. 2 vols, Scolar Press, Aldershot 1991) vol. 1, 44. I give the following text from *The illustrated book of Scottish songs from the sixteenth to the nineteenth century* (London, n.d.) 89–90:

1.   But are ye sure the news is true?
And are ye sure she's weel?
Is this a time to think o' wark?
Ye jauds, fling bye your wheel!
For there's nae luck about the house,
There's nae luck at a';
There's nae luck about the house,
When our gudeman's awa.

2.   Is this a time to think o' wark,
When Colin's at the door?
Rax down my cloak — I'll to the quay,
And see him come ashore.

3.   Rise up and make a clean fireside,
Put on the muckle pat;
Gie little Kate her cotton gown,
And Jock his Sunday coat.

4.   Mak their shoon as black as slaes,
Their stockins white as snaw;
It's a' to pleasure our gudeman —
He likes to see them braw.

5.   There are twa hens into the crib
Hae fed this month or mair;
Mak haste and traw their necks about,
That Colin weel may fare.

6. My Turkey slippers I'll put on,
   My stockins pearl-blue —
   It's a' to pleasure our gudeman,
   For he's baith leal and true.

7. Sae sweet his voice, sae smooth his tongue,
   His breath like cauler air;
   His very foot has music in't,
   As he comes up he stair.

8. And will I see his face again,
   And will I hear him speak?
   I'm downright dizzy wi' the thought,
   In troth I'm like to greet.

9. Thare's nae luck about the house,
   There's nae luck at a';
   There's nae luck about the house,
   When our gudeman's awa'.

Robbie Burns described this as 'positively the finest love-ballad in the Scotch, or perhaps in any other language'. There is a short 'jig-tune' parody (concerning whiskey) in CBÉ 616, 190 (Kerry 1939), and CBÉ 843, 206 & 208 (Kerry 1942). *Delaney's Scotch song book* has vv. 1, 2, 7, and 8 above, and the following two verses:

The cauld blasts a' the winter wind that thirl'd through my heart.
They're a' blawn by, I ha'e him safe, till death we'll never part;

But what puts parting in my head? it may be for awa',
The present moment is over ain — the neist we never saw.

183

There was a farmer all in this town

Child 272 **Laws** H 42 **Note** Title only from two of Bess's song-lists. **Notes** According to Tom Munnelly, this is Bess's version of the song otherwise known as *The Holland Handkerchief* or *The Suffolk Miracle* (for which see CBÉ 283, 257–59). Francis Child reported having acquired a copy of the song 'in the north of Ireland in 1850', in which the events are played out 'between Armagh and County Clare'; see *Engish and Scottish popular ballads* 5, 58–59. It is a great pity that Bess's version was not recorded or noted down, as the story is a very interesting one.

184

There was a lady in her father's garden^{2/16}

1. There was a lady in her father's garden,
   A gentleman being passing by;
   He stood a while and gazed upon her
   And said: 'Fair lady, would you marry me?'
   'I'm not a lady but a poor girl,
   And a poor girl of low degree;
   So therefore, young man, choose some other sweetheart,
   For I'm not fit your servant girl to be'.

2. 'I have houses and a good living,
    And I have money to set you free;
    And I will make you a nice young lady
    And you'll have servants to wait on thee'.
    ''Tis seven years since I had a sweetheart,
    And seven more since I did him see;
    And seven more I'll be waiting for him,
    For if he's alive he'll come home to me'.

3. 'If he is sick, I wish him better;
    If he is dead, I wish him rest;
    And if he's alive, I'll be waiting for him,
    For he's the young man that I love the best'.
    He put his hand down in his pocket,
    His lily-white fingers being thin and small;
    And up between them he pulled a gold ring,
    And when she saw it she down did fall.

4. He took her up all in her arms
    And gave her kisses most tenderly,
    Saying: 'I am your true love and single sailor
    That now came home for to wed with thee'.
    If you're my true love and single sailor
    Your face and features look strange to me;
    But sure seven years makes a great alteration
    And the raging seas between you and me'.

5. So all young maidens, I pray, take warning,
    Not to distrust your true love while on the sea;
    For if he's over across the ocean,
    He's sure to come back and marry thee.

Laws N 42. **Recording** JR–GP (24 Nov. 1952). **Text** From the JR–GP recording. There is a second text in CBÉ 283, 178–80.
Printed Sources Freeman, 'Irish folk songs', *JFSS* 6/5, No. 25 (Sept. 1921) 272–73, No. 59; Henry, 'Songs of the People', *Northern Constitution* (10 Dec. 1932), No. 471 (*The Broken Ring*, 7 vv.) = Huntington & Hermann, *Sam Henry's Songs of the People*, 317; Hughes, *Irish country songs* 4, 63–65; Ó Lochlainn, *Irish street ballads*, 4–5, No. 2; Laws, *American balladry from British broadsides*, 225–26. **Notes** In the recorded version, Bess has accidentally omitted the first half of verse 3:

3. 'If it is seven years since you had a sweetheart,
    And seven more since you did him see;
    And seven more you'll be waiting for him —
    Perhaps that young man you ne'er would see'

This is followed by 'If he is sick', etc., as in our text. Hence v. 4 should begin with 'He put his hand', etc., and end with 'That now came home', etc. Verse 5 then properly begins with 'If you're my true love', etc., and should end with 'He's sure to come back and marry thee'. In v. 2d 'And you'll have servants to wait on thee' reads 'If you will say that you'd marry me' in the CBÉ text. Freeman, in his Ballyvourney collection, has a version in seven verses from Conny Coughlan of Derrynasagart, which goes as follows:

A. There was a lady in her father's garden,
    And a bonny sailor being passing by,
    The more he viewed her, he stepped up to her,
    And said 'Fair maid, won't you fancy me?'

There was   a lad - y   in   her   fa - ther's   gar - den, __

A gent - le-man   be - ing pas-sing   by;

He stood a   while   and___   gazed u - pon her___

And said: 'Fair lad - y   would you mar - ry   me?'

'I'm ___   not a   lad - y   but a   poor girl, _____

And a   poor gir-l   of (a) low   de-gree;

So __ there-fore, young man, choose some ot - her sweet-heart, ___

For I'm not   fit your   ser - vant girl   to be.'

B.   'O no, kind sir, you're a man of honour,
     And a man of honour you seems to be,
     Far to impose you on any poor girrul
     That is scarce able your servant to be.'

C.   'And if you tell me you're a poor girrul,
     The more regard I shall have for thee;
     Come with me, and I'll make you quite happy,
     And you will have servants to wait on thee.'

D.   O no, kind sir, I once had a sweetheart,
     And those seven long years he is away from me,
     And for seven more I will wait for him,
     And if he's alive, he will return to me.'

E.   'Seven years makes an alteration,
     Perhaps that young man is dead and gone.'
     'If he is dead, I'd wish him rested,
     And if he is alive I'd wish him happy;
     For no other young man shall ever join me,
     For he is the darling young boy that I love the best.'

<blockquote>

F.　　And he put his hand all in his pocket,
　　　And his lovely fingers being thin and small,
　　　He pulled out a ring that was broke between them,
　　　And when she saw it, she down did fall.

G.　　He took her up closely in his arams,
　　　And gave her kisses most tenderly,
　　　Saying: 'I am your dear and loving sailor,
　　　That now came home for to marry thee.'

</blockquote>

According to Lucy Broadwood, in the notes to Freeman's text, this is a version of the popular song better known under the title *The Young and Single Sailor*. She mentions an edition with nine verses in the *JFSS* 4(1902) This is still one of the most popular songs in recent oral tradition in Ireland.

185

Three leaves of shamrock

1.　　I was leaving dear old Ireland in the merry month of June,
　　　When the birds were sweetly singing and all nature seemed in bloom;
　　　When an Irish girl accosted me with the sad tear in her eye,
　　　And while those words to me she said, she bitterly did cry:
　　　'Kind sir, I ask a favour, will you grant it, if you please?
　　　It is not much I'll ask of you, but 'twill set my heart at my ease.
　　　Take this bunch of shamrocks to my brother o'er the sea,
　　　And will you kindly tell him that they were sent by me?'

　　　Three leaves of shamrock, the Irishman's shamrock
　　　From his own sister Nora, her blessing too she gave.
　　　'Take them to Phelim, and will you kindly tell him,
　　　'Tis the three leaves of shamrock from his dear mother's grave?'

2.　　'You tell him, since he left us, what has happened to our lot;
　　　How the landlord came one winter's day and turned us from our cot.
　　　Our troubles they were plenty, and friends we had but few.
　　　Dear brother, these were all I had, and these I've sent to you'.

　　　Three leaves of shamrock, the Irishman's shamrock
　　　From his own sister Nora, her blessing too she gave.
　　　'Take them to Phelim, and will you kindly tell him,
　　　'Tis the three leaves of shamrock from his dear mother's grave?'

3.　　'Come back, come back, my darling son!', she oftentimes would say;
　　　But alas! one day she sickened and soon was laid away.
　　　Her grave I've watered with my tears, it's there these flowers grew.
　　　Dear brother, these were all I had, and these I've sent to you'.

　　　Three leaves of shamrock, the Irishman's shamrock
　　　From his own sister Nora, her blessing too she gave.
　　　'Take them to Phelim, and will you kindly tell him
　　　'Tis the three leaves of shamrock from his dear mother's grave?'

4. Old Tom Moore's fancies, rich and rare, my mind enraptured keeps.
    Long may the tiny shamrock grow, where Ireland's poet sleeps!
    Let other patriots boast of power or land that gave them birth!
    My voice I'll raise in Ireland's praise, the sweetest spot on earth!

    Three leaves of shamrock, the Irishman's shamrock
    From his own sister Nora, her blessing too she gave.
    'Take them to my brother, for I have got none other,
    And tell him they're the shamrocks from his dear mother's grave'.

Text From Bess's handwritten collection of songs.   **Printed Sources** *The three-Leafed Shamrock; or Take them to Phelim*, a broadside ballad published by J. Nicholson, Cheapside Song House, 36 Church Lane, Belfast, now in a scrapbook in the Belfast Public Library collection of broadside ballads. According to a communication from John Moulden, Nicholson was active from c. 1894 to 1916; cf. also *Delaney's Irish song book* No. 1, 2 *(Three Leaves of Shamrock)*; *Wehman's 617 Irish songs*, 82 (3 vv.).   **Notes** A note in *Delaney's song book* states 'words and music by James McGuire'. The texts published in *Delaney* and by J. Nicholson are very similar to Bess's:

> I was leaving dear old Ireland in the merry month of June,
> The birds were sweetly singing, and all nature was in tune,
> An Irish girl accosted me, the salt tear in her eye,
> And as she said these words to me she bitterly did cry —
> Kind sir, I ask a favour will you grant it to me, please,
> It is not much I ask, but it would set my heart at ease,
> Take this bunch of Shamrocks to my brother o'er the sea,
> And will you kindly tell him, sir, that they have come from me.
>
> Chorus —
>
> The three-leafed Shamrock, the Irishman's Shamrock,
> His own darling Norah her blessing she gave,
> Take them to Phelim, then kindly tell him,
> They're Shamrocks from his dear mother's grave.
>
> Tell him since he went away how bitter was out lot,
> The landlord came one winter day, and turned us from our cot,
> Our troubles they were many, and friends we had but few,
> And Phelim dear, my mother used to often sigh for you,
> My darling son come back to me, she often used to say,
> And saying so, she sickened, and soon was laid away;
> Her grave I watered with my tears, and there those flowers grew,
> Dear brother they were all I had, and these I sent to you.

Nicholson's text also has the following verse (which is clearly extraneous):

> Our Tom Moore's fancies, rich and rare,
> My mind enraptured keeps,
> Long may the tiny Shamrock grow
> Where Ireland's poet sleeps.
> Let other patients boast of power,
> Or land that gave them birth
> My voice I'll raise, in Ireland's praise,
> The sweetest spot on earth.

A version played by the North Carolina banjo-player, Charlie Poole (1892–1931) was very popular in the 1920s [John Moulden informs me]. Called *Leaving Dear Old Ireland*, it was re-issued on the LP, *The Legend of Charlie Poole*, County Records. County 516 (Virginia, n. d.).

186

Ticky-tack-too

1.   Ticky-tack-too, tack-too,
      Ticky-tack-too, tack-tay,
      Ticky-tack-too, tack-too,
      Ticky-tack-too, tack-tay.

Text From a DÓC notebook.   **Notes** A note to DÓC's text says 'for children, etc.'. A cobbler's song, there is a BBC recording of it, from Mary Murphy, Draperstown, in BBC 19973 (recorded 21 May 1953).

187

'Tis ten weary years[2/12]

1.   'Tis ten weary years since I left Ireland's shore
      To a far distant country to roam.
      Shall I ever return to the land of my birth,
      To the friends or the old folks at home?
      Last night as I slumbered I had a strange dream,
      One that seemed to bring distant friends near;
      I dreamt of old Ireland, the land of my birth,
      To the hearts of her sons ever dear.

      I saw the old homesteads and faces I loved,
      Yes, I saw Ireland's valleys and dells;
      And I listened with joy, as I did when a boy,
      To the sound of the old Shandon bells.
      For the turf was burning brightly;
      That night would banish all sin.
      The bells were ringing the old year out
      And the New Year in.

2.   As the joy bells rang, swift I wended my way
      To the cot where I lived when a boy.
      I looked in through the window, there by the fireside
      Sat my parents — my heart filled with joy.
      The tears trickled down my bronzed cheeks
      As I gazed on my mother so dear;
      For I knew in her heart she was breathing a prayer
      For the boy that she dreamt not so near.

      I saw the old homesteads and faces I loved.
      I saw Ireland's valleys and dells.
      And I listened with joy, as I did when a boy,
      To the sound of the old Shandon bells.

'Tis ten wear-y years since I left Ire-land's shore,
To a far dis-tant coun-try to roam.
Shall I ev-er re-turn to the land of my birth,
To the friends or the old folks at home?
Last night as I slum-bered I had a strange dream,
One that seemed to bring dis-tant friends near;
I dreamt of old Ire-land, the land of my_ birth,
To the hearts of her sons ev-er dear.

I saw the old home-steads and fa-ces I loved,
Yes, I saw Ire-land's vall-eys and dells;
And I list-ened with joy, as I did when a boy,
To the sound of the old Shan-don bells.

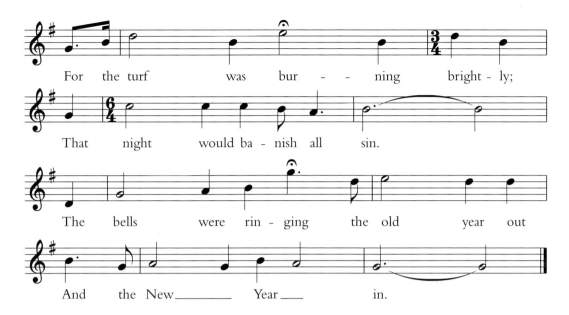

For the turf was burning brightly.
That night would banish all sin.
The bells were ringing the old year out
And the New Year in.

3. At the door of the cabin we met face to face,
    'Twas the first time for ten weary years.
    Soon the past was forgotten, we stood hand in hand,
    My parents they wondered in tears.
    Once more by the fireplace the turf burned brightly
    I promised no more would I roam.
    As I sat in the old vacant chair by the fire
    I sang that sweet song, Home Sweet Home.

    I saw the old homesteads and faces I loved.
    I saw Ireland's valleys and dells.
    And I listened with joy, as I did when a boy,
    To the sound of the old Shandon bells.
    For the turf was burning brightly;
    That night would banish all sin.
    The bells were ringing the old year out
    And the New Year in.

Recording JR–GP (2 Nov. 1952).   **Text** From the JR–GP recording; there is another in Bess's handwritten collection of songs.
Printed Sources Cf. *News Chronicle song book*, No. 2, Old-Time Variety Songs, 10–12.   **Notes** This is a slightly altered version of
The Miner's Dream of Home, written and composed by Will Goodwin and Leo Dryden, and sung by the latter in music halls. It was
popular with soldiers in the 1914–18 war. Dryden was a particularly patriotic song writer at the time of the Boer War and the First
World War; he was born on 6 June 1863 as George Dryden Wheeler. The song is pastiched by D. Kinsella as *An Irishman's Dream of
Home* in Walton's *New treasury of Irish songs and ballads* 2 (Dublin, n. d.) 23. Also known as *The Wanderer's Dream of Home*, it is found also
in CBÉ 1442, 10–11 (Kildare 1956). Not to be confused with the song called *The Bells of Shandon*, composed by the Rev. Francis
O'Mahony ('Father Prout'), which is commonplace in collections; e.g. Pádraig Breathnach, *Songs of the Gael* 1, 242–43.

188

Tom Toozick, the gentleman[1/23]

1. Éistíg go neosfaidh mé scéal,
    agus geallaim nach bréag a chanfad libh:
    Gur i dti'n tabhairne fhágas mo spré
    agus, geallaim, trí thaobh na scillinge.
    Creidíg mo scéal faoi dhó,
    gur minic a bhí coróinn 'na bhill' orm;
    Gur i dti'n tabhairne fhágas mo stór,
    agus cailiní óga am' chuileachtain.

    A dhuine, bí ciúin go fóill —
    éist le glór a' tseanachais!
    Leog dos na mná 'gus don ól,
    agus diúlthaigh go deo dos na beartaibh seo!

2. Dé Domhnaigh, nuair a théim go ti'n óil,
    bíonn an *landlady* romham go hinnealtha:
    'Fachtar dó cathaoir nó stól,
    agus bainíg de a bhróga agus triomaíg iad!'
    Mar do bhíodh mo dhúil insa liúnn,
    do deintí breis dúthracht go minic dom —
    Come landlady open the door,
    chun go dtéimíd sa rúimín is cluthaire!'

    A dhuine, bí ciúin go fóill —
    éist le glór a' tseanachais!
    Leog dos na mná 'gus don ól,
    agus diúlthaigh go deo dosna beartaibh seo.

3. Ní raibh ann ach triúr ar dtúis,
    is ba ghearr go raibh cúigear 'ár gcuileachtain:
    '*Come, bring us some toddy, my jewel,*
    for here is Tom Toozick the Gentleman!'
    Nuair airíos-sa m'ainm á ghlaoch,
    's an *title* go léir á thabhairt orm,
    D'fhanas ansúd ar mo phréic,
    chun gur ólas-sa saothar mo sheachtaine.

    A dhuine, bí ciúin go fóill —
    éist le glór a' tseanachais!
    Leog dos na mná 'gus don ól,
    agus diúlthaigh go deo dos na beartaibh seo!

4. Thuiteas lag marbh gan céill,
    's ní raibh scilling ná raol i dtaisce agam,
    Ach graithin is glamar a' tsléibh',
    is an *landlady* féin is í a' magadh fúm.
    [...   ...   .]
    [...   ...   .]

A dhuine, bí ciúin go fóill —
éist le glór a' tseanachais!
Leog dos na mná 'gus don ól,
agus diúlthaigh go deo dos na beartaibh seo!

5. D'éiríos go tapaidh im' shuí
'S do ghlaos mo chuid dí ar mo *landlady*:
'Le h-anmain t'athar!' ar sí,
's nár dhiúgais-se dríodar a' bharaille!'
Do bhí réasún aice leis siúd,
mar d'aithin sí gur cráite bhí an spaga agam,
'S dá dtagadh fear scillinge ar ball,
ní deasca do gheobhadh as a' mbaraille.

A dhuine, bí ciúin go fóill —
éist le glór a' tseanachais!
Leog dos na mná agus don ól,
agus diúlthaigh go deó dos na beartaibh seo!

6. Do bhíos-sa sealad dem' shaol,
's nuair a thuilinn mo shaol, do chaithinn í —
'*Mister Tom Cusack*' á ghlaoch
ag an *landlady* fhéin i dtigh a' tabhairne.
'Nois nuair ná fuil agam scilling ná raol,
ná aon stór i n-aon chor i dtaisce agam,
Fachtar dom Tomás Céasóg,
chun go mbainfead a bhróga 's a hata dhe!

A dhuine, bí ciúin go fóill —
éist le glór a' tseanachais!
Leog dos na mná 'gus do'n ól,
agus diúlthaigh go deo dos na beartaibh seo!

7. Leogfad-sa feasta dhon ól,
agus cnósfaidh mé ór agus airgead;
Beidh agam macha breá bó —
is mo mhallacht go deo dos na dramannaibh!
Sin tuillleadh dom' ghníomhartha ar lár:
leogfad do mhná is do rabaireacht;
Agus guím-se chun Íosa go h-árd,
Rí geal na nGrást á mhaitheamh dom!

English Summary A drinking-song, in which 'Tom Toozick' recounts his exploits in the local hostelry, where he habitually spent all his earnings. In the end he resolves to mend his ways, and asks God's forgiveness for his previous misbehaviour.
Recording CBÉ 397b (1947).   **Text** From the CBÉ recording (2 vv. only, with chorus) + Seamus Ennis CBÉ transcription (dated 7 May 1947) entitled *Tom Cusack, The Gentleman (Tomás Céasóg)*.   **Printed Sources** Freeman, 'Irish folk songs', *JFSS* 6/4 (Jan. 1921) 235–37, No. 44; Breathnach, *Ceól ár sínsear* (1923) 153–55 (4 vv.).   **Notes** In one of Bess's handwritten song-lists as *Eistig go nosamay sgeul*. Ennis has the complete text (7 vv.); another text (v. 1 + chorus only) in a DÓC notebook (dated 2 Jan. 1947); a third (7 vv.) in another notebook. I have also used the manuscript collection of Ballyvourney songs formerly in the possession of Caitlín Ní Bhuachalla, dated 1943. Breathnach's text in *Ceól ár sínsear*, 153–55, is more-or-less identical with ours. Note that Bess has replaced the 2nd two lines of v. 1 with the 1st two lines of v. 2, and run together the 2nd two lines of v. 2 with the 1st two lines of v. 3 of our text. An identical inversion has taken place in the Caitlín Ní Bhuachalla collection. There also appears to be a lacuna in v. 4; 3g *ar mo phréic* cf. *An Lóchrann* (Bealtaine 1918) 2 *Domhnall na Gréine* 'Fear *fréic* agus frolic, / I seomra ná i halla, / Seadh Domhnall na Gréine, / A gcualúir a thréithe', etc. Cf. **95** (4 (h)). Compare the song collected by Freeman from Conny Coughlan of Doire na Sagart (Baile Mhúirne) and published by him in the *JFSS* 6/4, No. 24 (Jan. 1921) 235–37, No. 44 *Éistig go n-ínsead mo scéal*, which has the same opening words as *Tom Toozick* (as Freeman pointed out), and whose tune is also related. I give the full text of the song here, for comparison [I have normalised Freeman's quasi-phonetic spelling]

Éis - tíg   go   neos - faidh   mé   scéal, _____

ag-us geal-laim nach breág___ a chan-fad libh:___

Gur i dti'n tab - hair - ne fhá - gas mo spré___

a - gus, geal-laim, trí thaobh na _ scil -lin -ge. _____

Dé   Domh- naigh, nuair a théim   go tí- 'n óil, ___

bíonn an *land - la - dy* rom-ham go hin - neal - tha: ___

'Fach - tar   dó   cath - aoir   nó   stól, _____

a-gus bai- níg de a bhró- ga 'gus triom- aíg iad!' (n)

A   dhui- ne, bí ciúin   go fóill -

éist ____   le glór ___ a' tsean - ach - ais! ___

Leog dos mn - á   'gus don   ól, _____

a - gus diúl - thaigh - go deo dos   na bear - taibh seo! (n)

1. Éistig go n-ínsead mo scéal,
    'Gus nách fhonn liom-sa bréag a dh'aithris,
    Má mheathann na prátaí sa chré,
    Go bhfuil buachaillí an tsaoil faoi tharcuisne.

    Fail-de-di, ail-de-deal-dá,
    Fail-al-de-deal-dá-rail, de-deal-de-di.
    Fail-de-di, ail-de-deal-dá,
    Fail-ail-de-di-á-rail-de-reail-dei-di.

2. Go moch, le h-amharc a' lae,
    Nuair a chuirthear le chéile as a' leabaidh iad,
    'Sé deirtear leo: 'Tuilíg úr bpá,
    Mar is suarach le rá 'n úr gcuid alais sibh!'

    Fail-de-di, etc.

3. 'S isé deir na feirmeoirí le chéile:
    'Cuirfear, is baol, as a' dtalamh sinn;
    Tá an iomarca taxanna a' glaoch,
    Is ní ghlacfar leathscéal gan a' t-airgead.'

    Fail-de-di, etc.

4. Bíonn a' cíos is a t-íoc ortha a' glaoch,
    Agus a mealataí mél sa tseachtain,
    Míle 'liú ag fear a' fuaréad,
    'Sé siúd is tréine nuair a thagann sé.

    Fail-de-di, etc.

5. 'S bíonn a' gabha, a' fiodóir 's a' siúinéar,
    'S a' táilliúir chun éadaigh a ghearradh dhóibh,
    Trifle beag eile 'on chúipéar,
    Do dhéanfadh cíléirí chun bainne dhóibh.

    Fail-de-di, etc.

Lucy Broadwood, in an additional note to Freeman's comments, points out that the tune 'is probably an English dance-tune and has a strong likeness to "Ragged and torn, and true", and a considerable likeness to "Old Simon the King", both in Playford's *Dancing Master* (see also Chappell's *Pop[ular] M[usic]*.' (237).

189

True friends and relations of high and low stations

1. True friends and relations of high and low stations,
    My little orations I'll give you quite clear
    About our good neighbours, who had some nice capers,
    Heaps of good nature and friendship that's near.
    Indeed, until lately we were banded completely,
    Stuck into ale-houses drinking strong beer.
    But it's now we're preparing, for war we're declaring.
    I hear people say we'll have corpses this year.

2. Our ranks they are broken, as I have just spoken,
    And everything looking like troublesome times.
    Some sheep they were stolen and false oaths were sworn,
    And hundreds of more things that were not too fine.
    The trenches are opened, the powers are opposing.
    The fences are closing, commencing the strife.
    When these are approaching no chance of controlling,
    The tide it is flowing — we'll have war to the knife!

3. One dark Monday morning old Forbus went crawling
    Around to the borders, on duty, we hear.
    Not very long after we found he was talking
    To Patsy Dearmawn, and so it appeared.
    Suspecting according, our sides we were guarding,
    Well knowing that our party couldn't get clear.
    My heart it is scalded to hear it recorded
    That tinkers rewarded are living out here.

4. If I was the farmer they style The Informer
    I'd go to headquarters and see myself clear.
    Immediately after, on leaving the altar,
    I'd stand on the walls of the church that is near.
    In every form I'd quell the alarum,
    And out of the storm my barque I would steer.
    If you don't act according you'll soon be discarded —
    The tinker won't solder your kettle, I fear!

5. The times they are awful, the Irish unlawful —
    A split in our party forever, I fear!
    When I hear people calling, shouting and bawling,
    I find it appalling, I tremble with fear
    When I think of those farmers that should be in their gardens,
    Weaned from their fathers, encumbered in years.
    But I hope without fear that God will reward us,
    To guide and to guard us throughout our career.

6. These terrible cases are spread through all nations,
    And innocent faces are greatly surprised.
    The rocks they are blazing, the people half-crazy,
    And nobody dreaming of quenching the fires.
    Through friends and relations of angry vexations
    I hear them declaring 'twas all done for spite.
    But I pity the creature that sold his good neighbour,
    For any foul traitor that's watching us tight.

7. So now in conclusion I'll make an allusion
    Through all the confusion that's here in Glenlee;
    Which left me disputing and often computing
    That forever in future we cannot agree.
    This little amusement has no signs of improvement;
    Our neighbours are wounded, I'm sorry to see;
    Which left me abusing this mean rotten Super'
    That sent our five troopers to the gaol of Tralee.

Text From the collection of Bess's handwritten songs. There is another, more-or-less identical, in a DÓC notebook. **Notes** This song was composed by Johnny Nóra Aodha [= Seán Ó Tuama], of Na hInsí, Cill Gharbháin (c. 1886–1928). For another song featuring Patsy Dearmawn see *You jolly young fellows, come listen to me* [No. **196**]. In v. 5g 'without farther', Bess's handwritten text has 'father' (which looks like it has been accidentally taken over from the previous line).

190

Uncle Rat[1/10]

1.   Uncle Rat went out to ride, Kitty alone, Kitty alone,
    Uncle Rat went out to ride, Kitty alone and I.
    Uncle Rat went out to ride, sword and buckle by his side,
    To me cax macaree duck-in-a-dill, Kitty alone and I.

2.   'Lady Mouse, will you marry me?', Kitty alone, Kitty alone,
    'Lady Mouse, will you marry me?', Kitty alone and I.
    'Lady Mouse will you marry me?' — 'Ask my Uncle rat', says she,
    To me cax ma-caree duck-in — a-dill, Kitty alone and I.

3.   'Uncle Rat, will I marry Lady Mouse?', Kitty alone, Kitty alone,
    'Uncle Rat, will I marry Lady Mouse?', Kitty alone and I.
    'Uncle Rat, will I marry Lady Mouse?' — 'Yes, kind sir, and half my house'
    To me cax ma-caree duck-in-a-dill, Kitty alone and I.

4.   'Lady Mouse, where will the wedding be?', Kitty alone, Kitty alone,
    'Lady Mouse, where will the wedding be?', Kitty alone and I.
    'Lady Mouse, where will the wedding be?' — 'Ask my Uncle Rat', says she,
    To me cax ma-caree duck-in-a-dill, Kitty alone and I.

5.   'Uncle Rat, where will the wedding be?', Kitty alone, Kitty alone,
    'Uncle Rat , where will the wedding be?', Kitty alone and I.
    'Uncle Rat, where will the wedding be?' — 'Up in the top of a holly tree',
    To me cax ma-caree duck-in-a-dill, Kitty alone and I.

Recordings BBC 11989 (7 Aug. 1947) — BBC 13774 (19 Sept. 1949) = Kennedy, *Folktracks* F–60–160 (1981) A6 = Kennedy & Lomax, *Songs of animals and other marvels* [= *The folk songs of Britain* 10], Topic Records 12T198 (London 1961) A 7b. **Text** From both BBC recordings. There is a separate copy in Seamus Ennis's CBÉ copybooks (Sept. 1946). **Printed Sources** See Rollins, *An analytical index of ballad-entries (1557–1709) in the registers of the Company of Stationers of London*, 158 No. 1815 'most Strange weddinge of the ffrogge and the mouse', A (Nov. 21, 1580, II 382, Ed. White). Beg. "It was a frog in the well", with 2nd st. beg. "The Frogge would a woing ride", *Melismata* (London 1611) = William Chappell, *The ballad literature and popular music of the olden time*, 2, 88 text and music. See Petrie & Stanford, *The complete collection of Irish music*, 162, No. 647 *Cousin frog went out to ride* (music only, without clef or signature); Wheeler, 'Uncle Rat' *JIFSS* 4 (1906) 22; see also Mackenzie, *Ballads and sea songs from Nova Scotia*, 407, No. 155 *A frog would a wooing go*, a few lines (with music); Shepard, *The broadside ballad. A study in origins and meaning*, has facsimile reproductions of *A new Ditty on a high Amour at St Jameses* and *The Frog and Mouse*; see Kennedy, *Folksongs of Britain and Ireland*, 649, No. 294 (and notes, 674–75). **Notes** Kennedy points out, *Folksongs of Britain and Ireland*, 674, that this song goes back to 1549 'This remarkable wedding was the theme of a song *The Frog Came to the Myl-dur*, which was sung by sheperds in Wedderburn's *Complaynt of Scotland* (1549)'. The version collected by Edith Wheeler and published in the *JIFSS* 4 (1906) 22, reads as follows:

        1.   Uncle Rat went out to ride,
                Hi, ho! little lady, O!
                With a sword and buckler by his side,
                With a ring, ding, ding, ding-a-dandy, O!

2. He rode till he came to Lady Mouse's hall,
    Hi, ho! little lady, O!
    And there he rapped and there he called,
    With a ring, ding, ding, ding-a-dandy, O!

3. 'Lady Mouse, are you within?'
    Hi, ho! little lady, O!
    'Yes; kind sir, will you walk in!'
    With a ring, ding, ding, ding-a-dandy, O!

4. She set her table neat and fine,
    Hi, ho! little lady, O!
    Saying, 'Here's a farthing, fetch me wine!'
    With a ring, ding, ding, ding-a-dandy, O!

5. In came Tabby the big black cat,
    Hi, ho! little lady, O!
    And seized poor mousey by the back,
    With a ring, ding, ding, ding-a-dandy, O!

6. Uncle Rat ran up the wall,
    Hi, ho! little lady, O!
    Saying, 'Muckla ban, be with you all.'
    With a ring, ding, ding, ding-a-dandy, O!

The piece is described as an old nurse's song, which was sung to Ms. Miller as a child in Co. Tyrone. Her mother remembered it being sung to her as a child by her father. That would take it back to the early nineteenth century. Mrs Costello of Birmingham had a similar fragment (*The frog and the mouse*), in which the theme is more explicit:

Lady mouse, will you be wed?
When will you lose your maidenhead?

See Slocombe & Shuldham-Shaw, *Jnl of the Engl. Folk Dance & Song Soc.* 7/2 (1953) 96–105: 105.

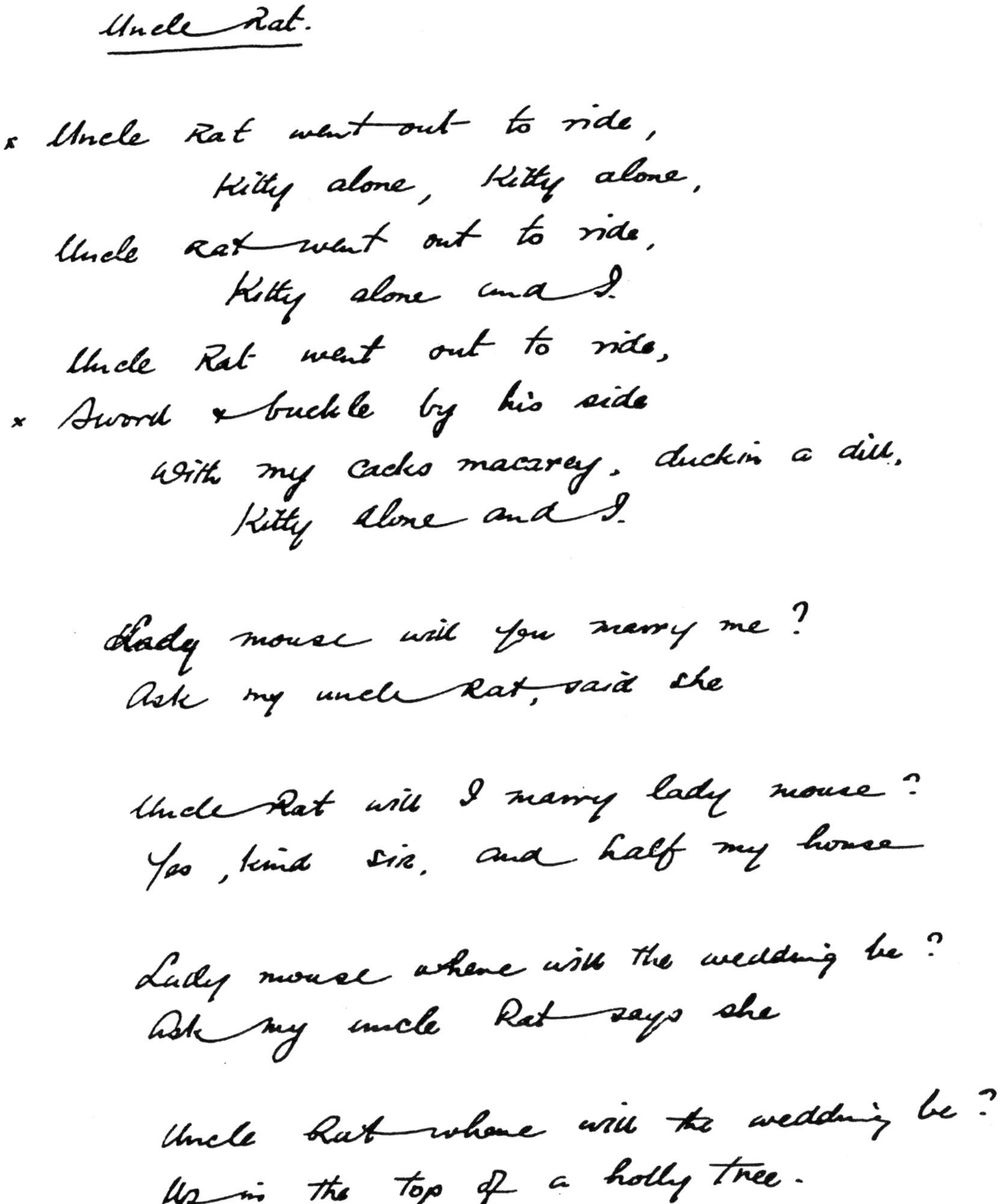

Uncle Rat.

x Uncle Rat went out to ride,
     Kitty alone, Kitty alone,
Uncle Rat went out to ride,
     Kitty alone and I.
Uncle Rat went out to ride,
x Sword & buckle by his side
     With my cacks macarey, duckin a dill.
     Kitty alone and I.

Lady mouse will you marry me?
Ask my uncle Rat, said she

Uncle Rat will I marry lady mouse?
Yes, kind sir, and half my house

Lady mouse where will the wedding be?
Ask my uncle Rat says she

Uncle Rat where will the wedding be?
Up in the top of a holly tree.

'Uncle Rat' transcribed from Bess Cronin by Seamus Ennis (CBÉ, UCD).

191

What would you do if you married a soldier?[2/14]

1.   What would you do if you married a soldier?
What would I do but to carry his gun.
And what would you do if he died on the ocean?
What would I do but to marry again.

2.   What would you do if the kettle boiled over?
What would I do but to fill it again.
And what would you do if the cows ate the clover?
What would I do but to set it again.

    Dee idle-dee didle-dee didle-dee-um
    Dee didle-dee idle-dee idle-dee diddle-dee
    Idle-dee -i-dee idle-dee-i-dee
    I-dee-dee i-dee-dee idle-dee-um

3.   What would you do if you married a soldier?
What would I do put to follow his gun.
And what would you do if he died on the ocean?
What would I do but to marry again.

Dee didle-dee didle-dee didle-dee-um
Dee didle-dee idle-dee idle-dee-diddle-dee
Idle-dee-i-dee idle-dee-i-dee
I-dee-dee i-dee-dee idle-dee-um

Recordings CBÉ 387c and 392c (1947) — BBC 12614 (7 Aug. 1947) = Kennedy, *Folktracks* FSP–60–160, A3, B3 (1981)— Lomax, *Columbia World Library* (1955), B 31 — JR–GP (2 Nov. 1952).   **Text** From the JR–GP recording; a second text in a DÓC notebook, with slightly different wording.   **Notes** The DÓC notebook text has another verse:

A.   The praties are boiling, the herrings are roasting,
Molly sit over close to the wall!
The praties are boiling, the herrings are roasting,
Molly sit over close to the wall!

This is Kennedy, *Folktracks* FSP–60–160, B3 ('The Taties are Boilin'). Seamus Ennis has this verse also in his RTÉ interview with Pádraic Ó Raghallaigh (2 March 1978). The tune is also known as *The Frost is All Over*, and is given as a jig in O'Neill's *1001 gems: The dance music of Ireland*, 66, No. 313.

192

When you call to an Irishman's door

1.   I left bonny Scotland, the land of brown heath,
And to Ireland I quickly sailed o'er,
Where no shelter to gain from wind or from rain
Till I called to an Irishman's door.
Says Pat, 'Sir, come in, though my roof it is thin;
Though humble and plain is my store.
You may always depend on meeting a friend
When you call to an Irishman's door'.

2.   'Although that I have but one hen on the roost,
One meal of potatoes in store,
Draw near to the fire, which is at your desire,
For this is an Irishman's door.
For tomorrow those dear little children you see,
Their poor darling mother and I,
Will be forced for to roam without cabin or home,
No roof but the cold winter sky'.

3.   For the agent came down with an angry frown,
And tomorrow I'm sorely afraid
That from this small abode we'll be thrust on the road
By the hard-hearted crowbar brigade.
But said Pat: 'Sir, come in, though my roof it is thin,
Though humble and plain is my store.
You may always depend on meeting a friend
When you call to an Irishman's door'.

Text From Bess's collection of handwritten songs.   **Note** Also known as *The Hard-Hearted Brigade* (see v. 3e), there is a version of this song in CBÉ 1592, 81–82 (Cork 1960).

193

Where were you all the day?

1. Where were you all the day, all the day, all the day?
   Where were you all the day,? — 'broad in the bush.

Text From a DÓC notebook.   **Notes** A note by DÓC says this was sung to the air of *Óró bog liom í, cailín deas donn*. Another jingle, sung to the same air, is given in the same notebook:

> High for Tadhg Leahy, high for Tadhg Leahy,
> High for Tadhg Leahy thiar ar a' gCnoc!

There is a reference to another one also, described as a 'Rócán making sport' (doubtless of some local lass):

> Iníon Bhiní Fíodóra, iníon Bhiní Fíodóra,
> Iníon Bhiní Fíodóra pósta ag Tadhg Leor.

There may have been more than this: a note reads *Tuille dhe*? ['More of it?'].

194

Whiskey in the jar

1. I am a young fellow that ever was undaunted,
   Grabbing for gold, though seldom I wanted;
   Grabbing for gold, for it was my only folly,
   And I'd venture my life with you, my lovely Molly.

   > To me ringdum dingdum da,
   > To me rights foll the da,
   > To me ringdum tooriladdy,
   > There's whiskey in the jar.

2. As I went over to sweet Gilbert Mountain
   I met Colonel Pepper and his money he was counting.
   I first drew my pistol and boldly drew my rifle,
   Saying: 'Stand and deliver, for I am a bold deceiver!'

   > To me ringdum dingdum da,
   > To me rights foll the da,
   > To me ringdum tooriladdy,
   > There is whiskey in the jar.

3. When I had it all it was a pretty penny.
   I brought it home and I gave it to my Molly.
   She vowed and she swore that she never would deceive me,
   But the devil is on the women and they never can be easy.

> To me ringdum dingdum da,
> To me rights foll the da,
> To me ringdum tooriladdy,
> There is whiskey in the jar.

4.   As I went in to my Molly's bed-chamber
     I laid down my head for to take a little slumber.
     She unloaded my pistol and filled it up with water —
     Bad luck to the woman that reared up such a daughter!

> To me ringdum dingdum da,
> To me rights foll the da,
> To me ringdum tooriladdy,
> There's whiskey in the jar.

5.   Early next morning, between six and seven,
     A large guard surrounded me and the Captain at eleven.
     I ran for my pistol, but found I was mistaken,
     For I fired off the water and a prisoner I was taken.

> To me ringdum dingdum da,
> To me rights foll the da,
> To me ringdum tooriladdy,
> There's whiskey in the jar.

6.   Johnny, lovely Johnny, you are a gallant soldier,
     You carry your blunderbuss over your right shoulder.
     When you meet a gentleman, you're sure to make him tremble,
     Put your whistle to your lips and your party will assemble.

> To me ringdum dingdum da,
> To me rights foll the da,
> To me ringdum tooriladdy,
> There's whiskey in the jar.

Laws L 13 A   **Text:** From the collection of Bess's hand-written songs. There is another text (v. 2 only, with chorus) in CBÉ 476, 58.   **Printed Sources:** cf. Henry, 'Songs of the People', *Northern Constitution* (28 Jan. 1939), No. 792 (5 vv.) = Huntington & Hermann, *Sam Henry's Songs of the People,* 122; Ó Lochlainn, *Irish street ballads,* 24–25, No. 12. See also Laws, *American balladry,* 173.   **Notes:** Sam Henry's version opens with our v. 2, followed by variants on vv. 3–5. His final verse reads as follows:

> I stood in the hall when the roll was a-calling,
> I stood in the hall when the turnkey was a-bawling,
> And by a metal ball I put the sentry down,
> And I made my escape into Londonderry town.

195

You feeling-hearted Christians

1.   You feeling-hearted Christians, I hope you will draw near!
     It's about a cruel step-mother I mean to let you hear.
     She poisoned two fine children that lived near Wexford Town,
     Their father was a farmer, and his name was Robert Brown.

2.   Their mother died all in her youth, she left a store of gold;
     And to each of her two children she left five-hundred pounds.
     Their father, he got married soon unto another wife,
     And she was the cruel step-mother that took away their lives.

3.   It being on a Sunday morning, the farmer that did say:
     'Get ready my dear children, we'll go to Mass this day'.
     But the farmer's daughter and step-mother, they both stayed at home,
     Saying: 'I think we'll have a cup of tea, as we're here all alone'.

4.   The farmer's daughter baked a cake, and that without delay;
     The step-mother into it the poison did convey.
     Young Johnny Brown came home from Mass — his father did delay —
     She locked him up in a room quite close and gave him bread and tea.

5.   When Robert Brown came home from Mass at ten o'clock at night,
     Finding his two children dead, it gave him a great fright.
     He sent for the doctor, who came immediately,
     Saying: 'Where is the poison which you have bought from me?'

6.   She flew into a parlour and locked the door quite close,
     And with a razor that was there she cut her guilty throat.
     When Robert Brown saw them all dead, distracted he did run,
     He wrung his hands and tore his hair and said: 'I am undone!'

7.   It was scarcely three months after — I mean to let you hear —
     When her hoarse voice and dreadful ghost to the farmer did appear,
     Saying: 'My case, it is now wretched, for the crime that I have done,
     For I poisoned your fine daughter, and likewise your darling son'.

Text CBÉ 283, 186–88.   **Notes** Also known as *Robert Brown*; for another text see CBÉ 134, 383–85 (Mayo 1936).

196

You jolly young fellows

1. You jolly young fellows, come listen to me,
   Till I'll sing a few verses to keep you in glee,
   About these distillers that came to Glenlee —
   The handsomest lot in the nation.
   My subject is funny, as you shall behold,
   'Tis highly becoming and very well told;
   For a stream that is running, that never gets cold,
   After its grand distillation.

2. To see that machinery there in a pile
   With wheels and triangles all working in style,
   Indeed you would ponder, I think, for a while,
   Believing the place was enchanted.
   The features of Bacchus were seen in the room,
   Wearing his mantle and godly costume;
   Praising McCarthy, that man from old Coom,
   For keeping his able long charter.

3. 'Tis long I'll remember that comical night,
   When to Buailey's we rambled to see the grand sight;
   Those worthy mechanics, they did us invite,
   To share and partake of their sample.
   We had the doctor and Patsy Diarmán,
   Also Tim Kelly and old Paddy Bán;
   Rafferty and Harrington, down from Bonane,
   We gave them a tasty example.

4. The first in the faction was young Mr. Lyons,
   A gentleman Yankee well up in the times;
   For a home-manufacture they tell me he's fine —
   'Take care and don't raise the alarm!'
   His brave and good prospects are grand, to be sure,
   His brave and stout heart is both candid and pure;
   From the town of New Ross to the banks of the Suir,
   I declare such a rake is not formed!

5. He spoke to poor Tom Jack, who lived near the place,
   And asked a few questions about the old race;
   Saying how he had travelled through many campaigns,
   And drank a few tréats with his father.
   It was his intention when passing the way
   To see their invention before going away;
   He had no objection, he gave them the sway,
   And promised his favours hereafter.

6.   We had our supper in very good time —
       Heaps of fresh butter and things that were fine;
       Old Nancy in a pucker was a very long time
       Arranging the cups and the saucers.
       I made myself handy in collecting the spoons
       And calling the officers down from the room;
       An abundance of coffee we drank very soon,
       And Lypton's black tea before morning.

7.   When supper was ended we sat in a throng,
       Surrounding poor Harrington's nice little gong;
       But when someone insisted we should have a song
       For a long time he was meditating.
       When up comes the Yankee, just like a brown trout,
       With a bucket of brandy quite fresh from the spout;
       We took off our hats and we began to shout,
       And believe me, he got an ovation!

8.   Around went the whiskey, as I said before,
       But soon we insisted on drinking no more;
       But they having plenty of that in their store,
       And in spilling they cared not a farthing.
       When Noll Buailey went dancing, she fell on the floor,
       Blind out from tobacco, her eyes they were sore;
       And in counting the glasses she drank twenty-four —
       You'd hear her complaining and yawning!

9.   We mounted the garret both lofty and steep;
       Creeping like rabbits to have a long peep;
       We met an old parrot as black as a sweep,
       She received us indeed very saucy.
       I told this young damsel she'd better look out,
       That there was a rat coming scratching about;
       On the day of our threshing we'd given him a clout,
       That'd sweep him away from the border.

Text From handwritten notes of SÓC.   **Notes** This much only in the notes; there appears to be some of the song missing. A note accompanying it says 'Buailey made poteen and gave a dance. A Yank attended'. See CBÉ 1591, 182–85 (Cork 1961). For another song, also featuring Patsy Diarmán and his neighbours around Glanlee, see *True Friends and Relations of High and Low Stations* [No. **189**].

APPENDIX I

AN DUINE BOCHT UASAL AR LORG NA DÉIRCE[1]

Go mbeannaí Dia agus Muire agus Pádraig, Rí an Domhnaigh, mná na gCeannaithe agus dhá cheann Chorcaí dhuit, iníon na dea-athar le togha máthar, riamh nár cáineadh i dtigh an tábhairne, agus gur maith buan a mhairfir-se i seilbh na háite.

Sea, conas tá'n tú, a bhean álainn? Ar ndóin, dar na miona, tá'n tú go maith mar ba dhual agus mar ba dhúchas duit a bheith. Conas tá Diarmuid 's a chlann? Ar ndóin, táid go biamhar teann agus maith ó Dhia 'na gceann.

Sea, a bhean mhaith a' tí is a rúin ghil mo chroí, seo cam-chuaird, cuireadh gan iarraidh, fada go dtáinig, éadan meirgeach, siúl go deireannach, dalla na daoi agus cúl le haghaidh do tháinig it' fhiafraí lena scéalta, agus le moladh le Dia, is maith an t-ionad do féin san.

Is tú síol na saoithe agus mar shlua iníona do mhaithibh na tíre, agus do bhéarfainn uait ó chroí é le dea-intinn. Dá iarraidh ar Dhia gan oiread na déirce seo de spré scaoilteach, éag daoine, bualadh bás, sileadh rosc, lomadh láithrí, ná rith teine gan taisearcan, ná torthama, ná cróchar d'imeacht ort féin ná ar aon duine is duine dhuit ó anocht go bliain ó anocht; agus dein an déirc ar an bpáiste bocht gan gharraí gan ghort, gan snáth ar a chorp, ná fós píosa h-ocht 'na phóca bheag anocht; go bhfuair a athair bás lá cruaidh fuar earraig agus gur bádhadh a mháthair i dtor mór aitinn; míle milleón moladh, glóire, onóir agus buíochas le Dia.

Mac do Chaitlín Ní Neais agus do Sheán bhocht Ó Murchú ó Thobar Rí an Domhnaigh agus ó Bhéal Croise Fírinne isea mise; agus mura ndéanfaidh mé na seacht nglan dturais déag so ar chroí mo dhá dheárnainn agus ar scáthán mo dhá ghlún thíos i Sráid na mBioránach bíodh sé fé bhráid anama mo shuime. Ach má tá sé i ndán dom go dtabharfaidh mé aghaidh siar ó dheas ar Bhaile Mhúirne na mór-chómhachta, agus éirigh id' sheasamh agus cur romhat an t-aon chrochaire cruaidh rua leath-phingne sin ag rinnce istigh ar úrlár do phóicín.

Ó, airiú, dein, agus go seirbhí Dia dhuit, agus go n-éirí grian ort, agus gura maith ramhar geal a rachas bia dhuit. Ná gaibh leathscéal liom anois, a bhean a' tí, agus ná bíodh an t-eiteach agam le fáil uait, dáltha do mháthar, agus a fhios agat féin gur bocht an earra an bhréag ar an abhar go lobhann sí an fhiacal, go mbréanann sí an anál, agus go mbeireann sí an t-anam bocht léi síos go fíor-íochtar Ifrinn dá phianadh an fhaid a bheidh Dia ag caitheamh na glóire.

Dá bhrí sin, a iníon ó, tuig féin gur mó scríob ó sceich, snaidhm ó chloich, agus madra géar scalaoideach do chuireas-sa dhíom ag teacht a' d'iarraidh na déirce seo ort-sa, agus ná tabharfá dhom í. Agus do bhéarfainn teagasc agus ní hé amháin le hanam do charaid atá le cian i dtalamh, agus a fhios agat féin nuair a bheadh an breith dá bhreith agus an t-anam dá mheáchaint ag Mícheál Naofa an t-Ardaingeal agus na ceithre feara fichead 'na seasamh ar dhóirse Ifrinn, agus crúcaí mór cama, agus úird mhóra ghabha i láimh gach duine acu; och mo léan! B'fhéidir gur

---

1   There is an incomplete copy of this text in CBÉ 173, 545–55, copied by Proinsias Ó Ceallaigh from Bess Cronin in 1935. An accompanying note states that she had heard the recitation 35 years before from her father. This would date the text to 1899/1900, which is precisely the date of Bess's first public performance (at the Feis in Macroom) reported in *Fáinne an Lae* 8 Jan. 1899, where the recitation is listed amongst the items she performed. I have a second, handwritten text (possibly by Seán Ó Cróinín) whose readings I have sometimes preferred to the CBÉ version. I have modernised the spelling throughout.

déirc leat mo bheannacht-sa a bheith agat an uair sin ag fuascailt suas go Flaithis mór na naomh; agus dá bhrí sin féach go taidhseach truaimhéileach ar an nduine bocht uasal atá ag feitheamh ar do ghrásta.

An gcluineann tú leat me, a bhean na coise míne gan speach; crích maith agus cion ort, agus luí tar éis mic ort, agus éirí briosc ort, dá iarraidh ar Dhia gan leanbh treasna ná easna briste ionat; agus éirigh id' sheasamh agus nár fhaghaidh tú treascairt, agus cuir romhat an déirc daonnachtach so i moch-éirí an Luain, i ndéanaí an tSatharain, in aon-phian na ndaor-pheacaí, go mallaithe, dian, dána, doirgeach. Éirigh, a bhean a' tí, agus tabhair chughainn dhá chuid cáise, trí chuid aráin, *soirloin* mairtfheola, urchar de phíosa trí scillinge, pic cruithneachta, nú púnt olna, nú céad ime, agus scaoil mé uait le géar geimhridh.[2]

Sea anois, a bhean a' tí, mura bhfuil dúil agat an déirc seo do thabhairt dom, scaoil do chailín caoin cneasta liom, agus socaróidh mé uirthi na seacht málaí: mála an t-saill, mála an tslinneáin, mála an tearpáin, an pocaire, an pacaire, agus an mealbhóg mór; na seacht dteachtairí: cóta cathánach dathannach priobánach, crios, scian, agus cainín agus fallaing fada mar fhéirín agus geallfaidh mé dhi go mbeidh airgead croise á bualadh dhi ins gach baile margaidh ar fuaid na hÉireann.

'Sé críoch mo scéil ná fuair mar dhéirc
Ach clabaireacht bhéil, go ndúirt sé léi:

A chrón-chailligh dhó-smeartha mhínáireach
Is dóigh leat gur cóir duit bheith béal-láidir.
Ní cóir, agus dar an fhóid seo dá mba mhaith liom
Do ghabhfainn ort de dhóirnibh go plaoscánta!
Ní lú orm beagán teine luaith' mhór,
Ná loiscre caillí le ceisneamh mór;
Ná bean óg bradach mínáireach;
Ná bean-tí gan allus gan náire.
Ní h-ait liom cailín ríghin salach,
Ná seanabhean gruama bhuartha bradach.
                                        Críoch.

2   The text in CBÉ 173 breaks off at this point, with the collector's note: '*Tá tuilleadh ann so, ach ní chuimníonn sí air*' ['There's more of this, but she doesn't remember it'].

APPENDIX II

LIST OF SONGS COLLECTED BY MÍCHEÁL Ó BRIAIN (1866–1942) FROM PEOPLE IN BALLYVOURNEY[1]

1. Trí'm aislinn dom ar leabaidh chluthmhair
2. Cois abhainn seal i gcéin dom, im' aonar a bhíos-sa
3. A fharaire shaor ghlain mhic Shéamais ón dtaoibh seo
4. Araoir dom trí'm shuan sea bhíogas-sa suas
5. Araoir ar mo leabaidh is me ag machnamh trí'm néaltaibh
6. Maidin álainn gréine agus me ar taobh Cnoc na Buaile
7. Araoir is me gan amhras
8. Ar maidin Luan Cásca tríd an mBlárnain soir
10. Dé bheatha-sa, a Rodire
11. Níor fhágas-sa coillthe, bun scairte ná díge
12. Maidin teas ó éadan
13. Cat Dhiarmaid na Bearnan
14. Tá gleanntáinín aoibhinn 'dir Laoi theas is Bannda **(101)**
15. Téim-se féd' scéithibh-se, a Athair na nGrás
16. Admhuím féin
17. Aréir dom go déanach cois taoibh Fleasga an ghaorthaidh
18. Is dubhach liom leagadh na seabhac
19. Tráth is me ag machnamh do ghluaisíos im' aonar
20. Is tá maide draighin craoiric (Aonach Barracha Ruaidh)
21. Céad slán leat, a shláinte 'bhí agam
22. Sealad aréir agus me ar mo leabaidh
23. Is é an creachairín éithigh
24. Cois abhainn gleanna an ghaorthaigh agus Claedeach na gcíonna
25. An Giolla Ruadh
26. Ag bun Ros na Coille ar thitim an drúcht araoir
27. Tráthnóna breá gréine i gcéin cois gleanna dom
28. Fiagaí an chúil bháin
29. Mh'osna go cruaidh (Caoineadh Uí Shúilleabháin Bhéara)
30. Ó'n nGaillimh a thánag (Beannacht an Scoláire)
31. In Uíbh Laoghaire, i gcúm cnoic sea bhíonn
32. Bacach fada an Tóchair
34. An Cailín Donn
35. Tá ainnir mhodhail mhaorga ar an mbaile seo taobh linn

---

1 This list was compiled by Proinsias Ó Ceallaigh, and is also to be found in CBÉ 173. I have indicated in bold numbers the songs that are also in Bess Cronin's collection, and in the case of the 'new songs' (*Amhráin Nua*, Nos 163–81, and Nos 36, 75, 81, 109, 140, 142, and 142 (a, i)) the names of the modern local authors, in italic, where they are given in the manuscript.

36. Tráthnóinín aoibhinn do bhíos go déanach *(Amhlaoibh Ó Loingsigh)*
37. Tráthnóinín saoire is me im shuí ar an mbuaile (Na Gamhna)
38. Is dubhach me le sealad, gan aiteas im bréithribh
39. Sin séala anois ceangailte i dteachtaireacht chruinn
40. Ar bruach na Laoi san oíche casadh me **(23)**
41. Go mbeannaí Rí na Naomh duit
42. A chairde trí láimh liom gan cháim
43. Mo chumha, mo léan, mo dheacair
44. A fharaire shaor ghlain dob' fhéile is dob' fhearr gníomhartha
45. An Fíodóir Gallda
46. Tráthnóinín saoire ar bhuíochtaint na gréine **(37)**
47. Tráth is me ag machnamh do ghluaisíos im aonar
48. Giolla dubh an ghluaireáin
49. Tréis gach púnc do'n taragraicht *(sic)*
50. Ní thuigeann an sáthach sámh don ocrach riamh
51. Cáit an Bhunáin
52. An Spealadóir **(21)**
53. Ba mhór an náire anois don mháistir
54. Ar mo thaisteal siúl *(sic)* do thangaidh liúm san oíche aréir
55. Linn na héigse cois taoibh an Ghaorthaidh
56. Cuir mo shál san áit is ruí' do'n stéil
57. Mo chruatan, a' t-uaigneas go léir im chiúnn
58. Cois sléibhe bhig uaignigh im aonar ghluaiseas
59. Mo chúrsa trí Éire le chéile gan fuíoll
60. Innis-se do Sheán gheal Clárach úr-uasal
61. Éistidh lem' scéal-sa, a charaid, cé gurb annamh ar siúl mo bhéal
62. Cailín na gruaige donne
63. Cé thaistealas ó Thráigh Lí
64. Mo mhuinntir gan ghasta
65. A Mháire Ní Laoghaire ó bhéal a' Chéama
66. Jack Buí, *you are easy*, do traochadh chun deiridh tu
67. An Spailpín Fánach
68. 'Sé mo bhrón-chreach nach Domhnall is ainm dom féin
69. Ar maidin Dé Máirt dom is sásta bhí m'aigne (An Banbh)
70. Ar mo thrácht dom ó Bhéara go Lén-loch im shiúlaibh
71. Leogaim slán le ceapadh dánta
72. Eachtra Capaill a' Chuimín
73. Bhíos i nDroichead Bandan, ar aonach ceart na Samhna
74. Trí Choill Ruisg im' aonar
75. Greadadh ort is cás, a fhiolair an fháin *(Driofúr don Phápar)*
76. Maidin chiúin cheoidh i dtosach an Fhómhair
77. Lá breá is me ag tráchtaint dom féin
78. Is danaid an scéal mo léan gan luadhail
79. A Dhiarmaid na n-ae istigh
80. Is díth 's is léan liom
81. Fáilthe 'gus míle *(Domhnall a' tSiopa)*

82. Eibhlín a Rúin

83. Seilg Ghleanna an Smóil, nó Eachtra na Mná Móire thar lear

84. Éistidh liom tréimhse go n-innse mé scéal díbh

85. A Dhomhnaill, ba chóir go mbeadh snaois agat

86. Táimse im' chodladh is ná dúistear mé

87. An Phaidrín Pháidreach

88. Is danaid an scéal dom fhéin le n-aithris

89. Sealad araoir i gcéin cois leasa dhom

90. Is fúnn liom scéal beag anois do léigheadh díbh

91. Éistidh, a dhaoine, go n-innse mé scéal díbh

92. Dá mba cléireach fónta me

93. Seán Ó Duibhir an Ghleanna

94. Cailín deas crúite na mbó

95. Cois leasa is me go huaigneach ar uair na maidne im aonar

96. Do déanadh aisling aréir dom do chlaoidh go léir me

97. Teagasc a bheirim díbh gan chealg óm' chroí

98. Ar maidin go moch is me amuigh le fáinnín an lae

99. Slán le Baile Mhúirne

100. An Chúil Duibh-ré **(16)**

101. Tráth ar buaireamh, tréis mo thuaith-bhirt

102. Barántas

103. Eibhlín Ní Ghrádaigh

104. A shaor-shliocht na Caesar do'n tréan-fhuil do chím

105. Ceo draíochta sheol oíche ar fán me **(38)**

106. An Mheánail

107. An Táilliúir agus an Píobaire

108. Nellie Murphy ag tarranc aoiligh

109. Mo chreach fhada cruaidh, arsa Nainí go duairc *(Neill Ní Mhurchú)*

110. San oíche aréir agus me chun suain

111. Bhéarsaí

112. Is díth is is léan liom agus is dubhach liom na scéaltha so

113. Óró, is do thugas seacht seachtaine

114. Tá bó agam ar sliabh is gan éinne beo 'na diaidh

115. Tá scéilín beag nua agam-sa dhíbhse

116. Ní fada liom lá thabharfainn spás ag Túirín an Chéim *(sic)*

117. Ar maidin dom féin agus me ag déanamh mo smaointe

118. Araoir is me ag machnamh in uaigneas an ghleanna

119. Cois Brice dom go déanach

120. Maidin ceoidh nuair éiríos

121. Is mithid dom trácht go hard

122. Is anaba is éachtach an scéal le n-aithris

123. An Brianach óg

124. Raca breá a cinn

125. Beir leitir uaim scríofa (Go dtí Pead Buí)

126. Freagra ag Pead Buí

127. Tráthnóinín déanach i gcéin cois leasa dom

128. Ar teacht Oíche Nollag
129. A Dhé 's a Mhuire
130. Idir Corcaigh is Eochaill ar nóint seal do bhíos
131. Trí Coill-ros im' aonar
132. Cáitín Ní Shéaghdha
133. An Gamhain Geal Bán **(18)**
134. Bhíos-sa riamh aerach, bhí greann ag an saol orm
135. Bhíos i Sasana, in Éire, is in Albain
136. Is sámh an duine me (Aisling Sheáin Aerach)
137. Tráth i gcéin dom, is ea ghluaisíos féinig
138. Tráthnóinín déanach is me 'dul ag bhálcaereacht **(144)**
139. A dhaoine, mar mheasaim le háthas daoibh innsead scéal
140. Tráthnóinín Fómhair ar leataoibh an róid *(Paddy na Daraí)*
141. An Mangalum ó, deabhdar ó
142. Glóire shíor leis an Athair aoibhinn is mór le rá *(Neill Ní Mhurchú)*
142 (a) Bhéarsaí reatha: —
    (i) Ochón, mo ghrá thu *(Máire Ní nAirt)*
    (ii) Mo ghrá thu 'gus mo shearc
    (iii) Mo chreach is mo chás an áit 'nar leagadh an corp
    (iv) D'aithníos féin ar dtúis
143. Agus éistidh a dhaoine go n-innse mé scéal díbh (An rámhann bhreá leathan)
144. Níl súgar ná aiteas cois abhainn an Ghaorthaidh
145. Is greannúr an taidhreamh a deineadh aréir dom (An Coran)
146. Is fada dom ar buaireamh
147. Agus, is buachaillín fíor-óg me **(19)**
148. Araoir is me go huaigneach im luí ar leabaidh shuain dom
149. Ar mo dhul dom go haonach i gCuiríní
150. Lá dá rabhas agus me i ngleann im' aonar
151. Trí bliana an Fhómhair seo d'fhágas an treo seo
152. Is, má théann tu go dtí an t-aonach beir an chaora leat 's a' t-uan
153. Is dubhach me le sealad
154. Ag déanamh smaointe 'sea bhíos go déanach
155. An cailín deas rua
156. Cois abhainn gleanna an Chéama
157. Cat Bhiní Fíodóra
158. An Banbh
159. Tá gleann i Magh Chromtha **(101)**
160. Ar maidin Dé Luain cois coille 'sea chuas
161. Mairneamh: Uíbh Laoghaire -á -í -ú
162. Cum(h)a Ailne : Bean Meargaidh na nglas lann i ndiaidh a fir agus a dís mhac do thit ar Chnoc an Áir

AMHRÁIN NUA

163. A mhuintir na hÉireann 's a Chonnradh na Gaeilge *(Mathghamhain Ó Tuama)*

164. Díleagra don Athair Tadhg Ó Cearbhaill *(Conchúr Ó Deasúna)*

165. Aisling an Mhuimhnigh *(Tadhg Mac Suibhne)*

166. A Dhiarmaid, a stóraigh *(Mícheál Ó Tuama)*

167. Mo chreach is mo chás (— —)

168. *Although I have travelled far over the seas* (— —) **(174)**

169. Baile Mhúirne *(Pádraig Ó Crodhlaoi)*

170. I gcóir an Oireachtais (— —)

171. Sin agaibh mo theastas le dúracht

172. Do Thadhg Ó Ríordáin *(Tadhg Ó Crodhlaoi)*

173. Do Thadhg Ó Ríordáin (— —)

174. A mháthair och nách brónach an sceol so anois im' láimh *(C. Ó Deasúna)*

175. Ar aireabhair an gháróid do bhí ag an gCáitigh *(M. Ó Tuama)*

176. Ar bhás Chonchúir Uí Dheasúna

177. Ar bhás Eoghain mhic Thaidhg Uí Chrodhlaoi *(Gael na nGael)*

178. Ar bhás Thaidhg Uí Ríordáin

179. Na Cleaganna *(Mícheál Ó Tuama)*

180. Gael na nGael *(Tadhg Ó Crodhlaoi)*

181. Ar an nGaeilge *(Seán Ó Murchú)*

APPENDIX III

THE CDS 'SONGS OF ELIZABETH CRONIN' VOLS 1–2

The two compact discs of the singing of Elizabeth Cronin which accompany this book contain 59 songs and song fragments selected from the some 130 recordings of her singing known to exist, and they are intended to represent the range both of her songs and of the recordings. On them, in Irish and English, contemporary local songs from west Cork rub shoulders with immemorial Munster songs of wide distribution, Irish songs with British and American favourites; the comic is found with the serious, the sentimental with the impersonal, the historical with the timeless. Particularly noteworthy are the little-documented women's songs of the hearth: lullabies, dance-songs and dandling songs.

The first compact disc is drawn from institutional field recordings on acetate disc, made by the Irish Folklore Commission in 1947 and 1951 and by the BBC in 1947, 1952 and 1954. The second disc is drawn from private field recordings made on magnetic tape by the American collectors Alan Lomax in 1951. Jean Ritchie and George Pickow in 1952, and the late Diane Hamilton in 1955. The actual recordings presented are indicated by the abbreviations used in the Index of Field Recordings above, where their dates of recording will be found.

Each recording session had its own ethos, as well as its distinctive audio character, and the recordings reflect this: the Irish Folklore Commission recorded for cultural preservation and towards paper transcription and academic study, the BBC for radio broadcasting, Jean Ritchie and George Pickow for academic research, and Alan Lomax and Diane Hamilton for publication on commercial LP. All the recordings were made in the Cronin family home; some of the recordists were friends of Mrs Cronin, others met her only at the time of recording. Her songs in Irish were favoured in the earlier sessions, her songs in English in the later. Recorded only during the last nine years of her life when she was in her sixties and seventies and in varying states of health, Mrs Cronin's singing is that of an elderly woman, but what the recordings lack in youthful vigour, they compensate for in subtlety of rhythm and maturity of style, and they demonstrate the variety of her musical taste and her still remarkable powers of recall.

The original recordings used here are of varying physical condition and sound quality. They have been transferred by Harry Bradshaw, music producer, RTÉ Radio 1. The CDs were edited and produced by the writer and compiled by Glenn Cumiskey, sound engineer, Irish Traditional Music Archive. Items were generally selected for their musical, regional and genre interest rather than for sound quality, but some recordings were considered too noisy or damaged for use.

All the field recordings considered for inclusion can be heard by the public in the Irish Traditional Music Archive, except for those recorded originally by the Irish Folklore Commission and now in the Department of Irish Folklore, University College Dublin. The originals of the Ritchie-Pickow recordings can also be heard by the public in the Library of the National University of Ireland, Galway.

NICHOLAS CAROLAN
Irish Traditional Music Archive
15 November 1999

BIBLIOGRAPHY & DISCOGRAPHY
OF WORKS CITED

MANUSCRIPTS AND PRINTED EPHEMERA

Belfast, *Central Public Library* (broadsides).

Cambridge, *University Library*, Henry Bradshaw collection of Irish broadside ballads (Hib. 2. 867. 1; Hib. 2. 867. 2; Hib. 1. 867. 1; Hib. 1. 867. 2; Madden 24; Madden 25).

— *A catalogue of the Bradshaw collection of Irish books in the University Library Cambridge*, 3 vols. Cambridge *University Library* (Cambridge 1916) [vol. 3 = index of titles].

Cambridge (Massachusetts), *Harvard University, Houghton Library* (Bute broadsides).

— Hugh Amory, *Bute Broadsides in the Houghton Library, Harvard University, guide & index to the microfilm collection* (Cambridge, Mass. 1905).

Dublin, *City of Dublin Library*, Gilbert Collection (broadside ballads).

— *National Library of Ireland*, General Collection (broadsides in general alphabetical portfolio series).

— *Royal Irish Academy*, RR 66 H 17. *A collection of Common Irish Ballads sold at fairs and markets and sung or recited by the Irish Peasantry at their meetings and gatherings, whether social, political, or otherwise, from the beginning of the 19th century to the present time* = Lord Moyne collection (broadsides).

— *Royal Irish Academy*, S. R. 3 C 37 (broadsides, numbered 1–148).

— *Royal Irish Academy*, 3 C 38. *Set of Ballets (26 in number) bought at the fair of Casteltown Berehaven, Monday Oct. 11, 1854.*

— *Royal Irish Academy, 3 C 39* (broadsides).

— *An tOireachtas*, Collection of Baile Mhúirne songs made by Máire Amhlaoibh Ní Loingsigh (mostly from her father, Amhlaoibh Ó Loingsigh), which won 1st Prize in Comórtas Cuimhneacháin an Mhairtínigh, 1941.

Galway, *National University of Ireland*, James Hardiman Library, Douglas Hyde Manuscript, No. 57 (a collection of Munster songs compiled by Cáit Ní Dhonnchú).

Ní Bhuachalla, Caitlín, P. O., Scoil na gCailíní, Achadh Cóiste, Co. Cork (copy of a collection of Baile Mhúirne songs, compiled by Mícheal Ó Briain, dated 1943) [private possession].

COMMERCIAL RECORDINGS

Clancy, Willie, *The pipering of Willie Clancy* 1, Claddagh CC32 (Dublin 1980).

Clayton, Paul, *British broadside ballads in popular tradition*. Folkways Records, FW8708 (New York 1957).

The drones and the chanters: Irish piping, Claddagh CC11 (Dublin 1971).

Kennedy, Peter, *Classic ballads of Britain 1 (F. J. Child: 2–84)*. Folktracks FSP–90–501 (Gloucester 1976).

— *Diddle Daddle: Mouth music of Britain and Ireland*. Folktracks FSD–60–301 (Gloucester 1979).

— *Cuckanandy, Irish lilts and lovesongs*. Folktracks, FSP–60–160 (Gloucester 1981).

Kennedy, Peter & Alan Lomax, *The Child Ballads 1:'The English and Scottish popular ballads' Nos 2–95 = The folk songs of Britain 4*, Topic Records 12T160 (London 1961) [originally Caedmon TC 1145].

— *Sailormen and servingmaids = The folk songs of Britain 6*, Topic Records 12T194 (London 1961) [originally Caedmon TC 1162].

— *Songs of courtship = The folk songs of Britain 1*, Topic Records 12T157 (London 1961) [originally Caedmon TC 1142].

— *Songs of animals and other marvels = The folk songs of Britain 10*. Topic Records 12T198 (London 1961) [originally Caedmon TC 1225].

Lomax, Alan, *Columbia world library of folk and primitive music 1*. Columbia Records SL–204 (New York 1955).

McColl, Ewan & Peggy Seeger, *The long harvest 3*. Argo Records (London 1967).

McConnell, Cathal & Robin Morton, *An Irish Jubilee. Traditional Irish songs and music*. Mercier Press (Cork 1970); reissued by Topic Records, Topic 12T290 (London 1976).

McQuaid, Sarah, *When two lovers meet*, Mongrel Music MMCD001 (Dublin 1997).

Ritchie, Jean & George Pickow, *Jean Ritchie field trip. Field recordings in England, Scotland and Ireland by Jean Ritchie and George Pickow.* Collector Limited Editions CLE 1201 (Port Washington, New York *c*.1955).

— *As I roved out. Field recordings from Ireland.* Smithsonian Folkways Recordings (Washington, D. C. 1960); reissued by Ossian Publications OSS–15 (Cork 1990).

Seoda Ceoil. Comhaltas Ceoltóirí Éireann, CEF018 (Dublin 1968).

Tunney, Paddy, *A wild bee's nest.* Topic Records 12T139 (London 1965).

BOOKS & ARTICLES

Anderson, Hugh, *The story of Australian song.* Oak Publications (New York 1970; rev., enlarged, re-titled ed.).

[—], *The illustrated book of Scottish songs from the sixteenth to the nineteenth century* (London, n. d.).

[—], *The Sarsfield song and recitation book.* James Duffy & Co. (Dublin, n. d.)

[—], 'Poirtíní Béil', *An Lóchrann* (Feabhra 1926) 32.

[—], 'Racaireacht ghrinn na tuaithe', *An Lóchrann* (Bealtaine 1925) 143–44.

[—], *The Kerryman* (n. d., but probably *c*.1952).

Baring-Gould, Sabine, H. Fleetwood Sheppard, F.W. Bussell, *Songs of the West: folk songs of Devon and Cornwall.* Methuen (London 1890; repr. 1913).

Borthwick, Norma, *Ceól-Sídhe* 1, 2 (I, II, III and IV, V agus VI).

— *Irish Songs* I, II, III, and IV, V & VI. The Léigheann Éireann Series. The Irish Book Co. (Dublin 1905).

Boswell, C. S., 'Placenames from our older literature II,' *Irisleabhar na Gaedhilge* 14, Uimh. 169 (Deireadh Foghmhair 1904) 641–46.

Breathnach, Breandán, 'The man and his music — Willie Clancy', *Ceol* 2/3 (1965) 70–77.

— *Ceol rínce na hÉireann* 2. Oifig an tSoláthair (Baile Átha Cliath 1976).

Breathnach, Pádraig, *Fuinn na smól* 3 (Baile Átha Cliath 1913).

— *Fuinn na smól* 5 (Baile Átha Cliath 1915).

— *Songs of the Gael* 1: *a collection of Anglo-Irish songs and ballads wedded to traditional Irish airs.* Browne & Nolan (Dublin 1915; repr. 1922).

— *Ceól ár sínsear.* Brún 7 Ó Nualláin (1913; repr. 1923).

— *Ar gceól féinig.* Brún 7 Ó Nóláin (Baile Átha Cliath 1920).

— *Cnuasachd bheag amhrán* 1. Brún 7 Ó Nualláin (Baile Átha Cliath, n. d.).

— *Cnuasachd bheag amhrán* 3. Brún 7 Ó Nualláin (Baile Átha Cliath, n. d.)

— *Sídh-Cheól* 1, 2. Brún 7 Ó Nualláin (Baile Átha Cliath 1924, 1926).

Broadwood, Lucy & J. A. Fuller Maitland, *English county songs.* The Leadenhall Press (London 1893).

Bronson, Bertrand H., *The traditional tunes of the Child ballads*, 4 vols (Princeton, N. J. 1957–72).

Buchan, Norman, *101 Scottish songs.* Collins (Glasgow 1962).

Chappell, William, *The ballad literature and popular music of the olden time*, 2 vols (London 1859); repr. Dover Publications (New York 1965).

Child, Francis James, *The English and Scottish popular ballads*, 10 parts in 5 vols (Boston 1882–98); repr. Cooper Square Publications (New York 1965).

Cole, William, *Folksongs of England, Ireland, Scotland and Wales* (New York 1961).

Colum, Padraic, *Broad-sheet ballads, being a collection of Irish popular songs* (Dublin & London 1956).

Comyn, David, 'Neithe toghtha agus bailighthe ó leabhraibh, xii–xv' ['Peata an Mhaoir' & 'Fa'n gcoill ghlais'], *Fáinne an Lae* (12 Márta 1898) 3.

Connolly, Frank (ed), *The Christy Moore songbook.* Brandon (Dingle 1984).

Corcoran, Seán, 'Two songs', *Ceol* 3/3 (June 1969) 66–70.

Craig, J. P., *An ceoltóir* 1. D. G. Craig & Co. (Derry 1910).

Crawfurd, Andrew *see* Lyle, Emily B.

Creighton, Helena & Calum McLeod (eds), *Gaelic songs and ballads from Nova Scotia. National Museum of Canada Bulletin No. 198, Anthropological Series No. 60.* (Ottawa 1964; repr. 1979).

Davison, Peter, *Songs of the British music-hall* (New York 1977).

Dean, Margaret C., *The flying cloud* (Virginia, Minnesota 1920).

Delaney's Irish song book, No. 1–No. 5, William W. Delaney (New York, n. d. [*c*.1900?]).

Delaney's Scotch song book, No. 1–No. 10. William W. Delaney (New York, n. d. [*c.*1900?]).

De Bhaldraithe, Tomás, 'Na Connerys', in Seamus Grimes & Gearóid Ó Tuathaigh (eds), *The Irish-Australian connection/An Caidreamh Gael-Astrálach* (Worcester 1989) 25–42.

De Brún, Pádraig, *Clár lámhscríbhinní Gaeilge Choláiste Ollscoile Chorcaí: Cnuasach Thórna*, 1. Cló Bhréanainn (Baile Átha Cliath 1967).

De Noraidh, Liam, *Ceol ón Mumhain*. An Clóchomhar (Baile Átha Cliath 1965).

Dublin College of Music Publications, 1st ser. ['Mrs Mulligan']. Walton's (Dublin 1921).

Edwards, Ron, 'On board of the Kangaroo', *Australian Folklore Soc. Jnl 23* (Oct. 1993) 444–45.

Fitzgerald, John, 'An account of the old street ballads of Cork', *Jnl Cork Hist. & Arch. Soc.* 1/4 (1892) 63–71.

Ford, Robert, *Children's rhymes, children's games, children's songs, children's stories: a book for bairns and big folk* (Paisley *c.*1900).

Fox, Charlotte Milligan, 'Twelve Ulster folk songs from the neighbourhood of Coleraine', *Jnl of the Irish Folk Song Soc.* 8 (Jan.-June 1910) 10–18.

Fox, C. M. & Edith Wheeler, 'Some ballads collected by C. M. Fox and Edith Wheeler', *Jnl of the Irish Folk Song Soc.* 4 (1906) 19–23.

Freeman, A. Martin, 'Irish folk songs' [The Ballyvourney Collection], *Jnl of the Folk Song Soc.*, pt 6, No. 23 (Jan. 1920) iii–xxviii, 95–205; No. 24 (Jan. 1921) 205–66; No. 25 (Sept.1921) [265]–342.

Geckle, George I., 'The "Dead Lass of Aughrim"', *Éire-Ireland* 9/3 (Autumn 1974) 86–96.

Greig, Gavin, *Folk-song of the North-East* (Peterhead [Scotland] 1909, 1914); repr. Folklore Associates (Hatboro, Pennsylvania 1963).

Goodman, P., *The Irish minstrel: a collection of songs for use in Irish schools*, No. 1. M. H. Gill (Dublin, n. d.).

Graves, A. P., *The Irish song book*. T. Fisher Unwin (London 1903).

Grimes, Seamus & Gearóid Ó Tuathaigh (eds), *The Irish-Australian connection/An Caidreamh Gael-Astrálach* (Worcester 1989).

Harding's Dublin songster, new series. N. Harding (Dublin, n. d.).

Healy, James N., *The Mercier book of old Irish street ballads* 1. Mercier Press (Cork 1967).

— *The second book of Irish ballads*. Mercier Press (Cork 1962; repr. 1964).

— *Ballads from the pubs of Ireland*. Mercier Press (Cork 1965).

— *The Mercier book of Irish street ballads* 4. Mercier Press (Cork 1969).

— *Ballads from an Irish fireside*. Mercier Press (Cork 1986).

Henry, Sam, 'Songs of the People', published in the the *Northern Constitution* from 12 Nov. 1923 to 2 Dec. 1939; see Huntington & Hermann.

Herd, David, *Ancient and modern Scottish songs, heroic ballads, etc.*, 2 vols (Edinburgh 1776); repr. Scottish Academic Press (Edinburgh & London 1973).

Holloway, John & John Black, *Later English broadside ballads* 2 (London 1979).

Hughes, Herbert, *Irish country songs* 4. Boosey & Co. (London 1936).

Hugill, Stan, *Shanties from the seven seas. Shipboard work-songs and songs used as work-songs from the great days of sail*. Routledge & Kegan Paul (London 1961; repr. 1974).

Huntington, Gale & Lani Hermann, with John Moulden (eds), *Sam Henry's Songs of the People*, University of Georgia Press (Athens, Georgia & London 1990).

Hyde, Douglas, 'An Irish ballad', *Ériu* 2 (1905) 77–81.

Johnson, James & Robert Burns, *The Scots musical museum 1787–1803*; repr. 2 vols, Scolar Press (Aldershot 1991).

Jolliffe, Maureen, *The third book of Irish ballads*. Mercier Press (Cork 1970).

Joyce, P. W., *Ancient Irish music*. M. H. Gill (Dublin 1872; repr. 1906).

— *Irish music and songs: a collection of songs in the Irish language*. M. H. Gill (Dublin 1888; repr. 1903).

— *Old Irish folk music and songs*. Dublin University Press (Dublin 1909).

Karpeles, Maud, *Cecil Sharp's collection of English folk songs*, 2 vols. Oxford University Press (London, New York, Toronto 1974).

— *The crystal spring: English folk songs collected by Cecil Sharp*. Oxford University Press (Oxford 1987).

— *Folk songs from Newfoundland*, Archon Books (Hamden, Conn. 1970).

Kennedy, Peter, *Folksongs of Britain and Ireland*. Schirmer Books (New York 1975); repr. Oak Publications (London, New York 1984).

Kidson, Frank, & Andrew Moffatt, *A garland of English folk-songs*. Ascherberg, Hopwood & Crew (London 1926).

Kiely, Brendan, *The Connerys: the origins of a Waterford legend* (Dungarvan 1989).

Laoide, Seosamh (ed), *An cúigeadh leabhar* (Baile Átha Cliath 1914).

Laws, George Malcolm, *American balladry from British broadsides: a guide for students and collectors of traditional song*. The American Folklore Society, Publications of the American Folklore Society, Bibliographical & Special Series, Vol. 8 (Philadelphia 1957).

Lomax, Alan, *The folk songs of North America in the English language*. Cassell (London 1960).

Lomax, John, *Cowboy songs and other frontier ballads*. Macmillan (New York 1936).

Lover, Samuel, *Songs and ballads* (London 1839).

Lyle, Emily B. (ed), *Andrew Crawfurd's collection of ballads and songs*, 2 vols. Scottish Texts Society (Edinburgh 1975).

Lyons, J. J., 'O'Sullivan's frolics', *An Gaodhal* 8/12 (Aug. 1891) 131.

McCarthy, Tony, *Bawdy British folk songs*. Wolfe Publishing Ltd (London 1972).

McClaskey, J. P., *200 favorite songs & hymns for schools & homes, nursery & fireside*, No. 3 (New York 1885).

McColl, Ewan, *Folk songs and ballads of Scotland*. Oak Publications (New York 1965).

Mac Coluim, Fionán [= Finghin na Leamhna], *Smóilín na rann*, Leabhairiní Gaedhilge le haghaidh an tsluaigh 32. Connradh na Gaedhilge (Baile Átha Cliath 1908).

— *Sean-amhráin na Mumhan* 1. Connradh na Gaedhilge (Baile Átha Cliath 1908).

— *Duanaireacht do leanbhaíbh*, Connradh na Gaedhilge (Baile Átha Cliath 1914).

— *Bolg an tsoláthair: cnuasach sean-rócán*. Connradh na Gaedhilge (Baile Átha Cliath 1919).

— (ed), *Racaireacht ghrinn na tuaithe*. Cló-Chualacht Seandúna (Corcaigh 1925).

— *Amhráin na ngleann*. Folklore Soc. of Ireland (Baile Átha Cliath 1939).

— 'Cúcúin, a chuaichín', *An Saoghal Gaelach* [Vocational Education Bulletin Supplement 8 ('Um Fhéile Mhichíl 1953') 4.

Mac Coluim, Fionán [= Finghin na Leamhna] & Pádraig Pléimion, *Cosa buidhe arda* 1, 2. An Lóchrann (Baile Átha Cliath 1922, 1923).

Mac Giolla Choille, Breandán, 'Na Connerys sa bhaile', *Comhar* 44/4 (Aibreán 1985) 20–21.

Mackenzie, William Roy, *Ballads and sea songs from Nova Scotia* (Cambridge, Mass. 1928); repr. Folklore Associates Inc. (Hatboro, Penn. 1963).

Mac Mathúna, Séamus, *Traditional songs and singers*. Comhaltas Ceoltóirí Éireann (Baile Átha Cliath 1977).

McPheeley, James, *More than 1000 songs and dances of the Irish people*. Hansen House (New York 1976).

McWilliams, Hugh, *Poems and songs on various subjects* (Belfast 1831).

Madden, Richard R., *Literary remains, etc., and selections from other popular lyrics of their times, with an essay on the authorship of "The Exile of Erin"*. James Duffy & Sons (Dublin 1887).

Maguidhir, Éamon, *Mo stóirín cheóil*. Brún 7 Ó Nualláin (Baile Átha Cliath, n. d.).

— *Pilib an Cheóil*. Brún 7 Ó Nualláin (Baile Átha Cliath, n. d.).

Meek, Bill, *The Land of Libertie: songs of the Irish in America*. Gilbert Dalton (Skerries, Dublin 1978).

— *Moon Penny, a collection of rhymes, songs and play-verse for children*. Ossian (Cork 1985).

Meredith, John, *The Wild Colonial Boy: Bushranger Jack Donaghue, 1806–1830* (Ascot Vale, Victoria 1982).

Meredith, John & Hugh Anderson, *Folk songs of Australia and the men and women who sang them*. Ure Smith (Sydney 1967).

Milner, Dan, *The bonnie bunch of roses*. Oak Publications (New York, etc. 1983).

Moffatt, Alfred, *The minstrelsy of Ireland*. Augener & Co. (London 1897).

Morton, Robbie, *Folksongs sung in Ulster*. Mercier Press (Cork 1970).

Moulden, John, *Songs of Hugh McWilliams, Schoolmaster, 1831*. Ulstersongs (Portrush 1993).

Munnelly, Tom, 'The long song singer', *Dal gCais* 8 (1966) 82–83.

— *The Mount Callan garland: songs from the repertoire of Tom Lenihan of Knockbrack, Milltown Malbay, County Clare* (Dublin 1994).

News Chronicle song book, No. 2, Old-time variety songs (London, n. d.).

Ní Annagáin, Maighréad & Séamus Clainndiolúin, *An londubh*. Connradh na Gaedhilge (Baile Átha Cliath 1904).

— *Londubh an chairn, being songs of the Irish Gaels*. Oxford University Press (London 1927).

Nicholson, J., *The Three-Leafed Shamrock; or Take them to Phelim*, a broadside ballad published by Cheapside Song House, 36 Church Lane, Belfast [n. d.].

Ní Chróinín, Siobhán [= 'Siobhán an tSagairt'], 'Amhrán chrúidhte na bó', *Timthiridh an Chroidhe Naomhtha* 6/3 (1916) 15.

— 'Seán 'ac Séamais', *An Lóchrann* 1 (Abrán 1916) 5.

Ní Ógáin, Róis, *Duanaire Gaedhilge* 1, 2. Comhlucht Oideachais na hÉireann (Baile Átha Cliath 1921, 1922).

Ní Shúilleabháin, Gobnait, 'Comhartha cuimhneacháin ar chomóradh céad blian Sgoil Bharr d'Inse, 1883–1983', *Múscraí* 1 (1983) 5–7.

Norris, T. D., 'As Bacchus frequented his frolics', *An Gaodhal* 9/3 (Aibreán 1892) 171.

Ó Baoill, Seán Óg & Mánus Ó Baoill, *Ceolta Gael*. Mercier Press (Cork & Dublin 1975).

Ó Briain, Mícheál, 'Casfam araon na géanna romhainn', *An Lóchrann* (Deire Fóghmhair 1916) 5.

Ó Buachalla, Mícheál, 'Sean-amhrán ó'n Mumhain', *Irishleabhar na Gaedhilge* 12/137 (Feabhra 1902) 21–22.

Ó Cadhlaigh, Cormac, 'Réidh-chnoc mná duibhe', *Irisleabhar na Gaedhilge* 14/162 (Márta 1904) 510–11.

— 'Níl sé 'na lá', *An Lóchrann* 1 (Abrán 1916) 1.

Ó Canainn, Tomás, *Songs of Cork*. Gilbert Dalton (Dublin 1978).

Ó Caoimh, Seán, 'Ar bhruach na Laoi', *Fáinne an Lae* (Meadhon Foghmhair 1926) 3.

Ó Catháin, Séamus, *The bedside book of Irish folklore*. Mercier Press (Cork 1980).

Ó Ceallaigh, Pádraig, 'Amhráin ó Mhúscraighe', *Béaloideas* 7/1 (1937) 19–44 [also publ. separately].

O'Conor, Manus, *Irish come-all-ye's and ballads of Ireland*. Popular Publishing Co. (New York 1901).

Ó Criomhthain, Tomás, 'Duanaireacht do leanbhaíbh', *An Lóchrann* (Samhain 1920) 2.

Ó Cróinín, Seán [= 'Seán Saor'], 'An Béiceachán agus an Chaillichín', *Irish Press* (13 Feb. 1953) 2.

Ó Cróinín, Seán & Donncha Ó Cróinín, *Seanachas Phádraig Í Chrualaoi*. Comhairle Bhéaloideas Éireann, Scríbhinní Béaloidis/Folklore Studies 10 (Baile Átha Cliath 1982).

O'Daly, John, *The Irish language miscellany, being a selection of poems by the Munster bards of the last century*. John O'Daly (Dublin 1876).

O'Daly, John & James Clarence Mangan, *The poets and poetry of Munster*, James Duffy & Co. (Dublin 1849; 4th ed., Dublin 1925).

Ó Donnchadha, Tadhg, 'Guth na mbard' ['O'Sullivan's Frolics'], *An Claidheamh Soluis* (2 Bealtaine 1914) 3.

Ó Donnchadha, Tadhg & Pádraig Mac Piarais (eds), *An tAithriseoir* 1 (Baile Átha Cliath 1900).

Ó Duibhginn, Séamus, *Dónall Óg. Taighde ar an amhrán*. An Clóchomhar (Baile Átha Cliath 1960).

Ó Foghludha, Diarmuid, 'Sean-aimsireacht', *Banba* (Nollaig 1902) 103.

Ó Gráda, Diarmuid, 'Na Connerys', *Comhar* 44/3 (Márta 1985) 22–25.

Ó Laoghaire, Donnchadh, 'Dán-mholadh Bhaile Mhúirne', *An Claidheamh Soluis* (Aibreán 20, 1901) 83.

Ó Laoghaire, Pádraig, 'Oídhche Fhéile Bríghde, agus mé go h-aoibhin', *An Gaodhal* 8/10 (Sept. 1891) 120.

— 'Ag seoladh na ngamhan faoi'n bhfásach', *Irisleabhar na Gaedhilge* 12/140 (Bealtaine 1902) 77–78.

Ó Lochlainn, Colm, *An Claisceadal*, Duilleacháin 1–31 (Dublin 1930–40).

— *Irish street ballads*. Three Candles (Dublin 1939); repr. Pan Books (London 1978).

— *More Irish street ballads* (Dublin 1965); repr. Pan Books (London 1978).

Ó Máille, Mícheál & Tomás Ó Máille (eds), *Amhráin chlainne Gaedheal* 1. Connradh na Gaedhilge (Baile Átha Cliath 1905).

Ó Muirithe, Diarmuid, *An t-amhrán macarónach*. Leabhair Thaighde 32. An Clóchomhar (Baile Átha Cliath 1980).

— *Cois an Ghaorthaidh. Filíocht ó Mhúscraí 1700–1840*. An Clóchomhar (Baile Átha Cliath 1987).

Ó Murchadha, Mícheál, 'Dán-mholadh an t-Suláin', *Irisleabhar na Gaedhilge* 12/140 (Bealtaine 1902) 74–75.

O'Neill, Capt. Francis, *1001 Gems: The dance music of Ireland*. (Chicago 1907); repr. Walton's (Dublin 1965).

— *Irish minstrels and musicians*. The Regan Publication House (Chicago 1913).

Ó hÓgáin, Dáithí, *Binneas thar meon 1, Cnuasach d'amhráin agus de cheolta a dhein Liam de Noraidh in oirthear Mumhan*. Comhairle Bhéaloideas Éireann (Baile Átha Cliath 1994).

Opie, Iona & Peter Opie, *The Oxford dictionary of nursery rhymes*. Oxford University Press (Oxford 1951).

— *The lore and language of schoolchildren*. Oxford University Press (Oxford 1959).

— *The singing game*. Oxford University Press (Oxford, New York 1985).

Ó Scanaill, Tadhg, 'A chuthaigh mhalluighthe', *Proceedings of the 3rd Oireachtas 1899*. Gaelic League (Dublin 1900) 163–64.

Ó Súilleabháin, Eoin Mikey, 'Abair Amhrán' ['I'll tell you a comical story'], *An Múscraíoch* (Bealtaine 1994) 8.

Ó Tuama, Seán, *An chóisir cheoil*. An Claisceadal (Baile Átha Cliath, n. d.).

Ó Tuama, Seán Óg, *Cóisir cheoil* 4 (Baile Átha Cliath 1957).

Ó Tuathaigh, Pádraig, *Filí an tSuláin*. Tower Books (Cork 1993).

Palmer, Roy (ed), *Songs of the Midlands*. E. P. Publishing (Wakefield 1972).

— *Everyman's book of British ballads*. J. M. Dent (London 1980).

Partridge, Eric, *A dictionary of slang and unconventional English* (New York 1937).

Petrie, George, *The Petrie collection of the ancient music of Ireland*. M. H. Gill (Dublin 1855); repr. (Farnborough 1967), (Heppenheim 1969).

Petrie, George & Charles Villiers Stanford (eds), *The complete collection of Irish music*. Boosey & Co. (London 1902–5).

Purslow, Frank, *The wanton seed: more English folk songs from the Hammond and Gardiner Mss*. EFDS Publications (London 1968).

— *The constant lovers: more English folk songs from the Hammond and Gardiner Mss*. EFDS Publications (London 1972).

Reeves, James, *The idiom of the people. English traditional verse, edited with an introduction and notes, from the manuscripts of Cecil J. Sharp*. Heinemann (London 1958).

Ritchie, Jean, *From fair to fair: folk songs of the British Isles*. Henry Z. Walck (New York 1966).

Roche, Frank, *The Roche collection of traditional Irish music*, 3 vols (Dublin 1927); repr., 3 vols in 1, Ossian Publications (Cork 1982).

Rollins, Hyder E., *A Pepysian garland. Black-letter broadside ballads of the years 1595–1639, chiefly from the collection of Samuel Pepys*. Cambridge University Press (Cambridge 1922).

— *An analytical index of ballad-entries (1557–1709) in the registers of the Company of Stationers of London*. Tradition Press (Hatboro, Penn. 1969).

Sedley, Stephen, *The seeds of love*. EFDS/Essex Music Ltd (London 1967).

Sharp, Cecil & C. L. Manson, *Folk-songs of Somerset* (London 1904).

Shepard, Leslie, *The broadside ballad: a study in origins and meaning*. Herbert Jenkins (London 1962).

Shields, Hugh, 'A latter-day "pastourelle": The Factory Girl', *Ceol* 1/3 (1963) 5–10.

— 'Four songs from Glendalough', *Ceol* 1/4 (1964) 4–14.

— 'Some songs and ballads in use in the province of Ulster … 1845', *Ulster Folklife* 17 (1971) 3–24.

— *Shamrock, rose and thistle: folk singing in north Derry*. Blackstaff Press (Belfast 1981).

— 'A history of *The Lass of Aughrim*', in Gerard Gillen & Harry White (eds), *Musical Studies* 1: Musicology in Ireland (Dublin 1990) 58–73.

Shields, Hugh, Douglas Sealy, & Cathal Goan (eds), *Scéalamhráin Cheilteacha*. Clólann Uí Mhathúna (Dublin 1985).

Sigerson, George, *Bards of the Gael and Gall. Examples of the poetic literature of Erinn*. Talbot Press/T. Fisher Unwin (Dublin & London 1897; 3rd ed. 1925).

Slocombe, Marie & Patrick Shuldham-Shaw, 'Seven songs recorded by the B.B.C. from Mrs Costello of Birmingham', *Jnl of the Engl. Folk Dance and Song Soc.* 7/2 (1953) 96–105.

Sparling, H. Halliday (ed), *Irish minstrelsy. A selection of Irish songs and ballads, orginal and translated*. Walter Scott (3rd ed., London *c*.1888).

Tunney, Paddy, *The stone fiddle: my way to traditional song*. Gilbert Dalton (Dublin 1979).

— *Where songs do thunder: travels in traditional song* (Belfast 1991).

Ua Braoin, Donnchadh, *An cuaichín ceoil*. Brún & Ó Nualláin (Baile Átha Cliath, n. d.).

Ua Duinnín, Pádraig, *Amhráin Eoghain Ruaidh Uí Shúilleabháin*. Connradh na Gaedhilge (Baile Átha Cliath 1901).

Vaughan Williams, Ralph & A. A. Lloyd, *The Penguin book of English folksongs* (London 1959).

Walton, Jake (ed), *Keltische Folksongs*. Fischer Taschenbücher (Frankfurt a. M. 1983).

Waltons new treasury of Irish songs and ballads 2 (Dublin, n. d.).

Walsh, Edward, *Irish popular songs* (Dublin 1847).

Wannan, Bill (ed), *The wearing of the green. The lore, literature, legend and balladry of the Irish in Australia* (London 1965; New English Library ed. 1968).

Ward, John, *Collection of Irish comic songs*. Ward Music Publishing Co. (Chicago, Ill. 1947).

Wehman's 617 Irish Songs (New York, n. d., but *c*.1900).

Wheeler, Edith, 'Notes on an Irish song (The Irish Girl)', *Jnl of the Irish Folk Song Soc.* 3/3–4 (1905) 26–28.

— 'Some ballads collected by C. M. Fox & Edith Wheeler', *Jnl of the Irish Folk Song Soc.* 4 (1906) 19–23.

Williams, Alfred, *Folk-songs of the Upper Thames* (London 1923).

[Witmark, M.], *Echoes from Erin: An album of ballads, novelties, comics (old and new), compiled expressly for and dedicated to those who love IRISH SONGS*. M. Witmark & Sons (New York 1926).

Wright, Robert L., *Irish emigrant ballads and songs*, Bowling Green University Press (Bowling Green, Ohio 1975).

Zimmermann, Georges-Denis, *Songs of Irish rebellion: Political street ballads and songs of rebellion 1780–1900*. Allen Figgis (Dublin 1967).

INDEX OF SONG TITLES

INDEX OF FIRST LINES

Boldface numbers between round brackets refer to the song-numbers in the Song-Book. **Boldface titles** refer to songs for which I have no text, and therefore no first line (except for Nos **2** and **65**, which are acephalous). First lines between square brackets [ ] indicate songs for which I have no text of Bess Cronin's, but which can be identified with reasonable certainty.

INDEX OF FIELD RECORDINGS

64.	Good night, Molly darling, good night	BBC 19021	8 Sept. 1952
65.	*Grá mo chléibh*		
66.	Green grows the rushes-o		
67.	Hang it up, boys, for sale!		
68.	High Germany	BBC 19025	8 Sept. 1952
69.	I am a maid that sleeps in love	JR-GP ER 4	24 Nov. 1952
70.	I have a bonnet trimmed with blue	JR-GP ER 1	2 Nov. 1952
71.	I'll tell you a comical story		
72.	If I was a fair maid		
73.	In Kerry long ago	CBÉ 395a	1947
74.	*Insa Ghaorthaidh thuit*		
75.	It was early, early in the month of spring		
76.	Johnny, get your hair cut!		
77.	Just like the ivy	JR-GP ER 4	24 Nov. 1952
78.	Kitty got a clinking coming from the races		
79.	Lackagh Bawn		
80.	Lanigan's Ball	JR-GP ER4	24 Nov. 1952
81.	Last night being windy	BBC 19023	14 Sept. 1952
82.	Little girleen with the curling poll, would you buy brooms?		
83.	Lord Gregory	BBC 18759	29 Aug. 1952
		JR-GP ER 3	24 Nov. 1952
84.	Lord Randal	BBC 21996	Aug. 1954
85.	Lovely Molly	CBÉ 1064a	1947
86.	*Maidean álainn gréine*		
87.	*Maidean bhog aoibhinn*		
88.	Marrowbones	BBC 19022	14 Sept. 1952
89.	*Mo leastar beag*	CBÉ 388a	1947
90.	*Mo mhúirnín bán*		
91.	*Mo theaghlach*		
92.	Molly Bawn	JR-GP ER 3	24 Nov. 1952
93.	Mount Massey, the flower of Macroom		
94.	Mrs Mulligan, the pride of the Coombe		
95.	Muirisheen went to Bonane		
96.	*Mullach na ré*		
97.	My father and mother are minding sheep		
98.	My name is Bold Hewson the Cobbler		
99.	My true love's face is as bright		
100.	*Na Conairigh*		
101.	*Na gleannta*	BBC 19026	21 Sept. 1952
102.	*Ní thaithneann liom fear a bhíonn sásta*		
103.	Nice little Jenny from Ballinasloe	BBC 19025	21 Sept. 1952
		JR-GP ER 4	24 Nov. 1952
104.	*Níl mo shláinte ar fónamh*	BBC 11988	7 Aug. 1947
		CBÉ 379	1947
105.	*Níl sé 'na lá*	BBC 18760	29 Aug. 1952
		DH EI Cork 2	1955

TRACK LISTING FOR CDS

CD 1 (FROM DISK)

			Durations
1.	*Níl mo shláinte ar fónamh*	BBC 11988	4'26"
2.	The lover and darling	BBC 19023	3'12"
3.	Cuckanandy	BBC 12614	1'11"
4.	*Mo leastar beag*	CBÉ 388a	1'39"
5.	On board the *Kangaroo*	BBC 8760	3'38"
6.	*Baile Mhúirne*	BBC 19026	1'05"
7.	*Cu-cúc, a chuaichín*	CBÉ 393b	0'30"
8.	All ye that's pierced by Cupid's darts	BBC 19026	2'23"
9.	*An botháinín íseal gan fálthas*	BBC 19027	1'54"
10.	Uncle Rat	BBC 11989	1'30"
11.	*Raghad-sa ó thuaidh leat, a bhó*	BBC 12614	1'18"
12.	The prayer book	BBC 19022	2'34"
13.	*An gamhain geal bán*	CBÉ 390a	1'35"
14.	Sweet Boney, will I e'er see you more?	BBC 11990	4'14"
15.	*Seoithín-seó*	BBC 11988	1'44"
16.	The braes of Balquidder	BBC 18758	1'36"
17.	*Cois abhainn na séad*	CBÉ 418	2'19"
18.	The Buachaill Rua	BBC 19023	2'44"
19.	*Na gleannta*	BBC 19026	1'56"
20.	The Cappabwee murder	BBC 19022	3'33"
21.	*Dá mba liomsa an ainnir*	CBÉ 388b	0'58"
22.	*Siúil, a rúin*	BBC 21535	2'05"
23.	Tom Toozick, the gentleman	CBÉ 397b	1'26"
24.	The banks of Sullane	BBC 11991	3'06"
25.	*Níl sé 'na lá*	BBC 18760	2'35"
26.	*A chaipín-ar-leathstuaic*	CBÉ 394b	0'44"
27.	Sweet Lisbweemore	BBC 11989	4'28"
28.	*Anonn 's anall, is tríd an abhainn*	CBÉ 395b	1'07"
29.	*Táim cortha ó bheith im' aonar im' luí*	CBÉ 389	3'42"
30.	Down by the groves of Tullig	BBC 11991	4'22"

CD 2 (FROM TAPE)

			Durations
1.	Lord Gregory	JR-GP ER 3	4'43"
2.	*Cuir a chodladh*	JR-GP ER 3	1'26"
3.	Down the green fields	JR-GP ER 1	0'32"
4.	Pussycat's party	JR-GP ER 1	1'02"
5.	The sun is gone down in the west, love	JR-GP ER 1	3'50"

6.	I have a bonnet trimmed with blue	JR-GP ER 1	0'40"
7.	*An bínsín luachra*	JR-GP ER 3	4'05"
8.	The little pack of tailors	JR-GP ER 3	0'35"
9.	The bonny blue-eyed lassie	DH EI Cork 2	2'40"
10.	Bold Jack Donohue	JR-GP ER 3	2'37"
11.	Dance for your daddy-o	Lomax	0'30"
12.	'Tis ten weary years	JR-GP ER 1	3'33"
13.	I am a maid that sleeps in love	JR-GP ER 4	4'10"
14.	What would you do if you married a soldier?	JR-GP ER 1	0'48"
15.	Sweet Killydysart	JR-GP ER 1	2'26"
16.	There was a lady in her father's garden	JR-GP ER 3	2'45"
17.	Derby ram	JR-GP ER 3	2'12"
18.	The Yorkshire farmer	JR-GP ER 3	4'32"
19.	Girleen, don't be idle	JR-GP ER 1	2'25"
20.	*Seothó-leó, a thoil*	JR-GP ER 2	2'40"
21.	The charming sweet girl that I love	JR-GP ER 1	3'45"
22.	The Kerry cow	JR-GP ER 3	1'09"
23.	Nice little Jenny from Ballinasloe	JR-GP ER 4	3'00"
24.	*Do thugas grá cléibh duit*	DH EI Cork 2	2'40"
25.	Did you see my man?	JR-GP ER 1	0'33"
26.	Molly Bawn	JR-GP ER 3	2'30"
27.	*Faiche bhreá aerach an cheoil*	DH EI Cork 2	3'14"
28.	Barbara Allen	DH EI Cork 1	2'12"
29.	The bells of heaven (with company)	JR-GP ER 1	1'07"